A HISTORY OF SANSKRIT LITERATURE

A HISTORY OF SANSKRIT LITERATURE

By

ARTHUR A. MACDONELL, M.A. Ph.D.

GYAN

Published by

GYAN

Gyan Publishing House
5, Ansari Road
Daryaganj, New Delhi-110002
Phone: 011-47034999, 9811692060
E-mail: books@gyanbooks.com

Distribution Network
gyanbooks.com
India, USA, Canada, UK, Australia, France

ISBN : 978-81-212-6502-7 (PB)
First Published, 1900

2nd Impression 2022

Printed at: Gyan Press, Delhi.

A HISTORY OF SANSKRIT LITERATURE
Author: ARTHUR A. MACDONELL

A HISTORY OF
SANSKRIT LITERATURE

BY

ARTHUR A. MACDONELL, M. A., PH. D.

OF CORPUS CHRISTI COLLEGE, OXFORD
BODEN PROFESSOR OF SANSKRIT AND FELLOW OF BALLIOL

1900

PREFACE

It is undoubtedly a surprising fact that down to the present time no history of Sanskrit literature as a whole has been written in English. For not only does that literature possess much intrinsic merit, but the light it sheds on the life and thought of the population of our Indian Empire ought to have a peculiar interest for the British nation. Owing chiefly to the lack of an adequate account of the subject, few, even of the young men who leave these shores every year to be its future rulers, possess any connected information about the literature in which the civilisation of Modern India can be traced to its sources, and without which that civilisation cannot be fully understood. It was, therefore, with the greatest pleasure that I accepted Mr. Gosse's invitation to contribute a volume to this series of *Literatures of the World;* for this appeared to me to be a peculiarly good opportunity for diffusing information on a subject in which more than twenty years of continuous study and teaching had instilled into me an ever-deepening interest.

Professor Max Müller's valuable *History of Ancient Sanskrit Literature* is limited in its scope to the Vedic period. It has long been out of print; and Vedic research has necessarily made great strides in the forty years which have elapsed since its publication.

The only book accessible to the English reader on

the history of Sanskrit literature in general has hitherto been the translation of Professor Weber's *Academical Lectures on Indian Literature*, as delivered nearly half a century ago at Berlin. The numerous and often very lengthy notes in this work supply the results of research during the next twenty-five years; but as these notes often modify, or even cancel, the statements of the unaltered original text of 1852, the result is bewildering to the student. Much new light has been thrown on various branches of Sanskrit literature since 1878, when the last notes were added to this translation, which, moreover, is not in any way adapted to the wants of the general reader. The only work on the subject appealing to the latter is the late Sir M. Monier-Williams's *Indian Wisdom*. That book, however, although it furnishes, in addition to the translated specimens, some account of the chief departments of Sanskrit literature, is not a history. There is thus distinctly a twofold demand in this country for a history of Sanskrit literature. The student is in want of a guide setting forth in a clear and trustworthy manner the results of research down to the present time, and the cultivated English reader looks for a book presenting in an intelligible and attractive form information which must have a special interest to us owing to our close relations with India.

To lack of space, no less than to the scope of the present series, is due the exclusion of a full account of the technical literature of law, science, and art, which contains much that would interest even the general reader; but the brief epitome given in the Appendix will, I hope, suffice to direct the student to all the most important authorities.

As to the bibliographical notes, I trust that, though

necessarily restricted in extent, they will enable the student to find all further information he may want on matters of detail; for instance, the evidence for approximate dates, which had occasionally to be summarily stated even in the text.

In writing this history of Sanskrit literature, I have dwelt more on the life and thought of Ancient India, which that literature embodies, than would perhaps have appeared necessary in the case of a European literature. This I have done partly because Sanskrit literature, as representing an independent civilisation entirely different from that of the West, requires more explanation than most others; and partly because, owing to the remarkable continuity of Indian culture, the religious and social institutions of Modern India are constantly illustrated by those of the past.

Besides the above-mentioned works of Professors Max Müller and Weber, I have made considerable use of Professor L. von Schroeder's excellent *Indiens Literatur und Cultur* (1887). I have further consulted in one way or another nearly all the books and monographs mentioned in the bibliographical notes. Much of what I have written is also based on my own studies of Sanskrit literature.

All the quotations which I have given by way of illustration I have myself carefully selected from the original works. Excepting the short extracts on page 333 from Cowell and Thomas's excellent translation of the *Harshacharita*, all the renderings of these are my own. In my versions of Rigvedic stanzas I have, however, occasionally borrowed a line or phrase from Griffith. Nearly all my renderings are as close as the use of metre permits. I have endeavoured to reproduce, as far as possible, the measures of the original, except in the quotations from the dramas, where I have always employed blank verse. I have throughout refrained from rhyme, as misrepresenting the original Sanskrit.

In the transliteration of Sanskrit words I have been guided by the desire to avoid the use of letters which might mislead those who do not know Sanskrit. I have therefore departed in a few particulars from the system on which Sanskrit scholars are now almost unanimously agreed, and which I otherwise follow myself. Hence for *c* and *ch* I have written *ch* and *chh* respectively, though in the rare cases where these two appear in combination I have retained *cch* (instead of *chchh*). I further use *sh* for the lingual *ṣ*, and *ç* for the palatal *ś*, and *ṛi* for the vowel *ṛ*. I have not thought it necessary to distinguish the guttural *ṅ* and the palatal *ñ* by diacritical marks, simply printing, for instance, *anga* and *pancha*. The reader who is unacquainted with Sanskrit will thus pronounce all words correctly by simply treating all the consonants as in English; remembering only that the vowels should be sounded as in Italian, and that *e* and *o* are always long.

I am indebted for some suggestions to my friend Mr. F. C. S. Schiller, Fellow and Tutor of Corpus Christi College, who looked through the final proof of the chapter on Philosophy. To my pupil Mr. A. B. Keith, Boden Sanskrit scholar and Classical scholar of Balliol, who has read all the final proofs with great care, I owe not only the removal of a number of errors of the press, but also several valuable criticisms regarding matters of fact.

107 BANBURY ROAD, OXFORD,
December 1, 1899.

CONTENTS

A HISTORY OF

SANSKRIT LITERATURE

CHAPTER I

INTRODUCTORY

SINCE the Renaissance there has been no event of such world-wide significance in the history of culture as the discovery of Sanskrit literature in the latter part of the eighteenth century. After Alexander's invasion, the Greeks became to some extent acquainted with the learning of the Indians; the Arabs, in the Middle Ages, introduced the knowledge of Indian science to the West; a few European missionaries, from the sixteenth century onwards, were not only aware of the existence of, but also acquired some familiarity with, the ancient language of India; and Abraham Roger even translated the Sanskrit poet Bhartṛihari into Dutch as early as 1651. Nevertheless, till about a hundred and twenty years ago there was no authentic information in Europe about the existence of Sanskrit literature, but only vague surmise, finding expression in stories about the wisdom of the Indians. The enthusiasm with which Voltaire in his *Essai sur les Mœurs et l'Esprit des Nations* greeted the lore of the *Ezour Vedam*, a work brought from India and introduced to his notice in the middle of the last century, was premature. For this work was later proved to be a forgery made in the seventeenth century by a Jesuit missionary. The scepticism justified by this fabrication, and indulged in when the discovery of the genuine Sanskrit literature was announced, survived far into the present century. Thus, Dugald Stewart, the philosopher, wrote an essay in which he endeavoured to prove that not only Sanskrit literature, but also the Sanskrit language, was a forgery made by the crafty Brahmans on the model of Greek after Alexander's conquest. Indeed, this view was elaborately defended by a professor at Dublin as late as the year 1838.

The first impulse to the study of Sanskrit was given by the practical administrative needs of our Indian possessions. Warren Hastings, at that time Governor-General, clearly seeing the advantage of ruling the Hindus as far as possible according to their own laws and customs, caused a number of Brahmans to prepare a digest based on the best ancient Indian legal authorities. An English version of this Sanskrit compilation, made through the medium of a Persian translation, was published in 1776. The introduction to this work, besides giving specimens of the Sanskrit script, for the first time supplied some trustworthy information about the ancient Indian language and literature. The earliest step, however, towards making Europe acquainted with actual Sanskrit writings was taken by Charles Wilkins, who, having, at the instigation of Warren Hastings, acquired a considerable knowledge of Sanskrit at Benares, published in 1785 a translation of the *Bhagavad-gītā*, or *The Song of the Adorable One*, and two years later, a version of the well-known collection of fables entitled *Hitopadeça*, or *Friendly Advice.*

Sir WILLIAM JONES (1746–94) was, however, the pioneer of Sanskrit studies in the West. It was this brilliant and many-sided Orientalist who, during his too brief career of eleven years in India, first aroused a keen interest in the study of Indian antiquity by his unwearied literary activity and by the foundation of the Asiatic Society of Bengal in 1784. Having rapidly acquired an accurate knowledge of Sanskrit, he published in 1789 a translation of *Çakuntalā*, the finest Sanskrit drama, which was greeted with enthusiasm by such judges as Herder and Goethe. This was followed by a translation of the *Code of Manu*, the most important of the Sanskrit law-books. To Sir William Jones also belongs the credit of having been the first man who ever printed an edition of a Sanskrit text. This was a short lyrical poem entitled *Ṛitusaṃhāra*, or *Cycle of the Seasons*, published in 1792.

We next come to the great name of HENRY THOMAS COLEBROOKE (1765–1837), a man of extraordinary industry, combined with rare clearness of intellect and sobriety of judgment. The first to handle the Sanskrit language and literature on scientific principles, he published many texts, translations, and essays dealing with almost every branch of Sanskrit learning, thus laying the solid foundations on which later scholars have built.

While Colebrooke was beginning his literary career in India during the opening years of the century, the romance of war led to the practical knowledge of Sanskrit being introduced on the Continent of Europe. ALEXANDER HAMILTON (1765–1824), an Englishman who had acquired a good knowledge of Sanskrit in India, happened to be passing through France on his way home in 1802. Hostilities breaking out afresh just then, a decree of Napoleon, directed against all Englishmen in the country, kept Hamilton a prisoner in Paris. During his long involuntary stay in that city he taught Sanskrit to some French scholars, and especially to the German romantic poet FRIEDRICH SCHLEGEL. One of the results of these studies was the publication by Schlegel of his work *On the Language and Wisdom of the Indians* (1808). This book produced nothing less than a revolution in the science of language by the introduction of the comparative and the historical method. It led to the foundation of the science of comparative philology by FRANZ BOPP in his treatise on the conjugational system of Sanskrit in comparison with that of Greek, Latin, Persian, and German (1816). Schlegel's work, moreover, aroused so much zeal for the study of Sanskrit in Germany, that the vast progress made since his day in this branch of learning has been mainly due to the labours of his countrymen.

In the early days of Sanskrit studies Europeans became acquainted only with that later phase of the ancient language of India which is familiar to the Pandits, and is commonly called Classical Sanskrit. So it came about that the literature composed in this dialect engaged the attention of [illegible]s almost exclusively down to the middle of the century. Colebrooke had, it is true, supplied as early as 1805 valuable information about the literature of the older period in his essay *On the Vedas*. Nearly a quarter of a century later, F. ROSEN, a German scholar, had conceived the plan of making this more ancient literature known to Europe from the rich collection of manuscripts at the East India House; and his edition of the first eighth of the *Rigveda* was actually brought out in 1838, shortly after his premature death. But it was not till RUDOLF ROTH (1821–95), the founder of Vedic philology, published his epoch-making little book *On the Literature and History of the Veda* in 1846, that the studies of Sankritists received a lasting impulse in the direction of the earlier and more important literature of the Vedas. These studies have since been prosecuted with such zeal, that nearly all the most valuable works of the Vedic, as well as the later period, have within the last fifty years been made accessible in thoroughly trustworthy editions.

In judging of the magnitude of the work thus accomplished, it should be borne in mind that the workers have been far fewer in this than in other analogous fields, while the literature of the Vedas at least equals in extent what survives of the writings of ancient Greece. Thus in the course of a century the whole range of Sanskrit literature, which in quantity exceeds that of Greece and Rome put together, has been explored. The great bulk of it has been edited, and most of its valuable productions have been translated, by competent hands. There has long been at the service of scholars a Sanskrit dictionary, larger and more scientific than any either of the classical languages yet possesses. The detailed investigations in every department of Sanskrit literature are now so numerous, that a comprehensive work embodying the results of all these researches has become a necessity. An encyclopædia covering the whole domain of Indo-Aryan antiquity has accordingly been planned on a more extensive scale than that of any similar undertaking, and is now being published at Strasburg in parts, contributed to by about thirty specialists of various nationalities. By the tragic death, in April 1898, of its eminent editor, Professor BÜHLER of Vienna, Sanskrit scholarship has sustained an irreparable loss. The work begun by him is being completed by another very distinguished Indianist, Professor KIELHORN of Göttingen.

Although so much of Sanskrit literature has already been published, an examination of the catalogues of Sanskrit manuscripts, of which an enormous number are preserved in European and Indian libraries, proves that there are still many minor works awaiting, and likely to repay, the labours of an editor.

The study of Sanskrit literature deserves far more attention than it has yet received in this country. For in that ancient heritage the languages, the religious and intellectual life and thought, in short, the whole civilisation of the Hindus, who form the vast majority of the inhabitants of our Indian Empire, have their roots. Among all the ancient literatures, that of India is, moreover, undoubtedly in intrinsic value and æsthetic merit second only to that of Greece. To the latter it is, as a source for the study of human evolution, even superior. Its earliest period, being much older than any product of Greek literature, presents a more primitive form of belief, and therefore gives a clearer picture of the development of religious ideas than any other literary monument of the world. Hence it came about that, just as the discovery of the Sanskrit language led to the foundation of the science of Comparative Philology, an acquaintance with the literature of the Vedas resulted in the foundation of the science of Comparative Mythology by ADALBERT KUHN and MAX MÜLLER.

Though it has touched excellence in most of its

branches, Sanskrit literature has mainly achieved greatness in religion and philosophy. The Indians are the only division of the Indo-European family which has created a great national religion—Brahmanism—and a great world-religion—Buddhism; while all the rest, far from displaying originality in this sphere, have long since adopted a foreign faith. The intellectual life of the Indians has, in fact, all along been more dominated by religious thought than that of any other race. The Indians, moreover, developed independently several systems of philosophy which bear evidence of high speculative powers. The great interest, however, which these two subjects must have for us lies, not so much in the results they attained, as in the fact that every step in the evolution of religion and philosophy can be traced in Sanskrit literature.

The importance of ancient Indian literature as a whole largely consists in its originality. Naturally isolated by its gigantic mountain barrier in the north, the Indian peninsula has ever since the Aryan invasion formed a world apart, over which a unique form of Aryan civilisation rapidly spread, and has ever since prevailed. When the Greeks, towards the end of the fourth century B.C., invaded the North-West, the Indians had already fully worked out a national culture of their own, unaffected by foreign influences. And, in spite of successive waves of invasion and conquest by Persians, Greeks, Scythians, Muhammadans, the national development of the life and literature of the Indo-Aryan race remained practically unchecked and unmodified from without down to the era of British occupation. No other branch of the Indo-European stock has experienced an isolated evolution like this. No other country except

China can trace back its language and literature, its religious beliefs and rites, its domestic and social customs, through an uninterrupted development of more than three thousand years.

A few examples will serve to illustrate this remarkable continuity in Indian civilisation. Sanskrit is still spoken as the tongue of the learned by thousands of Brahmans, as it was centuries before our era. Nor has it ceased to be used for literary purposes, for many books and journals written in the ancient language are still produced. The copying of Sanskrit manuscripts is still continued in hundreds of libraries in India, uninterrupted even by the introduction of printing during the present century. The Vedas are still learnt by heart as they were long before the invasion of Alexander, and could even now be restored from the lips of religious teachers if every manuscript or printed copy of them were destroyed. A Vedic stanza of immemorial antiquity, addressed to the sun-god Savitṛi, is still recited in the daily worship of the Hindus. The god Vishṇu, adored more than 3000 years ago, has countless votaries in India at the present day. Fire is still produced for sacrificial purposes by means of two sticks, as it was in ages even more remote. The wedding ceremony of the modern Hindu, to single out but one social custom, is essentially the same as it was long before the Christian era.

The history of ancient Indian literature naturally falls into two main periods. The first is the Vedic, which beginning perhaps as early as 1500 B.C., extends in its latest phase to about 200 B.C. In the former half of the Vedic age the character of its literature was creative and poetical, while the centre of culture lay in the territory of the Indus and its tributaries, the modern Panjāb; in the latter half, literature was theologically speculative in matter and prosaic in form, while the centre of intellectual life had shifted to the valley of the Ganges. Thus in the course of the Vedic age Aryan civilisation had overspread the whole of Hindustan Proper, the vast tract extending from the mouths of the Indus to those of the Ganges, bounded on the north by the Himālaya, and on the south by the Vindhya range. The second period, concurrent with the final offshoots of Vedic literature and closing with the Muhammadan conquest after 1000 A.D., is the Sanskrit period, strictly speaking. In a certain sense, owing to the continued literary use of Sanskrit, mainly for the composition of commentaries, this period may be regarded as coming down to the present day. During this second epoch Brahmanic culture was introduced into and overspread the southern portion of the continent called the Dekhan or "the South." In the course of these two periods taken together, Indian literature attained noteworthy results in nearly every department. The Vedic age, which, unlike the earlier epoch of Greece, produced only religious works, reached a high standard of merit in lyric poetry, and later made some advance towards the formation of a prose style.

The Sanskrit period embracing in general secular subjects, achieved distinction in many branches of literature, in national as well as court epic, in lyric and especially didactic poetry, in the drama, in fairy tales, fables, and romances. Everywhere we find much true poetry, the beauty of which is, however, marred by obscurity of style and the ever-increasing taint of artificiality. But this period produced few works which, regarded as a whole, are dominated by a sense of harmony and proportion. Such considerations have had little influence on the æsthetic notions of India. The tendency has been rather towards exaggeration, manifesting itself in all directions. The almost incredible development of detail in ritual observance; the extraordinary excesses of asceticism; the grotesque representations of mythology in art; the frequent employment of vast numbers in description; the immense bulk of the epics; the unparalleled conciseness of one of the forms of prose; the huge compounds habitually employed in the later style, are among the more striking manifestations of this defect of the Indian mind.

In various branches of scientific literature, in phonetics, grammar, mathematics, astronomy, medicine, and law, the Indians also achieved notable results. In some of these subjects their attainments are, indeed, far in advance of what was accomplished by the Greeks.

History is the one weak spot in Indian literature. It is, in fact, non-existent. The total lack of the historical sense is so characteristic, that the whole course of Sanskrit literature is darkened by the shadow of this defect, suffering as it does from an entire absence of exact chronology. So true is this, that the very date of KĀLIDĀSA, the greatest of Indian poets, was long a matter of controversy within the limits of a thousand years, and is even now doubtful to the extent of a century or two. Thus the dates of Sanskrit authors are in the vast majority of cases only known approximately, having been inferred from the indirect evidence of interdependence, quotation or allusion, development of language or style. As to the events of their lives, we usually know nothing at all, and only in a few cases one or two general facts. Two causes seem to have combined to bring about this remarkable result. In the first place, early India wrote no history because it never made any. The ancient Indians never went through a struggle for life, like the Greeks in the Persian and the Romans in the Punic wars, such as would have welded their tribes into a nation and developed political greatness. Secondly, the Brahmans, whose task it would naturally have been to record great deeds, had early embraced the doctrine that all action and existence are a positive evil, and could therefore have felt but little inclination to chronicle historical events.

Such being the case, definite dates do not begin to appear in Indian literary history till about 500 A.D. The chronology of the Vedic period is altogether conjectural, being based entirely on internal evidence. Three main literary strata can be clearly distinguished in it by differences in language and style, as well as in religious and social views. For the development of each of these strata a reasonable length of time must be allowed; but all we can here hope to do is to approximate to the truth by centuries. The lower limit of the second Vedic stratum cannot, however, be fixed later that 500 B.C., because its latest doctrines are presupposed by Buddhism, and the date of the death of Buddha has been with a high degree of probability calculated, from the recorded dates of the various Buddhist councils, to be 480 B.C. With regard to the commencement of the Vedic age, there seems to have been a decided tendency among Sanskrit scholars to place it too high. 2000 B.C. is commonly represented as its starting-point. Supposing this to be correct, the truly vast period of 1500 years is required to account for a development of language and thought hardly greater than that between the Homeric and the Attic age of Greece. Professor Max Müller's earlier estimate of 1200 B.C., formed forty years ago, appears to be much nearer the mark. A lapse of three centuries, say from 1300–1000 B.C., would amply account for the difference between what is oldest and newest in Vedic hymn poetry. Considering that the affinity of the oldest form of the Avestan language with the dialect of the Vedas is already so great that, by the mere application of phonetic laws, whole Avestan stanzas may be translated word for word into Vedic, so as to produce verses correct not only in form but in poetic spirit; considering further, that if we knew the Avestan language at as early a stage as we know the Vedic, the former would necessarily be almost identical with the latter, it is impossible to avoid the conclusion that the Indian branch must have separated from the Iranian only a very short time before the beginnings of Vedic literature, and can therefore have hardly entered the North-West of India even as early as 1500 B.C. All previous estimates of the antiquity of the Vedic period have been outdone by the recent theory of Professor Jacobi of Bonn, who supposes that period goes back to at least 4000 B.C. This theory is based on astronomical calculations connected with a change in the beginning of the seasons, which Professor Jacobi thinks has taken place since the time of the *Rigveda*. The whole estimate is, however, invalidated by the assumption of a doubtful, and even improbable, meaning in a Vedic word, which forms the very starting-point of the theory. Meanwhile we must rest content with the certainty that Vedic literature in any case is of considerably higher antiquity than that of Greece.

For the post-Vedic period we have, in addition to the

results of internal evidence, a few landmarks of general chronological importance in the visits of foreigners. The earliest date of this kind is that of the invasion of India by Alexander in 326 B.C. This was followed by the sojourn in India of various Greeks, of whom the most notable was MEGASTHENES. He resided for some years about 300 B.C. at the court of Pāṭaliputra (the modern Patna), and has left a valuable though fragmentary account of the contemporary state of Indian society. Many centuries later India was visited by three Chinese Buddhist pilgrims, FA HIAN (399 A.D.), HIOUEN THSANG (630–645), and I TSING (671–695). The records of their travels, which have been preserved, and are all now translated into English, shed much light on the social conditions, the religious thought, and the Buddhist antiquities of India in their day. Some general and specific facts about Indian literature also can be gathered from them. Hiouen Thsang especially supplies some important statements about contemporary Sanskrit poets. It is not till his time that we can say of any Sanskrit writer that he was alive in any particular year, excepting only the three Indian astronomers, whose exact dates in the fifth and sixth centuries have been recorded by themslves. It was only the information supplied by the two earlier Chinese writers that made possible the greatest archæological discovery of the present century in India, that of the site of Buddha's birthplace, Kapila-vastu, identified in December 1896. At the close of our period we have the very valuable account of the country at the time of the Muhammadan conquest by the Arabic author ALBĒRŪNĪ, who wrote his *India* in 1030 A.D.

It is evident from what has been said, that before 500 A.D. literary chronology, even in the Sanskrit period, is almost entirely relative, priority or posteriority being determined by such criteria as development of style or thought, the mention of earlier authors by name, stray political references as to the Greeks or to some well-known dynasty, and allusions to astronomical facts which cannot have been known before a certain epoch. Recent research, owing to increased specialisation, has made considerable progress towards greater chronological definiteness. More light will doubtless in course of time come from the political history of early India, which is being reconstructed, with great industry and ability, by various distinguished scholars from the evidence of coins, copper-plate grants, and rock or pillar inscriptions. These have been or are being published in the *Corpus Inscriptionum Indicarum*, the *Epigraphia Indica*, and various journals devoted to the study of Indian antiquities. The rise in the study of epigraphy during the last twenty years has, indeed, already yielded some direct information of importance about the literary and religious history of India, by fixing the date of some of the later poets as well as by throwing light on religious systems and whole classes of literature. Thus some metrical inscriptions of considerable length have been deciphered, which prove the existence of court poetry in Sanskrit and vernacular dialects from the first century of our era onwards. No direct evidence of this fact had previously been known.

The older inscriptions are also important in connection with Sanskrit literature as illustrating both the early history of Indian writing and the state of the language at the time. The oldest of them are the rock and pillar inscriptions, dating from the middle of the third century B.C., of the great Buddhist king AÇOKA, who ruled over Northern India from 259 to 222 B.C., and during whose reign was held the third Buddhist council, at which the canon of the Buddhist scriptures was probably fixed. The importance of these inscriptions can hardly be over-rated for the value of the information to be derived from them about the political, religious, and linguistic conditions of the age. Found scattered all over India, from Girnar (Giri-nagara) in Kathiawar to Dhauli in Orissa, from Kapur-di-Giri, north of the Kabul river, to Khalsi, they have been reproduced, deciphered, and translated. One of them, engraved on a pillar erected by Açoka to commemorate the actual birthplace of Buddha, was discovered only at the close of 1896.

These Açoka inscriptions are the earliest records of Indian writing. The question of the origin and age of writing in India, long involved in doubt and controversy, has been greatly cleared up by the recent palæographical researches of Professor BÜHLER. That great scholar has shown, that of the two kinds of script known in ancient India, the one called *Kharoshṭhī*, employed in the country of Gandhāra (Eastern Afghanistan and Northern Panjāb) from the fourth century B.C. to 200 A.D., was borrowed from the Aramaic type of Semitic writing in use during the fifth century B.C. It was always written from right to left, like its original. The other ancient Indian script, called *Brāhmī*, is, as Bühler shows, the true national writing of India, because all later Indian alphabets are descended from it, however dissimilar many of them may appear at the present day. It was regularly written from left to right; but that this was not its original direction is indicated by a coin of the fourth century B.C., the inscription on which runs from right to left. Dr. Bühler has shown that this writing is based on the oldest Northern Semitic or Phœnician type, represented on Assyrian weights and on the Moabite stone, which dates from about 890 B.C. He argues, with much probability, that it was introduced about 800 B.C. into India by traders coming by way of Mesopotamia.

References to writing in ancient Indian literature are, it is true, very rare and late; in no case, perhaps, earlier than the fourth century B.C., or not very long before the date of the Açoka inscriptions. Little weight, however, can be attached to the *argumentum ex silentio* in this instance. For though writing has now been extensively in use for an immense period, the native learning of the modern Indian is still based on oral tradition. The sacred scriptures as well as the sciences can only be acquired from the lips of a teacher, not from a manuscript; and as only memorial knowledge is accounted of value, writing and MSS. are rarely mentioned. Even modern poets do not wish to be read, but cherish the hope that their works may be recited. This immemorial practice, indeed, shows that the beginnings of Indian poetry and science go back to a time when writing was unknown, and a system of oral tradition, such as is referred to in the *Rigveda*, was developed before writing was introduced. The latter could, therefore, have been in use long before it began to be mentioned. The palæographical evidence of the Açoka inscriptions, in any case, clearly shows that writing was no recent invention in the third century B.C., for most of the letters have several, often very divergent forms, sometimes as many as nine or ten. A considerable length of time was, moreover, needed to elaborate from the twenty-two borrowed

Semitic symbols the full *Brāhmī* alphabet of forty-six letters. This complete alphabet, which was evidently worked out by learned Brahmans on phonetic principles, must have existed by 500 B.C., according to the strong arguments adduced by Professor Bühler. This is the alphabet which is recognised in Pāṇini's great Sanskrit grammar of about the fourth century B.C., and has remained unmodified ever since. It not only represents all the sounds of the Sanskrit language, but is arranged on a thoroughly scientific method, the simple vowels (short and long) coming first, then the diphthongs, and lastly the consonants in uniform groups according to the organs of speech with which they are pronounced. Thus the dental consonants appear together as *t*, *th*, *d*, *dh*, *n*, and the labials as *p*, *ph*, *b*, *bh*, *m*. We Europeans, on the other hand, 2500 years later, and in a scientific age, still employ an alphabet which is not only inadequate to represent all the sounds of our languages, but even preserves the random order in which vowels and consonants are jumbled up as they were in the Greek adaptation of the primitive Semitic arrangement of 3000 years ago.

In the inscriptions of the third century B.C. two types, the Northern and the Southern, may be distinguished in the *Brāhmī* writing. From the former is descended the group of Northern scripts which gradually prevailed in all the Aryan dialects of India. The most important of them is the *Nāgarī* (also called *Devanāgarī*), in which Sanskrit MSS. are usually written, and Sanskrit as well as Marāthī and Hindī books are regularly printed. It is recognisable by the characteristic horizontal line at the top of the letters. The oldest inscription engraved entirely in *Nāgarī* belongs to the eighth, and the oldest MS. written in it to the eleventh century. From the Southern variety of the *Brāhmī* writing are descended five types of script, all in use south of the Vindhya range. Among them are the characters employed in the Canarese and the Telugu country.

Owing to the perishability of the material on which they are written, Sanskrit MSS. older than the fourteenth century A.D. are rare. The two ancient materials used in India were strips of birch bark and palm leaves. The employment of the former, beginning in the North-West of India, where extensive birch forests clothe the slopes of the Himālaya, gradually spread to Central, Eastern, and Western India. The oldest known Sanskrit MS. written on birch bark dates from the fifth century A.D., and a Pāli MS. in *Kharoshṭhī*, which became known in 1897, is still older, but the use of this material doubtless goes back to far earlier days. Thus we have the statement of Quintus Curtius that the Indians employed it for writing on at the time of Alexander. The testimony of classical Sanskrit authors, as well as of Alberūnī, shows that leaves of birch bark (*bhūrja-pattra*) were also regularly used for letter-writing in early mediæval India.

The first example of a palm leaf Sanskrit MS. belongs to the sixth century A.D. It is preserved in Japan, but there is a facsimile of it in the Bodleian Library. According to the Chinese pilgrim Hiouen Thsang, the use of the palm leaf was common all over India in the seventh century; but that it was known many centuries earlier is proved by the fact that an inscribed copper-plate, dating from the first century A.D. at the latest, imitates a palm leaf in shape.

Paper was introduced by the Muhammadan conquest, and has been very extensively used since that time for the writing of MSS. The oldest known example of a paper Sanskrit MS. written in India is one from Gujarat, belonging to the early part of the thirteenth century. In Northern India, where ink was employed for writing, palm leaves went out of use after the introduction of paper. But in the South, where a stilus has always been employed for scratching in the character, palm leaves are still common for writing both MSS. and letters. The birch bark and palm leaf MSS. are held together by a cord drawn through a single hole in the middle, or through two placed some distance apart. This explains how the Sanskrit word for "knot," *grantha*, came to acquire the sense of "book."

Leather or parchment has never been utilised in India for MSS., owing to the ritual impurity of animal materials. For inscriptions copper-plates were early and frequently employed. They regularly imitate the shape of either palm leaves or strips of birch bark.

The actual use of ink (the oldest Indian name of which is *mashi*) is proved for the second century B.C. by an inscription from a Buddhist relic mound, and is rendered very probable for the fourth century B.C. by the statements of Nearchos and Quintus Curtius.

All the old palm leaf, birch bark, and paper Sanskrit MSS. have been written with ink and a reed pen, usually called *kalama* (a term borrowed from the Greek *kalamos*). In Southern India, on the other hand, it has always been the practice to scratch the writing on palm leaves with a stilus, the characters being subsequently blackened by soot or charcoal being rubbed into them.

Sanskrit MSS. of every kind are usually kept between thin strips of wood with cords wound round them, and wrapped up in coloured, sometimes embroidered, cloths. They have been, and still are, preserved in the libraries of temples, monasteries, colleges, the courts of princes, as well as private houses. A famous library was owned by King Bhoja of Dhār in the eleventh century. That considerable private libraries existed in fairly early times is shown by the fact that the Sanskrit author BĀṆA (about 620 A.D.) had in his employment a reader of manuscripts. Even at the present day there are many excellent libraries of Sanskrit MSS. in the possession of Brahmans all over India.

The ancient Indian language, like the literature composed in it, falls into the two main divisions of Vedic and Sanskrit. The former differs from the latter on the whole about as much as Homeric from classical Greek, or the Latin of the Salic hymns from that of Varro. Within the Vedic language, in which the sacred literature of India is written, several stages can be distinguished. In its transitions from one to the other it gradually grows more modern till it is ultimately merged in Sanskrit. Even in its earliest phase Vedic cannot be regarded as a popular tongue, but is rather an artificially archaic dialect, handed down from one generation to the other within the class of priestly singers. Of this the language itself supplies several indications. One of them is the employment side by side of forms belonging to different linguistic periods, a practice in which, however, the Vedic does not go so far as the Homeric dialect. The spoken language of the Vedic priests probably differed from this dialect of the hymns only in the absence of poetical constructions and archaisms. There was, in fact, even in the earlier Vedic age, a caste language, such as is to be found more or less wherever a literature has grown up ; but in India it has been more strongly marked than in any other country.

If, however, Vedic was no longer a natural tongue, but was already the scholastic dialect of a class, how much truer is this of the language of the later literature! Sanskrit differs from Vedic, but not in conformity with the natural development which appears in living languages. The phonetic condition of Sanskrit remains almost exactly the same as that of the earliest Vedic. In the matter of grammatical forms, too, the language shows itself to be almost stationary; for hardly any new formations or inflexions have made their appearance. Yet even from a grammatical point of view the later language has become very different from the earlier. This change was therefore brought about, not by new creations, but by successive losses. The most notable of these were the disappearance of the subjunctive mood and the reduction of a dozen infinitives to a single one. In declension the change consisted chiefly in the dropping of a number of synonymous by-forms. It is probable that the spoken Vedic, more modern and less complex than that of the hymns, to some extent affected the later literary language in the direction of simplification. But the changes in the language were mainly due to the regulating efforts of the grammarians, which were more powerful in India than anywhere else, owing to the early and exceptional development of grammatical studies in that country. Their influence alone can explain the elaborate nature of the phonetic combinations (called *Sandhi*) between the finals and initials of words in the Sanskrit sentence.

It is, however, the vocabulary of the language that has undergone the greatest modifications, as is indeed the case in all literary dialects; for it is beyond the power of grammarians to control change in this direction. Thus we find that the vocabulary has been greatly extended by derivation and composition according to recognised types. At the same time there are numerous words which, though old, seem to be new only because they happen by accident not to occur in the Vedic literature. Many really new words have, however, come in through continual borrowings from a lower stratum of language, while already existing words have undergone great changes of meaning.

This later phase of the ancient language of India was stereotyped by the great grammarian PĀṆINI towards the end of the fourth century B.C. It came to be called Sanskrit, the "refined" or "elaborate" (*saṃskṛi-ta,* literally "put together"), a term not found in the older grammarians, but occurring in the earliest epic, the *Rāmāyaṇa.* The name is meant to be opposed to that of the popular dialects called *Prākṛita,* and is so opposed, for instance, in the *Kāvyādarça,* or *Mirror of Poetry,* a work of the sixth century A.D. The older grammarians themselves, from YĀSKA (fifth century B.C.) onwards, speak of this classical dialect as *Bhāshā,* "the speech," in distinction from Vedic. The remarks they make about it point to a spoken language. Thus one of them, PATANJALI, refers to it as used "in the world," and designates the words of his Sanskrit as "current in the world." Pāṇini himself gives many rules which have no significance except in connection with living speech; as when he describes the accent or the lengthening of vowels in calling from a distance, in salutation, or in question and answer. Again, Sanskrit cannot have been a mere literary and school language, because there are early traces of its having had dialectic variations. Thus Yāska and Pāṇini mention the peculiarities of the "Easterns" and "Northerners," Kātyāyana refers to local divergences, and Patanjali specifies words occurring in single districts only. There is, indeed, no doubt that in the second century B.C. Sanskrit was actually spoken in the whole country called by Sanskrit writers Āryāvarta, or "Land of the Aryans," which lies between the Himālaya and the Vindhya range. But who spoke it there? Brahmans certainly did; for Patanjali speaks of them as the "instructed" (*çishṭa*), the employers of correct speech. Its use, however, extended beyond the Brahmans; for we read in Patanjali about a head-groom disputing with a grammarian as to the etymology of the Sanskrit word for "charioteer" (*sūta*). This agrees with the distribution of the dialects in the Indian drama, a distribution doubtless based on a tradition much older than the plays themselves. Here the king and those of superior rank speak Sanskrit, while the various forms of the popular dialect are assigned to women and to men of the people. The dramas also show that whoever did not speak Sanskrit at any rate understood it, for Sanskrit is there employed in conversation with speakers of Prākrit. The theatrical public, and that before which, as we know from frequent references in the literature, the epics were recited, must also have understood Sanskrit. Thus, though classical Sanskrit was from the beginning a literary and, in a sense, an artificial dialect, it would be erroneous to deny to it altogether the character of a colloquial language. It is indeed, as has already been mentioned, even now actually spoken in India by learned Brahmans, as well as written by them, for every-day purposes. The position of Sanskrit, in short, has all along been, and still is, much like that of

Hebrew among the Jews or of Latin in the Middle Ages.

Whoever was familiar with Sanskrit at the same time spoke one popular language or more. The question as to what these popular languages were brings us to the relation of Sanskrit to the vernaculars of India. The linguistic importance of the ancient literary speech for the India of to-day will become apparent when it is pointed out that all the modern dialects—excepting those of a few isolated aboriginal hill tribes—spoken over the whole vast territory between the mouths of the Indus and those of the Ganges, between the Himālaya and the Vindhya range, besides the Bombay Presidency as far south as the Portuguese settlement of Goa, are descended from the oldest form of Sanskrit. Starting from their ancient source in the north-west, they have overflowed in more and more diverging streams the whole peninsula except the extreme south-east. The beginnings of these popular dialects go back to a period of great antiquity. Even at the time when the Vedic hymns were composed, there must have existed a popular language which already differed widely in its phonetic aspect from the literary dialect. For the Vedic hymns contain several words of a phonetic type which can only be explained by borrowings on the part of their composers from popular speech.

We further know that in the sixth century B.C., Buddha preached his gospel in the language of the people, as opposed to that of the learned, in order that all might understand him. Thus all the oldest Buddhist literature dating from the fourth or fifth century B.C. was composed in the vernacular, originally doubtless in the dialect of Magadha (the modern Behar), the birthplace of Buddhism. Like Italian, as compared with Latin, this early popular speech is characterised by the avoidance of conjunct consonants and by fondness for final vowels. Thus the Sanskrit *sūtra*, "thread," and *dharma*, "duty," become *sutta* and *dhamma* respectively, while *vidyut*, "lightning," is transformed into *vijju*. The particular form of the popular language which became the sacred idiom of Southern Buddhism is known by the name of Pāli. Its original home is still uncertain, but its existence as early as the third century B.C. is proved beyond the range of doubt by the numerous rock and pillar inscriptions of Açoka. This dialect was in the third century B.C. introduced into Ceylon, and became the basis of Singhalese, the modern language of the island. It was through the influence of Buddhism that, from Açoka's time onwards, the official decrees and documents preserved in inscriptions were for centuries composed exclusively in Middle Indian (Prākrit) dialects. Sanskrit was not familiar to the chanceries during these centuries, though the introduction of Sanskrit verses in Prākrit inscriptions shows that Sanskrit was alive during this period, and proves its continuity for literary purposes. The older tradition of both the Buddhist and the Jain religion, in fact, ignored Sanskrit entirely, using only the popular dialects for all purposes.

But in course of time both the Buddhists and the Jains endeavoured to acquire a knowledge of Sanskrit. This led to the formation of an idiom which, being in the main Prākrit, was made to resemble the old language by receiving Sanskrit endings and undergoing other adaptations. It is therefore decidedly wrong to consider this artificial dialect an intermediate stage between Sanskrit and Pāli. This peculiar type of language is most pronounced in the poetical pieces called *gāthā* or "song," which occur in the canonical works of the Northern Buddhists, especially in the *Lalita-vistara*, a life of Buddha. Hence it was formerly called the Gāthā dialect. The term is, however, inaccurate, as Buddhist prose works have also been written in this mixed language.

The testimony of the inscriptions is instructive in showing the gradual encroachment of Sanskrit on the popular dialects used by the two non-Brahmanical religions. Thus in the Jain inscriptions of Mathurā (now Muttra), an almost pure Prākrit prevails down to the first century A.D. After that Sanskritisms become more and more frequent, till at last simple Sanskrit is written. Similarly in Buddhist inscriptions pure Prākrit is relieved by the mixed dialect, the latter by Sanskrit. Thus in the inscriptions of Nāsik, in Western India, the mixed dialect extends into the third, while Sanskrit first begins in the second century A.D. From the sixth century onwards Sanskrit prevails exclusively (except among the Jains) in inscriptions, though Prākritisms often occur in them. Even in the literature of Buddhism the mixed dialect was gradually supplanted by Sanskrit. Hence most of the Northern Buddhist texts have come down to us in Sanskrit, which, however, diverges widely in vocabulary from that of the sacred texts of the Brahmans, as well as from that of the classical literature, since they are full of Prākrit words. It is expressly attested by the Chinese pilgrim, Hiouen Thsang, that in the seventh century the Buddhists used Sanskrit even in oral theological discussions. The Jains finally did the same, though without entirely giving up Prākrit. Thus by the time of the Muhammadan conquest Sanskrit was almost the only written language of India. But while Sanskrit was recovering its ancient supremacy, the Prākrits had exercised a lasting influence upon it in two respects. They had supplied its vocabulary with a number of new words, and had transformed into a stress accent the old musical accent which still prevailed after the days of Pāṇini.

In the oldest period of Prākrit, that of the Pāli Açoka inscriptions and the early Buddhistic and Jain literature, two main dialects, the Western and the Eastern, may be distinguished. Between the beginning of our era and about 1000 A.D., mediæval Prākrit, which is still synthetic in character, is divided into four chief dialects. In the west we find *Apabhraṃça* ("decadent") in the valley of the Indus, and *Çaurasenī* in the Doab, with Mathurā as its centre. Subdivisions of the latter were *Gaurjarī* (*Gujaratī*), *Avantī* (Western *Rājputānī*), and *Mahārāshṭrī* (Eastern *Rājputānī*). The Eastern Prākrit now appears as *Māgadhī*, the dialect of Magadha, now Behar, and *Ardha-Māgadhī* (Half-Māgadhī), with Benares as its centre. These mediæval Prākrits are important in connection with Sanskrit literature, as they are the vernaculars employed by the uneducated classes in the Sanskrit drama.

They are the sources of all the Aryan languages of modern India. From the *Apabhraṃça* are derived *Sindhī*, Western *Panjābī*, and *Kashmīrī;* from *Çaurasenī* come Eastern *Panjabī* and *Hindī* (the old *Avantī*), as well as *Gujaratī;* while from the two forms of *Māgadhī* are descended *Marāthī* on the one hand, and the various dialects of Bengal on the other. These modern vernaculars, which began to develop from about 1000 A.D., are no longer inflexional languages, but are analytical like English, forming an interesting parallel in their development from ancient Sanskrit to the Romance dialects in their derivation from Latin. They have developed literatures of their own, which are based entirely on that of Sanskrit. The non-Aryan languages of the Dekhan, the Dravidian group, including Telugu, Canarese, Malāyalam, and Tamil, have not indeed been ousted by Aryan tongues, but they are full of words borrowed from Sanskrit, while their literature is dominated by Sanskrit models.

CHAPTER II

THE VEDIC PERIOD

ON the very threshold of Indian literature more than three thousand years ago, we are confronted with a body of lyrical poetry which, although far older than the literary monuments of any other branch of the Indo-European family, is already distinguished by refinement and beauty of thought, as well as by skill in the handling of language and metre. From this point, for a period of more than a thousand years, Indian literature bears an exclusively religious stamp; even those latest productions of the Vedic age which cannot be called directly religious are yet meant to further religious ends. This is, indeed, implied by the term "Vedic." For *veda*, primarily signifying "knowledge" (from *vid*, "to know"), designates "sacred lore," as a branch of literature. Besides this general sense, the word has also the restricted meaning of "sacred book."

In the Vedic period three well-defined literary strata are to be distinguished. The first is that of the four Vedas, the outcome of a creative and poetic age, in which hymns and prayers were composed chiefly to accompany the pressing and offering of the Soma juice or the oblation of melted butter (*ghṛita*) to the gods. The four Vedas are "collections," called *saṃhitā*, of hymns and prayers made for different ritual purposes. They are of varying age and significance. By far the most important as well as the oldest—for it is the very foundation of all Vedic literature—is the *Rigveda*, the "Veda of verses" (from *ṛich*, "a laudatory stanza"), consisting entirely of lyrics, mainly in praise of different gods. It may, therefore, be described as the book of hymns or psalms. The *Sāma-veda* has practically no independent value, for it consists entirely of stanzas (excepting only 75) taken from the *Rigveda* and arranged solely with reference to their place in the Soma sacrifice. Being meant to be sung to certain fixed melodies, it may be called the book of chants (*sāman*). The *Yajur-veda* differs in one essential respect from the *Sāma-veda*. It consists not only of stanzas (*ṛich*), mostly borrowed from the *Rigveda*, but also of original prose formulas. It resembles the *Sāma-veda*, however, in having its contents arranged in the order in which it was actually employed in various sacrifices. It is, therefore, a book of sacrificial prayers (*yajus*). The matter of this Veda has been handed down in two forms. In the one, the sacrificial formulas only are given; in the other, these are to a certain extent intermingled with their explanations. These three Vedas alone were at first recognised as canonical scriptures, being in the next stage of Vedic literature comprehensively spoken of as "the threefold knowledge" (*trayī vidyā*).

The fourth collection, the *Atharva-veda*, attained to this position only after a long struggle. Judged both by its language and by that portion of its matter which is analogous to the contents of the *Rigveda*, the *Atharva-veda* came into existence considerably later than that Veda. In form it is similar to the *Rigveda*, consisting for the most part of metrical hymns, many of which are taken from the last book of the older collection. In spirit, however, it is not only entirely different from the *Rigveda*, but represents a much more primitive stage of thought. While the *Rigveda* deals almost exclusively with the higher gods as conceived by a comparatively advanced and refined sacerdotal class, the *Atharva-veda* is, in the main, a book of spells and incantations appealing to the demon world, and teems with notions about witchcraft current among the lower grades of the population, and derived from an immemorial antiquity. These two, thus complementary to each other in contents, are obviously the most important of the four Vedas. As representing religious ideas at an earlier stage than any other literary monuments of the ancient world, they are of inestimable value to those who study the evolution of religious beliefs.

The creative period of the Vedas at length came to an end. It was followed by an epoch in which there no longer seemed any need to offer up new prayers to the gods, but it appeared more meritorious to repeat those made by the holy seers of bygone generations, and handed down from father to son in various priestly families. The old hymns thus came to be successively gathered together in the Vedic collections already mentioned, and in this form acquired an ever-increasing sanctity. Having ceased to produce poetry, the priesthood transferred their creative energies to the elaboration of the sacrificial ceremonial. The result was a ritual system far surpassing in complexity of detail anything the world has elsewhere known. The main importance of the old Vedic hymns and formulas now came to be their application to the innumerable details of the sacrifice. Around this combination of sacred verse and rite a new body of doctrine grew up in sacerdotal tradition, and finally assumed definite shape in the guise of distinct theological treatises entitled *Brāhmaṇas*, "books dealing with devotion or prayer" (*brahman*). They evidently did not come into being till a time when the hymns were already deemed ancient and sacred revelations, the priestly custodians of which no longer fully understood their meaning owing to the change undergone by the language. They are written in prose throughout, and are in some cases accented, like the Vedas themselves. They are thus notable as representing the oldest prose writing of the Indo-European family. Their style is, indeed, cumbrous, rambling, and disjointed, but distinct progress towards greater facility is observable within this literary period.

The chief purpose of the Brāhmaṇas is to explain the mutual relation of the sacred text and the ceremonial, as well as their symbolical meaning with reference to each other. With the exception of the occasional legends and striking thoughts which occur in them, they cannot be said to be at all attractive as literary productions. To support their explanations of the ceremonial, they interweave exegetical, linguistic, and etymological observations, and introduce myths and philosophical speculations in confirmation of their cosmogonic and theosophic theories. They form an aggregate of shallow and pedantic discussions, full of sacerdotal conceits, and fanciful, or even absurd, identifications, such as is doubtless unparalleled anywhere else. Yet, as the oldest treatises on ritual practices extant in any literature, they are of great interest to the student of the history of religions in general, besides furnishing much important material to the student of Indian antiquity in particular.

It results from what has been said that the contrasts between the two older phases of Vedic literature are strongly marked. The Vedas are poetical in matter and form; the Brāhmaṇas are prosaic and written in prose. The thought of the Vedas is on the whole natural and concrete; that of the Brāhmaṇas artificial and abstract. The chief significance of the Vedas lies in their mythology; that of the Brāhmaṇas in their ritual.

The subject-matter of the Brāhmaṇas which are attached to the various Vedas, differs according to the divergent duties performed by the kind of priest connected with each Veda. The Brāhmaṇas of the *Rigveda*, in explaining the ritual, usually limit themselves to the duties of the priest called *hoṭṛi* or "reciter," on whom it was incumbent to form the canon (*çastra*) for each particular rite, by selecting from the hymns the verses applicable to it. The Brāhmaṇas of the *Sāma-veda* are concerned only with the duties of the *udgātṛi* or "chanter" of the Sāmans; the Brāhmaṇas of the *Yajur-veda* with those of the *adhvaryu*, or the priest who is the actual sacrificer. Again, the Brāhmaṇas of the *Rigveda* more or less follow the order of the ritual, quite irrespectively of the succession of the hymns in the Veda itself. The Brāhmaṇas of the *Sāma-* and the *Yajur-veda*, on the other hand, follow the order of their respective Vedas, which are already arranged in the ritual sequence. The Brāhmaṇa of the *Sāma-veda*, however, rarely explains individual verses, while that of the *Yajur-veda* practically forms a running commentary on all the verses of the text.

The period of the Brāhmaṇas is a very important one in the history of Indian society. For in it the system of the four castes assumed definite shape, furnishing the frame within which the highly complex network of the castes of to-day has been developed. In that system the priesthood, who even in the first Vedic period had occupied an influential position, secured for themselves the dominant power which they have maintained ever since. The life of no other people has been so saturated with sacerdotal influence as that of the Hindus, among whom sacred learning is still the monopoly of the hereditary priestly caste. While in other early societies the chief power remained in the hands of princes and warrior nobles, the domination of the priesthood became possible in India as soon as the energetic life of conquest during the early Vedic times in the north-west was followed by a period of physical inactivity or indolence in the plains. Such altered conditions enabled the cultured class, who alone held the secret of the all-powerful sacrifice, to gain the supremacy of intellect over physical force.

The Brāhmaṇas in course of time themselves acquired a sacred character, and came in the following period to be classed along with the hymns as *çruti* or "hearing," that which was directly heard by or, as we should say, revealed to, the holy sages of old. In the sphere of revelation are included the later portions of the Brāhmaṇas, which form treatises of a specially theosophic character, and being meant to be imparted or studied in the solitude of the forest, are called *Āraṇyakas* or "Forest-books." The final part of these, again, are philosophical books named *Upanishads*, which belong to the latest stage of Brāhmaṇa literature. The pantheistic groundwork of their doctrine was later developed into the Vedānta system, which is still the favourite philosophy of the modern Hindus.

Works of Vedic "revelation" were deemed of higher authority in cases of doubt than the later works on religious and civil usage, called *smṛiti* or "memory," as embodying only the tradition derived from ancient sages.

We have now arrived at the third and last stage ot Vedic literature, that of the Sūtras. These are compendious treatises dealing with Vedic ritual on the one hand, and with customary law on the other. The rise of this class of writings was due to the need of reducing the vast and growing mass of details in ritual and custom, preserved in the Brāhmaṇas and in floating tradition, to a systematic shape, and of compressing them within a compass which did not impose too great a burden on the memory, the vehicle of all teaching and learning. The main object of the Sūtras is, therefore, to supply a short survey of the sum of these scattered details. They are not concerned with the interpretation of ceremonial or custom, but aim at giving a plain and methodical account of the whole course of the rites or practices with which they deal. For this purpose the utmost brevity was needed, a requirement which was certainly met in a manner unparalleled elsewhere. The very name of this class of literature, *sūtra*, "thread" or "clue" (from *siv*, "to sew"), points to its main characteristic and chief object—extreme conciseness. The prose in which these works are composed is so compressed that the wording of the most laconic telegram would often appear diffuse compared with it. Some of the Sūtras attain to an almost algebraic mode of expression, the formulas of which cannot be understood without the help of detailed commentaries. A characteristic aphorism has been preserved, which illustrates this straining after brevity. According to it, the composers of grammatical Sūtras delight as much in the saving of a short vowel as in the birth of a son. The full force of this remark can only be understood when it is remembered that a Brahman is deemed incapable of gaining heaven without a son to perform his funeral rites.

Though the works comprised in each class of Sūtras are essentially the same in character, it is natural to suppose that their composition extended over some length of time, and that those which are more concise and precise in their wording are the more recent; for the evolution of their style is obviously in the direction of increased succinctness. Research, it is true, has hitherto failed to arrive at any definite result as to the date of their composition. Linguistic investigations, however, tend to show that the Sūtras are closely connected in time with the grammarian Pāṇini, some of them appearing to be considerably anterior to him. We shall, therefore, probably not go very far wrong in assigning 500 and 200 B.C. as the chronological limits within which the Sūtra literature was developed.

The tradition of the Vedic ritual was handed down in two forms. The one class, called *Çrauta Sūtras,* because based on *çruti* or revelation (by which in this case the Brāhmaṇas are chiefly meant), deal with the ritual of the greater sacrifices, for the performance of which three or more sacred fires, as well as the ministrations of priests, are necessary. Not one of them presents a complete picture of the sacrifice, because each of them, like the Brāhmaṇas, describes only the duties of one or other of the three kinds of priests attached to the respective Vedas. In order to obtain a full description of each ritual ceremony, it is therefore needful to supplement the account given by one Çrauta Sūtra from that furnished by the rest.

The other division of the ritual Sūtras is based on *smṛiti* or tradition. These are the *Gṛihya Sūtras*, or "House Aphorisms," which deal with the household ceremonies, or the rites to be performed with the domestic fire in daily life. As a rule, these rites are not performed by a priest, but by the householder himself in company with his wife. For this reason there is, apart from deviations in arrangement and expression, omission or addition, no essential difference between the various Gṛihya Sūtras, except that the verses to be repeated which they contain are taken from the Veda to which they belong. Each Gṛihya Sūtra, besides being attached to and referring to the Çrauta Sūtra of the same school, presupposes a knowledge of it. But though thus connected, the two do not form a unity.

The second class of Sūtras, which deal with social and legal usage, is, like the Gṛihya Sūtras, also based on *smṛiti* or tradition. These are the *Dharma Sūtras*, which are in general the oldest sources of Indian law. As is implied by the term *dharma*, "religion and morality," their point of view is chiefly a religious one. They are closely connected with the Veda, which they quote, and which the later law-books regard as the first and highest source of *dharma*.

From the intensely crabbed and unintelligible nature of their style, and the studied baldness with which they present their subjects, it is evident that the Sūtras are inferior even to the Brāhmaṇas as literary productions. Judged, however, with regard to its matter, this strange phase of literature has considerable value. In all other ancient literatures knowledge of sacrificial rites can only be gained by collecting stray references. But in the ritual Sūtras we possess the ancient manuals which the priests used as the foundation of their sacrificial lore. Their statements are so systematic and detailed that it is possible to reconstruct from them various sacrifices without having seen them performed. They are thus of great importance for the history of religious institutions. But the Sūtras have a further value. For, as the life of the Hindu, more than that of any other nation, was, even in the Vedic age, surrounded with a network of religious forms, both in its daily course and in its more important divisions, the domestic ritual as well as the legal Sūtras are our most important sources for the study of the social conditions of ancient India. They are the oldest Indian records of all that is included under custom.

Besides these ritual and legal compendia, the Sūtra period produced several classes of works composed in this style, which, though not religious in character, had a religious origin. They arose from the study of the Vedas, which was prompted by the increasing difficulty of understanding the hymns, and of reciting them correctly, in consequence of the changes undergone by the language. Their chief object was to ensure the right recitation and interpretation of the sacred text. One of the most important classes of this ancillary literature comprises the *Prātiçākhya Sūtras*, which, dealing with accentuation, pronunciation, metre, and other matters, are chiefly concerned with the phonetic changes undergone by Vedic words when combined in a sentence. They contain a number of minute observations, such as have only been made over again by the phoneticians of the present day in Europe. A still more important branch of this subsidiary literature is grammar, in which the results attained by the Indians in the systematic analysis of language surpass those arrived at by any other nation. Little has been preserved of the earliest attempts in this direction, for all that had been previously done was superseded by the great Sūtra work of PĀṆINI. Though belonging probably to the middle of the Sūtra period, Pāṇini must be regarded as the starting-point of the Sanskrit age, the literature of which is almost entirely dominated by the linguistic standard stereotyped by him.

In the Sūtra period also arose a class of works specially designed for preserving the text of the Vedas from loss or change. These are the *Anukramaṇīs* or "Indices," which quote the first words of each hymn, its author, the deity celebrated in it, the number of verses it contains, and the metre in which it is composed. One of them states the total number of hymns, verses, words, and even syllables, contained in the *Rigveda*, besides supplying other details.

From this general survey of the Vedic period we now turn to a more detailed consideration of the different phases of the literature it produced.

CHAPTER III

THE RIGVEDA

In the dim twilight preceding the dawn of Indian literature the historical imagination can perceive the forms of Aryan warriors, the first Western conquerors of Hindustan, issuing from those passes in the north-west through which the tide of invasion has in successive ages rolled to sweep over the plains of India. The earliest poetry of this invading race, whose language and culture ultimately overspread the whole continent, was composed while its tribes still occupied the territories on both sides of the Indus now known as Eastern Kabulistan and the Panjāb. That ancient poetry has come down to us in the form of a collection of hymns called the *Rigveda*. The cause which gathered the poems it contains into a single book was not practical, as in the case of the *Sāma-* and *Yajur-veda*, but scientific and historical. For its ancient editors were undoubtedly impelled by the motive of guarding this heritage of olden time from change and destruction. The number of hymns comprised in the *Rigveda*, in the only recension which has been preserved, that of the Çākala school, is 1017, or, if the eleven supplementary hymns (called *Vālakhilya*) which are inserted in the middle of the eighth book are added, 1028. These hymns are grouped in ten books, called *maṇḍalas*, or "cycles," which vary in length, except that the tenth contains the same number of hymns as the first. In bulk the hymns of the *Rigveda* equal, it has been calculated, the surviving poems of Homer.

The general character of the ten books is not identical in all cases. Six of them (ii.–vii.) are homogeneous. Each of these, in the first place, is the work of a different seer or his descendants according to the ancient tradition, which is borne out by internal evidence. They were doubtless long handed down separately in the families to which they owed their being. Moreover, the hymns contained in these "family books," as they are usually called, are arranged on a uniform plan differing from that of the rest. The first, eighth, and tenth books are not the productions of a single family of seers respectively, but consist of a number of groups based on identity of authorship. The arrangement of the ninth book is in no way connected with its composers; its unity is due to all its hymns being addressed to the single deity Soma, while its groups depend on identity of metre. The family books also contain groups; but each of these is formed of hymns addressed to one and the same deity.

Turning to the principle on which the entire books of the *Rigveda* are arranged in relation to one another, we find that Books II.–VII., if allowance is made for later additions, form a series of collections which contain a successively increasing number of hymns. This fact, combined with the uniformity of these books in general character and internal arrangement, renders it probable that they formed the nucleus of the *Rigveda*, to which the remaining books were successively added. It further seems likely that the nine shorter collections, which form the second part of Book I., as being similarly based on identity of authorship, were subsequently combined and prefixed to the family books; which served as the model for their internal arrangement.

The hymns of the eighth book in general show a mutual affinity hardly less pronounced than that to be found in the family books. For they are connected by numerous repetitions of similar phrases and lines running through the whole book. The latter, however, does not form a parallel to the family books. For though a single family, that of the Kaṇvas, at least predominates among its authors, the prevalence in it of the strophic form of composition impresses upon it a character of its own. Moreover, the fact that the eighth book contains fewer hymns than the seventh, in itself shows that the former did not constitute one of the family series.

The first part (1–50) of Book I. has considerable affinities with the eighth, more than half its hymns being attributed to members of the Kaṇva family, while in the hymns composed by some of these Kaṇvas the favourite strophic metre of the eighth book reappears. There are, moreover, numerous parallel and directly identical passages in the two collections. It is, however, at present impossible to decide which of the two is the earlier, or why it is that, though so nearly related, they should have been separated. Certain it is that they were respectively added at the beginning and the end of a previously existing collection, whether they were divided for chronological reasons or because composed by different branches of the Kaṇva family.

As to the ninth book, it cannot be doubted that it came into being as a collection after the first eight books had been combined into a whole. Its formation was in fact the direct result of that combination. The hymns to

Soma Pavamāna ("the clearly flowing") are composed by authors of the same families as produced Books II.–VII., a fact, apart from other evidence, sufficiently indicated by their having the characteristic refrains of those families. The Pavamāna hymns have affinities to the first and eighth books also. When the hymns of the different families were combined into books, and clearly not till then, all their Pavamāna hymns were taken out and gathered into a single collection. This of course does not imply that the Pavamāna hymns themselves were of recent origin. On the contrary, though some of them may date from the time when the tenth book came into existence, there is good reason to suppose that the poetry of the Soma hymns, which has many points in common with the Avesta, and deals with a ritual going back to the Indo-Iranian period, reached its conclusion as a whole in early times among the Vedic singers. Differences of age in the hymns of the ninth book have been almost entirely effaced; at any rate, research has as yet hardly succeeded in distinguishing chronological stages in this collection.

With regard to the tenth book, there can be no doubt that its hymns came into being at a time when the first nine already existed. Its composers grew up in the knowledge of the older books, with which they betray their familiarity at every turn. The fact that the author of one of its groups (20–26) begins with the opening words (*agnim īḷe*) of the first stanza of the *Rigveda*, is probably an indication that Books I.–IX. already existed in his day even as a combined collection. That the tenth book is indeed an aggregate of supplementary hymns is shown by its position after the Soma book, and by the number of its hymns being made up to that of the first book (191). The unity which connects its poetry is chronological; for it is the book of recent groups and recent single hymns. Nevertheless the supplements collected in it appear for the most part to be older than the additions which occur in the earlier books.

There are many criteria, derived from its matter as well as its form, showing the recent origin of the tenth book. With regard to mythology, we find the earlier gods beginning to lose their hold on the imagination of these later singers. Some of them seem to be disappearing, like the goddess of Dawn, while only deities of widely established popularity, such as Indra and Agni, maintain their position. The comprehensive group of the *Viçve devās*, or "All gods," has alone increased in prominence. On the other hand, an altogether new type, the deification of purely abstract ideas, such as "Wrath" and "Faith," now appears for the first time. Here, too, a number of hymns are found dealing with subjects foreign to the earlier books, such as cosmogony and philosophical speculation, wedding and burial rites, spells and incantations, which give to this book a distinctive character besides indicating its recent origin.

Linguistically, also, the tenth book is clearly distinguished as later than the other books, forming in many respects a transition to the other Vedas. A few examples will here suffice to show this. Vowel contractions occur much more frequently, while the hiatus has grown rarer. The use of the letter *l*, as compared with *r*, is, in agreement with later Sanskrit, strikingly on the increase. In inflexion the employment of the Vedic nominative plural in *āsas* is on the decline.

With regard to the vocabulary, many old words are going out of use, while others are becoming commoner. Thus the particle *sīm*, occurring fifty times in the rest of the *Rigveda*, is found only once in the tenth book. A number of words common in the later language are only to be met with in this book; for instance, *labh*, "to take," *kāla*, "time," *lakshmī*, "fortune," *evam*, "thus." Here, too, a number of conscious archaisms can be pointed out.

Thus the tenth book represents a definitely later stratum of composition in the *Rigveda*. Individual hymns in the earlier books have also been proved by various recognised criteria to be of later origin than others, and some advance has been made towards assigning them to three or even five literary epochs. Research has, however, not yet arrived at any certain results as to the age of whole groups in the earlier books. For it must be borne in mind that posteriority of collection and incorporation does not necessarily prove a later date of composition.

Some hundreds of years must have been needed for all the hymns found in the *Rigveda* to come into being. There was also, doubtless, after the separation of the Indians from the Iranians, an intermediate period, though it was probably of no great length. In this transitional age must have been composed the more ancient poems which are lost, and in which the style of the earliest preserved hymns, already composed with much skill, was developed. The poets of the older part of the *Rigveda* themselves mention predecessors, in whose wise they sing, whose songs they desire to renew, and speak of ancestral hymns produced in days of yore. As far as linguistic evidence is concerned, it affords little help in discriminating periods within the *Rigveda* except with regard to the tenth book. For throughout the hymns, in spite of the number of authors, essentially the same language prevails. It is quite possible to distinguish differences of thought, style, and poetical ability, but hardly any differences of dialect. Nevertheless, patient and minute linguistic research, combined with the indications derived from arrangement, metre, and subject-matter, is beginning to yield evidence which may lead to the recognition of chronological strata in the older books of the *Rigveda.*

Though the aid of MSS. for this early period entirely fails, we yet happily possess for the *Rigveda* an abundant mass of various readings over 2000 years old. These are contained in the other Vedas, which are largely composed of hymns, stanzas, and lines borrowed from the *Rigveda.* The other Vedas are, in fact, for the criticism of the *Rigveda,* what manuscripts are for other literary monuments. We are thus enabled to collate with the text of the *Rigveda* directly handed down, various readings considerably older than even the testimony of Yāska and of the Prātiçākhyas.

The comparison of the various readings supplied by the later Vedas leads to the conclusion that the text of the *Rigveda* existed, with comparatively few exceptions, in its present form, and not in a possibly different recension, at the time when the text of the *Sāma-veda,* the oldest form of the *Yajur-veda,* and the *Atharva-veda* was constituted. The number of cases is infinitesimal in which the *Rigveda* shows a corruption from which the others are free. Thus it appears that the kernel of Vedic tradition, as represented by the *Rigveda*, has come down to us, with a high degree of fixity and remarkable care for verbal integrity, from a period which can hardly be less remote than 1000 B.C.

It is only natural that a sacred collection of poetry, historical in its origin, and the heritage of oral tradition before the other Vedas were composed and the details of the later ritual practice were fixed, should have continued to be preserved more accurately than texts formed mainly by borrowing from it hymns which were arbitrarily cut up into groups of verses or into single verses, solely in order to meet new liturgical needs. For those who removed verses of the *Rigveda* from their context and mixed them up with their own new creations would not feel bound to guard such verses from change as strictly as those who did nothing but continue to hand down, without any break, the ancient text in its connected form. The control of tradition would be wanting where quite a new tradition was being formed.

The criticism of the text of the *Rigveda* itself is concerned with two periods. The first is that in which it existed alone before the other Vedas came into being; the second is that in which it appears in the phonetically modified form called the Saṃhitā text, due to the labours of grammatical editors. Being handed down in the older period exclusively by oral tradition, it was not preserved in quite authentic form down to the time of its final redaction. It did not entirely escape the fate suffered by all works which, coming down from remote antiquity, survive into an age of changed linguistic conditions. Though there are undeniable corruptions in detail belonging to the older period, the text maintained a remarkably high level of authenticity till such modifications as it had undergone reached their conclusion in the Saṃhitā text. This text differs in hundreds of places from that of the composers of the hymns; but its actual words are nearly always the same as those used by the ancient seers. Thus there would be no uncertainty as to whether the right word, for instance, was *sumnam* or *dyumnam*. The difference lies almost entirely in the phonetic changes which the words have undergone according to the rules of *Sandhi* prevailing in the classical language. Thus what was formerly pronounced as *tuaṃ hi agne* now appears as *tvaṃ hy agne*. The modernisation of the text thereby produced is, however, only partial, and is often inconsistently applied. The euphonic combinations introduced in the Saṃhitā text have interfered with the metre. Hence by reading according to the latter the older text can be restored. At the same time the Saṃhitā text has preserved the smallest minutiæ of detail most liable to corruption, and the slightest difference in the matter of accent and alternative forms, which might have been removed with the greatest ease. Such points furnish an additional proof that the extreme care with which the verbal integrity of the text was guarded goes back to the earlier period itself. Excepting single mistakes of tradition in the first, and those due to grammatical theories in the second period, the old text of the *Rigveda* thus shows itself to have been preserved from a very remote antiquity with marvellous accuracy even in the smallest details.

From the explanatory discussions of the Brāhmaṇas in connection with the *Rigveda*, it results that the text of the latter must have been essentially fixed in their time, and that too in quite a special manner, more, for instance, than the prose formulas of the *Yajurveda*. For the *Çatapatha Brāhmaṇa*, while speaking of the possibility of varying some of these formulas, rejects the notion of changing the text of a certain Rigvedic verse, proposed by some teachers, as something not to be thought of. The Brāhmaṇas further often mention the fact that such and such a hymn or liturgical group contains a particular number of verses. All such numerical statements appear to agree with the extant text of the *Rigveda*. On the other hand, transpositions and omissions of Rigvedic verses are to be found in the Brāhmaṇas. These, however, are only connected with the ritual form of those verses, and in no way show that the text from which they were taken was different from ours.

The Sūtras also contain altered forms of Rigvedic verses, but these are, as in the case of the Brāhmaṇas, to be explained not from an older recension of the text, but from the necessity of adapting them to new ritual technicalities. On the other hand, they contain many statements which confirm our present text. Thus all that the Sūtra of Çānkhāyana says about the position occupied by verses in a hymn, or the total number of verses contained in groups of hymns, appears invariably to agree with our text.

We have yet to answer the question as to when the Saṃhitā text, which finally fixed the canonical form of the *Rigveda*, was constituted. Now the Brāhmaṇas contain a number of direct statements as to the number of syllables in a word or a group of words, which are at variance with the Saṃhitā text owing to the vowel contractions made in the latter. Moreover, the old part of the Brāhmaṇa literature shows hardly any traces of speculations about phonetic questions connected with the Vedic text. The conclusion may therefore be drawn that the Saṃhitā text did not come into existence till after the completion of the Brāhmaṇas. With regard to the Āraṇyakas and Upanishads, which form supplements to the Brāhmaṇas, the case is different. These works not only mention technical grammatical terms for certain groups of letters, but contain detailed doctrines about the phonetic treatment of the Vedic text. Here, too, occur for the first time the names of certain theological grammarians, headed by Çākalya and Māṇḍūkeya, who are also recognised as authorities in the Prātiçākhyas. The Āraṇyakas and Upanishads accordingly form a transition, with reference to the treatment of grammatical questions, between the age of the Brāhmaṇas and that of Yāska and the Prātiçākhyas. The Saṃhitā text must have been created in this intermediate period, say about 600 B.C.

This work being completed, extraordinary precautions soon began to be taken to guard the canonical text thus fixed against the possibility of any change or loss. The result has been its preservation with a faithfulness unique in literary history. The first step taken in this direction was the constitution of the Pada, or "word" text, which being an analysis of the Saṃhitā, gives each separate word in its independent form, and thus to a considerable extent restores the Saṃhitā text to an older stage. That the Pada text was not quite contemporaneous in origin with the other is shown by its containing some undoubted misinterpretations and misunderstandings. Its composition can, however, only be separated by a short interval from that of the Saṃhitā, for it appears to have been known to the writer of the *Aitareya Āraṇyaka*, while its author, Çākalya, is older than both Yāska, who quotes him, and Çaunaka, composer of the *Rigveda Prātiçākhya*, which is based on the Pada text.

The importance of the latter as a criterion of the authenticity of verses in the *Rigveda* is indicated by the following fact. There are six verses in the *Rigveda*[1] not analysed in the Pada text, but only given there over again in the Saṃhitā form. This shows that Çākalya did not acknowledge them as truly Rigvedic, a view justified by internal evidence. This group of six, which is doubtless exhaustive, stands midway between old additions which Çākalya recognised as canonical, and the new appendages called *Khilas*, which never gained admission into the Pada text in any form.

A further measure for preserving the sacred text from alteration with still greater certainty was soon taken in the form of the *Krama-pāṭha*, or "step-text." This is old, for it, like the *Pada-pāṭha*, is already known to the author of the *Aitareya Āraṇyaka*. Here every word of the Pada text occurs twice, being connected both with that which precedes and that which follows. Thus the first four words, if represented by *a*, *b*, *c*, *d*, would be read as *ab*, *bc*, *cd*. The *Jaṭā-pāṭha*, or "woven-text," in its turn based on the *Krama-pāṭha*, states each of its combinations three times, the second time in reversed order (*ab*, *ba*, *ab*; *bc*, *cb*, *bc*). The climax of complication is reached in the *Ghana-pāṭha*, in which the order is *ab*, *ba*, *abc*, *cba*, *abc*; *bc*, *cb*, *bcd*, &c.

The Prātiçākhyas may also be regarded as safeguards

[1] vii. 59, 12; x. 20, 1; 121, 10; 190, 1–3.

of the text, having been composed for the purpose of exhibiting exactly all the changes necessary for turning the Pada into the Saṃhitā text.

Finally, the class of supplementary works called Anukramaṇīs, or "Indices," aimed at preserving the *Rigveda* intact by registering its contents from various points of view, besides furnishing calculations of the number of hymns, verses, words, and even syllables, contained in the sacred book.

The text of the *Rigveda* has come down to us in a single recension only; but is there any evidence that other recensions of it existed in former times?

The *Charaṇa-vyūha*, or "Exposition of Schools," a supplementary work of the Sūtra period, mentions as the five *çākhās* or "branches" of the *Rigveda*, the Çākalas, the Vāshkalas, the Āçvalāyanas, the Çānkhāyanas, and the Māṇḍūkeyas. The third and fourth of these schools, however, do not represent different recensions of the text, the sole distinction between them and the Çākalas having been that the Āçvalāyanas recognised as canonical the group of the eleven *Vālakhilya* or supplementary hymns, and the Çānkhāyanas admitted the same group, diminished only by a few verses. Hence the tradition of the Purāṇas, or later legendary works, mentions only the three schools of Çākalas, Vāshkalas, and Māṇḍūkas. If the latter ever possessed a recension of an independent character, all traces of it were lost at an early period in ancient India, for no information of any kind about it has been preserved. Thus only the two schools of the Çākalas and the Vāshkalas come into consideration. The subsidiary Vedic writings contain sufficient evidence to show that the text of the Vāshkalas differed from that of the Çākalas only in admitting eight additional hymns, and in assigning another position to a group of the first book. But in these respects it compares unfavourably with the extant text. Thus it is evident that the Çākalas not only possessed the best tradition of the text of the *Rigveda*, but handed down the only recension, in the true sense, which, as far as we can tell, ever existed.

The text of the *Rigveda*, like that of the other Saṃhitās, as well as of two of the Brāhmaṇas (the *Çatapatha* and the *Taittirīya*, together with its Āraṇyaka), has come down to us in an accented form. The peculiarly sacred character of the text rendered the accent very important for correct and efficacious recitation. Analogously the accent was marked by the Greeks in learned and model editions only. The nature of the Vedic accent was musical, depending on the pitch of the voice, like that of the ancient Greeks. This remained the character of the Sanskrit accent till later than the time of Pāṇini. But just as the old Greek musical accent, after the beginning of our era, was transformed into a stress accent, so by the seventh century A.D. (and probably long before) the Sanskrit accent had undergone a similar change. While, however, in modern Greek the stress accent has remained, owing to the high pitch of the old acute, on the same syllable as bore the musical accent in the ancient language, the modern pronunciation of Sanskrit has no connection with the Vedic accent, but is dependent on the quantity of the last two or three syllables, much the same as in Latin. Thus the penultimate, if long, is accented, *e.g.* *Kālidấsa*, or the antepenultimate, if long and followed by a short syllable, *e.g.* *brấhmaṇa* or *himấlaya* ("abode of snow"). This change of accent in Sanskrit was brought about by the influence of Prākrit, in which, as there is evidence to show, the stress accent is very old, going back several centuries before the beginning of our era.

There are three accents in the *Rigveda* as well as the other sacred texts. The most important of these is the rising accent, called *ud-ātta* ("raised"), which corresponds to the Greek acute. Comparative philology shows that in Sanskrit it rests on the same syllable as bore it in the proto-Aryan language. In Greek it is generally on the same syllable as in Sanskrit, except when interfered with by the specifically Greek law restricting the accent to one of the last three syllables. Thus the Greek *heptá* corresponds to the Vedic *saptá*, "seven." The low-pitch accent, which precedes the acute, is called the *anudātta* ("not raised"). The third is the falling accent, which usually follows the acute, and is called *svarita* ("sounded").

Of the four different systems of marking the accent in Vedic texts, that of the *Rigveda* is most commonly employed. Here the acute is not marked at all, while the low-pitch *anudātta* is indicated by a horizontal stroke below the syllable bearing it, and the *svarita* by a vertical stroke above. Thus *y̱ajnasyà* ("of sacrifice") would mean that the second syllable has the acute and the third the *svarita* (*yajnásyà*). The reason why the acute is not marked is because it is regarded as the middle tone between the other two.[1]

The hymns of the *Rigveda* consist of stanzas ranging in number from three to fifty-eight, but usually not

[1] The other three systems are: (1) that of the *Maitrāyaṇī* and *Kāṭhaka* Saṃhitās (two recensions of the Black *Yajurveda*), which mark the acute with a vertical stroke above; (2) that of the *Çatapatha Brāhmaṇa*, which marks the acute with a horizontal stroke below; and (3) that of the *Sāmaveda*, which indicates the three accents with the numerals 1, 2, 3, to distinguish three degrees of pitch, the acute (1) here being the highest.

exceeding ten or twelve. These stanzas (often loosely called verses) are composed in some fifteen different metres, only seven of which, however, are at all frequent. Three of them are by far the commonest, claiming together about four-fifths of the total number of stanzas in the *Rigveda*.

There is an essential difference between Greek and Vedic prosody. Whereas the metrical unit of the former system is the foot, in the latter it is the line (or verse), feet not being distinguished. Curiously enough, however, the Vedic metrical unit is also called *pāda*, or "foot," but for a very different reason; for the word has here really the figurative sense of "quarter" (from the foot of a quadruped), because the most usual kind of stanza has four lines. The ordinary *pādas* consist of eight, eleven, or twelve syllables. A stanza or *ṛich* is generally formed of three or four lines of the same kind. Four or five of the rarer types of stanza are, however, made up of a combination of different lines.

It is to be noted that the Vedic metres have a certain elasticity to which we are unaccustomed in Greek prosody, and which recalls the irregularities of the Latin Saturnian verse. Only the rhythm of the last four or five syllables is determined, the first part of the line not being subject to rule. Regarded in their historical connection, the Vedic metres, which are the foundation of the entire prosody of the later literature, occupy a position midway between the system of the Indo-Iranian period and that of classical Sanskrit. For the evidence of the Avesta, with its eight and eleven syllable lines, which ignore quantity, but are combined into stanzas otherwise the same as those of the *Rigveda*, indicates that the metrical practice of the period when Persians and Indians were still one people, depended on no other principle than the counting of syllables. In the Sanskrit period, on the other hand, the quantity of every syllable in the line was determined in all metres, with the sole exception of the loose measure (called *çloka*) employed in epic poetry. The metrical regulation of the line, starting from its end, thus finally extended to the whole. The fixed rhythm at the end of the Vedic line is called *vṛitta*, literally "turn" (from *vṛit*, Lat. *vert-ere*), which corresponds etymologically to the Latin *versus*.

The eight-syllable line usually ends in two iambics, the first four syllables, though not exactly determined, having a tendency to be iambic also. This verse is therefore the almost exact equivalent of the Greek iambic dimeter.

Three of these lines combine to form the *gāyatrī* metre, in which nearly one-fourth (2450) of the total number of stanzas in the *Rigveda* is composed. An example of it is the first stanza of the *Rigveda*, which runs as follows:—

Agním īle puróhitaṃ
Yajnásya devám ṛitvíjam
Hótāraṃ ratnadhā́tamam.

It may be closely rendered thus in lines imitating the rhythm of the original:—

I praise Agni, domestic priest,
God, minister of sacrifice,
Herald, most prodigal of wealth.

Four of these eight-syllable lines combine to form the *anushṭubh* stanza, in which the first two and the last two are more closely connected. In the *Rigveda* the number of stanzas in this measure amounts to only about one-third of those in the *gāyatrī*. This relation is gradually reversed, till we reach the post-Vedic period, when the *gāyatrī* is found to have disappeared, and the *anushṭubh* (now generally called *çloka*) to have become the predominant measure of Sanskrit poetry. A development in the character of this metre may be observed within the *Rigveda* itself. All its verses in the oldest hymns are the same, being iambic in rhythm. In later hymns, however, a tendency to differentiate the first and third from the second and fourth lines, by making the former non-iambic, begins to show itself. Finally, in the latest hymns of the tenth book the prevalence of the iambic rhythm disappears in the odd lines. Here every possible combination of quantity in the last four syllables is found, but the commonest variation, nearly equalling the iambic in frequency, is ⏑——⏓. The latter is the regular ending of the first and third line in the post-Vedic *çloka*.

The twelve-syllable line ends thus: —⏑—⏑⏓. Four of these together form the *jagatī* stanza. The *trishṭubh* stanza consists of four lines of eleven syllables, which are practically catalectic *jagatīs*, as they end —⏑—⏓. These two verses being so closely allied and having the same cadence, are often found mixed in the same stanza. The *trishṭubh* is by far the commonest metre, about two-fifths of the *Rigveda* being composed in it.

Speaking generally, a hymn of the *Rigveda* consists entirely of stanzas in the same metre. The regular and typical deviation from this rule is to conclude a hymn with a single stanza in a metre different from that of the rest, this being a natural method of distinctly marking its close.

A certain number of hymns of the *Rigveda* consist

not merely of a succession of single stanzas, but of equal groups of stanzas. The group consists either of three stanzas in the same simple metre, generally *gāyatrī*, or of the combination of two stanzas in different mixed metres. The latter strophic type goes by the name of *Pragātha*, and is found chiefly in the eighth book of the *Rigveda*.

CHAPTER IV

POETRY OF THE RIGVEDA

BEFORE we turn to describe the world of thought revealed in the hymns of the *Rigveda*, the question may naturally be asked, to what extent is it possible to understand the true meaning of a book occupying so isolated a position in the remotest age of Indian literature? The answer to this question depends on the recognition of the right method of interpretation applicable to that ancient body of poetry. When the *Rigveda* first became known, European scholars, as yet only acquainted with the language and literature of classical Sanskrit, found that the Vedic hymns were composed in an ancient dialect and embodied a world of ideas far removed from that with which they had made themselves familiar. The interpretation of these hymns was therefore at the outset barred by almost insurmountable difficulties. Fortunately, however, a voluminous commentary on the *Rigveda*, which explains or paraphrases every word of its hymns, was found to exist. This was the work of the great Vedic scholar SĀYAṆA, who lived in the latter half of the fourteenth century A.D. at Vijayanagara ("City of Victory"), the ruins of which lie near Bellary in Southern India. As his commentary constantly referred to ancient authorities, it was thought to have preserved the true meaning of the *Rigveda* in a traditional interpretation going back to the most ancient times. Nothing further seemed to be necessary than to ascertain the explanation of the original text which prevailed in India five centuries ago, and is laid down in Sāyaṇa's work. This view is represented by the translation of the *Rigveda* begun in 1850 by H. H. Wilson, the first professor of Sanskrit at Oxford.

Another line was taken by the late Professor Roth, the founder of Vedic philology. This great scholar propounded the view that the aim of Vedic interpretation was not to ascertain the meaning which Sāyaṇa, or even YĀSKA, who lived eighteen centuries earlier, attributed to the Vedic hymns, but the meaning which the ancient poets themselves intended. Such an end could not be attained by simply following the lead of the commentators. For the latter, though valuable guides towards the understanding of the later theological and ritual literature, with the notions and practice of which they were familiar, showed no continuity of tradition from the time of the poets; for the tradition supplied by them was solely that which was handed down among interpreters, and only began when the meaning of the hymns was no longer fully comprehended. There could, in fact, be no other tradition; interpretation only arising when the hymns had become obscure. The commentators, therefore, simply preserved attempts at the solution of difficulties, while showing a distinct tendency towards misinterpreting the language as well as the religious, mythological, and cosmical ideas of a vanished age by the scholastic notions prevalent in their own.

It is clear from what Yāska says that some important discrepancies in opinion prevailed among the older expositors and the different schools of interpretation which flourished before his time. He gives the names of no fewer than seventeen predecessors, whose explanations of the Veda are often conflicting. Thus one of them interprets the word *Nāsatyau*, an epithet of the Vedic Dioskouroi, as "true, not false;" another takes it to mean "leaders of truth," while Yāska himself thinks it might mean "nose-born"! The gap between the poets and the early interpreters was indeed so great that one of Yāska's predecessors, named Kautsa, actually had the audacity to assert that the science of Vedic exposition was useless, as the Vedic hymns and formulas were obscure, unmeaning, or mutually contradictory. Such criticisms Yāska meets by replying that it was not the fault of the rafter if the blind man did not see it. Yāska himself interprets only a very small portion of the hymns of the *Rigveda*. In what he does attempt to explain, he largely depends on etymological considerations for the sense he assigns. He often gives two or more alternative or optional senses to the same word. The fact that he offers a choice of meanings shows that he had no earlier authority for his guide, and that his renderings are simply conjectural; for no one can suppose that the authors of the hymns had more than one meaning in their minds.

It is, however, highly probable that Yāska, with all the appliances at his command, was able to ascertain the sense of many words which scholars who, like Sāyaṇa, lived nearly two thousand years later, had no means of discovering. Nevertheless Sāyaṇa is sometimes found to depart from Yāska. Thus we arrive at the dilemma that either the old interpreter is wrong or the later one does not follow the tradition. There are also many instances in which Sāyaṇa, independently of Yāska, gives a variety of inconsistent explanations of a word, both in interpreting a single passage or in commenting on different passages. Thus *çārada*, "autumnal," he explains in one place as "fortified for a year," in another as "new or fortified for a year," and in a third as "belonging to a demon called Çarad." One of the defects of Sāyaṇa is, in fact, that he limits his view in most cases to the single verse he has before him. A detailed examination of his explanations, as well as those of Yāska, has shown that there is in the *Rigveda* a large number of the most difficult words, about the proper sense of which neither scholar had any certain information from either tradition or etymology. We are therefore justified in saying about them that there is in the hymns no unusual or difficult word or obscure text in regard to which the authority of the commentators should be received as final, unless it is supported by probability, by the context, or by parallel passages. Thus no translation of the *Rigveda* based exclusively on Sāyaṇa's commentary can possibly be satisfactory. It would, in fact, be as unreasonable to take him for our sole guide as to make our understanding of the Hebrew books of the Old Testament dependent on the Talmud and the Rabbis. It must, indeed, be admitted that from a large proportion of Sāyaṇa's interpretations most material help can be derived, and that he has been of the greatest service in facilitating and accelerating the comprehension of the Veda. But there is little information of value to be derived from him, that, with our knowledge of later Sanskrit, with the other remains of ancient Indian literature, and with our various philological appliances, we might not sooner or later have found out for ourselves.

Roth, then, rejected the commentators as our chief guides in interpreting the *Rigveda,* which, as the earliest literary monument of the Indian, and indeed of the Aryan race, stands quite by itself, high up on an isolated peak of remote antiquity. As regards its more peculiar and difficult portions, it must therefore be interpreted mainly through itself; or, to apply in another sense the words of an Indian commentator, it must shine by its own light and be self-demonstrating. Roth further expressed the view that a qualified European is better able to arrive at the true meaning of the *Rigveda* than a Brahman interpreter. The judgment of the former is unfettered by theological bias; he possesses the historical faculty, and he has also a far wider intellectual horizon, equipped as he is with all the resources of scientific scholarship. Roth therefore set himself to compare carefully all passages parallel in form and matter, with due regard to considerations of context, grammar, and etymology, while consulting, though, perhaps, with insufficient attention, the traditional interpretations. He thus subjected the *Rigveda* to a historical treatment within the range of Sanskrit itself. He further called in the assistance rendered from without by the comparative method, utilising the help afforded not only by the *Avesta,* which is so closely allied to the *Rigveda* in language and matter, but also by the results of comparative philology, resources unknown to the traditional scholar.

By thus ascertaining the meaning of single words, the foundations of the scientific interpretation of the Vedas were laid in the great Sanskrit Dictionary, in seven volumes, published by Roth in collaboration with Böhtlingk between 1852 and 1875. Roth's method is now accepted by every scientific student of the Veda. Native tradition is, however, being more fully exploited than was done by Roth himself, for it is now more clearly recognised that no aid to be derived from extant Indian scholarship ought to be neglected. Under the guidance of such principles the progress already made in solving many important problems presented by Vedic literature has been surprising, when we consider the shortness of the time and the fewness of the labourers, of whom only two or three have been natives of this country. As a general result, the historical sense has succeeded in grasping the spirit of Indian antiquity, long obscured by native misinterpretation. Much, of course, still remains to be done by future generations of scholars, especially in detailed and minute investigation. This could not be otherwise when we remember that Vedic research is only the product of the last fifty years, and that, notwithstanding the labours of very numerous Hebrew scholars during several centuries, there are, in the Psalms and the Prophetic Books of the Old Testament, still many passages which remain obscure and disputed. There can be no doubt that many problems at present insoluble will in the end be solved by that modern scholarship which has already deciphered the cuneiform writings of Persia as well as the rock inscriptions of India, and has discovered the languages which lay hidden under these mysterious characters.

Having thus arrived at the threshold of the world of Vedic thought, we may now enter through the portals opened by the golden key of scholarship. By far the greater part of the poetry of the *Rigveda* consists of religious lyrics, only the tenth book containing some secular poems. Its hymns are mainly addressed to the various gods of the Vedic pantheon, praising their mighty deeds, their greatness, and their beneficence, or beseeching them for wealth in cattle, numerous offspring, prosperity, long life, and victory. The *Rigveda* is not a collection of primitive popular poetry, as it was apt to be described at an earlier period of Sanskrit studies. It is rather a body of skilfully composed hymns, produced by a sacerdotal class and meant to accompany the Soma oblation and the fire sacrifice of melted butter, which were offered according to a ritual by no means so simple as was at one time supposed, though undoubtedly much simpler than the elaborate system of the Brāhmaṇa period. Its poetry is consequently marred by frequent references to the sacrifice, especially when the two great ritual deities, Agni and Soma, are the objects of praise. At the same time it is on the whole much more natural than might under these conditions be expected. For the gods who are invoked are nearly all personifications of the phenomena of Nature, and thus give occasion for the employment of much beautiful and even noble imagery. The diction of the hymns is, generally speaking, simple and unaffected. Compound words are sparingly used, and are limited to two members, in marked contrast with the frequency and length of compounds in classical Sanskrit. The thought, too, is usually artless and direct, except in the hymns to the ritual deities, where it becomes involved in conceit and mystical obscurity. The very limited nature of the theme, in these cases, must have forced the minds of the priestly singers to strive after variety by giving utterance to the same idea in enigmatical phraseology.

Here, then, we already find the beginnings of that fondness for subtlety and difficult modes of expression which is so prevalent in the later literature, and which is betrayed even in the earlier period by the saying in one of the Brāhmaṇas that the gods love the recondite. In some hymns, too, there appears that tendency to play with words which was carried to inordinate lengths in late Sanskrit poems and romances. The hymns of the *Rigveda*, of course, vary much in literary merit, as is naturally to be expected in the productions of many poets extendng over some centuries. Many display a high order of poetical excellence, while others consist of commonplace and mechanical verse. The degree of skill in composition is on the average remarkably high, especially when we consider that here we have by far the oldest poetry of the Aryan race. The art which these early seers feel is needed to produce a hymn acceptable to the gods is often alluded to, generally in the closing stanza. The poet usually compares his work to a car wrought and put together by a deft craftsman. One Rishi also likens his prayers to fair and well-woven garments; another speaks of having adorned his song of praise like a bride for her lover. Poets laud the gods according to knowledge and ability (vi. 21, 6), and give utterance to the emotions of their hearts (x. 39, 15). Various individual gods are, it is true, in a general way said to have granted seers the gift of song, but of the later doctrine of revelation the Rigvedic poets know nothing.

The remark which has often been made that monotony prevails in the Vedic hymns contains truth. But the impression is produced by the hymns to the same deity being commonly grouped together in each book. A similar effect would probably arise from reading in succession twenty or thirty lyrics on Spring, even in an anthology of the best modern poetry. When we consider that nearly five hundred hymns of the *Rigveda* are addressed to two deities alone, it is surprising that so many variations of the same theme should be possible.

The hymns of the *Rigveda* being mainly invocations of the gods, their contents are largely mythological. Special interest attaches to this mythology, because it represents an earlier stage of thought than is to be found in any other literature. It is sufficiently primitive to enable us to see clearly the process of personification by which natural phenomena developed into gods. Never observing, in his ordinary life, action or movement not caused by an acting or moving person, the Vedic Indian, like man in a much less advanced state, still refers such occurrences in Nature to personal agents, which to him are inherent in the phenomena. He still looks out upon the workings of Nature with childlike astonishment. One poet asks why the sun does not fall from the sky; another wonders where the stars go by day; while a third marvels that the waters of all rivers constantly flowing into it never fill the ocean. The unvarying regularity of sun and moon, and the unfailing recurrence of the dawn, however, suggested to these ancient singers the idea of the unchanging order that prevails in Nature. The notion of this general law, recognised under the name *ṛita* (properly the "course" of things), we find in the *Rigveda* extended first to the fixed rules of the sacrifice (rite), and then to those of morality (right). Though the mythological phase presented by the *Rigveda* is comparatively primitive, it yet contains many conceptions inherited from previous ages. The parallels of the *Avesta* show that several of the Vedic deities go back to the time when the ancestors of Persians and Indians were still one people. Among these may be mentioned

Yama, god of the dead, identical with Yima, ruler of paradise, and especially Mitra, the cult of whose Persian counterpart, Mithra, obtained from 200–400 A.D. a world-wide diffusion in the Roman Empire, and came nearer to monotheism than the cult of any other god in paganism.

Various religious practices can also be traced back to that early age, such as the worship of fire and the cult of the plant *Soma* (the Avestan *Haoma*). The veneration of the cow, too, dates from that time. A religious hymn poetry must have existed even then, for stanzas of four eleven-syllable (the Vedic *trishṭubh*) and of four or three eight-syllable lines (*anushṭubh* and *gāyatrī*) were already known, as is proved by the agreement of the *Avesta* with the *Rigveda.*

From the still earlier Indo-European period had come down the general conception of "god" (*deva-s*, Lat. *deu-s*) and that of heaven as a divine father (*Dyauṣ pitā*, Gr. *Zeus patēr*, Lat. *Jūpiter*). Probably from an even remoter antiquity is derived the notion of heaven and earth as primeval and universal parents, as well as many magical beliefs.

The universe appeared to the poets of the *Rigveda* to be divided into the three domains of earth, air, and heaven, a division perhaps also known to the early Greeks. This is the favourite triad of the *Rigveda*, constantly mentioned expressly or by implication. The solar phenomena are referred to heaven, while those of lightning, rain, and wind belong to the air. In the three worlds the various gods perform their actions, though they are supposed to dwell only in the third, the home of light. The air is often called a sea, as the abode of the celestial waters, while the great rainless clouds are conceived sometimes as rocks or mountains, sometimes as the castles of demons who war against the gods. The thundering rain-clouds become lowing cows, whose milk is shed and bestows fatness upon the earth.

The higher gods of the *Rigveda* are almost entirely personifications of natural phenomena, such as Sun, Dawn, Fire, Wind. Excepting a few deities surviving from an older period, the gods are, for the most part, more or less clearly connected with their physical foundation. The personifications being therefore but slightly developed, lack definiteness of outline and individuality of character. Moreover, the phenomena themselves which are behind the personifications have few distinctive traits, while they share some attributes with other phenomena belonging to the same domain. Thus Dawn, Sun, Fire have the common features of being luminous, dispelling darkness, appearing in the morning. Hence the character of each god is made up of only a few essential qualities combined with many others which are common to all the gods, such as brilliance, power, beneficence, and wisdom. These common attributes tend to obscure those which are distinctive, because in hymns of prayer and praise the former naturally assume special importance. Again, gods belonging to different departments of nature, but having striking features in common, are apt to grow more like each other. Assimilation of this kind is encouraged by a peculiar practice of the Vedic poets—the invocation of deities in pairs. Such combinations result in attributes peculiar to the one god attaching themselves to the other, even when the latter appears alone. Thus when the Fire-god, invoked by himself, is called a slayer of the demon Vṛitra, he receives an attribute distinctive of the thunder-god Indra, with whom he is often coupled. The possibility of assigning nearly every power to every god rendered the identification of one deity with another an easy matter. Such identifications are frequent enough in the *Rigveda*. For example, a poet addressing the fire-god exclaims: "Thou at thy birth, O Agni, art Varuṇa; when kindled thou becomest Mitra; in thee, O Son of Might, all gods are centred; thou art Indra to the worshipper" (v. 3, 1).

Moreover, mystical speculations on the nature of Agni, so important a god in the eyes of a priesthood devoted to a fire-cult, on his many manifestations as individual fires on earth, and on his other aspects as atmospheric fire in lightning and as celestial fire in the sun—aspects which the Vedic poets are fond of alluding to in riddles—would suggest the idea that various deities are but different forms of a single divine being. This idea is found in more than one passage of the later hymns of the *Rigveda*. Thus the composer of a recent hymn (164) of the first book says: "The one being priests speak of in many ways; they call it Agni, Yama, Mātariçvan." Similarly, a seer of the last book (x. 114) remarks: "Priests and poets with words make into many the bird (*i.e.* the sun) which is but one." Utterances like these show that by the end of the Rigvedic period the polytheism of the Rishis had received a monotheistic tinge.

Occasionally we even find shadowed forth the pantheistic idea of a deity representing not only all the gods, but Nature as well. Thus the goddess Aditi is identified with all the deities, with men, with all that has been and shall be born, with air, and heaven (i. 89); and in a cosmogonic hymn (x. 121) the Creator is not only described as the one god above all gods, but is said[1] to embrace all things. This germ of pantheism developed through the later Vedic literature till it assumed its final shape in the

[1] In verse 10, which is a late addition; see p. 51, footnote.

Vedānta philosophy, still the most popular system of the Hindus.

The practice of the poets, even in the older parts of the *Rigveda*, of invoking different gods as if each of them were paramount, gave rise to Professor Max Müller's theory of Henotheism or Kathenotheism, according to which the seers held "the belief in individual gods alternately regarded as the highest," and for the moment treated the god addressed as if he were an absolutely independent and supreme deity, alone present to the mind. In reality, however, the practice of the poets of the *Rigveda* hardly amounts to more than the exaggeration—to be found in the Homeric hymns also—with which a singer would naturally magnify the particular god whom he is invoking. For the Rishis well knew the exact position of each god in the Soma ritual, in which nearly every member of the pantheon found a place.

The gods, in the view of the Vedic poets, had a beginning; for they are described as the offspring of heaven and earth, or sometimes of other gods. This in itself implies different generations, but earlier gods are also expressly referred to in several passages. Nor were the gods regarded as originally immortal; for immortality is said to have been bestowed upon them by individual deities, such as Agni and Savitṛi, or to have been acquired by drinking soma. Indra and other gods are spoken of as unaging, but whether their immortality was regarded by the poets as absolute there is no evidence to show. In the post-Vedic view it was only relative, being limited to a cosmic age.

The physical aspect of the Vedic gods is anthropomorphic. Thus head, face, eyes, arms, hands, fee ,

6

and other portions of the human frame are ascribed to them. But their forms are shadowy and their limbs or parts are often simply meant figuratively to describe their activities. Thus the tongue and limbs of the fire-god are merely his flames; the arms of the sun-god are simply his rays, while his eye only represents the solar orb. Since the outward shape of the gods was thus vaguely conceived, while their connection with natural phenomena was in many instances still evident, it is easy to understand why no mention is made in the *Rigveda* of images of the gods, still less of temples, which imply the existence of images. Idols first begin to be referred to in the Sūtras.

Some of the gods appear equipped as warriors, wearing coats of mail and helmets, and armed with spears, battle-axes, bows and arrows. They all drive through the air in luminous cars, generally drawn by horses, but in some cases by kine, goats, or deer. In their cars the gods come to seat themselves at the sacrifice, which, however, is also conveyed to them in heaven by Agni. They are on the whole conceived as dwelling together in harmony; the only one who ever introduces a note of discord being the warlike and overbearing Indra.

To the successful and therefore optimistic Vedic Indian, the gods seemed almost exclusively beneficent beings, bestowers of long life and prosperity. Indeed, the only deity in whom injurious features are at all prominent is Rudra. The lesser evils closely connected with human life, such as disease, proceed from minor demons, while the greater evils manifested in Nature, such as drought and darkness, are produced by powerful demons like Vṛitra. The conquest of these demons brings out all the more strikingly the beneficent nature of the gods.

The character of the Vedic gods is also moral. They are "true" and "not deceitful," being throughout the friends and guardians of honesty and virtue. But the divine morality only reflects the ethical standard of an early civilisation. Thus even the alliance of Varuṇa, the most moral of the gods, with righteousness is not such as to prevent him from employing craft against the hostile and the deceitful man. Moral elevation is, on the whole, a less prominent characteristic of the gods than greatness and power.

The relation of the worshipper to the gods in the *Rigveda* is in general one of dependence on their will, prayers and sacrifices being offered to win their favour or forgiveness. The expectation of something in return for the offering is, however, frequently apparent, and the keynote of many a hymn is, "I give to thee that thou mayst give to me." The idea is also often expressed that the might and valour of the gods is produced by hymns, sacrifices, and especially offerings of soma. Here we find the germs of sacerdotal pretensions which gradually increased during the Vedic age. Thus the statement occurs in the *White Yajurveda* that the Brahman who possesses correct knowledge has the gods in his power. The Brāhmaṇas go a step farther in saying that there are two kinds of gods, the Devas and the Brahmans, the latter of whom are to be held as deities among men. In the Brāhmaṇas, too, the sacrifice is represented as all-powerful, controlling not only the gods, but the very processes of nature.

The number of the gods is stated in the *Rigveda* itself to be thirty-three, several times expressed as thrice eleven, when each group is regarded as corresponding to one of the divisions of the threefold universe. This aggregate could not always have been deemed exhaustive, for sometimes other gods are mentioned in addition to the thirty-three. Nor can this number, of course, include various groups, such as the storm-gods.

There are, however, hardly twenty individual deities important enough in the *Rigveda* to have at least three entire hymns addressed to them. The most prominent of these are Indra, the thunder-god, with at least 250 hymns, Agni with about 200, and Soma with over 100; while Parjanya, god of rain, and Yama, god of the dead, are invoked in only three each. The rest occupy various positions between these two extremes. It is somewhat remarkable that the two great deities of modern Hinduism, Vishṇu and Çiva, who are equal in importance, should have been on the same level, though far below the leading deities, three thousand years ago, as Vishṇu and Rudra (the earlier form of Çiva) in the *Rigveda*. Even then they show the same general characteristics as now, Vishṇu being specially benevolent and Rudra terrible.

The oldest among the gods of heaven is Dyaus (identical with the Greek Zeus). This personification of the sky as a god never went beyond a rudimentary stage in the *Rigveda*, being almost entirely limited to the idea of paternity. Dyaus is generally coupled with Pṛithivī, Earth, the pair being celebrated in six hymns as universal parents. In a few passages Dyaus is called a bull, ruddy and bellowing downwards, with reference to the fertilising power of rain no less than to the lightning and thundering heavens. He is also once compared with a black steed decked with pearls, in obvious allusion to the nocturnal star-spangled sky. One poet describes this god as furnished with a bolt, while another speaks of him as "Dyaus smiling through the clouds," meaning the lightening sky. In several other passages of the *Rigveda* the verb "to smile" (*smi*) alludes to lightning, just as in classical Sanskrit a smile is constantly compared with objects of dazzling whiteness.

A much more important deity of the sky is Varuṇa, in whom the personification has proceeded so far that the natural phenomenon which underlies it can only be inferred from traits in his character. This obscurity of origin arises partly from his not being a creation of Indian mythology, but a heritage from an earlier age, and partly from his name not at the same time designating a natural phenomenon, like that of Dyaus. The word *varuṇa-s* seems to have originally meant the "encompassing" sky, and is probably the same word as the Greek *Ouranos*, though the identification presents some phonetic difficulties. Varuṇa is invoked in far fewer hymns than Indra, Agni, or Soma, but he is undoubtedly the greatest of the Vedic gods by the side of Indra. While Indra is the great warrior, Varuṇa is the great upholder of physical and moral order (*ṛita*). The hymns addressed to him are more ethical and devout in tone than any others. They form the most exalted portion of the Veda, often resembling in character the Hebrew psalms. The peaceful sway of Varuṇa is explained by his connection with the regularly recurring celestial phenomena, the course of the heavenly bodies seen in the sky; Indra's warlike and occasionally capricious nature is accounted for by the variable and uncertain strife of the elements in the thunderstorm. The character and power of Varuṇa may be sketched as nearly as possible in the words of the Vedic poets themselves as follows. By the law of Varuṇa heaven and earth are held apart. He made the golden swing (the sun) to shine in heaven. He has made a wide path for the sun. The wind which resounds through the air is Varuṇa's breath. By his ordinances the moon shining brightly moves at night, and the stars placed up on high are seen at night but disappear by day. He causes the rivers to flow; they stream unceasingly according to his ordinance. By his occult power the rivers swiftly pouring into the ocean do not fill it with water. He makes the inverted cask to pour its waters and to moisten the ground, while the mountains are wrapt in cloud. It is chiefly with these aërial waters that he is connected, very rarely with the sea.

Varuṇa's omniscience is often dwelt on. He knows the flight of the birds in the sky, the path of ships in the ocean, the course of the far-travelling wind. He beholds all the secret things that have been or shall be done. He witnesses men's truth and falsehood. No creature can even wink without him. As a moral governor Varuṇa stands far above any other deity. His wrath is roused by sin, which is the infringement of his ordinances, and which he severely punishes. The fetters with which he binds sinners are often mentioned. A dispeller, hater, and punisher of falsehood, he is gracious to the penitent. He releases men not only from the sins which they themselves commit, but from those committed by their fathers. He spares the suppliant who daily transgresses his laws, and is gracious to those who have broken his ordinances by thoughtlessness. There is, in fact, no hymn to Varuṇa in which the prayer for forgiveness of guilt does not occur, as in the hymns to other deities the prayer for worldly goods.

With the growth of the conception of the creator, Prajāpati, as a supreme deity, the characteristics of Varuṇa as a sovereign god naturally faded away, and the dominion of waters, only a part of his original sphere, alone remained. This is already partly the case in the *Atharva-veda*, and in post-Vedic mythology he is only an Indian Neptune, god of the sea.

The following stanzas from a hymn to Varuṇa (vii. 89) will illustrate the spirit of the prayers addressed to him:—

May I not yet, King Varuṇa,
Go down into the house of clay:
Have mercy, spare me, mighty Lord.

Thirst has come on thy worshipper
Though standing in the waters' midst:[1]
Have mercy, spare me, mighty Lord.

O Varuṇa, whatever the offence may be
That we as men commit against the heavenly folk
When through our want of thought we violate thy laws,
Chastise us not, O God, for that iniquity.

There are in the *Rigveda* five solar deities, differentiated as representing various aspects of the activity of the sun. One of the oldest of these, Mitra, the "Friend," seems to have been conceived as the beneficent side of the sun's power. Going back to the Indo-Iranian period, he has in the *Rigveda* almost entirely lost his individuality, which is practically merged in that of Varuṇa. With the latter he is constantly invoked, while only one single hymn (iii. 59) is addressed to him alone.

Sūrya (cognate in name to the Greek Hēlios) is the most concrete of the solar deities. For as his name also designates the luminary itself, his connection with the

[1] A reference to dropsy, with which Varuṇa is thought to afflict sinners.

latter is never lost sight of. The eye of Sūrya is often mentioned, and Dawn is said to bring the eye of the gods. All-seeing, he is the spy of the whole world, beholding all beings and the good or bad deeds of mortals. Aroused by Sūrya, men pursue their objects and perform their work. He is the soul or guardian of all that moves and is fixed. He rides in a car, which is generally described as drawn by seven steeds. These he unyokes at sunset:—

> *When he has loosed his coursers from their station,*
> *Straightway Night over all spreads out her garment* (i. 115, 4).

Sūrya rolls up the darkness like a skin, and the stars slink away like thieves. He shines forth from the lap of the dawns. He is also spoken of as the husband of Dawn. As a form of Agni, the gods placed him in heaven. He is often described as a bird or eagle traversing space. He measures the days and prolongs life. He drives away disease and evil dreams. At his rising he is prayed to declare men sinless to Mitra and Varuṇa. All beings depend on Sūrya, and so he is called "all-creating."

Eleven hymns, or about the same number as to Sūrya, are addressed to another solar deity, Savitṛi, the "Stimulator," who represents the quickening activity of the sun. He is pre-eminently a golden deity, with golden hands and arms and a golden car. He raises aloft his strong golden arms, with which he blesses and arouses all beings, and which extend to the ends of the earth. He moves in his golden car, seeing all creatures, on a downward and an upward path. He shines after the path of the dawn. Beaming with the rays of the sun, yellow-haired, Savitṛi raises up his light continually from the east. He removes evil dreams and drives away demons and sorcerers. He bestows immortality on the gods as well as length of life on man. He also conducts the departed spirit to where the righteous dwell. The other gods follow Savitṛi's lead ; no being, not even the most powerful gods, Indra and Varuṇa, can resist his will and independent sway. Savitṛi is not infrequently connected with the evening, being in one hymn (ii. 38) extolled as the setting sun :—

Borne by swift coursers, he will now unyoke them :
The speeding chariot he has stayed from going.
He checks the speed of them that glide like serpents :
Night has come on by Savitṛi's commandment.
The weaver rolls her outstretched web together,
The skilled lay down their work in midst of toiling,
The birds all seek their nests, their shed the cattle :
Each to his lodging Savitṛi disperses.

To this god is addressed the most famous stanza of the *Rigveda*, with which, as the Stimulator, he was in ancient times invoked at the beginning of Vedic study, and which is still repeated by every orthodox Hindu in his morning prayers. From the name of the deity it is called the *Sāvitrī*, but it is also often referred to as "the *Gāyatrī*," from the metre in which it is composed :—

May we attain that excellent
Glory of Savitṛi the god,
That he may stimulate our thoughts (iii. 62, 10).

A peculiarity of the hymns to Savitṛi is the perpetual play on his name with forms of the root *sū*, "to stimulate," from which it is derived.

Pūshan is invoked in some eight hymns of the *Rigveda*. His name means "Prosperer," and the conception underlying his character seems to be the beneficent power of the sun, manifested chiefly as a pastoral deity. His car is drawn by goats and he carries a goad. Knowing the ways of heaven, he conducts the dead on the far path to the fathers. He is also a guardian of roads, protecting cattle and guiding them with his goad. The welfare which he bestows results from the protection he extends to men and cattle on earth, and from his guidance of mortals to the abodes of bliss in the next world.

Judged by a statistical standard, Vishṇu is only a deity of the fourth rank, less frequently invoked than Sūrya, Savitṛi, and Pūshan in the *Rigveda*, but historically he is the most important of the solar deities. For he is one of the two great gods of modern Hinduism. The essential feature of his character is that he takes three strides, which doubtless represent the course of the sun through the three divisions of the universe. His highest step is heaven, where the gods and the fathers dwell. For this abode the poet expresses his longing in the following words (i. 154, 5):—

May I attain to that, his well-loved dwelling,
Where men devoted to the gods are blessèd:
In Vishṇu's highest step—he is our kinsman,
Of mighty stride—there is a spring of nectar.

Vishṇu seems to have been originally conceived as the sun, not in his general character, but as the personified swiftly moving luminary which with vast strides traverses the three worlds. He is in several passages said to have taken his three steps for the benefit of man.

To this feature may be traced the myth of the

Brāhmaṇas in which Vishṇu appears in the form of a dwarf as an artifice to recover the earth, now in the possession of demons, by taking his three strides. His character for benevolence was in post-Vedic mythology developed in the doctrine of the Avatārs ("descents" to earth) or incarnations which he assumed for the good of humanity.

Ushas, goddess of dawn, is almost the only female deity to whom entire hymns are addressed, and the only one invoked with any frequency. She, however, is celebrated in some twenty hymns. The name, meaning the "Shining One," is cognate to the Latin *Aurora* and the Greek *Ēōs*. When the goddess is addressed, the physical phenomenon of dawn is never absent from the poet's mind. The fondness with which the thoughts of these priestly singers turned to her alone among the goddesses, though she received no share in the offering of soma like the other gods, seems to show that the glories of the dawn, more splendid in Northern India than those we are wont to see, deeply impressed the minds of these early poets. In any case, she is their most graceful creation, the charm of which is unsurpassed in the descriptive religious lyrics of any other literature. Here there are no priestly subtleties to obscure the brightness of her form, and few allusions to the sacrifice to mar the natural beauty of the imagery.

To enable the reader to estimate the merit of this poetry I will string together some utterances about the Dawn goddess, culled from various hymns, and expressed as nearly as possible in the words of their composers. Ushas is a radiant maiden, born in the sky, daughter of Dyaus. She is the bright sister of dark Night. She shines with the light of her lover, with the light of Sūrya, who beams after her path and follows her as a young man a maiden. She is borne on a brilliant car, drawn by ruddy steeds or kine. Arraying herself in gay attire like a dancer, she displays her bosom. Clothed upon with light, the maiden appears in the east and unveils her charms. Rising resplendent as from a bath, she shows her form. Effulgent in peerless beauty, she withholds her light from neither small nor great. She opens wide the gates of heaven; she opens the doors of darkness, as the cows (issue from) their stall. Her radiant beams appear like herds of cattle. She removes the black robe of night, warding off evil spirits and the hated darkness. She awakens creatures that have feet, and makes the birds fly up: she is the breath and life of everything. When Ushas shines forth, the birds fly up from their nests and men seek nourishment. She is the radiant mover of sweet sounds, the leader of the charm of pleasant voices. Day by day appearing at the appointed place, she never infringes the rule of order and of the gods; she goes straight along the path of order; knowing the way, she never loses her direction. As she shone in former days, so she shines now and will shine in future, never aging, immortal.

The solitude and stillness of the early morning sometimes suggested pensive thoughts about the fleeting nature of human life in contrast with the unending recurrence of the dawn. Thus one poet exclaims:—

Gone are the mortals who in former ages
Beheld the flushing of the earlier morning.
We living men now look upon her shining;
They are coming who shall in future see her (i. 113, 11).

In a similar strain another Rishi sings :—

Again and again newly born though ancient,
Decking her beauty with the self-same colours,
The goddess wastes away the life of mortals,
Like wealth diminished by the skilful player (i. 92, 10).

The following stanzas from one of the finest hymns to Dawn (i. 113) furnish a more general picture of this fairest creation of Vedic poetry :—

This light has come, of all the lights the fairest,
The brilliant brightness has been born, far-shining.
Urged onward for god Savitṛi's uprising,
Night now has yielded up her place to Morning.

The sisters' pathway is the same, unending:
Taught by the gods, alternately they tread it.
Fair-shaped, of different forms and yet one-minded,
Night and Morning clash not, nor do they linger.

Bright leader of glad sounds, she shines effulgent:
Widely she has unclosed for us her portals.
Arousing all the world, she shows us riches:
Dawn has awakened every living creature.

There Heaven's Daughter has appeared before us,
The maiden flushing in her brilliant garments.
Thou sovran lady of all earthly treasure,
Auspicious Dawn, flush here to-day upon us.

In the sky's framework she has shone with splendour;
The goddess has cast off the robe of darkness.
Wakening up the world with ruddy horses,
Upon her well-yoked chariot Dawn is coming.

Bringing upon it many bounteous blessings,
Brightly shining, she spreads her brilliant lustre.
Last of the countless mornings that have gone by,
First of bright morns to come has Dawn arisen.

Arise! the breath, the life, again has reached us:
Darkness has gone away and light is coming.
She leaves a pathway for the sun to travel:
We have arrived where men prolong existence.

Among the deities of celestial light, those most frequently invoked are the twin gods of morning named Açvins. They are the sons of Heaven, eternally young and handsome. They ride on a car, on which they are accompanied by the sun-maiden Sūryā. This car is bright and sunlike, and all its parts are golden. The time when these gods appear is the early dawn, when "darkness still stands among the ruddy cows." At the yoking of their car Ushas is born.

Many myths are told about the Açvins as succouring divinities. They deliver from distress in general, especially rescuing from the ocean in a ship or ships. They are characteristically divine physicians, who give sight to the blind and make the lame to walk. One very curious myth is that of the maiden Viçpalā, who having had her leg cut off in some conflict, was at once furnished by the Açvins with an iron limb. They agree in many respects with the two famous horsemen of Greek mythology, the Dioskouroi, sons of Zeus and brothers of Helen. The two most probable theories as to the origin of these twin deities are, that they represent either the twilight, half dark, half light, or the morning and evening star.

In the realm of air Indra is the dominant deity. He is, indeed, the favourite and national god of the Vedic Indian. His importance is sufficiently indicated by the fact that more than one-fourth of the *Rigveda* is devoted to his praise. Handed down from a bygone age, Indra has become more anthropomorphic and surrounded by mythological imagery than any other Vedic god. The significance of his character is nevertheless sufficiently clear. He is primarily the thunder-god, the conquest of the demon of drought or darkness named Vṛitra, the

"Obstructor," and the consequent liberation of the waters or the winning of light, forming his mythological essence. This myth furnishes the Rishis with an ever-recurring theme. Armed with his thunderbolt, exhilarated by copious draughts of soma, and generally escorted by the Maruts or Storm-gods, Indra enters upon the fray. The conflict is terrible. Heaven and earth tremble with fear when Indra smites Vṛitra like a tree with his bolt. He is described as constantly repeating the combat. This obviously corresponds to the perpetual renewal of the natural phenomena underlying the myth. The physical elements in the thunderstorm are seldom directly mentioned by the poets when describing the exploits of Indra. He is rarely said to shed rain, but constantly to release the pent-up waters or rivers. The lightning is regularly the " bolt," while thunder is the lowing of the cows or the roaring of the dragon. The clouds are designated by various names, such as cow, udder, spring, cask, or pail. They are also rocks (*adri*), which encompass the cows set free by Indra. They are further mountains from which Indra casts down the demons dwelling upon them. They thus often become fortresses (*pur*) of the demons, which are ninety, ninety-nine, or a hundred in number, and are variously described as "moving," "autumnal," "made of iron or stone." One stanza (x. 89, 7) thus brings together the various features of the myth : " Indra slew Vṛitra, broke the castles, made a channel for the rivers, pierced the mountain, and delivered over the cows to his friends." Owing to the importance of the Vṛitra myth, the chief and specific epithet of Indra is *Vṛitrahan*, "slayer of Vṛitra." The following stanzas are from one of the most graphic of the hymns which celebrate the conflict of Indra with the demon (i. 32):—

I will proclaim the manly deeds of Indra,
The first that he performed, the lightning-wielder.
He smote the dragon, then discharged the waters,
And cleft the caverns of the lofty mountains.

Impetuous as a bull, he chose the soma,
And drank in threefold vessels of its juices.
The Bounteous god grasped lightning for his missile,
He struck down dead that first-born of the dragons.

Him lightning then availed naught, nor thunder,
Nor mist nor hailstorm which he spread around him:
When Indra and the dragon strove in battle,
The Bounteous god gained victory for ever.

Plunged in the miast of never-ceasing torrents,
That stand not still but ever hasten onward,
The waters bear off Vṛitra's hidden body:
Indra's fierce foe sank down to lasting darkness.

With the liberation of the waters is connected the winning of light and the sun. Thus we read that when Indra had slain the dragon Vṛitra with his bolt, releasing the waters for man, he placed the sun visibly in the heavens, or that the sun shone forth when Indra blew the dragon from the air.

Indra naturally became the god of battle, and is more frequently invoked than any other deity as a helper in conflicts with earthly enemies. In the words of one poet, he protects the Aryan colour (*varṇa*) and subjects the black skin; while another extols him for having dispersed 50,000 of the black race and rent their citadels. His combats are frequently called *gavishṭi*, "desire of cows," his gifts being considered the result of victories.

The following stanzas (ii. 12, 2 and 13) will serve as a

specimen of the way in which the greatness of Indra is celebrated :—

Who made the widespread earth when quaking steadfast,
Who brought to rest the agitated mountains,
Who measured out air's intermediate spaces,
Who gave the sky support: he, men, is Indra.

Heaven and earth themselves bow down before him,
Before his might the very mountains tremble.
Who, known as Soma-drinker, armed with lightning,
Is wielder of the bolt: he, men, is Indra.

To the more advanced anthropomorphism of Indra's nature are due the occasional immoral traits which appear in his character. Thus he sometimes indulges in acts of capricious violence, such as the slaughter of his father or the destruction of the car of Dawn. He is especially addicted to soma, of which he is described as drinking enormous quantities to stimulate him in the performance of his warlike exploits. One entire hymn (x. 119) consists of a monologue in which Indra, inebriated with soma, boasts of his greatness and power. Though of little poetic merit, this piece has a special interest as being by far the earliest literary description of the mental effects, braggadocio in particular, produced by intoxication. In estimating the morality of Indra's excesses, it should not be forgotten that the exhilaration of soma partook of a religious character in the eyes of the Vedic poets.

Indra's name is found in the *Avesta* as that of a demon. His distinctive Vedic epithet, *Vṛitrahan,* also occurs there in the form of *verethraghna,* as a designation of the god of victory. Hence there was probably in the Indo-Iranian period a god approaching to the Vedic form of the Vṛitra-slaying and victorious Indra.

7

In comparing historically Varuṇa and Indra, whose importance was about equal in the earlier period of the *Rigveda,* it seems clear that Varuṇa was greater in the Indo-Iranian period, but became inferior to Indra in later Vedic times. Indra, on the other hand, became in the Brāhmaṇas and Epics the chief of the Indian heaven, and even maintained this position under the Puranic triad, Brahmā-Vishṇu-Çiva, though of course subordinate to them.

At least three of the lesser deities of the air are connected with lightning. One of these is the somewhat obscure god Trita, who is only mentioned in detached verses of the *Rigveda.* The name appears to designate the "third" (Greek, *trito-s*), as the lightning form of fire. His frequent epithet, *Āptya,* seems to mean the "watery." This god goes back to the Indo-Iranian period, as both his name and his epithet are found in the *Avesta.* But he was gradually ousted by Indra as being originally almost identical in character with the latter. Another deity of rare occurrence in the *Rigveda,* and also dating from the Indo-Iranian period, is Apāṃ napāt, the "Son of Waters." He is described as clothed in lightning and shining without fuel in the waters. There can, therefore, be little doubt that he represents fire as produced from the rain-clouds in the form of lightning. Mātariçvan, seldom mentioned in the *Rigveda,* is a divine being described as having, like the Greek Prometheus, brought down the hidden fire from heaven to earth. He most probably represents the personification of a celestial form of Agni, god of fire, with whom he is in some passages actually identified. In the later Vedas, the Brāhmaṇas, and the subsequent literature, the name has become simply a designation of wind.

The position occupied by the god Rudra in the *Rigveda* is very different from that of his historical successor in a later age. He is celebrated in only three or four hymns, while his name is mentioned slightly less often than that of Vishṇu. He is usually said to be armed with bow and arrows, but a lightning shaft and a thunderbolt are also occasionally assigned to him. He is described as fierce and destructive like a wild beast, and is called "the ruddy boar of heaven." The hymns addressed to him chiefly express fear of his terrible shafts and deprecation of his wrath. His malevolence is still more prominent in the later Vedic literature. The euphemistic epithet *Çiva*, "auspicious," already applied to him in the *Rigveda*, and more frequently, though not exclusively, in the younger Vedas, became his regular name in the post-Vedic period. Rudra is, of course, not purely malevolent like a demon. He is besought not only to preserve from calamity but to bestow blessings and produce welfare for man and beast. His healing powers are mentioned with especial frequency, and he is lauded as the greatest of physicians.

Prominent among the gods of the *Rigveda* are the Maruts or Storm-gods, who form a group of thrice seven or thrice sixty. They are the sons of Rudra and the mottled cloud-cow Pṛiçni. At birth they are compared with fires, and are once addressed as "born from the laughter of lightning." They are a troop of youthful warriors armed with spears or battle-axes and wearing helmets upon their heads. They are decked with golden ornaments, chiefly in the form of armlets or of anklets:—

They gleam with armlets as the heavens are decked with stars;
Like cloud-born lightnings shine the torrents of their rain (ii. 34, 2).

They ride on golden cars which gleam with lightning, while they hold fiery lightnings in their hands :—

The lightnings smile upon the earth below them
What time the Maruts sprinkle forth their fatness.
—(i. 168, 8).

They drive with coursers which are often described as spotted, and they are once said to have yoked the winds as steeds to their pole.

The Maruts are fierce and terrible, like lions or wild boars. With the fellies of their car they rend the hills :—

The Maruts spread the mist abroad,
And make the mountains rock and reel,
When with the winds they go their way (viii. 7, 4).

They shatter the lords of the forest and like wild elephants devour the woods :—

Before you, fierce ones, even woods bow down in fear,
The earth herself, the very mountain trembles (v. 60, 2).

One of their main functions is to shed rain. They are clad in a robe of rain, and cover the eye of the sun with showers. They bedew the earth with milk; they shed fatness (ghee); they milk the thundering, the never-failing spring; they wet the earth with mead; they pour out the heavenly pail :—

The rivers echo to their chariot fellies
What time they utter forth the voice of rain-clouds.
—(i. 168, 8).

In allusion to the sound of the winds the Maruts are often called singers, and as such aid Indra in his fight with the demon. They are, indeed, his constant associates in all his celestial conflicts.

The God of Wind, called Vāyu or Vāta, is not a

prominent deity in the *Rigveda*, having only three entire hymns addressed to him. The personification is more developed under the name of Vāyu, who is mostly associated with Indra, while Vāta is coupled only with the less anthropomorphic rain-god, Parjanya. Vāyu is swift as thought and has roaring velocity. He has a shining car drawn by a team or a pair of ruddy steeds. On this car, which has a golden seat and touches the sky, Indra is his companion. Vāta, as also the ordinary designation of wind, is celebrated in a more concrete manner. His name is often connected with the verb *vā*, "to blow," from which it is derived. Like Rudra, he wafts healing and prolongs life; for he has the treasure of immortality in his house. The poet of a short hynm (x. 168) devoted to his praise thus describes him:—

Of Vāta's car I now will praise the greatness:
Crashing it speeds along; its noise is thunder.
Touching the sky, it goes on causing lightnings;
Scattering the dust of earth it hurries forward.

In air upon his pathways hastening onward,
Never on any day he tarries resting.
The first-born order-loving friend of waters,
Where, pray, was he born? say, whence came he hither?

The soul of gods, and of the world the offspring,
This god according to his liking wanders.
His sound is heard, but ne'er is seen his figure.
This Vāta let us now with offerings worship.

Another deity of air is Parjanya, god of rain, who is invoked in but three hymns, and is only mentioned some thirty times in the *Rigveda*. The name in several passages still means simply "rain-cloud." The personification is therefore always closely connected with the phenomenon of the rain-storm, in which the rain-cloud itself becomes an udder, a pail, or a water-skin. Often likened to a bull, Parjanya is characteristically a shedder of rain. His activity is described in very vivid strains (v. 83):—

The trees he strikes to earth and smites the demon crew:
The whole world fears the wielder of the mighty bolt.
The guiltless man himself flees from the potent god,
What time Parjanya thund'ring smites the miscreant.

Like a car-driver urging on his steeds with whips,
He causes to bound forth the messengers of rain.
From far away the lion's roar reverberates,
What time Parjanya fills the atmosphere with rain.

Forth blow the winds, to earth the lightning flashes fall,
Up shoot the herbs, the realm of light with moisture streams;
Nourishment in abundance springs for all the world,
What time Parjanya quickeneth the earth with seed.

Thunder and roar: the vital germ deposit!
With water-bearing chariot fly around us!
Thy water-skin unloosed to earth draw downward:
With moisture make the heights and hollows equal!

The Waters are praised as goddesses in four hymns of the *Rigveda.* The personification, however, hardly goes beyond representing them as mothers, young wives, and goddesses who bestow boons and come to the sacrifice. As mothers they produce Agni, whose lightning form is, as we have seen, called Apāṃ Napāt, "Son of Waters." The divine waters bear away defilement, and are even invoked to cleanse from moral guilt, the sins of violence, cursing, and lying. They bestow remedies, healing, long life, and immortality. Soma delights in the waters as a young man in lovely maidens; he approaches them as a lover; they are maidens who bow down before the youth.

Several rivers are personified and invoked as deities

in the *Rigveda.* One hymn (x. 75) celebrates the Sindhu or Indus, while another (iii. 33) sings the praises of the sister streams Vipāç and Çutudrī. Sarasvatī is, however, the most important river goddess, being lauded in three entire hymns as well as in many detached verses. The personification here goes much further than in the case of other streams; but the poets never lose sight of the connection of the goddess with the river. She is the best of mothers, of rivers, and of goddesses. Her unfailing breast yields riches of every kind, and she bestows wealth, plenty, nourishment, and offspring. One poet prays that he may not be removed from her to fields which are strange. She is invoked to descend from the sky, from the great mountain, to the sacrifice. Such expressions may have suggested the notion of the celestial origin and descent of the Ganges, familiar to post-Vedic mythology. Though simply a river deity in the *Rigveda,* Sarasvatī is in the Brāhmaṇas identified with Vāch, goddess of speech, and has in post-Vedic mythology become the goddess of eloquence and wisdom, invoked as a muse, and regarded as the wife of Brahmā.

Earth, Pṛithivī, the Broad One, hardly ever dissociated from Dyaus, is celebrated alone in only one short hymn of three stanzas (v. 84). Even here the poet cannot refrain from introducing references to her heavenly spouse as he addresses the goddess,

Who, firmly fixt, the forest trees
With might supportest in the ground:
When from the lightning of thy cloud
The rain-floods of the sky pour down.

The personification is only rudimentary, the attributes of the goddess being chiefly those of the physical earth.

The most important of the terrestrial deities is Agni,

god of fire. Next to Indra he is the most prominent of the Vedic gods, being celebrated in more than 200 hymns. It is only natural that the personification of the sacrificial fire, the centre around which the ritual poetry of the Veda moves, should engross so much of the attention of the Rishis. *Agni* being also the regular name of the element (Latin, *igni-s*), the anthropomorphism of the deity is but slight. The bodily parts of the god have a clear connection with the phenomena of terrestrial fire mainly in its sacrificial aspect. In allusion to the oblation of ghee cast in the fire, Agni is "butter-backed," "butter-faced," or "butter-haired." He is also "flame-haired," and has a tawny beard. He has sharp, shining, golden, or iron teeth and burning jaws. Mention is also often made of his tongue or tongues. He is frequently compared with or directly called a steed, being yoked to the pole of the rite in order to waft the sacrifice to the gods. He is also often likened to a bird, being winged and darting with rapid flight to the gods. He eats and chews the forest with sharp tooth. His lustre is like the rays of dawn or of the sun, and resembles the lightnings of the rain-cloud; but his track and his fellies are black, and his steeds make black furrows. Driven by the wind, he rushes through the wood. He invades the forests and shears the hairs of the earth, shaving it as a barber a beard. His flames are like the roaring waves of the sea. He bellows like a bull when he invades the forest trees; the birds are terrified at the noise when his grass-devouring sparks arise. Like the erector of a pillar, he supports the sky with his smoke; and one of his distinctive epithets is "smoke-bannered." He is borne on a brilliant car, drawn by two or more steeds, which are ruddy or tawny and wind-impelled. He yokes them to summon the gods, for he is the charioteer of the sacrifice.

The poets love to dwell on his various births, forms, and abodes. They often refer to the daily generation of Agni by friction from the two fire-sticks. These are his parents, producing him as a new-born infant who is hard to catch. From the dry wood the god is born living; the child as soon as born devours his parents. The ten maidens said to produce him are the ten fingers used in twirling the upright fire-drill. Agni is called "Son of strength" because of the powerful friction necessary in kindling a flame. As the fire is lit every morning for the sacrifice, Agni is described as "waking at dawn." Hence, too, he is the "youngest" of the gods; but he is also old, for he conducted the first sacrifice. Thus he comes to be paradoxically called both "ancient" and "very young" in the same passage.

Agni also springs from the aërial waters, and is often said to have been brought from heaven. Born on earth, in air, in heaven, Agni is frequently regarded as having a triple character. The gods made him threefold, his births are three, and he has three abodes or dwellings. "From heaven first Agni was born, the second time from us (*i.e.* men), thirdly in the waters." This earliest Indian trinity is important as the basis of much of the mystical speculation of the Vedic age. It was probably the prototype not only of the later Rigvedic triad, Sun, Wind, Fire, spoken of as distributed in the three worlds, but also of the triad Sun, Indra, Fire, which, though not Rigvedic, is still ancient. It is most likely also the historical progenitor of the later Hindu trinity of Brahmā, Vishṇu, Çiva. This triad of fires may have suggested and would explain the division of a single sacrificial fire into the three which form an essential feature of the cult of the Brāhmaṇas.

Owing to the multiplicity of terrestrial fires, Agni is also said to have many births; for he abides in every family, house, or dwelling. Kindled in many spots, he is but one; scattered in many places, he is one and the same king. Other fires are attached to him as branches to a tree. He assumes various divine forms, and has many names; but in him are comprehended all the gods, whom he surrounds as a felly the spokes. Thus we find the speculations about Agni's various forms leading to the monotheistic notion of a unity pervading the many manifestations of the divine.

Agni is an immortal who has taken up his abode among mortals; he is constantly called a "guest" in human dwellings; and is the only god to whom the frequent epithet *gṛihapati*, "lord of the house," is applied.

As the conductor of sacrifice, Agni is repeatedly called both a "messenger" who moves between heaven and earth and a priest. He is indeed the great priest, just as Indra is the great warrior.

Agni is, moreover, a mighty benefactor of his worshippers. With a thousand eyes he watches over the man who offers him oblations; but consumes his worshippers' enemies like dry bushes, and strikes down the malevolent like a tree destroyed by lightning. All blessings issue from him as branches from a tree. All treasures are collected in him, and he opens the door of wealth. He gives rain from heaven and is like a spring in the desert. The boons which he confers are, however, chiefly domestic welfare, offspring, and general prosperity, while Indra for the most part grants victory, booty, power, and glory.

Probably the oldest function of fire in regard to its cult is that of burning and dispelling evil spirits and hostile magic. It still survives in the *Rigveda* from an earlier age, Agni being said to drive away the goblins with his light and receiving the epithet *raksho-han*, "goblin-slayer." This activity is at any rate more characteristic of Agni than of any other deity, both in the hymns and in the ritual of the Vedas.

Since the soma sacrifice, beside the cult of fire, forms a main feature in the ritual of the *Rigveda*, the god Soma is naturally one of its chief deities. The whole of the ninth book, in addition to a few scattered hymns elsewhere, is devoted to his praise. Thus, judged by the standard of frequency of mention, Soma comes third in order of importance among the Vedic gods. The constant presence of the soma plant and its juice before their eyes set limits to the imagination of the poets who describe its personification. Hence little is said of Soma's human form or action. The ninth book mainly consists of incantations sung over the soma while it is pressed by the stones and flows through the woollen strainer into the wooden vats, in which it is finally offered as a beverage to the gods on a litter of grass. The poets are chiefly concerned with these processes, overlaying them with chaotic imagery and mystical fancies of almost infinite variety. When Soma is described as being purified by the ten maidens who are sisters, or by the daughters of Vivasvat (the rising sun), the ten fingers are meant. The stones used in pounding the shoots on a skin "chew him on the hide of a cow." The flowing of the juice into jars or vats after passing through the filter of sheep's wool is described in various ways. The streams of soma rush to the forest of the vats like buffaloes. The god flies like a bird to settle in the vats. The Tawny One settles in the bowls like a bird sitting on a tree. The juice being mixed with water in the vat, Soma is said to rush into the lap of the waters like a roaring bull on the herd. Clothing himself in waters, he rushes around the vat, impelled by the singers. Playing in the wood, he is cleansed by the ten maidens. He is the embryo or child of waters, which are called his mothers. When the priests add milk to soma "they clothe him in cow-garments."

The sound made by the soma juice flowing into the vats or bowls is often referred to in hyperbolical language. Thus a poet says that "the sweet drop flows over the filter like the din of combatants." This sound is constantly described as roaring, bellowing, or occasionally even thundering. In such passages Soma is commonly compared with or called a bull, and the waters, with or without milk, are termed cows.

Owing to the yellow colour of the juice, the physical quality of Soma mainly dwelt upon by the poets is his brilliance. His rays are often referred to, and he is frequently assimilated to the sun.

The exhilarating and invigorating action of soma led to its being regarded as a divine drink that bestows everlasting life. Hence it is called *amṛita*, the "immortal" draught (allied to the Greek *ambrosia*). Soma is the stimulant which conferred immortality upon the gods. Soma also places his worshipper in the imperishable world where there is eternal light and glory, making him immortal where King Yama dwells. Thus soma naturally has medicinal power also. It is medicine for a sick man, and the god Soma heals whatever is sick, making the blind to see and the lame to walk.

Soma when imbibed stimulates the voice, which it impels as the rower his boat. Soma also awakens eager thought, and the worshippers of the god exclaim, "We have drunk soma, we have become immortal, we have entered into light, we have known the gods." The intoxicating power of soma is chiefly, and very frequently, dwelt on in connection with Indra, whom it stimulates in his conflict with the hostile demons of the air.

Being the most important of herbs, soma is spoken of as lord of plants or their king, receiving also the epithet *vanaspati*, "lord of the forest."

Soma is several times described as dwelling or growing on the mountains, in accordance with the statements of the *Avesta* about Haoma. Its true origin and abode is regarded as heaven, whence it has been brought down to earth. This belief is most frequently embodied in the myth of the soma-bringing eagle (*çyena*), which is probably only the mythological account of the simple phenomenon of the descent of lightning and the simultaneous fall of rain.

In some of the latest hymns of the *Rigveda* Soma begins to be somewhat obscurely identified with the moon. In the *Atharva-veda* Soma several times means the moon, and in the *Yajurveda* Soma is spoken of as having the lunar mansions for his wives. The identification is a commonplace in the Brāhmaṇas, which explain the waning of the moon as due to the gods and fathers eating up the ambrosia of which it consists. In one of the Upanishads, moreover, the statement occurs that the moon is King Soma, the food of the gods, and is drunk up by them. Finally, in post-Vedic literature Soma is a regular name of the moon, which is regarded as being consumed by the gods, and consequently waning till it is filled up again by the sun. This somewhat remarkable coalescence of Soma with the moon doubtless sprang from the hyperbolical terms in which the poets of the *Rigveda* dwell on Soma's celestial nature and brilliance, which they describe as dispelling darkness. They sometimes speak of it as swelling in the waters, and often refer to the sap as a "drop" (*indu*). Comparisons with the moon would thus easily suggest themselves. In one passage of the *Rigveda*, for instance, Soma in the bowls is said to appear like the moon in the waters. The mystical speculations with which the Soma poetry teems would soon complete the symbolism.

A comparison of the *Avesta* with the *Rigveda* shows clearly that soma was already an important feature in the mythology and cult of the Indo-Iranian age. In both it is described as growing on the mountains, whence it is brought by birds; in both it is king of plants; in both a medicine bestowing long life and removing death. In both the sap was pressed and mixed with milk; in both its mythical home is heaven, whence it comes down to earth; in both the draught has become a mighty god; in both the celestial Soma is distinguished from the terrestrial, the god from the beverage. The similarity goes so far that Soma and Haoma have even some individual epithets in common.

The evolution of thought in the Rigvedic period shows a tendency to advance from the concrete to the abstract. One result of this tendency is the creation of abstract deities, which, however, are still rare, occurring for the most part in the last book only. A few of them are deifications of abstract nouns, such as Çraddhā

"Faith," invoked in one short hymn, and Manyu, "Wrath," in two. These abstractions grow more numerous in the later Vedas. Thus Kāma, "Desire," first appears in the *Atharva-veda*, where the arrows with which he pierces hearts are already referred to; he is the forerunner of the flower-arrowed god of love, familiar in classical literature. More numerous is the class of abstractions comprising deities whose names denote an agent, such as *Dhātṛi*, "Creator," or an attribute, such as *Prajāpati*, "Lord of Creatures." These do not appear to be direct abstractions, but seem to be derived from epithets designating a particular aspect of activity or character, which at first applying to one or more of the older deities, finally acquired an independent value. Thus *Prajāpati*, originally an epithet of such gods as Savitṛi and Soma, occurs in a late verse of the last book as a distinct deity possessing the attribute of a creator. This god is in the *Atharva-veda* and the *Vājasaneyi-Saṃhitā* often, and in the Brāhmaṇas regularly, recognised as the chief deity, the father of the gods. In the Sūtras, Prajāpati is identified with Brahmā, his successor in the post-Vedic age.

A hymn of the tenth book furnishes an interesting illustration of the curious way in which such abstractions sometimes come into being. Here is one of the stanzas:—

By whom the mighty sky, the earth so steadfast,
The realm of light, heaven's vault, has been established,
Who in the air the boundless space traverses:
What god should we with sacrifices worship?

The fourth line here is the refrain of nine successive stanzas, in which the creator is referred to as unknown, with the interrogative pronoun *ka*, "what?" This *ka* in the later Vedic literature came to be employed not only as an epithet of the creator Prajāpati, but even as an independent name of the supreme god.

A deity of an abstract character occurring in the oldest as well as the latest parts of the *Rigveda* is Bṛihaspati, "Lord of Prayer." Roth and other distinguished Vedic scholars regard him as a direct personification of devotion. In the opinion of the present writer, however, he is only an indirect deification of the sacrificial activity of Agni, a god with whom he has undoubtedly much in common. Thus the most prominent feature of his character is his priesthood. Like Agni, he has been drawn into and has obtained a firm footing in the Indra myth. Thus he is often described as driving out the cows after vanquishing the demon Vala. As the divine *brahmā* priest, Bṛihaspati seems to have been the prototype of the god Brahmā, chief of the later Hindu trinity. But the name Bṛihaspati itself survived in post-Vedic mythology as the designation of a sage, the teacher of the gods, and regent of the planet Jupiter.

Another abstraction, and one of a very peculiar kind, is the goddess Aditi. Though not the subject of any separate hymn, she is often incidentally celebrated. She has two, and only two, prominent characteristics. She is, in the first place, the mother of the small group of gods called Ādityas, of whom Varuṇa is the chief. Secondly, she has, like her son Varuṇa, the power of releasing from the bonds of physical suffering and moral guilt. With the latter trait her name, which means "unbinding," "freedom," is clearly connected. The unpersonified sense seems to survive in a few passages of the *Rigveda*. Thus a poet prays for the "secure and unlimited gift of *aditi*." The origin of the abstraction is probably to be explained as follows. The expression "sons of Aditi," which is several times applied to the Ādityas, when first used in all likelihood meant "sons of liberation," to emphasise a salient trait of their character, according to a turn of language common in the *Rigveda*. The feminine word "liberation" (*aditi*) used in this connection would then have become personified by a process which has more than one parallel in Sanskrit. Thus Aditi, a goddess of Indian origin, is historically younger than some at least of her sons, who can be traced back to a pre-Indian age.

Goddesses, as a whole, occupy a very subordinate position in Vedic belief. They play hardly any part as rulers of the world. The only one of any consequence is Ushas. The next in importance, Sarasvatī, ranks only with the least prominent of the male gods. One of the few, besides Pṛithivī, to whom an entire hymn is addressed, is Rātrī, Night. Like her sister Dawn, with whom she is often coupled, she is addressed as a daughter of the sky. She is conceived not as the dark, but as the bright starlit night. Thus, in contrasting the twin goddesses, a poet says, "One decks herself with stars, with sunlight the other." The following stanzas are from the hymn addressed to Night (x. 127):—

Night coming on, the goddess shines
In many places with her eyes:
All-glorious she has decked herself.

Immortal goddess, far and wide
She fills the valleys and the heights:
Darkness with light she overcomes.

8

And now the goddess coming on
Has driven away her sister Dawn:
Far off the darkness hastes away.

Thus, goddess, come to us to-day,
At whose approach we seek our homes,
As birds upon the tree their nest.

The villagers have gone to rest,
Beasts, too, with feet and birds with wings:
The hungry hawk himself is still.

Ward off the she-wolf and the wolf,
Ward off the robber, goddess Night:
And take us safe across the gloom.

Goddesses, as wives of the great gods, play a still more insignificant part, being entirely devoid of independent character. Indeed, hardly anything about them is mentioned but their names, which are simply formed from those of their male consorts by means of feminine suffixes.

A peculiar feature of Vedic mythology is the invocation in couples of a number of deities whose names are combined in the form of dual compounds. About a dozen such pairs are celebrated in entire hymns, and some half-dozen others in detached stanzas. By far the greatest number of such hymns is addressed to Mitra-Varuṇa, but the names most often found combined in this way are those of Heaven and Earth (*Dyāvā-pṛithivī*). There can be little doubt that the latter couple furnished the analogy for this favourite formation. For the association of this pair, traceable as far back as the Indo-European period, appeared to early thought so intimate in nature, that the myth of their conjugal union is found widely diffused among primitive peoples.

Besides these pairs of deities there is a certain number of more or less definite groups of divine beings generally associated with some particular god. The largest and most important of these are the Maruts or Storm-gods, who, as we have seen, constantly attend Indra on his warlike exploits. The same group, under the name of Rudras, is occasionally associated with their father Rudra. The smaller group of the Ādityas is constantly mentioned in company with their mother Aditi, or their chief Varuṇa. Their number in two passages of the *Rigveda* is stated as seven or eight, while in the Brāhmaṇas and later it is regularly twelve. Some eight or ten hymns of the *Rigveda* are addressed to them collectively. The following lines are taken from one (viii. 47) in which their aid and protection is specially invoked :—

As birds extend their sheltering wings,
Spread your protection over us.

As charioteers avoid ill roads,
May dangers always pass us by.

Resting in you, O gods, we are
Like men that fight in coats of mail.

Look down on us, O Ādityas,
Like spies observing from the bank:

Lead us to paths of pleasantness,
Like horses to an easy ford.

A third and much less important group is that of the Vasus, mostly associated with Indra in the *Rigveda,* though in later Vedic texts Agni becomes their leader. They are a vague group, for they are not characterised, having neither individual names nor any definite number. The Brāhmaṇas, however, mention eight of them. Finally, there are the Viçvedevās or All-gods, to whom some sixty hymns are addressed. It is a factitious sacrificial group meant to embrace the whole pantheon in order that none should be excluded in invocations intended to be addressed to all. Strange to say, the All-gods are sometimes conceived as a narrower group, which is invoked with others like the Vasus and Ādityas.

Besides the higher gods the *Rigveda* knows a number of mythical beings not regarded as possessing the divine nature to the full extent and from the beginning. The most important of these are the Ṛibhus who form a triad, and are addressed in eleven hymns. Characteristically deft-handed, they are often said to have acquired the rank of deities by their marvellous skill. Among the five great feats of dexterity whereby they became gods, the greatest—in which they appear as successful rivals of Tvashṭṛi, the artificer god—consists in their having transformed his bowl, the drinking vessel of the gods, into four shining cups. This bowl perhaps represents the moon, the four cups being its phases. It has also been interpreted as the year with its division into seasons. The Ṛibhus are further said to have renewed the youth of their parents, by whom Heaven and Earth seem to have been meant. With this miraculous deed another myth told about them appears to be specially connected. They rested for twelve days in the house of the sun, Agohya ("who cannot be concealed"). This sojourn of the Ṛibhus in the house of the sun in all probability alludes to the winter solstice, the twelve days being the addition which was necessary to bring the lunar year of 354 into harmony with the solar year of nearly 366 days, and was intercalated before the days begin to grow perceptibly longer. On the whole, it seems likely that the Ṛibhus were originally terrestrial or aërial elves, whose dexterity gradually attracted to them various myths illustrative of marvellous skill.

In a few passages of the *Rigveda* mention is made of a celestial water-nymph called Apsaras ("moving in the waters"), who is regarded as the spouse of a corresponding male genius called Gandharva. The Apsaras, in the words of the poet, smiles at her beloved in the highest heaven. More Apsarases than one are occasionally spoken of. Their abode is in the later Vedas extended to the earth, where they especially frequent trees, which resound with the music of their lutes and cymbals. The Brāhmaṇas describe them as distinguished by great beauty and devoted to dance, song, and play. In the post-Vedic period they become the courtesans of Indra's heaven. The Apsarases are loved not only by the Gandharvas but occasionally even by men. Such an one was Urvaçī. A dialogue between her and her earthly spouse, Purūravas, is contained in a somewhat obscure hymn of the *Rigveda* (x. 95). The nymph is here made to say :—

Among mortals in other form I wandered,
And dwelt for many nights throughout four autumns.

Her lover implores her to return ; but, though his request is refused, he (like Tithonus) receives the promise of immortality. The *Çatapatha Brāhmaṇa* tells the story in a more connected and detailed form. Urvaçī is joined with Purūravas in an alliance, the permanence of which depends on a condition. When this is broken by a stratagem of the Gandharvas, the nymph immediately vanishes from the sight of her lover. Purūravas, distracted, roams in search of her, till at last he observes her swimming in a lotus lake with other Apsarases in the form of an aquatic bird. Urvaçī discovers herself to him, and in response to his entreaties, consents to return for once after the lapse of a year. This myth in the post-Vedic age furnished the theme of Kālidāsa's play *Vikramorvaçī*.

Gandharva appears to have been conceived originally as a single being. For in the *Rigveda* the name nearly always occurs in the singular, and in the *Avesta*, where it is found a few times in the form of Gandarewa, only in the singular. According to the *Rigveda*, this genius, the lover of the water-nymph, dwells in the fathomless spaces of air, and stands erect on the vault of heaven. He is also a guardian of the celestial soma, and is sometimes, as in the *Avesta*, connected with the waters. In the later Vedas the Gandharvas form a class, their association with the Apsarases being so frequent as to amount to a stereotyped phrase. In the post-Vedic age they have become celestial singers, and the notion of their home being in the realm of air survives in the expression "City of the Gandharvas" as one of the Sanskrit names for "mirage."

Among the numerous ancient priests and heroes of the *Rigveda* the most important is Manu, the first sacrificer and the ancestor of the human race. The poets refer to him as "our father," and speak of sacrificers as "the people of Manu." The *Çatapatha Brāhmaṇa* makes Manu play the part of a Noah in the history of human descent.

A group of ancient priests are the Angirases, who are closely associated with Indra in the myth of the capture of the cows. Another ancient race of mythical priests are the Bhṛigus, to whom the Indian Prometheus, Mātariçvan, brought the hidden Agni from heaven, and whose function was the establishment and diffusion of the sacrificial fire on earth.

A numerically definite group of ancestral priests, rarely mentioned in the *Rigveda*, are the seven Rishis or seers. In the Brāhmaṇas they came to be regarded as the seven stars in the constellation of the Great Bear, and are said to have been bears in the beginning. This curious identification was doubtless brought about partly by the sameness of the number in the two cases, and partly by the similarity of sound between *ṛishi*, "seer," and *ṛiksha*, which in the *Rigveda* means both "star" and "bear."

Animals play a considerable part in the mythological and religious conceptions of the Veda. Among them the horse is conspicuous as drawing the cars of the gods, and in particular as representing the sun under various names. In the Vedic ritual the horse was regarded as symbolical of the sun and of fire. Two hymns of the *Rigveda* (i. 162–163) which deal with the subject, further show that horse-sacrifice was practised in the earliest age of Indian antiquity.

The cow, however, is the animal which figures most largely in the *Rigveda*. This is undoubtedly due to the important position, resulting from its pre-eminent utility, occupied by this animal even in the remotest period of Indian life. The beams of dawn and the clouds are cows. The rain-cloud, personified under the name of Pṛiçni, "the speckled one," is a cow, the mother of the Storm-gods. The bountiful clouds on which all wealth in India depended, were doubtless the prototypes of the many-coloured cows which yield all desires in the heaven of the blest described by the *Atharva-veda*, and which are the forerunners of the "Cow of Plenty" (*Kāmaduh*) so familiar to post-Vedic poetry. The earth itself is often spoken of by the poets of the *Rigveda* as a cow. That this animal already possessed a sacred character is shown by the fact that one Rishi addresses a cow as Aditi and a goddess, impressing upon his hearers that she should not be slain. *Aghnyā* ("not to be killed"), a frequent designation of the cow in the *Rigveda*, points in the same direction. Indeed the evidence of the *Avesta* proves that the sanctity of this animal goes back even to the Indo-Iranian period. In the *Atharva-veda* the worship of the cow is fully recognised, while the *Çatapatha Brāhmaṇa* emphasises the evil consequences of eating beef. The sanctity of the cow has not only survived in India down to the present day, but has even gathered strength with the lapse of time. The part played by the greased cartridges in the Indian Mutiny is sufficient to prove this statement. To no other animal has mankind owed so much, and the debt has been richly repaid in India with a veneration unknown in other lands. So important a factor has the cow proved in Indian life and thought, that an exhaustive account of her influence from the earliest times would form a noteworthy chapter in the history of civilisation.

Among the noxious animals of the *Rigveda* the serpent is the most prominent. This is the form which the powerful demon, the foe of Indra, is believed to possess. The serpent also appears as a divine being in the form of the rarely mentioned Ahi budhnya, "the Dragon of the Deep," supposed to dwell in the fathomless depths of the aërial ocean, and probably representing the beneficent side of the character of the serpent Vṛitra. In the later Vedas the serpents are mentioned as a class of semi-divine beings along with the Gandharvas and others; and in the Sūtras offerings to them are prescribed. In the latter works we meet for the first time with the Nāgas, in reality serpents, and human only in form. In post-Vedic times serpent-worship is found all over India. Since there is no trace of it in the *Rigveda*, while it prevails widely among the non-Aryan Indians, there is reason to believe that when the Aryans spread over India, the land of serpents, they found the cult diffused among the aborigines and borrowed it from them.

Plants are frequently invoked as divinities, chiefly in enumerations along with waters, rivers, mountains, heaven, and earth. One entire hymn (x. 97) is, however, devoted to the praise of plants (*oshadhi*) alone, mainly with regard to their healing powers. Later Vedic texts mention offerings made to plants and the adoration paid to large trees passed in marriage processions. One hymn of the *Rigveda* (x. 146) celebrates the forest as a whole, personified as Araṇyānī, the mocking genius of the woods. The weird sights and sounds of the gloaming are here described with a fine perception of nature. In the dark solitudes of the jungle

Sounds as of grazing cows are heard,
A dwelling-house appears to loom,
And Araṇyānī, Forest-nymph,
Creaks like a cart at eventide.

Here some one calls his cow to him,
Another there is felling wood;
Who tarries in the forest-glade
Thinks to himself, "I heard a cry."

Never does Araṇyānī hurt
Unless one goes too near to her:
When she has eaten of sweet fruit
At her own will she goes to rest.

Sweet-scented, redolent of balm,
Replete with food, yet tilling not,
Mother of beasts, the Forest-nymph,
Her I have magnified with praise.

On the whole, however, the part played by plant, tree, and forest deities is a very insignificant one in the *Rigveda.*

A strange religious feature pointing to a remote antiquity is the occasional deification and worship even of objects fashioned by the hand of man, when regarded as useful to him. These are chiefly sacrificial implements. Thus in one hymn (iii. 8) the sacrificial post (called "lord of the forest") is invoked, while three hymns of the tenth book celebrate the pressing stones used in preparing soma. The plough is invoked in a few stanzas; and an entire hymn (vi. 75) is devoted to the praise of various implements of war, while one in the *Atharva-veda* (v. 20) glorifies the drum.

The demons so frequently mentioned in the *Rigveda* are of two classes. The one consists of the aërial adversaries of the gods. The older view is that of a conflict waged between a single god and a single demon. This gradually developed into the notion of the gods and the demons in general being arrayed against each other as two opposing hosts. The Brāhmaṇas regularly represent the antagonism thus. Asura is the ordinary name of the aërial foes of the gods. This word has a remarkable history. In the *Rigveda* it is predominantly a designation of the gods, and in the *Avesta* it denotes, in the form of Ahura, the highest god of Zoroastrianism. In the later parts of the *Rigveda*, however, *asura*, when used by itself, also signifies "demon," and this is its only sense in the *Atharva-veda.* A somewhat unsuccessful attempt has been made to explain how a word signifying "god" came to mean "devil," as the result of national conflicts, the Asuras or gods of extra-Vedic tribes becoming demons to the Vedic Indian, just as the *devas* or gods of the Veda are demons in the *Avesta*. There is no traditional evidence in support of this view, and it is opposed by the fact that to the Rigvedic Indian *asura* not only in general meant a divine being, but was especially appropriate to Varuṇa, the most exalted of the gods. The word must therefore have changed its meaning in course of time within the Veda itself. Here it seems from the beginning to have had the sense of "possessor of occult power," and hence to have been potentially applicable to hostile beings. Thus in one hymn of the *Rigveda* (x. 124) both senses seem to occur. Towards the end of the Rigvedic period the application of the word to the gods began to fall into abeyance. This tendency was in all likelihood accelerated by the need of a word denoting the hostile demoniac powers generally, as well as by an incipient popular etymology, which saw a negative (*a-sura*) in the word and led to the invention of *sura*, "god," a term first found in the Upanishads.

A group of aërial demons, primarily foes of Indra, are the Paṇis. The proper meaning of the word is "niggard," especially in regard to sacrificial gifts. From this signification it developed the mythological sense of demons resembling those originally conceived as withholding the treasures of heaven. The term *dāsa* or *dasyu*, properly the designation of the dark aborigines of India contrasted with their fair Aryan conquerors, is frequently used in the sense of demons or fiends.

By far the most conspicuous of the individual aërial

demons of the *Rigveda*, is Vṛitra, who has the form of a serpent, and whose name means "encompasser." Another demon mentioned with some frequency is Vala, the personification of the mythical cave in which the celestial cows are confined. In post-Vedic literature these two demons are frequently mentioned together and are regarded as brothers slain by Indra. The most often named among the remaining adversaries of Indra is Çushṇa, the "hisser" or "scorcher." A rarely-mentioned demon is Svarbhānu, who is described as eclipsing the sun with darkness. His successor in Sanskrit literature was Rāhu, regarded as causing eclipses by swallowing the sun or moon.

The second class of demons consists of goblins supposed to infest the earth, enemies of mankind as the Asuras are of the gods. By far the most common generic name for this class is Rakshas. They are hardly ever mentioned except in connection with some god who is invoked to destroy or is praised for having destroyed them. These goblins are conceived as having the shapes of various animals as well as of men. Their appearance is more fully described by the *Atharvaveda*, in which they are also spoken of as deformed or as being blue, yellow, or green in colour. According to the *Rigveda* they are fond of the flesh of men and horses, whom they attack by entering into them in order to satisfy their greed. They are supposed to prowl about at night and to make the sacrifice the special object of their attacks. The belief that the Rakshases actively interfere with the performance of sacrificial rites remains familiar in the post-Vedic period. A species of goblin scarcely referred to in the *Rigveda*, but often mentioned in the later Vedas, are the Piçāchas, described as devouring corpses and closely connected with the dead.

Few references to death and the future life are to be found in the hymns of the *Rigveda*, as the optimistic and active Vedic Indian, unlike his descendants in later centuries, seems to have given little thought to the other world. Most of the information to be gained about their views of the next life are to be found in the funeral hymns of the last book. The belief here expressed is that fire or the grave destroys the body only, while the real personality of the deceased is imperishable. The soul is thought to be separable from the body, not only after death, but even during unconsciousness (x. 58). There is no indication here, or even in the later Vedas, of the doctrine of the transmigration of souls, though it was already firmly established in the sixth century B.C. when Buddhism arose. One passage of the *Rigveda*, however, in which the soul is spoken of as departing to the waters or the plants, may contain the germs of the theory.

CHAPTER V

PHILOSOPHY OF THE RIGVEDA

ACCORDING to the Vedic view, the spirit of the deceased proceeded to the realm of eternal light on the path trodden by the fathers, whom he finds in the highest heaven revelling with Yama, king of the dead, and feasting with the gods.

In one of the funeral hymns (x. 14, 7) the dead man is thus addressed :—

Go forth, go forth along those ancient pathways
To where our early ancestors departed.
There thou shalt see rejoicing in libations
The two kings, Varuṇa the god and Yama.

Here a tree spreads its branches, in the shade of which Yama drinks soma with the gods, and the sound of the flute and of songs is heard. The life in heaven is free from imperfections or bodily frailties, and is altogether delectable. It is a glorified life of material joys as conceived by the imagination, not of warriors, but of priests. Heaven is gained as a reward by heroes who risk their lives in battle, but above all by those who bestow liberal sacrificial gifts on priests.

Though the *Atharva-veda* undoubtedly shows a belief in a place of future punishment, the utmost that can be inferred with regard to the *Rigveda* from the scanty evidence we possess, is the notion that unbelievers were consigned to an underground darkness after death. So little, indeed, do the Rishis say on this subject, and so vague is the little they do say, that Roth held the total annihilation of the wicked by death to be their belief. The early Indian notions about future punishment gradually developed, till, in the post-Vedic period, a complicated system of hells had been elaborated.

Some passages of the *Rigveda* distinguish the path of the fathers or dead ancestors from the path of the gods, doubtless because cremation appeared as a different process from sacrifice. In the Brāhmaṇas the fathers and the gods are thought to dwell in distinct abodes, for the "heavenly world" is contrasted with the "world of the fathers."

The chief of the blessed dead is Yama, to whom three entire hymns are addressed. He is spoken of as a king who rules the departed and as a gatherer of the people, who gives the deceased a resting-place and prepares an abode for him. Yama it was who first discovered the way to the other world :—

> *Him who along the mighty heights departed,*
> *Him who searched and spied out the path for many,*
> *Son of Vivasvat, gatherer of the people,*
> *Yama the king, with sacrifices worship.* (x. 14, 1).

Though death is the path of Yama, and he must consequently have been regarded with a certain amount of fear, he is not yet in the *Rigveda*, as in the *Atharva-veda* and the later mythology, a god of death. The owl and pigeon are occasionally mentioned as emissaries of Yama, but his regular messengers are two dogs which guard the path trodden by the dead proceeding to the other world.

With reference to them the deceased man is thus addressed in one of the funeral hymns (x. 14):—

Run on thy path straight forward past the two dogs,
The sons of Saramā, four-eyed and brindled,
Draw near thereafter to the bounteous fathers,
Who revel on in company with Yama.

Broad-nosed and brown, the messengers of Yama,
Greedy of lives, wander among the people:
May they give back to us a life auspicious
Here and to-day, that we may see the sunlight.

The name of Yama is sometimes used in the *Rigveda* in its primary sense of "twin," and the chief of the dead actually occurs in this character throughout a hymn (x. 10) of much poetic beauty, consisting of a dialogue between him and his sister Yamī. She endeavours to win his love, but he repels her advances with these words:—

The spies sent by the gods here ever wander,
They stand not still, nor close their eyes in slumber:
Another man thine arms shall clasp, O Yamī,
Tightly as twines around the tree the creeper.

The incestuous union which forms the main theme of the poem, though rejected as contrary to the higher ethical standard of the *Rigveda*, was doubtless the survival of an already existing myth of the descent of mankind from primeval "twins." This myth, indeed, seems to have been handed down from the Indo-Iranian period, for the later Avestan literature makes mention of Yimeh as a sister of Yima. Even the name of Yama's father goes back to that period, for Yima is the son of Vivanhvant in the *Avesta* as Yama is of Vivasvat in the *Rigveda*.

The great bulk of the Rigvedic poems comprises invocations of gods or deified objects as described in the foregoing pages. Scattered among them are to be found, chiefly in the tenth book, about a dozen mythological pieces consisting of dialogues which, in a vague and fragmentary way, indicate the course of the action and refer to past events. In all likelihood they were originally accompanied by a narrative setting in prose, which explained the situation more fully to the audience, but was lost after these poems were incorporated among the collected hymns of the *Rigveda*. One of this class (iv. 42) is a colloquy between Indra and Varuṇa, in which each of these leading gods puts forward his claims to pre-eminence. Another, which shows considerable poetic merit and presents the situation clearly, is a dialogue in alternate verses between Varuṇa and Agni (x. 51), followed by a second (x. 52) between the gods and Agni, who has grown weary of his sacrificial office, but finally agrees to continue the performance of his duties.

A curious but prosaic and obscure hymn (x. 86), consists of a dialogue between Indra and his wife Indrāṇī on the subject of a monkey which has incurred the anger of the latter. The circumstances are much more clearly presented in a poem of great beauty (x. 108), in which Saramā, the messenger of Indra, having tracked the stolen cows, demands them back from the Paṇis. Another already referred to (p. 107) treats the myth of Urvaçī and Purūravas. The dialogue takes place at the moment when the nymph is about to quit her mortal lover for ever. A good deal of interest attaches to this myth, not only as the oldest Indo-European love-story, but as one which has had a long history in Indian literature. The dialogue of Yama and Yamī (x. 10) is, as we have seen, based on a still older myth. These mythological ballads, if I may use the expression, foreshadow the dramatic and epic poetry of a later age.

A very small number, hardly more than thirty altogether, of the hymns of the *Rigveda* are not addressed to the gods or deified objects. About a dozen poems, occurring almost exclusively in the tenth book, are concerned with magical notions, and therefore belong rather to the domain of the *Atharva-veda.* Two short ones (ii. 42–43) belong to the sphere of augury, certain birds of omen being invoked to utter auspicious cries. Two others consist of spells directed against poisonous vermin (i. 191), and the disease called *yakshma* (x. 163). Two are incantations to preserve the life of one lying at the point of death (x. 58; 60, 7–12). A couple of stanzas from one of the latter may serve as a specimen :—

Just as a yoke with leathern thong
They fasten on that it may hold :
So have I now held fast thy soul,
That thou mayst live and mayst not die,
Anon to be unhurt and well.

Downward is blown the blast of wind,
Downward the burning sunbeams shoot,
Adown the milk streams from the cow :
So downward may thy ailment go.

Here is a stanza from a poem intended as a charm to induce slumber (v. 55) :—

The man who sits and he who walks,
And he who sees us with his gaze :
Of these we now close up the eyes,
Just as we shut this dwelling-house.

The first three stanzas of this lullaby end with the refrain, "Fall fast asleep" (*ni shu shvapa*).

The purpose of one incantation (x. 183) is to procure children, while another (x. 162) is directed against the demon that destroys offspring. There is also a spell (x. 166) aiming at the destruction of enemies. We further find the incantation (x. 145) of a woman desiring to oust her rival wives from the affections of her husband. A sequel to it is formed by the song of triumph (x. 159) of one who has succeeded in this object:—

Up has arisen there the sun,
So too my fortunes now arise:
With craft victorious I have gained
Over my lord this victory.

My sons now mighty warriors are,
My daughter is a princess now,
And I myself have gained the day:
My name stands highest with my lord.

Vanquished have I these rival wives,
Rising superior to them all,
That over this heroic man
And all this people I may rule.

With regard to a late hymn (vii. 103), which is entirely secular in style, there is some doubt as to its original purpose. The awakening of the frogs at the beginning of the rainy season is here described with a graphic power which will doubtless be appreciated best by those who have lived in India. The poet compares the din of their croaking with the chants of priests exhilarated by soma, and with the clamour of pupils at school repeating the words of their teacher:—

Resting in silence for a year,
As Brahmans practising a vow,

The frogs have lifted up their voice,
Excited when Parjanya comes.

When one repeats the utterance of the other
Like those who learn the lesson of their teacher,
Then every limb of yours seems to be swelling,
As eloquent ye prate upon the waters.

As Brahmans at the mighty soma offering
Sit round the large and brimming vessel talking,
So throng ye round the pool to hallow
This day of all the year that brings the rain-time.

These Brahmans with their soma raise their voices,
Performing punctually their yearly worship;
And these Adhvaryus, sweating with their kettles,
These priests come forth to view, and none are hidden.

The twelvemonth's god-sent order they have guarded,
And never do these men neglect the season.
When in the year the rainy time commences,
Those who were heated kettles gain deliverance.

This poem has usually been interpreted as a satire upon the Brahmans. If such be indeed its purport, we find it difficult to conceive how it could have gained admittance into a collection like the *Rigveda*, which, if not entirely composed, was certainly edited, by priests. The Brahmans cannot have been ignorant of the real significance of the poem. On the other hand, the comparison of frogs with Brahmans would not necessarily imply satire to the Vedic Indian. Students familiar with the style of the *Rigveda* know that many similes which, if used by ourselves, would involve contempt or ridicule, were employed by the ancient Indian poets only for the sake of graphic effect. As the frogs are in the last stanza besought to grant wealth and length of days, it is much more likely that we have here a panegyric of frogs believed to have the magical power of bringing rain.

There remain about twenty poems the subject-matter of which is of a more or less secular character. They deal with social customs, the liberality of patrons, ethical questions, riddles, and cosmogonic speculations. Several of them are of high importance for the history of Indian thought and civilisation. As social usages have always been dominated by religion in India, it is natural that the poems dealing with them should have a religious and mythological colouring. The most notable poem of this kind is the long wedding-hymn (x. 85) of forty-seven stanzas. Lacking in poetic unity, it consists of groups of verses relating to the marriage ceremonial loosely strung together. The opening stanzas (1–5), in which the identity of the celestial soma and of the moon is expressed in veiled terms, are followed by others (6–17) relating the myth of the wedding of Soma the moon with the sun-maiden Sūryā. The Açvins, elsewhere her spouses, here appear in the inferior capacity of groomsmen, who, on behalf of Soma, sue for the hand of Sūryā from her father, the sun-god. Savitṛi consents, and sends his daughter, a willing bride, to her husband's house on a two-wheeled car made of the wood of the *çalmali* or silk-cotton tree, decked with red *kiṃçuka* flowers, and drawn by two white bulls.

Then sun and moon, the prototype of human marriage, are described as an inseparable pair (18–19):—

They move alternately with mystic power;
Like children playing they go round the sacrifice:
One of the two surveys all living beings,
The other, seasons meting out, is born again.

Ever anew, being born again, he rises,
He goes in front of dawns as daylight's token.
He, coming, to the gods their share apportions:
The moon extends the length of man's existence.

Blessings are then invoked on the wedding procession, and a wish expressed that the newly-married couple may have many children and enjoy prosperity, long life, and freedom from disease (20–33).

The next two stanzas (34–35), containing some obscure references to the bridal garments, are followed by six others (36–41) pronounced at the wedding rite, which is again brought into connection with the marriage of Sūryā. The bridegroom here thus addresses the bride :—

I grasp thy hand that I may gain good fortune,
That thou may'st reach old age with me thy husband.
Bhaga, Aryaman, Savitṛi, Puraṃdhi,
The gods have given thee to share my household.

The god of fire is at the same time invoked :—

To thee, O Agni, first they led
Bright Sūryā with the bridal throng:
So in thy turn to husbands give
A wife along with progeny.

The concluding verses (42–47) are benedictions pronounced on the newly-wedded couple after the bride has arrived at her future home :—

Here abide; be not divided;
Complete life's whole allotted span,
Playing with your sons and grandsons,
Rejoicing in your own abode.

The last stanza of all is spoken by the bridegroom :—

May all the gods us two unite,
May Waters now our hearts entwine;
May Mātariçvan and Dhātri,
May Deshṭrī us together join.

There are five hymns, all in the last book (x. 14–18), which are more or less concerned with funeral rites.

All but one of them, however, consist chiefly of invocations of gods connected with the future life. The first (14) is addressed to Yama, the next to the Fathers, the third to Agni, and the fourth to Pūshan, as well as Sarasvatī. Only the last (18) is a funeral hymn in the true sense. It is secular in style as well as in matter, being almost free from references to any of the gods. Grave and elevated in tone, it is distinguished by great beauty of language. It also yields more information about the funeral usages of those early days than any of the rest.

From this group of hymns it appears that burial was practised as well as cremation by the Vedic Indians. The composer of a hymn addressed to Varuṇa in Book VII. also mentions "the house of clay" in connection with death. Cremation was, however, the usual manner of disposing of the dead, and the later Vedic ritual practically knew this method alone, sanctioning only the burial of ascetics and children under two years of age. With the rite of cremation, too, the mythological notions about the future life were specially connected. Thus Agni conducts the corpse to the other world, where the gods and Fathers dwell. A goat was sacrificed when the corpse was burned, and this goat, according to the *Atharva-veda* (ix. 5, 1 and 3), preceded and announced the deceased to the fathers, just as in the *Rigveda* the goat immolated with the sacrificial horse goes before to announce the offering to the gods (i. 162–163). In the later Vedic ritual a goat or cow was sacrificed as the body was cremated.

In conformity with a custom of remotest antiquity still surviving in India, the dead man was provided with ornaments and clothing for use in the future life.

The fact that in the funeral obsequies of the *Rigveda* the widow lies down beside the body of her deceased husband and his bow is removed from the dead man's hand, shows that both were in earlier times burnt with his body to accompany him to the next world, and a verse of the *Atharva-veda* calls the dying of the widow with her husband an old custom. The evidence of anthropology shows that this was a very primitive practice widely prevailing at the funerals of military chiefs, and it can be proved to go back to the Indo-European age.

The following stanza (8) from the last funeral hymn (x. 18) is addressed to the widow, who is called upon to rise from the pyre and take the hand of her new husband, doubtless a brother of the deceased, in accordance with an ancient marriage custom :—

Rise up; come to the world of life, O woman;
Thou liest here by one whose soul has left him.
Come: thou hast now entered upon the wifehood
Of this thy lord who takes thy hand and woos thee.

The speaker then, turning to the deceased man, exclaims :—

From the dead hand I take the bow he wielded,
To gain for us dominion, might, and glory.
Thou there, we here, rich in heroic offspring,
Will vanquish all assaults of every foeman.

Approach the bosom of the earth, the mother,
This earth extending far and most propitious:
Young, soft as wool to bounteous givers, may she
Preserve thee from the lap of dissolution.

Open wide, O earth, press not heavily on him,
Be easy of approach, hail him with kindly aid;
As with a robe a mother hides
Her son, so shroud this man, O earth.

Referring to the bystanders he continues:—

These living ones are from the dead divided:
Our calling on the gods is now auspicious.
We have come forth prepared for dance and laughter,
Till future days prolonging our existence.

As days in order follow one another,
As seasons duly alternate with seasons,
As the later never forsakes the earlier,
So fashion thou the lives of these, Ordainer.

A few of the secular poems contain various historical references. These are the so-called *Dānastutis* or "Praises of Gifts," panegyrics commemorating the liberality of princes towards the priestly singers employed by them. They possess little poetic merit, and are of late date, occurring chiefly in the first and tenth books, or among the *Vālakhilya* (supplementary) hymns of the eighth. A number of encomia of this type, generally consisting of only two or three stanzas, are appended to ordinary hymns in the eighth book and, much less commonly, in most of the other books. Chiefly concerned in describing the kind and the amount of the gifts bestowed on them, the composers of these panegyrics incidentally furnish historical data about the families and genealogies of themselves and their patrons, as well as about the names and homes of the Vedic tribes. The amount of the presents bestowed—for instance, 60,000 cows—is sometimes enormously exaggerated. We may, however, safely conclude that it was often considerable, and that the Vedic chiefs possessed very large herds of cattle.

Four of the secular poems are didactic in character. One of these (x. 34), "The Lament of the Gambler," strikes a pathetic note. Considering that it is the oldest composition of the kind in existence, we cannot but regard this poem as a most remarkable literary product. The gambler deplores his inability to throw off the spell of the dice, though he sees the ruin they are bringing on him and his household :—

Downward they fall, then nimbly leaping upward,
They overpower the man with hands, though handless.
Cast on the board like magic bits of charcoal,
Though cold themselves, they burn the heart to ashes.

It pains the gambler when he sees a woman,
Another's wife, and their well-ordered household:
He yokes these brown steeds early in the morning,
And, when the fire is low, sinks down an outcast.

"Play not with dice, but cultivate thy cornfield;
Rejoice in thy goods, deeming them abundant:
There are thy cows, there is thy wife, O gambler."
This counsel Savitṛi the kindly gives me.

We learn here that the dice (*aksha*) were made of the nut of the Vibhīdaka tree (*Terminalia bellerica*), which is still used for the purpose in India.

The other three poems of this group may be regarded as the forerunners of the sententious poetry which flourished so luxuriantly in Sanskrit literature. One of them, consisting only of four stanzas (ix. 112), describes in a moralising strain of mild humour how men follow after gain in various ways :—

The thoughts of men are manifold,
Their callings are of diverse kinds:
The carpenter desires a rift,
The leech a fracture wants to cure.

A poet I; my dad's a leech;
Mama the upper millstone grinds:
With various minds we strive for wealth,
As ever seeking after kine.

Another of these poems (x. 117) consists of a collection of maxims inculcating the duty of well-doing and charity :—

Who has the power should give unto the needy,
Regarding well the course of life hereafter:
Fortune, like two chariot wheels revolving,
Now to one man comes nigh, now to another.

Ploughing the soil, the share produces nurture;
He who bestirs his feet performs his journey;
A priest who speaks earns more than one who's silent;
A friend who gives is better than the niggard.

The fourth of these poems (x. 71) is composed in praise of wise speech. Here are four of its eleven stanzas :—

Where clever men their words with wisdom utter,
And sift them as with flail the corn is winnowed,
There friends may recognise each other's friendship:
A goodly stamp is on their speech imprinted.

Whoever his congenial friend abandons,
In that man's speech there is not any blessing.
For what he hears he hears without advantage:
He has no knowledge of the path of virtue.

When Brahman friends unite to offer worship,
In hymns by the heart's impulse swiftly fashioned,
Then not a few are left behind in wisdom,
While others win their way as gifted Brahmans.

The one sits putting forth rich bloom of verses,
Another sings a song in skilful numbers,
A third as teacher states the laws of being,
A fourth metes out the sacrifice's measure.

Even in the ordinary hymns are to be found a few moralising remarks of a cynical nature about wealth and women, such as frequently occur in the ethical literature of the post-Vedic age. Thus one poet exclaims: "How many a maiden is an object of affection to her wooer for the sake of her admirable wealth!" (x. 27, 12); while another addresses the kine he desires with the words: "Ye cows make even the lean man fat, even the ugly man ye make of goodly countenance" (vi. 28, 6). A third observes: "Indra himself said this, 'The mind of woman is hard to instruct, and her intelligence is small'" (viii. 33, 17); and a fourth complains: "There are no friendships with women; their hearts are those of hyenas" (x. 95, 15). One, however, admits that "many a woman is better than the godless and niggardly man" (v. 61, 6).

Allied to the didactic poems are the riddles, of which there are at least two collections in the *Rigveda*. In their simplest form they are found in a poem (29) of the eighth book. In each of its ten stanzas a different deity is described by his characteristic marks, but without being mentioned, the hearer being left to guess his name. Vishṇu, for instance, is thus alluded to:—

Another with his mighty stride has made three steps
To where the gods rejoice in bliss.

A far more difficult collection, consisting of fifty-two stanzas, occurs in the first book (164). Nothing here is directly described, the language being always symbolical and mystical. The allusions in several cases are so obscurely expressed that it is now impossible to divine the meaning. Sometimes the riddle is put in the form of a question, and in one case the answer itself is also given. Occasionally the poet propounds a riddle of which he himself evidently does not know the solution. In general these problems are stated as enigmas. The subject of about one-fourth of them is the sun. Six or seven deal with clouds, lightning, and the production of rain; three or four with Agni and his various forms; about the same number with the year and its divisions; two with the origin of the world and the One Being. The dawn, heaven and earth, the metres, speech, and some other subjects which can hardly even be conjectured, are dealt with in one or two stanzas respectively. One of the more clearly expressed of these enigmas is the following, which treats of the wheel of the year with its twelve months and three hundred and sixty days:—

Provided with twelve spokes and undecaying,
The wheel of order rolls around the heavens;
Within it stand, O Agni, joined in couples,
Together seven hundred sons and twenty.

The thirteenth or intercalary month, contrasted with the twelve others conceived as pairs, is thus darkly alluded to: "Of the co-born they call the seventh single-born; sages call the six twin pairs god-born." The latter expression probably alludes to the intercalary month being an artificial creation of man. In the later Vedic age it became a practice to propound such enigmas, called "theological problems" (*brahmodya*), in contests for intellectual pre-eminence when kings instituted great sacrifices or Brahmans were otherwise assembled together.

Closely allied to these poetical riddles is the philosophical poetry contained in the six or seven cosmogonic hymns of the *Rigveda.* The question of the origin of the world here treated is of course largely mixed with mythological and theological notions. Though betraying much confusion of ideas, these early speculations are of great interest as the sources from which flow various streams of later thought. Most of these hymns handle the subject of the origin of the world in a theological, and only one in a purely philosophical spirit. In the view of the older Rishis, the gods in general, or various individual deities, "generated" the world. This view conflicts with the frequently expressed notion that heaven and earth are the parents of the gods. The poets thus involve themselves in the paradox that the children produce their own parents. Indra, for instance, is described in so many words as having begotten his father and mother from his own body (x. 54, 3). This conceit evidently pleased the fancy of a priesthood becoming more and more addicted to far-fetched speculations; for in the cosmogonic hymns we find reciprocal generation more than once introduced in the stages of creation. Thus Daksha is said to have sprung from Aditi, and Aditi from Daksha (x. 72, 4).

The evolution of religious thought in the *Rigveda* led to the conception of a creator distinct from any of the chief deities and superior to all the gods. He appears under the various names of Purusha, Viçvakarman, Hiraṇyagarbha, or Prajāpati in the cosmogonic hymns. Whereas creation, according to the earlier view, is regularly referred to as an act of natural generation with some form of the verb *jan*, "to beget," these cosmogonic poems speak of it as the manufacture or evolution from some original material. In one of them (x. 90), the well-known Hymn of Man (*purusha-sūkta*), the gods are still the agents, but the material out of which the world is made consists of the body of a primeval giant, Purusha (man), who being thousand-headed and thousand-footed, extends even beyond the earth, as he covers it. The fundamental idea of the world being created from the body of a giant is, indeed, very ancient, being met with in several primitive mythologies. But the manner in which the idea is here worked out is sufficiently late. Quite in the spirit of the Brāhmaṇas, where Vishṇu is identified with the sacrifice, the act of creation is treated as a sacrificial rite, the original man being conceived as a victim, the parts of which when cut up become portions of the universe. His head, we are told, became the sky, his navel the air, his feet the earth, while from his mind sprang the moon, from his eye the sun, from his breath the wind. "Thus they (the gods) fashioned the worlds." Another sign of the lateness of the hymn is its pantheistic colouring; for it is here said that "Purusha is all this world, what has been and shall be," and "one-fourth of him is all creatures, and three-fourths are the world of the immortals in heaven." In the Brāhmaṇas, Purusha is the same as the creator, Prajāpati, and in the Upanishads he is identified with the universe. Still later, in the dualistic Sānkhya philosophy, Purusha becomes the name of "soul" as opposed to "matter." In the Hymn of Man a being called Virāj is mentioned as produced from Purusha. This in the later Vedānta philosophy is a name of the personal creator as contrasted with Brahma, the universal soul. The Purusha hymn, then, may be regarded as the oldest product of the pantheistic literature of India. It is at the same time one of the very latest poems of the Rigvedic age; for it presupposes a knowledge of the three oldest Vedas, to which it refers together by name. It also for the first and only time in the *Rigveda* mentions the four castes; for it is here said that Purusha's mouth became the Brahman, his arms the Rājanya (warrior), his thighs the Vaiçya (agriculturist), and his feet the Çūdra (serf).

In nearly all the other poems dealing with the origin

of the world, not the gods collectively but an individual creator is the actor. Various passages in other hymns show that the sun was regarded as an important agent of generation by the Rishis. Thus he is described as "the soul of all that moves and stands" (i. 115, 1), and is said to be "called by many names though one" (i. 164, 46). Such statements indicate that the sun was in process of being abstracted to the character of a creator. This is probably the origin of Viçvakarman, "the all-creating," to whom two cosmogonic hymns (x. 81–82) are addressed. Three of the seven stanzas of the first deserve to be quoted :—

What was the place on which he gained a footing?
Where found he anything, or how, to hold by,
What time, the earth creating, Viçvakarman,
All-seeing, with his might disclosed the heavens?

Who has his eyes and mouth in every quarter,
Whose arms and feet are turned in all directions,
The one god, when the earth and heaven creating,
With his two arms and wings together welds them.

What was the wood, and what the tree, pray tell us,
From which they fashioned forth the earth and heaven?
Ye sages, in your mind, pray make inquiry,
Whereon he stood, when he the worlds supported?

It is an interesting coincidence that "wood," the term here used, was regularly employed in Greek philosophy to express "original matter" (*hūlē*).

In the next hymn (x. 82), the theory is advanced that the waters produced the first germ of things, the source of the universe and the gods.

Who is our father, parent, and disposer,
Who knows all habitations and all beings,
Who only to the gods their names apportions:
To him all other beings turn inquiring?

What germ primeval did the waters cherish,
Wherein the gods all saw themselves together,
Which is beyond the earth, beyond that heaven,
Beyond the mighty gods' mysterious dwelling?

That germ primeval did the waters cherish,
Wherein the gods together all assembled,
The One that in the goat's[1] *source is established,*
Within which all the worlds are comprehended.

Ye cannot find him who these worlds created:
That which comes nearer to you is another.

In a cosmogonic poem (x. 121) of considerable beauty the creator further appears under the name of Hiraṇyagarbha, "germ of gold," a notion doubtless suggested by the rising sun. Here, too, the waters are, in producing Agni, regarded as bearing the germ of all life.

The Germ of Gold at first came into being,
Produced as the one lord of all existence.
The earth he has supported and this heaven:
What god shall we with sacrifices worship?

Who gives the breath of life and vital power,
To whose commands the gods all render homage,
Whose shade is death and life immortal:
What god shall we with sacrifices worship?

What time the mighty waters came containing
All germs of life and generating Agni,
Then was produced the gods' one vital spirit:
What god shall we with sacrifices worship?

Who with his mighty power surveyed the waters
That intellect and sacrifice engendered,
The one god over all the gods exalted:
What god shall we with sacrifices worship?

---

[1] The sun is probably meant.

The refrain receives its answer in a tenth stanza (added to the poem at a later time), which proclaims the unknown god to be Prajāpati.

Two other cosmogonic poems explain the origin of the world philosophically as the evolution of the existent (*sat*) from the non-existent (*asat*). In the somewhat confused account given in one of them (x. 72), three stages of creation may be distinguished: first the world is produced, then the gods, and lastly the sun. The theory of evolution is here still combined with that of creation:—

Even as a smith, the Lord of Prayer,
Together forged this universe:
In earliest ages of the gods
From what was not arose what is.

A far finer composition than this is the Song of Creation (x. 129):—

Non-being then existed not, nor being:
There was no air, nor heaven which is beyond it.
What motion was there? Where? By whom directed?
Was water there, and fathomless abysses?

Death then existed not, nor life immortal;
Of neither night nor day was any semblance.
The One breathed calm and windless by self-impulse:
There was not any other thing beyond it.

Darkness at first was covered up by darkness;
This universe was indistinct and fluid.
The empty space that by the void was hidden,
That One was by the force of heat engendered.

Desire then at the first arose within it,
Desire, which was the earliest seed of spirit.
The bond of being in non-being sages
Discovered searching in their hearts with wisdom.

Who knows it truly? who can here declare it?
Whence was it born? whence issued this creation?
And did the gods appear with its production?
But then who knows from whence it has arisen?

This world-creation, whence it has arisen,
Or whether it has been produced or has not,
He who surveys it in the highest heaven,
He only knows, or ev'n he does not know it.

Apart from its high literary merit, this poem is most noteworthy for the daring speculations which find utterance in so remote an age. But even here may be traced some of the main defects of Indian philosophy—lack of clearness and consistency, with a tendency to make reasoning depend on mere words. Being the only piece of sustained speculation in the *Rigveda*, it is the starting-point of the natural philosophy which assumed shape in the evolutionary Sānkhya system. It will, moreover, always retain a general interest as the earliest specimen of Aryan philosophic thought. With the theory of the Song of Creation, that after the non-existent had developed into the existent, water came first, and then intelligence was evolved from it by heat, the cosmogonic accounts of the Brāhmaṇas substantially agree. Here, too, the non-existent becomes the existent, of which the first form is the waters. On these floats Hiraṇyagarbha, the cosmic golden egg, whence is produced the spirit that desires and creates the universe. Always requiring the agency of the creator Prajāpati at an earlier or a later stage, the Brāhmaṇas in some of their accounts place him first, in others the waters. This fundamental contradiction, due to mixing up the theory of creation with that of evolution, is removed in the Sānkhya system by causing Purusha, or soul, to play the part of a passive spectator, while *Prakṛiti*, or primordial matter, undergoes successive stages of development. The cosmogonic hymns of the *Rigveda* are not only thus the precursors of Indian philosophy, but also of the Purāṇas, one of the main objects of which is to describe the origin of the world.

CHAPTER VI

THE RIGVEDIC AGE

THE survey of the poetry of the *Rigveda* presented in the foregoing pages will perhaps suffice to show that this unique monument of a long-vanished age contains, apart from its historical interest, much of æsthetic value, and well deserves to be read, at least in selections, by every lover of literature. The completeness of the picture it supplies of early religious thought has no parallel. Moreover, though its purely secular poems are so few, the incidental references contained in the whole collection are sufficiently numerous to afford material for a tolerably detailed description of the social condition of the earliest Aryans in India. Here, then, we have an additional reason for attaching great importance to the *Rigveda* in the history of civilisation.

In the first place, the home of the Vedic tribes is revealed to us by the geographical data which the hymns yield. From these we may conclude with certainty that the Aryan invaders, after having descended into the plains, in all probability through the western passes of the Hindu Kush, had already occupied the north-western corner of India which is now called by the Persian name of Panjāb, or "Land of Five Rivers."[1] Mention is made in the hymns of some twenty-five

[1] The component parts of this name are in Sanskrit *pancha*, five, and *āp*, water.

streams, all but two or three of which belong to the Indus river system. Among them are the five which water the territory of the Panjāb, and, after uniting in a single stream, flow into the Indus. They are the Vitastā (now Jhelum), the Asiknī (Chenab), the Parushṇī (later called Irāvatī, "the refreshing," whence its present name, Ravi), the Vipāç (Beäs), and the largest and most easterly, the Çutudrī (Sutlej). Some of the Vedic tribes, however, still remained on the farther side of the Indus, occupying the valleys of its western tributaries, from the Kubhā (Kabul), with its main affluent to the north, the Suvāstu, river "of fair dwellings" (now Swat), to the Krumu (Kurum) and Gomatī, "abounding in cows" (now Gomal), farther south.

Few of the rivers of the *Rigveda* are mentioned more than two or three times in the hymns, and several of them not more than once. The only names of frequent occurrence are those of the Indus and the Sarasvatī. One entire hymn (x. 75) is devoted to its laudation, but eighteen other streams, mostly its tributaries, share its praises in two stanzas. The mighty river seems to have made a deep impression on the mind of the poet. He speaks of her as the swiftest of the swift, surpassing all other streams in volume of water. Other rivers flow to her as lowing cows hasten to their calf. The roar and rush of her waters are described in enthusiastic strains :—

From earth the sullen roar swells upward to the sky,
With brilliant spray she dashes up unending surge ;
As when the streams of rain pour thund'ring from the cloud,
The Sindhu onward rushes like a bellowing bull.

The Sindhu (now Sindh), which in Sanskrit simply means *the* "river," as the western boundary of the Aryan settlements, suggested to the nations of antiquity which first came into contact with them in that quarter a name for the whole peninsula. Adopted in the form of *Indos*, the word gave rise to the Greek appellation *India* as the country of the Indus. It was borrowed by the ancient Persians as *Hindu*, which is used in the *Avesta* as a name of the country itself. More accurate is the modern Persian designation *Hindustan*, "land of the Indus," a name properly applying only to that part of the peninsula which lies between the Himālaya and Vindhya ranges.

Mention is often made in the *Rigveda* of the *sapta sindhavaḥ*, or "seven rivers," which in one passage at least is synonymous with the country inhabited by the Aryan Indians. It is interesting to note that the same expression *hapta hindu* occurs in the *Avesta*, though it is there restricted to mean only that part of the Indian territory which lay in Eastern Kabulistan. If "seven" is here intended for a definite number, the "seven rivers" must originally have meant the Kabul, the Indus, and the five rivers of the Panjāb, though later the Sarasvatī may have been substituted for the Kabul. For the Sarasvatī is the sacred river of the *Rigveda*, more frequently mentioned, generally as a goddess, and lauded with more fervour than any other stream. The poet's descriptions are often only applicable to a large river. Hence Roth and other distinguished scholars concluded that Sarasvatī is generally used by the poets of the *Rigveda* simply as a sacred designation of the Indus. On the other hand, the name in a few passages undoubtedly means the small river midway between the Sutlej and the Jumna, which at a later period formed, with the Dṛishadvatī, the eastern boundary of the sacred region called Brahmāvarta, lying to the south of Ambāla, and commencing some sixty miles south of Simla.

This small river now loses itself in the sands of the desert, but the evidence of ancient river-beds appears to favour the conclusion that it was originally a tributary of the Çutudrī (Sutlej). It is therefore not improbable that in Vedic times it reached the sea, and was considerably larger than it is now. Considering, too, the special sanctity which it had already acquired, the laudations supposed to be compatible only with the magnitude of the Indus may not have seemed too exaggerated when applied to the lesser stream. It is to be noted that the Driṣhadvatī, the "stony" (now Ghogra or Ghugger), in the only passage in which the name occurs in the *Rigveda*, is associated with the Sarasvatī, Agni being invoked to flame on the banks of these rivers. This is perhaps an indication that even in the age of the *Rigveda* the most easterly limit of the Indus river system had already acquired a certain sanctity as the region in which the sacrificial ritual and the art of sacred poetry were practised in the greatest perfection. There are indications showing that by the end at least of the Rigvedic period some of the Aryan invaders had passed beyond this region and had reached the western limit of the Gangetic river system. For the Yamunā (now Jumna), the most westerly tributary of the Ganges in the north, is mentioned in three passages, two of which prove that the Aryan settlements already extended to its banks. The Ganges itself is already known, for its name is mentioned directly in one passage of the *Rigveda* and indirectly in another. It is, however, a noteworthy fact that the name of the Ganges is not to be found in any of the other Vedas.

The southward migration of the Aryan invaders does not appear to have extended, at the time when the hymns of the *Rigveda* were composed, much beyond the point where the united waters of the Panjāb flow into the Indus. The ocean was probably known only from hearsay, for no mention is made of the numerous mouths of the Indus, and fishing, one of the main occupations on the banks of the Lower Indus at the present day, is quite ignored. The word for fish (*matsya*), indeed, only occurs once, though various kinds of animals, birds, and insects are so frequently mentioned. This accords with the character of the rivers of the Panjāb and Eastern Kabulistan, which are poor in fish, while it contrasts with the intimate knowledge of fishing betrayed by the *Yajurveda*, which was composed when the Aryans had spread much farther to the east, and, doubtless, also to the south. The word which later is the regular name for "ocean" (*sam-udra*), seems therefore, in agreement with its etymological sense ("collection of waters"), to mean in the *Rigveda* only the lower course of the Indus, which, after receiving the waters of the Panjāb, is so wide that a boat in mid-stream is invisible from the bank. It has been noted in recent times that the natives in this region speak of the river as the "sea of Sindh;" and indeed the word *sindhu* ("river") itself in several passages of the *Rigveda* has practically the sense of "sea." Metaphors such as would be used by a people familiar with the ocean are lacking in the *Rigveda*. All references to navigation point only to the crossing of rivers in boats impelled by oars, the main object being to reach the other bank (*pāra*). This action suggested a favourite figure, which remained familiar throughout Sanskrit literature. Thus one of the poets of the *Rigveda* invokes Agni with the words, "Take us across all woes and dangers as across the river (*sindhu*) in a boat;" and in the later literature one who has accomplished his purpose or mastered his subject is very frequently described as "having reached the farther shore" (*pāraga*). The *Atharva-veda*, on the other hand, contains some passages showing that its composers were acquainted with the ocean.

Mountains are constantly mentioned in the *Rigveda*, and rivers are described as flowing from them. The Himālaya ("abode of snow") range in general is evidently meant by the "snowy" (*himavantaḥ*) mountains which are in the keeping of the Creator. But no individual peak is mentioned with the exception of Mūjavat, which is indirectly referred to as the home of Soma. This peak, it is to be inferred from later Vedic literature, was situated close to the Kabul Valley, and was probably one of the mountains to the south-west of Kashmir. The *Atharva-veda* also mentions two other mountains of the Himālaya. One of these is called Trikakud, the "three-peaked" (in the later literature Trikūṭa, and even now Trikōta), through the valley at the foot of which flows the Asiknī (Chenab). The other is Nāvaprabhraṃçana ("sinking of the ship"), doubtless identical with the Naubandhana ("binding of the ship") of the epic and the Manoravasarpaṇa of the *Çatapatha Brāhmaṇa*, on which the ship of Manu is said to have rested when the deluge subsided. The *Rigveda* knows nothing of the Vindhya range, which divides Northern India from the southern triangle of the peninsula called the Dekhan;[1] nor does it mention the Narmadā River (now Nerbudda),

[1] From the Sanskrit *dakshiṇa*, south, literally "right," because the Indians faced the rising sun when naming the cardinal points.

which flows immediately south of and parallel to that range.

From these data it may safely be concluded that the Aryans, when the hymns of the *Rigveda* were composed, had overspread that portion of the north-west which appears on the map as a fan-shaped territory, bounded on the west by the Indus, on the east by the Sutlej, and on the north by the Himālaya, with a fringe of settlements extending beyond those limits to the east and the west. Now the Panjāb of the present day is a vast arid plain, from which, except in the north-west corner at Rawal Pindi, no mountains are visible, and over which no monsoon storms break. Here there are no grand displays of the strife of the elements, but only gentle showers fall during the rainy season, while the phenomena of dawn are far more gorgeous than elsewhere in the north. There is, therefore, some probability in the contention of Professor Hopkins, that only the older hymns, such as those to Varuṇa and Ushas, were composed in the Panjāb itself, while the rest arose in the sacred region near the Sarasvatī, south of the modern Ambāla, where all the conditions required by the *Rigveda* are found. This is more likely than the assumption that the climate of the Panjāb has radically changed since the age of the Vedic poets.

That the home of the Aryans in the age of the *Rigveda* was the region indicated is further borne out by the information the poems yield about the products of the country, its flora and fauna. Thus the soma, the most important plant of the *Rigveda*, is described as growing on the mountains, and must have been easily obtainable, as its juice was used in large quantities for the daily ritual. In the period of the Brāhmaṇas it was brought from long distances, or substitutes had to be used on account of its rarity. Thus the identity of the original plant came to be lost in India. The plant which is now commonly used is evidently quite another, for its juice when drunk produces a nauseating effect, widely different from the feeling of exhilaration dwelt on by the poets of the *Rigveda.* Nor can the plant which the Parsis still import from Persia for the Haoma rite be identical with the old soma. Again, rice, which is familiar to the later Vedas and regarded in them as one of the necessaries of life, is not mentioned in the *Rigveda* at all. Its natural habitat is in the south-east, the regular monsoon area, where the rainfall is very abundant. Hence it probably did not exist in the region of the Indus river system when the *Rigveda* was composed, though, in later times, with the practice of irrigation, its cultivation spread to all parts of India. Corn (*yava*) was grown by the tillers of the *Rigveda*, but the term is probably not restricted, as later, to the sense of barley.

Among large trees mentioned in the *Rigveda*, the most important is the Açvattha ("horse-stand") or sacred fig-tree (*Ficus religiosa*). Its fruit (*pippala*) is described as sweet and the food of birds. Its sacredness is at least incipient, for its wood was used for soma vessels, and, as we learn from the *Atharva-veda*, also for the drill (later-called *pramantha*) employed in producing the sacred fire. The latter Veda further tells us that the gods are seated in the third heaven under an Açvattha, which may indeed have been intended in the *Rigveda* itself by the "tree with fair foliage," in whose shade the blessed revel with Yama. This tree, now called Peepal, is still considered so sacred that a Hindu would be afraid to utter a falsehood beside it. But the *Rigveda* does not mention at all, and the *Atharva-veda* only twice, the tree which is most characteristic of India, and shades with its wide-spreading foliage a larger area than any other tree on the face of the earth—the Nyagrodha ("growing downwards") or banyan (*Ficus indica*). With its lofty dome of foliage impenetrable to the rays of the sun and supported by many lesser trunks as by columns, this great tree resembles a vast temple of verdure fashioned by the hand of Nature. What the village oak is in England, that and much more is the banyan to the dwellers in the innumerable hamlets which overspread the face of agricultural India.

Among wild animals, one of the most familiar to the poets of the *Rigveda* is the lion (*siṃha*). They describe him as living in wooded mountains and as caught with snares, but the characteristic on which they chiefly dwell is his roaring. In the vast desert to the east of the Lower Sutlej and of the Indus, the only part of India suited for its natural habitat, the lion was in ancient times no doubt frequent, but he now survives only in the wooded hills to the south of the peninsula of Gujarat. The king of beasts has, however, remained conventionally familiar in Indian literature, and his old Sanskrit designation is still common in Hindu names in the form of Singh.

The tiger is not mentioned in the *Rigveda* at all, its natural home being the swampy jungles of Bengal, though he is now found in all the jungly parts of India. But in the other Vedas he has decidedly taken the place of the lion, which is, however, still known. His dangerous character as a beast of prey is here often referred to. Thus the *White Yājurvedā* compares a peculiarly hazardous undertaking with waking a sleeping tiger; and the *Atharva-veda* describes the animal as "man eating" (*purushād*). The relation of the tiger to the lion in the Vedas therefore furnishes peculiarly interesting evidence of the eastward migration of the Aryans during the Vedic period.

Somewhat similar is the position of the elephant. It is explicitly referred to in only two passages of the *Rigveda*, and the form of the name applied to it, "the beast (*mṛiga*) with a hand (*hastin*)," shows that the Rishis still regarded it as a strange creature. One passage seems to indicate that by the end of the Rigvedic period attempts were made to catch the animal. That the capture of wild elephants had in any case become a regular practice by 300 B.C. is proved by the evidence of Megasthenes. To the *Atharva-* and the *Yajur-vedas* the elephant is quite familiar, for it is not only frequently mentioned, but the adjective *hastin*, "possessing a hand" (*i.e.* trunk), has become sufficiently distinctive to be used by itself to designate the animal. The regular home of the elephant in Northern India is the Terai or lowland jungle at the foot of the Himālaya, extending eastward from about the longitude of Cawnpore.

The wolf (*vṛika*) is mentioned more frequently in the *Rigveda* than the lion himself, and there are many references to the boar (*varāha*), which was hunted with dogs. The buffalo (*mahisha*), in the tame as well as the wild state, was evidently very familiar to the poets, who several times allude to its flesh being cooked and eaten. There is only one reference to the bear (*ṛiksha*). The monkey (*kapi*) is only mentioned in a late hymn (x. 86), but in such a way as to show that the animal had already been tamed. The later and ordinary Sanskrit name for monkey, *vānara* ("forest-animal"), has survived in the modern vernaculars, and is known to readers of Mr.

Rudyard Kipling in the form of *Bunder-log* ("monkey-people").

Among the domestic animals known to the *Rigveda* those of lesser importance are sheep, goats, asses, and dogs. The latter, it may be gathered, were used for hunting, guarding, and tracking cattle, as well as for keeping watch at night. Cattle, however, occupy the chief place. Cows were the chief form of wealth, and the name of the sacrificial "fee,"[1] *dakshiṇā*, is properly an adjective meaning "right," "valuable," with the ellipse of *go*, "cow." No sight gladdened the eye of the Vedic Indian more than the cow returning from the pasture and licking her calf fastened by a cord; no sound was more musical to his ear than the lowing of milch kine. To him therefore there was nothing grotesque in the poet exclaiming, "As cows low to their calves near the stalls, so we will praise Indra with our hymns," or "Like unmilked kine we have called aloud (lowed) to thee, O hero (Indra)." For greater security cows were, after returning from pasture, kept in stalls during the night and let out again in the morning. Though the cow-killer is in the *White Yajurveda* already said to be punishable with death, the *Rigveda* does not express an absolute prohibition, for the wedding-hymn shows that even the cow was slaughtered on specially solemn occasions, while bulls are several times described as sacrificed to Indra in large numbers. Whilst the cows were out at pasture, bulls and oxen were regularly used for the purpose of ploughing and drawing carts.

Horses came next in value to cattle, for wealth in steeds is constantly prayed for along with abundance of cows. To a people so frequently engaged in battle,

[1] German, *vieh;* Latin, *pecus*, from which *pecunia*, "money."

the horse was of essential value in drawing the war-car; he was also indispensable in the chariot-race, to which the Vedic Indian was devoted. He was, however, not yet used for riding. The horse-sacrifice, moreover, was regarded as the most important and efficacious of animal sacrifices.

Of the birds of the *Rigveda* I need only mention those which have some historical or literary interest. The wild goose or swan (*haṃsa*), so familiar to the classical poets, is frequently referred to, being said to swim in the water and to fly in a line. The curious power of separating soma from water is attributed to it in the *White Yajurveda*, as that of extracting milk from water is in the later poetry. The latter faculty belongs to the curlew (*krunch*), according to the same Veda.

The *chakravāka* or ruddy goose, on the fidelity of which the post-Vedic poets so often dwell, is mentioned once in the *Rigveda*, the Açvins being said to come in the morning like a couple of these birds, while the *Atharva-veda* already refers to them as models of conjugal love. Peahens (*mayūrī*) are spoken of in the *Rigveda* as removing poison, and parrots (*çuka*) are alluded to as yellow. By the time of the *Yajurveda* the latter bird had been tamed, for it is there described as "uttering human speech."

A good illustration of the dangers of the *argumentum ex silentio* is furnished by the fact that salt, the most necessary of minerals, is never once mentioned in the *Rigveda*. And yet the Northern Panjāb is the very part of India where it most abounds. It occurs in the salt range between the Indus and the Jhelum in such quantities that the Greek companions of Alexander, according to Strabo, asserted the supply to be sufficient for the wants of the whole of India.

Among the metals, gold is the one most frequently mentioned in the *Rigveda.* It was probably for the most part obtained from the rivers of the north-west, which even at the present day are said to yield considerable quantities of the precious metal. Thus the Indus is spoken of by the poets as "golden" or "having a golden bed." There are indications that kings possessed gold in abundance. Thus one poet praises his royal benefactor for bestowing ten nuggets of gold upon him besides other bountiful gifts. Gold ornaments of various kinds, such as ear-rings and armlets, are often mentioned.

The metal which is most often referred to in the *Rigveda* next to gold is called *ayas* (Latin, *aes*). It is a matter of no slight historical interest to decide whether this signifies "iron" or not. In most passages where it occurs the word appears to mean simply "metal." In the few cases where it designates a particular metal, the evidence is not very conclusive; but the inference which may be drawn as to its colour is decidedly in favour of its having been reddish, which points to bronze and not iron. The fact that the *Atharva-veda* distinguishes between "dark" *ayas* and "red," seems to indicate that the distinction between iron and copper or bronze had only recently been drawn. It is, moreover, well known that in the progress of civilisation the use of bronze always precedes that of iron. Yet it would be rash to assert that iron was altogether unknown even to the earlier Vedic age. It seems quite likely that the Aryans of that period were unacquainted with silver, for its name is not mentioned in the *Rigveda,* and the knowledge of silver goes hand in hand with that of iron, owing to the manner in which these metals are intermingled in the ore which produces them. These two metals, moreover, are not found in any quantity in the north-west of India.

The evidence of the topography, the climate, and the products of the country thus shows that the people by whose poets the *Rigveda* was composed were settled in the north-west of India, from the Kabul to the Jumna. But they were still engaged in conflict with the aborigines, for many victories over them are referred to. Thus Indra is said to have bound 1000 or slain 30,000 of them for his allies. That the conquerors were bent on acquiring new territory appears from the rivers being frequently mentioned as obstacles to farther advance. The invaders, though split up into many tribes, were conscious of a unity of race and religion. They styled themselves Āryas or "kinsmen," as opposed to the aborigines, to whom they gave the name of *Dasyu* or *Dāsa*, "fiends," in later times also called *anārya*, or non-Aryans. The characteristic physical difference between the two races was that of colour (*varṇa*), the aborigines being described as "black" (*kṛishṇa*) or "black-skins," and as the "Dāsa colour," in contrast with the "Aryan colour" or "our colour." This contrast undoubtedly formed the original basis of caste, the regular name for which in Sanskrit is "colour."

Those of the conquered race who did not escape to the hills and were captured became slaves. Thus one singer receives from his royal patron a hundred asses, a hundred sheep, and a hundred Dāsas. The latter word in later Sanskrit regularly means servant or slave, much in the same way as "captive Slav" to the German came to mean "slave." When thoroughly subjected, the original inhabitants, ceasing to be called Dasyus, became the fourth caste under the later name of Çūdras. The Dasyus are described in the *Rigveda* as non-sacrificing, unbelieving, and impious. They are also doubtless meant by the phallus-worshippers mentioned in two passages. The Aryans in course of time came to adopt this form of cult. There are several passages in the *Mahābhārata* showing that Çiva was already venerated under the emblem of the phallus when that epic was composed. Phallus-worship is widely diffused in India at the present day, but is most prevalent in the south. The Dasyus appear to have been a pastoral race, for they possessed large herds, which were captured by the victorious Aryans. They fortified themselves in strongholds (called *pur*), which must have been numerous, as Indra is sometimes said to have destroyed as many as a hundred of them for his allies.

The *Rigveda* mentions many tribes among the Aryans. The most north-westerly of these are the Gandhāris, who, judged by the way they are referred to, must have been breeders of sheep. They were later well known as Gandhāras or Gāndhāras. The *Atharva-veda* mentions as contiguous to the Gandhāris the Mūjavats, a tribe doubtless settled close to Mount Mūjavat; evidently regarding these two as the extreme limit of the Aryan settlements to the north-west.

The most important part, if not the whole, of the Indian Aryans is meant by the "five tribes," an expression of frequent occurrence in the *Rigveda*. It is not improbable that by this term were meant five tribes which are enumerated together in two passages, the Pūrus, Turvaças, Yadus, Anus, and Druhyus. These are often mentioned as engaged in intertribal conflicts. Four of them, along with some other clans, are named as having formed a coalition under ten kings against Sudās, chief of the Tṛitsus. The opposing forces met on the banks of the Parushṇī, where the great "battle of the ten kings" was fought. The coalition, in their endeavours to cross the stream and to deflect its course, were repulsed with heavy loss by the Tṛitsus.

The Pūrus are described as living on both banks of the Sarasvatī. A part of them must, however, have remained behind farther west, as they were found on the Parushṇī in Alexander's time. The *Rigveda* often mentions their king, Trasadasyu, son of Purukutsa, and speaks of his descendant Tṛikshi as a powerful prince. The Turvaças are one of the most frequently named of the tribes. With them are generally associated the Yadus, among whom the priestly family of the Kaṇvas seems to have lived. It is to be inferred from one passage of the *Rigveda* that the Anus were settled on the Parushṇī, and the priestly family of the Bhṛigus, it would appear, belonged to them. Their relations to the Druhyus seem to have been particularly close. The Matsyas, mentioned only in one passage of the *Rigveda*, were also foes of the Tṛitsus. In the *Mahābhārata* we find them located on the western bank of the Yamunā.

A more important name among the enemies of Sudās is that of the Bharatas. One hymn (iii. 33) describes them as coming to the rivers Vipāç and Çutudrī accompanied by Viçvāmitra, who, as we learn from another hymn (iii. 53), had formerly been the chief priest of Sudās, and who now made the waters fordable for the Bharatas by his prayers. This is probably the occasion on which, according to another hymn (vii. 33), the

Bharatas were defeated by Sudās and his Tṛitsus, who were aided by the invocations of Vasishṭha, the successor and rival of Viçvāmitra. The Bharatas appear to be specially connected with sacrificial rites in the *Rigveda*; for Agni receives the epithet *Bhārata*, "belonging to the Bharatas," and the ritual goddess Bhāratī, frequently associated with Sarasvatī, derives her name from them. In a hymn to Agni (iii. 23), mention is made of two Bharatas named Devaçravas and Devavāta who kindled the sacred fire on the Dṛishadvatī, the Āpayā, and the Sarasvatī, the very region which is later celebrated as the holy land of Brahmanism under the names of Brahmāvarta and Kurukshetra. The family of the Kuçikas, to whom Viçvāmitra belonged, was closely connected with the Bharatas.

The Tṛitsus appear to have been settled somewhere to the east of the Parushṇī, on the left bank of which Sudās may be supposed to have drawn up his forces to resist the coalition of the ten kings attempting to cross the stream from the west. Five tribes, whose names do not occur later, are mentioned as allied with Sudās in the great battle. The Sṛinjayas were probably also confederates of the Tṛitsus, being, like the latter, described as enemies of the Turvaças.

Of some tribes we learn nothing from the *Rigveda* but the name, which, however, survives till later times. Thus the Uçīnaras, mentioned only once, were, at the period when the *Aitareya Brāhmaṇa* was composed, located in the middle of Northern India; and the Chedis, also referred to only once, are found in the epic age settled in Magadha (Southern Behar). Krivi, as a tribal name connected with the Indus and Asiknī, points to the north-west. In the *Çatapatha Brāhmaṇa* it is stated to be the old name of the Panchālas, who inhabited the country to the north of the modern Delhi.

The *Atharva-veda* mentions as remote tribes not only the Gandhāris and Mūjavats, but also the Magadhas (Behar) and the Angas (Bengal). We may therefore conclude that by the time that Veda was completed the Aryans had already spread to the Delta of the Ganges.

The Panchālas are not mentioned in either Veda, and the name of the Kurus is only found there indirectly in two or three compounds or derivatives. They are first referred to in the *White Yajurveda;* yet they are the two most prominent peoples of the Brāhmaṇa period. On the other hand, the names of a number of the most important of the Rigvedic tribes, such as the Pūrus, Turvaças, Yadus, Tṛitsus, and others, have entirely or practically disappeared from the Brāhmaṇas. Even the Bharatas, though held in high regard by the composers of the Brāhmaṇas, and set up by them as models of correct conduct, appear to have ceased to represent a political entity, for there are no longer any references to them in that sense, as to other peoples of the day. Their name, moreover, does not occur in the tribal enumerations of the *Aitareya Brāhmaṇa* and of *Manu,* while it is practically altogether ignored in the Buddhistic literature.

Such being the case, it is natural to suppose that the numerous Vedic tribes, under the altered conditions of life in vast plains, coalesced into nations with new names. Thus the Bharatas, to whom belonged the royal race of the Kurus in the epic, and from whom the very name of the *Mahābhārata,* which describes the great war of the Kurus, is derived, were doubtless absorbed in what came to be called the Kuru nation. In the genealogical system of the *Mahābhārata* the Pūrus are brought into close connection with the Kurus. This is probably an indication that they too had amalgamated with the latter people. It is not unlikely that the Tṛitsus, whose name disappears after the *Rigveda*, also furnished one of the elements of the Kuru nation.

As to the Panchālas, we have seen that they represent the old Krivis. It is, however, likely that the latter combined with several small tribes to make up the later nation. A Brāhmaṇa passage contains an indication that the Turvaças may have been one of these. Perhaps the Yadus, generally associated with the Turvaças in the *Rigveda*, were also one of them. The epic still preserves the name, in the patronymic form of Yādava, as that of the race in which Kṛishṇa was born. The name of the Panchālas itself (derived from *pancha*, five) seems to indicate that this people consisted of an aggregate of five elements.

Some of the tribes mentioned in the *Rigveda*, however, maintained their individual identity under their old names down to the epic period. These were the Uçīnaras, Sṛinjayas, Matsyas, and Chedis.

It is interesting to note that the *Rigveda* refers to a rich and powerful prince called Ikshvāku. In the epic this name recurs as that of a mighty king who ruled to the east of the Ganges in the city of Ayodhyā (Oudh) and was the founder of the Solar race.

It is clear from what has been said that the Vedic Aryans were split up into numerous tribes, which, though conscious of their unity in race, language, and religion, had no political cohesion. They occasionally formed coalitions, it is true, but were just as often at war with one another. The tribe, in fact, was the political unit, organised much in the same way as the Afghans are at the present day, or the Germans were in the time of Tacitus. The tribe (*jana*) consisted of a number of settlements (*viç*), which again were formed of an aggregate of villages (*grāma*). The fighting organisation of the tribe appears to have been based on these divisions. The houses forming the village seem to have been built entirely of wood, as they still were in the time of Megasthenes. In the midst of each house the domestic fire burnt. For protection against foes or inundations, fortified enclosures (called *pur*) were made on eminences. They consisted of earthworks strengthened with a stockade, or occasionally with stone. There is nothing to show that they were inhabited, much less that *pur* ever meant a town or city, as it did in later times.

The basis of Vedic society being the patriarchal family, the government of the tribe was naturally monarchical. The king (*rāja*) was often hereditary. Thus several successive members of the same family are mentioned as rulers of the Tṛitsus and of the Pūrus. Occasionally, however, the king was elected by the districts (*viç*) of the tribe; but whether the choice was then limited to members of the royal race, or was extended to certain noble families, does not appear. In times of peace the main duty of the king was to ensure the protection of his people. In return they rendered him obedience, and supplied him with voluntary gifts—not fixed taxes—for his maintenance. His power was by no means absolute, being limited by the will of the people expressed in the tribal assembly (*samiti*). As to the constitution and functions of the latter, we have unfortunately little or no information. In war, the king of course held the chief command. On important occasions, such as the eve of a battle, it was also his duty to offer sacrifice on behalf of his tribe, either performing the rites himself, or employing a priest to do so.

Every tribe doubtless possessed a family of singers who attended the king, praising his deeds as well as composing hymns to accompany the sacrifice in honour of the gods. Depending on the liberality of their patrons, these poets naturally did not neglect to lay stress on the efficacy of their invocations, and on the importance of rewarding them well for their services. The priest whom a king appointed to officiate for him was called a *purohita* or domestic chaplain. Vasishṭha occupied that position in the employ of King Sudās; and in one of his hymns (vii. 33) he does not fail to point out that the victory of the Tṛitsus was due to his prayers. The panegyrics on liberal patrons contain manifest exaggerations, partly, no doubt, intended to act as an incentive to other princes. Nevertheless, the gifts in gold, cows, horses, chariots, and garments bestowed by kings on their chief priests must often have been considerable, especially after important victories. Under the later Brahmanic hierarchy liberality to the priestly caste became a duty, while the amount of the sacrificial fee was fixed for each particular rite.

The employment of Purohitas by kings as their substitutes in the performance of sacrificial functions is to be regarded as the beginning and the oldest form of the priesthood in India. It became the starting-point of the historically unique hierarchical order in which the sacerdotal caste occupied the supreme position in society, and the State was completely merged in the Church. Such, indeed, was the ideal of the Catholic Church in the

West during the Middle Ages, but it never became an accomplished fact in Europe, as it did in India. No sooner had the priesthood become hereditary than the development of a caste system began, which has had no parallel in any other country. But during the period represented by Sudās and Vasishṭha, in which the older portion of the *Rigveda* was composed, the priesthood was not yet hereditary, still less had the warrior and sacerdotal classes became transformed into castes among the Aryan tribes settled in the Panjāb. This is confirmed by the fact that in the epic age the inhabitants of Madhyadeça or Mid-land, where the Brahmanic caste system grew up, regarded the people of the north-west as semi-barbarians.

In the simple social organisation of the Vedic tribes of this region, where occupations were but little differentiated, every man was a soldier as well a civilian, much as among the Afghans of to-day. As they moved farther to the east, society became more complex, and vocations tended to become hereditary. The population being now spread over wider tracts of territory, the necessity arose for something in the nature of a standing army to repel sudden attacks or quell risings of the subject aborigines. The nucleus would have been supplied by the families of the chiefs of lesser tribes which had amalgamated under some military leader. The agricultural and industrial part of the population were thus left to follow their pursuits without interruption. Meanwhile the religious ceremonial was increasing in complexity; its success was growing more dependent on correct performance, while the preservation of the ancient hymns was becoming more urgent. The priests had, therefore, to devote all their time and energies to the carrying out of their religious duties and the handing down of the sacred tradition in their families.

Owing to these causes, the three main classes of Aryan society became more and more separated. But how were they transformed into castes or social strata divided from one another by the impassable barriers of heredity and the prohibition of intermarrying or eating together? This rigid mutual exclusiveness must have started, in the first instance, from the treatment of the conquered aborigines, who, on accepting the Aryan belief, were suffered to form a part of the Aryan polity in the capacity of a servile class. The gulf between the two races need not have been wider than that which at the present day, in the United States, divides the whites from the negroes. When the latter are described as men of "colour," the identical term is used which, in India, came to mean "caste." Having become hereditary, the sacerdotal class succeeded in securing a position of sanctity and inviolability which raised them above the rest of the Aryans as the latter were raised above the Dāsas. When their supremacy was established, they proceeded to organise the remaining classes in the state on similar lines of exclusiveness. To the time when the system of the three Aryan castes, with the Çūdras added as a fourth, already existed in its fundamental principles, belong the greater part of the independent portions of the *Yajurveda*, a considerable part of the *Atharva-veda* (most of books viii. to xiii.), but of the *Rigveda*, besides the one (x. 90) which distinctly refers to the four castes by name, only a few of the latest hymns of the first, eighth, and tenth books. The word *brāhmaṇa*, the regular name for "man of the first caste," is still rare in the *Rigveda*, occurring only eight times, while *brahman*, which simply means sage or officiating priest, is found forty-six times.

We may now pass on to sketch rapidly the social conditions which prevailed in the period of the *Rigveda.* The family, in which such relationships as a wife's brother and a husband's brother or sister had special names, was clearly the foundation of society. The father was at its head as "lord of the house" (*gṛihapati*). Permission to marry a daughter was asked from him by the suitor through the mediation of an intimate friend. The wedding was celebrated in the house of the bride's parents, whither the bridegroom, his relatives, and friends came in procession. Here they were entertained with the flesh of cows slain in honour of the occasion. Here, too, the bridegroom took the bride's hand and led her round the nuptial fire. The *Atharva-veda* adds that he set down a stone on the ground, asking the bride to step upon it for the obtainment of offspring. On the conclusion of the wedding festivities, the bride, anointed and in festal array, mounted with her husband a car adorned with red flowers and drawn by two white bulls. On this she was conducted in procession to her new home. The main features of this nuptial ceremony of 3000 years ago still survive in India.

Though the wife, like the children, was subject to the will of her husband, she occupied a position of greater honour in the age of the *Rigveda* than in that of the Brāhmaṇas, for she participated with her husband in the offering of sacrifice. She was mistress of the house (*gṛihapatnī*), sharing the control not only of servants and slaves, but also of the unmarried brothers and sisters of her husband. From the *Yajurveda* we learn that it was customary for sons and daughters to marry in the order of their age, but the *Rigveda* more than once speaks of girls who remained unmarried and grew old in their father's house. As the family could only be continued in the male line, abundance of sons is constantly prayed for, along with wealth in cattle and land, and the newly wedded husband hopes that his bride may become a mother of heroes. Lack of sons was placed on the same level as poverty, and adoption was regarded as a mere makeshift. No desire for the birth of daughters is ever expressed in the *Rigveda;* their birth is deprecated in the *Atharva-veda*, and the *Yajurveda* speaks of girls being exposed when born. Fathers, even in the earliest Vedic times, would doubtless have sympathised with the sentiment of the *Aitareya Brāhmaṇa*, that "to have a daughter is a misery." This prejudice survives in India to the present day with unabated force.

That the standard of morality was comparatively high may be inferred from the fact that adultery and rape were counted among the most serious offences, and illegitimate births were concealed.

One or two passages indicate that the practice of exposing old men, found among many primitive peoples, was not unknown to the *Rigveda*.

Among crimes, the commonest appears to have been robbery, which generally took the form of cattle-lifting, mostly practised at night. Thieves and robbers are often mentioned, and the *Rigveda* contains many prayers for protection at home, abroad, and on journeys. Such criminals, when caught, were punished by being tied to stakes with cords. Debts (*ṛiṇa*) were often incurred, chiefly, it would seem, at play, and the *Rigveda* even speaks of paying them off by instalments.

From the references to dress which the *Rigveda* contains we may gather that a lower garment and a cloak were worn. Clothes were woven of sheep's wool, were often variegated, and sometimes adorned with gold. Necklets, bracelets, anklets, and ear-rings are mentioned in the way of ornaments. The hair was anointed and combed. The *Atharva-veda* even mentions a comb with a hundred teeth, and also speaks of remedies which strengthened or restored the growth of the hair. Women plaited their hair, while men occasionally wore it braided and wound like a shell. The gods Rudra and Pūshan are described as being thus adorned; and the Vasishṭhas, we learn, wore their hair braided on the right side of the head. On festive occasions wreaths were worn by men. Beards were usual, but shaving was occasionally practised. The *Atharva-veda* relates how, when the ceremony of shaving off his beard was performed on King Soma, Vāyu brought the hot water and Savitṛi skilfully wielded the razor.

The chief article of food was milk, which was either drunk as it came from the cow or was used for cooking grain as well as mixing with soma. Next in importance came clarified butter (*ghṛita*, now *ghee*), which, as a favourite food of men, was also offered to the gods. Grain was eaten after being parched, or, ground to flour between millstones, was made into cakes with milk or butter. Various kinds of vegetables and fruit also formed part of the daily fare of the Vedic Indian. Flesh was eaten only on ceremonial occasions, when animals were sacrificed. Bulls being the chief offerings to the gods, beef was probably the kind of meat most frequently eaten. Horse-flesh must have been less commonly used, owing to the comparative rarity of the horse-sacrifice. Meat was either roasted on spits or cooked in pots. The latter were made of metal or earthenware; but drinking-vessels were usually of wood.

The Indians of the *Rigveda* were acquainted with at least two kinds of spirituous liquor. Soma was the principal one. Its use was, however, restricted to occasions of a religious character, such as sacrifices and festivals. The genuine soma plant from which it was made also became increasingly difficult to obtain as the Aryans moved farther away from the mountains. The spirit in ordinary use was called *surā*. The knowledge of it goes back to a remote period, for its name, like that of soma, is found in the *Avesta* in the form of *hura*. It was doubtless prepared from some kind of grain, like the liquor made from rice at the present day in India. Indulgence in *surā* went hand in hand with gambling. One poet mentions anger, dice, and *surā* as the causes of various sins; while another speaks of men made arrogant with *surā* reviling the gods. Its use must have been common, for by the time of the *Vājasaneyi Saṃhitā*, the occupation of a "maker of surā" (*surākāra*) or distiller had become a profession.

One of the chief occupations of the Vedic Indians was of course warfare. They fought either on foot or on chariots. The latter had two occupants, the fighter and the driver. This was still the case in the *Mahābhārata*, where we find Kṛishṇa acting as charioteer to Arjuna. Cavalry is nowhere mentioned, and probably came into use at a considerably later period. By the time of Alexander's invasion, however, it formed one of the regular four divisions of the Indian army. There are some indications that riding on horseback was at least known to the *Rigveda*, and distinct references to it occur in the *Atharva-* and the *Yajur-vedas*. The Vedic warriors were protected with coats of mail and helmets of metal. The principal weapons were the bow and arrow, the latter being tipped with poisoned horn or with a metal point. Spears and axes are also frequently mentioned.

The principal means of livelihood to the Vedic Indian was cattle-breeding. His great desire was to possess large herds; and in the numerous prayers for protection, health, and prosperity, cattle are nearly always mentioned first.

The Vedic Aryans were, however, not merely a pastoral people. They had brought with them from beyond the valleys of Afghanistan at least a primitive knowledge of agriculture, as is shown by the Indians and Iranians having such terms as "to plough" (*kṛish*) in common. This had, indeed, by the time of the *Rigveda*, become an industry second only to cattle-breeding in importance. The plough, which we learn from the *Atharva-veda* had a metal share, was used for making furrows in the fields, and was drawn by bulls. When the earth was thus prepared, seed was strewn over the soil. Irrigation seems not to have been unknown, as dug-out channels for water are mentioned. When ripe, the corn (*yava*) was cut with a sickle. It was then laid in bundles on the threshing-floor, where it was threshed out and finally sifted by winnowing.

Though the Vedic Indians were already a pastoral and agricultural people, they still practised hunting to a considerable extent. The hunter pursued his game with bow and arrow, or used traps and snares. Birds were usually caught with toils or nets spread on the ground. Lions were taken in snares, antelopes secured in pits, and boars hunted with dogs.

Navigation in Rigvedic times was, as we have already seen, limited to the crossing of rivers. The boats (called *nau-s*, Greek *nau-s*) were propelled by what were doubtless paddles (*aritra*), and must have been of the most primitive type, probably dug-out tree-trunks. No mention is made of rudder or anchor, masts, or sails.

Trade in those days consisted in barter, the cow being the pecuniary standard by which the value of everything was measured. The transition to coinage was made by the use of gold ornaments and jewelry as a form of reward or payment, as was the case among the ancient Germans. Thus *nishka*, which in the *Rigveda* means a necklet, in later times became the name of a coin.

Though the requirements of life in early Vedic times were still primitive enough to enable every man more or less to supply his own wants, the beginnings of various trades and industries can be clearly traced in the *Rigveda*. References are particularly frequent to the labour of the worker in wood, who was still carpenter, joiner, and wheelwright in one. As the construction of chariots and carts required peculiar skill, we find that certain men already devoted themselves to it as a special art, and worked at it for pay. Hence felicity in the composition of hymns is often compared with the dexterity of the wheelwright. Mention is also sometimes made of the smith who smelts the ore in a forge, using the wing of a bird instead of a bellows to produce a draught. He is described as making kettles as well as other domestic utensils of metal. The *Rigveda* also refers to tanners and the skins of animals prepared by them. Women, it appears, were acquainted with sewing and with the plaiting of mats from grass or reeds. An art much more frequently alluded to in metaphors and similes is that of weaving, but the references are so brief that we obtain no insight into the process. The *Atharva-veda*, however, gives some details in a passage which describes how Night and Day, personified as two sisters, weave the web of the year alternately with threads that never break or come to an end. The division of labour had been greatly developed by the time of the *White Yajurveda*, in which a great many trades and vocations are enumerated. Among these we find the rope-maker, the jeweller, the elephant-keeper, and the actor.

Among the active and warlike Vedic Aryans the chariot-race was a favourite amusement, as is shown by the very metaphors which are borrowed from this form of sport. Though skilful driving was still a highly esteemed art in the epic period, the use of the chariot both for war and for racing gradually died out in Hindustan, partly perhaps owing to the enervating influence of the climate, and partly to the scarcity of horses, which had to be brought from the region of the Indus.

The chief social recreation of men when they met together was gambling with dice. The irresistible fascination exercised, and the ruin often entailed by this amusement, we have already found described in the Gambler's Lament. Some haunted the gaming-hall to such an extent that we find them jocularly described in the *Yajurveda* as "pillars of the playhouse" (*sabhā-sthāṇu*). No certain information can be gathered from the *Rigveda* as to how the game was played. We know, however, from one passage that four dice were used. The *Yajurveda* mentions a game played with five, each of which has a name. Cheating at play appears in the *Rigveda* as one of the most frequent of crimes; and one poet speaks of dice as one of the chief sources of sinning against the ordinances of Varuṇa. Hence the word used in the *Rigveda* for "gamester" (*kitava*) in classical Sanskrit came to mean "cheat," and a later word for "rogue" (*dhūrta*) is used as a synonym of "gamester."

Another amusement was dancing, which seems to have been indulged in by men as well as women. But when the sex of the dancers is distinctly referred to, they are nearly always maidens. Thus the Goddess of Dawn is compared to a dancer decked in gay attire. That dancing took place in the open air may be gathered from the line (x. 76, 6), "thick dust arose as from men who dance" (*nṛityatām*).

Various references in the *Rigveda* show that even in that early age the Indians were acquainted with different kinds of music. For we find the three main types of percussion, wind, and stringed instruments there represented by the drum (*dundubhi*), the flute (*vāṇa*), and the lute (*vīṇā*). The latter has ever since been the favourite musical instrument of the Indians down to the present day. That the Vedic Indians were fond of instrumental music may be inferred from the statement of a Rishi that the sound of the flute is heard in the abode of Yama, where the blessed dwell. From one of the Sūtras we learn that instrumental music was performed at some religious rites, the *vīṇā* being played at the sacrifice to the Manes.

By the time of the *Yajurveda* several kinds of professional musicians appear to have arisen, for lute-players, drummers, flute-players, and conch-blowers are enumerated in its list of callings. Singing is, of course, very often mentioned in the *Rigveda*. That vocal music had already got beyond the most primitive stage may be concluded from the somewhat complicated method of chanting the *Sāmaveda*, a method which was probably very ancient, as the Soma ritual goes back to the Indo-Iranian age.

CHAPTER VII

THE LATER VEDAS

OF the three later Vedas, the *Sāmaveda* is much the most closely connected with the *Rigveda.* Historically it is of little importance, for it contains hardly any independent matter, all its verses except seventy-five being taken directly from the *Rigveda.* Its contents are derived chiefly from the eighth and especially the ninth, the Soma book. The *Sāmaveda* resembles the *Yajurveda* in having been compiled exclusively for ritual application ; for the verses of which it consists are all meant to be chanted at the ceremonies of the soma sacrifice. Removed from their context in the *Rigveda,* they are strung together without internal connection, their significance depending solely on their relation to particular rites. In form these stanzas appear in the text of the *Sāmaveda* as if they were to be spoken or recited, differing from those of the *Rigveda* only in the way of marking the accent. The *Sāmaveda* is, therefore, only the book of words employed by the special class of Ugātṛi priests at the soma sacrifice. Its stanzas assume their proper character of musical *Sāmans* or chants only in the various song-books called *gānas,* which indicate the prolongation, the repetition, and the interpolation of syllables necessary in singing, just as is often done in European publications when the words are given below the musical notation. There are four of these song-books in existence, two belonging to each division of the Veda. The number of *Sāmans* here given of course admitted of being indefinitely increased, as each verse could be sung to many melodies.

The *Sāmaveda* consists of 1549 stanzas, distributed in two books called *ārchikas* or collections of *ṛich* verses. The principle of arrangement in these two books is different. The first is divided into six lessons (*prapāṭhaka*), each of which contains ten decades (*daçat*) of stanzas, except the sixth, which has only nine. The verses of the first twelve decades are addressed to Agni, those of the last eleven to Soma, while those of the intermediate thirty-six are chiefly invocations of Indra, the great soma-drinker. The second book contains nine lessons, each of which is divided into two, and sometimes three sections. It consists throughout of small groups of stanzas, which, generally three in number, are closely connected, the first in the group being usually found in the first book also. That the second book is both later in date and secondary in character is indicated by its repeating stanzas from the first book as well as by its deviating much less from the text of the *Rigveda*. It is also a significant fact in this connection that the verses of the first book which recur in the second agree more closely with the readings of the *Rigveda* than the other verses by which they are surrounded. This can only be accounted for by the supposition that they were consciously altered in order to accord with the same verses in the second book which were directly influenced by the *Rigveda*, while the readings of the first book had diverged more widely because that book had been handed down, since the original borrowing, by an independent tradition.

We know from statements of the *Çatapatha Brāhmaṇa*

that the divisions of the first book of the *Sāmaveda* existed at least as early as the period when the second part of that Brāhmaṇa was composed. There is, moreover, some reason to believe that the *Sāmaveda* as a collection is older than at least the *Taittirīya* and the *Vājasaneyi* recensions of the *Yajurveda*. For the latter contain verses, used also as *Sāman* chants, in a form which shows the variations of the *Sāmaveda* in contrast with the *Rigveda*. This is all the more striking as the *Vājasaneyi* text has an undoubted tendency to adhere to the readings of the *Rigveda*. On the other hand, the view expressed by Professor Weber that numerous variants in verses of the *Sāmaveda* contain archaic forms as compared with the *Rigveda*, and were therefore borrowed at a time before the existing redaction of the *Rigveda* took place, has been shown to be untenable. The various readings of the *Sāmaveda* are really due in part to inferior tradition, and in part to arbitrary alterations made in order to adapt verses detached from their context to the ritual purpose to which they were applied.

Two schools of the *Sāmaveda* are known—the Kauthumas and the Rāṇāyanīyas, the former of whom are said still to exist in Gujarat, while the latter, at one time settled mainly in the Mahratta country, are said to survive in Eastern Hyderabad. Their recensions of the text appear to have differed but little from each other. That of the Rāṇāyanīyas has been published more than once. The earliest edition, brought out by a missionary named Stevenson in 1842, was entirely superseded by the valuable work of Benfey, which, containing a German translation and glossary besides the text, came out in 1848. The *Sāmaveda* was thus the first of the Vedas to be edited in its entirety. The text of this Veda, according to the recension of the same school, together with the commentary of Sāyaṇa, was subsequently edited in India. Of the Kauthuma recension nothing has been preserved excepting the seventh *prapāṭhaka*, which, in the Naigeya subdivision of this school, forms an addition to the first *ārchika*, and was edited in 1868. Two indices of the deities and composers of the *Sāmaveda* according to the Naigeya school have also been preserved, and indirectly supply information about the text of the Kauthuma recension.

The *Yajurveda* introduces us not only to a geographical area different from that of the *Rigveda*, but also to a new epoch of religious and social life in India. The centre of Vedic civilisation is now found to lie farther to the east. We hear no more of the Indus and its tributaries; for the geographical data of all the recensions of the *Yajurveda* point to the territory in the middle of Northern India occupied by the neighbouring peoples of the Kurus and Panchālas. The country of the former, called Kurukshetra, is specifically the holy land of the *Yajurvedas* and of the Brāhmaṇas attached to them. It lay in the plain between the Sutlej and the Jumna, beginning with the tract bounded by the two small rivers Dṛishadvatī and Sarasvatī, and extending south-eastwards to the Jumna. It corresponds to the modern district of Sirhind. Closely connected with, and eastward of this region, was situated the land of the Panchālas, which, running south-east from the Meerut district to Allahabad, embraces the territory between the Jumna and the Ganges called the Doab ("Two Waters"). Kurukshetra was the country in which the Brahmanic religious and social system was developed, and from which it spread over the rest of India. It claims a further historical interest as being in later times the scene of the conflict, described in the *Mahābhārata*, between the Panchālas and Matsyas on the one hand, and the Kurus, including the ancient Bharatas, on the other. In the famous law-book of Manu the land of the Kurus is still regarded with veneration as the special home of Brahmanism, and as such is designated Brahmāvarta. Together with the country of the Panchālas, and that of their neighbours to the south of the Jumna, the Matsyas (with Mathurā, now Muttra, as their capital) and the Çūrasenas, it is spoken of as the land of Brahman sages, where the bravest warriors and the most pious priests live, and the customs and usages of which are authoritative.

Here the adherents of the *Yajurveda* split up into several schools, which gradually spread over other parts of India, the Kaṭhas, with their subdivision the Kapishṭhalas, being in the time of the Greeks located in the Panjāb, and later in Kashmir also. The Kaṭhas are now to be found in Kashmir only, while the Kapishṭhalas have entirely disappeared. The Maitrāyaṇīyas, originally called Kālāpas, appear at one time to have occupied the region around the lower course of the Narmadā for a distance of some two hundred miles from the sea, extending to the south of its mouth more than a hundred miles, as far as Nāsik, and northwards beyond the modern city of Baroda. There are now only a few remnants of this school to the north of the Narmadā in Gujarat, chiefly at Ahmedabad, and farther west at Morvi. Before the beginning of our era these two ancient schools must have been very widely diffused in India. For the grammarian Patanjali speaks of the Kaṭhas and Kālāpas as the universally known schools of the *Yajurveda*, whose doctrines were proclaimed in every village. From the *Rāmāyaṇa*, moreover, we learn that these two schools were highly honoured in Ayodhyā (Oudh) also. They were, however, gradually ousted by the two younger schools of the *Yajurveda*. Of these, the Taittirīyas have been found only to the south of the Narmadā, where they can be traced as far back as the fourth century A.D. Their most important subdivision, that of the Āpastambas, still survives in the territory of the Godāvarī, while another, the Hiraṇyakeçins, are found still farther south. The school of the Vājasaneyins spread towards the south-east, down the Ganges Valley. At the present day they occupy a wide area, embracing North-East and Central India.

Each of these four schools has preserved one or two recensions of the *Yajurveda*. The text of the *Maitrāyaṇī Saṃhitā*, which consists of four books (*kāṇḍa*), subdivided into fifty-four lessons (*prapāṭhaka*), has been edited by Professor L. v. Schroeder (1881–86). The same scholar is preparing an edition of the *Kāṭhaka Saṃhitā*, the recension of the Kaṭha school. These two recensions are nearly related in language, having many forms in common which are not found elsewhere. Of the *Kapishṭhala-Kaṭha Saṃhitā* only somewhat corrupt fragments have hitherto come to light, and it is very doubtful whether sufficient manuscript material will ever be discovered to render an edition of this text possible. The *Taittirīya Saṃhitā*, which comprises seven books, and is subdivided into forty-four lessons, is somewhat later in origin than the above-mentioned recensions. It was edited by Professor A. Weber in 1871–72. These texts of the *Yajurveda* form a closely connected group, for they are essentially the same in character. Their agreement is often even verbal, especially in the verses and formulas for recitation which they contain. They also agree in arranging their matter according to a similar principle, which is different from that of the *Vājasaneyi* recension.

The *Saṃhitā* of the latter consists entirely of the verses and formulas to be recited at the sacrifice, and is therefore clear (*çukla*), that is to say, separated from the explanatory matter which is collected in the Brāhmaṇa. Hence it is called the *White* (*çukla*) *Yajurveda*, while the others, under the general name of *Black* (*kṛishṇa*) *Yajurveda*, are contrasted with it, as containing both kinds of matter mixed up in the *Saṃhitā*. The text of the Vājasaneyins has been preserved in two recensions, that of the Mādhyaṃdinas and of the Kāṇvas. These are almost identical in their subject-matter as well as its arrangement. Their divergences hardly go beyond varieties of reading, which, moreover, appear only in their prose formulas, not in their verses. Agreeing thus closely, they cannot be separated in their origin by any wide interval of time. Their discrepancies probably arose rather from geographical separation, since each has its own peculiarities of spelling. The *White Yajurveda* in both these recensions has been edited by Professor Weber (1849–52).

It is divided into forty chapters, called *adhyāyas*. That it originally consisted of the first eighteen alone is indicated by external as well as internal evidence. This is the only portion containing verses and prose formulas (both having the common name of *mantras*) which recur in the *Taittirīya Saṃhitā*, the sole exceptions being a few passages relating to the horse-sacrifice in chapters 22–25. Otherwise the contents of the last twenty-two chapters are found again only in the Brāhmaṇa and the Āraṇyaka belonging to the *Taittirīya Saṃhitā*. Moreover, it is only the *mantras* of the first eighteen chapters of the *Vājasaneyi Saṃhitā* which are quoted and explained word by word in the first nine books of its own Brāhmaṇa, while merely a few *mantras* from the following seventeen chapters are mentioned in that work. According to the further testimony of an ancient index of the *White Yajurveda*, attributed to Kātyāyana, the ten chapters 26–35 form a supplement (*khila*).

The internal evidence of the *Vājasaneyi Saṃhitā* leads to similar conclusions. The fact that chapters 26–29 contain *mantras* relating to ceremonies dealt with in previous chapters and requiring to be applied to those ceremonies, is a clear indication of their supplementary character. The next ten chapters (30–39) are concerned with altogether new ceremonies, such as the human sacrifice, the universal sacrifice, and the sacrifice to the Manes. Lastly, the 40th chapter must be a late addition, for it stands in no direct relation to the ritual and bears the character of an Upanishad. Different parts of the *Saṃhitā*, moreover, furnish some data pointing to different periods of religious and social development. In the 16th chapter the god Rudra is described by a large number of epithets which are subsequently peculiar to Çiva. Two, however, which are particularly significant, *Īçāna*, "Ruler," and *Mahādeva*, "Great God," are absent here, but are added in the 39th chapter. These, as indicating a special worship of the god, represent a later development. Again, the 30th chapter specifies most of the Indian mixed castes, while the 16th mentions only a few of them. Hence, it is likely that at least some which are known to the former chapter did not as yet exist when the latter was composed.

On these grounds four chronological strata may be distinguished in the *White Yajurveda.* To the fundamental portion, comprising chapters 1–18, the next seven must first have been added, for these two parts deal with the general sacrificial ceremonial. The development of the ritual led to the compilation of the next fourteen chapters, which are concerned with ceremonies already treated (26–29) or entirely new (30–39). The last chapter apparently dates from a period when the excessive growth of ritual practices led to a reaction. It does not supply sacrificial *mantras,* but aims at establishing a mean between exclusive devotion to and total neglect of the sacrificial ceremonies.

Even the original portion of the *White Yajurveda* must have assumed shape somewhat later than any of the recensions of the *Black.* For the systematic and orderly distribution of matter by which the *mantras* are collected in the *Saṃhitā,* while their dogmatic explanation is entirely relegated to a Brāhmaṇa, can hardly be as old as the confused arrangement in which both parts are largely mixed up.

The two most important portions of the *Yajurvedas* deal with the new and full moon sacrifices, as well as the soma sacrifice, on the one hand, and with the construction of the fire-altar on the other. Chapters 1–10 of the *White Yajurveda* contain the *mantras* for the former, chapters 11–18 those for the latter part of the ceremonial. The corresponding ritual explanations are to be found in books 1–5 and 6–9 respectively of the *Çatapatha Brāhmaṇa.* In these fundamental portions even the *Black Yajurveda* does not intermingle the *mantras* with their explanations. The first book of the *Taittirīya Saṃhitā* contains in its first four lessons nothing but the verses and formulas to be recited at the fortnightly and the soma sacrifices; the fourth book, nothing but those employed in the fire-altar ritual. These books follow the same order as, and in fact furnish a parallel recension of, the corresponding parts of the *Vājasaneyi Saṃhitā.* On the other hand, the *Taittirīya Saṃhitā* contains within itself, but in a different part, the two corresponding Brāhmaṇas, which, on the whole, are free from admixture with *mantras.* The fifth book is the Brāhmaṇa of the fire ritual, and the sixth is that of the soma sacrifice; but the dogmatic explanation of the new and full moon sacrifice is altogether omitted here, being found in the third book of the *Taittirīya Brāhmaṇa.* In the *Maitrāyaṇī Saṃhitā* the distribution of the corresponding material is similar. The first three lessons of the first book contain the *mantras* only for the fortnightly and the soma sacrifices; the latter half of the second book (lessons 7–13), the *mantras* only for the fire ritual. The corresponding Brāhmaṇas begin with the sixth and the first lesson respectively of the third book. It is only in the additions to these fundamental parts of the *Black Yajurveda* that the separation of Mantra and Brāhmaṇa is not carried out. The main difference, then, between the *Black* and the *White* consists in the former combining within the same collection Brāhmaṇa as well as Mantra matter. As to its chief and fundamental parts, there is no reason to suppose that these two kinds of matter, which are kept separate and unmixed, are either chronologically or essentially more nearly related than are the *Vājasaneyi Saṃhitā* and the *Çatapatha Brāhmaṇa.*

The *Yajurveda* resembles the *Sāmaveda* in having been compiled for application to sacrificial rites only.

But while the *Sāmaveda* deals solely with one part of the ritual, the soma sacrifice, the *Yajurveda* supplies the formulas for the whole sacrificial ceremonial. Like the *Sāmaveda*, it is also connected with the *Rigveda;* but while the former is practically altogether extracted from the *Rigveda*, the *Yajurveda*, though borrowing many of its verses from the same source, is largely an original production. Thus somewhat more than one-fourth only of the *Vājasaneyi Saṃhitā* is derived from the *Rigveda*. One half of this collection consists of verses (*ṛich*) most of which (upwards of 700) are found in the *Rigveda;* the other half is made up of prose formulas (*yajus*). The latter, as well as the verses not borrowed from the *Rigveda*, are the independent creation of the composers of the *Yajurveda*. This partial originality was indeed a necessary result of the growth of entirely new ceremonies and the extraordinary development of ritual detail. It became impossible to obtain from the *Rigveda* even approximately suitable verses for these novel requirements.

The language of the Mantra portion of the *Yajurveda*, though distinctly representing a later stage, yet on the whole agrees with that of the *Rigveda*, while separated from that of classical Sanskrit by a considerable interval.

On its mythological side the religion of the *Yajurveda* does not differ essentially from that of the older Veda; for the pantheon is still the same. Some important modifications in detail are, however, apparent. The figure of Prajāpati, only foreshadowed in the latest hymns of the *Rigveda*, comes more and more into the foreground as the chief of the gods. The Rudra of the *Rigveda* has begun to appear on the scene as Çiva, being several times mentioned by that name as well as by other epithets later peculiar to Çiva, such as Çankara and Mahādeva. Vishṇu now occupies a somewhat more prominent position than in the *Rigveda*. A new feature is his constant identification with the sacrifice. The demons, now regularly called Asuras, perpetually appear as a group of evil beings opposed to the good gods. Their conflicts with the latter play a considerable part in the myths of the *Yajurveda*. The Apsarases, who, as a class of celestial nymphs endowed with all the seductive charms of female beauty, occupy so important a place in post-Vedic mythology, but are very rarely mentioned in the *Rigveda*, begin to be more prominent in the *Yajurveda*, in which many of them are referred to by individual names.

Certain religious conceptions have, moreover, been modified and new rites introduced. Thus the word *brahma*, which in the *Rigveda* meant simply "devotion," has come to signify the essence of prayer and holiness, an advance towards its ultimate sense in the Upanishads. Again, snake-worship, which is unknown to the *Rigveda*, now appears as an element in Indian religion. That, however, which impresses on the *Yajurveda* the stamp of a new epoch is the character of the worship which it represents. The relative importance of the gods and of the sacrifice in the older religion has now become inverted. In the *Rigveda* the object of devotion was the gods, for the power of bestowing benefits on mankind was believed to lie in their hands alone, while the sacrifice was only a means of influencing their will in favour of the offerer. In the *Yajurveda* the sacrifice itself has become the centre of thought and desire, its correct performance in every detail being all-important. Its power is now so great that it not merely influences, but compels the gods to do the will of the officiating priest. By means of it the Brahmans may, in fact, be said to hold the gods in their hands.

The religion of the *Yajurveda* may be described as a kind of mechanical sacerdotalism. A crowd of priests conducts a vast and complicated system of external ceremonies, to which symbolical significance is attributed, and to the smallest minutiæ of which the greatest weight is attached. In this stifling atmosphere of perpetual sacrifice and ritual, the truly religious spirit of the *Rigveda* could not possibly survive. Adoration of the power and beneficence of the gods, as well as the consciousness of guilt, is entirely lacking, every prayer being coupled with some particular rite and aiming solely at securing material advantages. As a natural result, the formulas of the *Yajurveda* are full of dreary repetitions or variations of the same idea, and abound with half or wholly unintelligible interjections, particularly the syllable *om*. The following quotation from the *Maitrāyaṇī Saṃhitā* is a good example: *Nidhāyo vā nidhāyo vā oṃ vā oṃ vā oṃ vā ē ai oṃ svarṇajyotiḥ.* Here only the last word, which means "golden light," is translatable.

Thus the ritual could not fail to become more and more of a mystery to all who did not belong to the Brahman caste. To its formulas, no less than to the sacrifice itself, control over Nature as well as the supernatural powers is attributed. Thus there are certain formulas for the obtainment of victory; by means of these, it is said, Indra constantly vanquished the demons. Again, we learn that, if the priest pro-

13

nounces a formula for rain while mixing a certain offering, he causes the rain to stream down. Hence the formulas are regarded as having a kind of magical effect by exercising compulsion. Similar miraculous powers later came to be attached to penance and asceticism among the Brahmans, and to holiness among the Buddhists. The formulas of the *Yajurveda* have not, as a rule, the form of prayers addressed to the gods, but on the whole and characteristically consist of statements about the result of employing particular rites and *mantras*. Together with the corresponding ritual they furnish a complex mass of appliances ready to hand for the obtainment of material welfare in general as well as all sorts of special objects, such as cattle or a village. The presence of a priest capable of using the necessary forms correctly is of course always presupposed. The desires which several rites are meant to fulfil amount to nothing more than childish absurdity. Thus some of them aim at the obtainment of the year. Formulas to secure possession of the moon would have had equal practical value.

Hand in hand with the elaboration of the sacrificial ceremonial went the growth and consolidation of the caste system, in which the Brahmans secured the social as well as the religious supremacy, and which has held India enchained for more than two thousand five hundred years. Not only do we find the four castes firmly established as the main divisions of Indian society in the *Yajurveda*, but, as one of the later books of the *Vājasaneyi Saṃhitā* shows, most of the mixed castes known in later times are already found to exist. The social as well as the religious conditions of the Indian people, therefore, now wear an aspect essentially differing from those revealed to us in the hymns of the *Rigveda*.

The *Rig-*, *Sāma-*, and *Yajur-vedas* alone were originally recognised as canonical collections. For they only were concerned with the great sacrificial ceremonial. The *Atharva-veda*, with the exception of the last book, which was obviously added in order to connect it with that ceremonial, is essentially unconnected with it. The ceremonial to which its hymns were practically applied is, with few exceptions, that with which the Gṛihya Sūtras deal, being domestic rites such as those of birth, marriage, and death, or the political rites relating to the inauguration of kings. Taken as a whole, it is a heterogeneous collection of spells. Its most salient teaching is sorcery, for it is mainly directed against hostile agencies, such as diseases, noxious animals, demons, wizards, foes, oppressors of Brahmans. But it also contains many spells of an auspicious character, such as charms to secure harmony in family and village life, reconciliation of enemies, long life, health, and prosperity, besides prayers for protection on journeys, and for luck in gambling. Thus it has a double aspect, being meant to appease and bless as well as to curse.

In its main contents the *Atharva-veda* is more superstitious than the *Rigveda*. For it does not represent the more advanced religious beliefs of the priestly class, but is a collection of the most popular spells current among the masses, who always preserve more primitive notions with regard to demoniac powers. The spirit which breathes in it is that of a prehistoric age. A few of its actual charms probably date with little modification from the Indo-European period;

for, as Adalbert Kuhn has shown, some of its spells for curing bodily ailments agree in purpose and content, as well as to some extent even in form, with certain old German, Lettic, and Russian charms. But with regard to the higher religious ideas relating to the gods, it represents a more recent and advanced stage than the *Rigveda*. It contains, indeed, more theosophic matter than any of the other Saṃhitās. For the history of civilisation it is on the whole more interesting and important than the *Rigveda* itself.

The *Atharva-veda* is extant in the recensions of two different schools. That of the Paippalādas is, however, known in a single birch-bark manuscript, which is ancient but inaccurate and mostly unaccented. It was discovered by Professor Bühler in Kashmir, and has been described by Professor Roth in his tract *Der Atharvaveda in Kaschmir* (1875). It will probably soon be accessible to scholars in the form of a photographic reproduction published by Professor Bloomfield. This recension is doubtless meant by the "Paippalāda Mantras" mentioned in one of the *Pariçishṭas* or supplementary writings of the *Atharva-veda*.

The printed text, edited by Roth and Whitney in 1856, gives the recension of the Çaunaka school. Nearly the whole of Sāyaṇa's commentary to the *Atharva-veda* has been edited in India. Its chief interest lies in the large number of readings supplied by it which differ from those of the printed edition of this Veda.

This Saṃhitā is divided into twenty books, containing 730 hymns and about 6000 stanzas. Some 1200 of the latter are derived from the *Rigveda*, chiefly from the tenth, first, and eighth books, a few also from each of the other books. Of the 143 hymns of Book XX., all but twelve are taken bodily from the established text of the *Rigveda* without any change. The matter borrowed from the *Rigveda* in the other books shows considerable varieties of reading, but these, as in the other Saṃhitās, are of inferior value compared with the text of the *Rigveda*. As is the case in the *Yajurveda*, a considerable part of the *Atharva* (about one-sixth) consists of prose. Upwards of fifty hymns, comprising the whole of the fifteenth and sixteenth, besides some thirty hymns scattered in the other books, are entirely unmetrical. Parts or single stanzas of over a hundred other hymns are of a similar character.

That the *Atharva-veda* originally consisted of its first thirteen books only is shown both by its arrangement and by its subject-matter. The contents of Books I.–VII. are distributed according to the number of stanzas contained in the hymns. In Book I. they have on the average four stanzas, in II. five, in III. six, in IV. seven, in V. eight to eighteen, in VI. three; and in VII. about half the hymns have only one stanza each. Books VIII.–XIII. contain longer pieces. The contents of all these thirteen books are indiscriminately intermingled.

The following five books, on the contrary, are arranged according to uniformity of subject-matter. Book XIV. contains the stanzas relating to the wedding rite, which consist largely of *mantras* from the tenth book of the *Rigveda*. Book XV. is a glorification of the Supreme Being under the name of Vrātya, while XVI. and XVII. contain certain conjurations. The whole of XV. and nearly the whole of XVI., moreover, are composed in prose of the type found in the Brāhmaṇas. Both XVI. and XVII. are very short, the former containing nine hymns occupying four printed pages, the latter consisting of only a single hymn, which extends to little more than two pages. Book XVIII. deals with burial and the Manes. Like XIV., it derives most of its stanzas from the tenth book of the *Rigveda*. Both these books are, therefore, not specifically Atharvan in character.

The last two books are manifestly late additions. Book XIX. consists of a mixture of supplementary pieces, part of the text of which is rather corrupt. Book XX., with a slight exception, contains only complete hymns addressed to Indra, which are borrowed directly and without any variation from the *Rigveda*. The fact that its readings are identical with those of the *Rigveda* would alone suffice to show that it is of later date than the original books, the readings of which show considerable divergences from those of the older Veda. There is, however, more convincing proof of the lateness of this book. Its matter relates to the Soma ritual, and is entirely foreign to the spirit of the *Atharva-veda*. It was undoubtedly added to establish the claim of the *Atharva* to the position of a fourth Veda, by bringing it into connection with the recognised sacrificial ceremonial of the three old Vedas. This book, again, as well as the nineteenth, is not noticed in the *Prātiçākhya* of the *Atharva-veda*. Both of them must, therefore, have been added after that work was composed. Excepting two prose pieces (48 and 49) the only original part of Book XX. is the so-called *kuntāpa* hymns (127–136). These are allied to the *dānastutis* of the *Rigveda*, those panegyrics of liberal kings or sacrificers which were the forerunners of epic narratives in praise of warlike princes and heroes.

The existence of the *Atharva*, as a collection of some kind, when the last books of the *Çatapatha Brāh-*

maṇa (xi., xiii., xiv.), the *Taittirīya Brāhmaṇa*, and the *Chhāndogya Upanishad* were composed, is proved by the references to it in those works. In Patanjali's *Mahābhāshya* the *Atharva* had already attained to such an assured position that it is even cited at the head of the Vedas, and occasionally as their only representative.

The oldest name of this Veda is *Atharvāngirasaḥ*, a designation occurring in the text of the *Atharva-veda*, and found at the beginning of its MSS. themselves. This word is a compound formed of the names of two ancient families of priests, the Atharvans and Angirases. In the opinion of Professor Bloomfield the former term is here synonymous with "holy charms," as referring to auspicious practices, while the latter is an equivalent of "witchcraft charms." The term *atharvan* and its derivatives, though representing only its benevolent side, would thus have come to designate the fourth Veda as a whole. In its plural form (*atharvāṇaḥ*) the word in this sense is found several times in the Brāhmaṇas, but in the singular it seems first to occur in an Upanishad. The adjective *ātharvaṇa*, first found as a neuter plural with the sense of "Atharvan hymns" in the *Atharva-veda* itself (Book XIX.), is common from that time onwards. The name *atharva-veda* first appears in Sūtras about as early as *ṛigveda* and similar designations of the other Saṃhitās. There are besides two other names of the *Atharva-veda*, the use of which is practically limited to the ritual texts of this Veda. In one of these, *Bhṛigu-angirasaḥ*, the name of another ancient family of fire-priests, the Bhṛigus, takes the place of that of the Angirases. The other, *brahma-veda*, has outside the Atharvan literature only been found once, and that in a Gṛihya Sūtra of the *Rigveda*.

A considerable time elapsed before the *Atharva-veda*, owing to the general character of its contents, attained to the rank of a canonical book. There is no evidence that even at the latest period of the *Rigveda* the charms constituting the *Atharva-veda* were formally recognised as a separate literary category. For the Purusha hymn, while mentioning the three sacrificial Vedas by the names of *Rik*, *Sāman*, and *Yajus*, makes no reference to the spells of the *Atharva-veda*. Yet the *Rigveda*, though it is mainly concerned with praises of the gods in connection with the sacrifice, contains hymns showing that sorcery was bound up with domestic practices from the earliest times in India. The only reference to the spells of the *Atharva-veda* as a class in the *Yajurvedas* is found in the *Taittirīya Saṃhitā*, where they are alluded to under the name of *angirasaḥ* by the side of *Rik*, *Sāman*, and *Yajus*, which it elsewhere mentions alone. Yet the formulas of the *Yajur-veda* are often pervaded by the spirit of the *Atharva-veda*, and are sometimes Atharvan even in their wording. In fact, the difference between the *Rigveda* and *Yajurveda* on the one hand, and the *Atharva* on the other, as regards sorcery, lies solely in the degree of its applicability and prominence.

The *Atharva-veda* itself only once mentions its own literary type directly (as *atharvāngirasaḥ*) and once indirectly (as *bheshajā* or "auspicious spells"), by the side of the other three Vedas, while the latter in a considerable number of passages are referred to alone. This shows that as yet there was no feeling of antagonism between the adherents of this Veda and those of the older ones.

Turning to the Brāhmaṇas, we find that those of the *Rigveda* do not mention the *Atharva-veda* at all, while the *Taittirīya Brāhmaṇa* (like the *Taittirīya Āraṇyaka*) refers to it twice. In the *Çatapatha Brāhmaṇa* it appears more frequently, occupying a more defined position, though not that of a Veda. This work very often mentions the three old Vedas alone, either explicitly as *Rik, Sāman, Yajus*, or as *trayī vidyā*, "the threefold knowledge." In several passages they are also mentioned along with other literary types, such as *itihāsa* (story), *purāṇa* (ancient legend) *gāthā* (song), *sūtra*, and *upanishad*. In these enumerations the *Atharva-veda* regularly occupies the fourth place, coming immediately after the three Vedas, while the rest follow in varying order. The Upanishads in general treat the *Atharva-veda* in the same way; the Upanishads of the *Atharva* itself, however, sometimes tacitly add its name after the three Vedas, even without mentioning other literary types. With regard to the Çrauta or sacrificial Sūtras, we find no reference to the *Atharva* in those of Kātyāyana (*White Yajurveda*) or Lāṭyāyana (*Sāmaveda*), and only one each in those of Çānkhāyana and Āçvalāyana (*Rigveda*).

In all this sacrificial literature there is no evidence of repugnance to the *Atharva*, or of exclusiveness towards it on the part of followers of the other Vedas. Such an attitude could indeed hardly be expected. For though the sphere of the Vedic sacrificial ritual was different from that of regular magical rites, it is impossible to draw a distinct line of demarcation between sacrifice and sorcery in the Vedic religion, of which witchcraft is, in fact, an essential element. The adherents of the three sacrificial Vedas would thus naturally recognise a work which was a repository of witchcraft. Thus the *Çatapatha Brāhmaṇa*, though characterising *yātu* or sorcery as devilish—doubtless because it may be dangerous to those who practise it—places *yātuvidaḥ* or sorcerers by the side of *bahvṛichas* or men skilled in Rigvedic verses. Just as the *Rigveda* contains very few hymns directly connected with the practice of sorcery, so the *Atharva* originally included only matters incidental and subsidiary to the sacrificial ritual. Thus it contains a series of formulas (vi. 47–48) which have no meaning except in connection with the three daily pressings (*savana*) of soma. We also find in it hymns (*e.g.* vi. 114) which evidently consist of formulas of expiation for faults committed at the sacrifice. We must therefore conclude that the followers of the *Atharva* to some extent knew and practised the sacrificial ceremonial before the conclusion of the present redaction of their hymns. The relation of the *Atharva* to the *çrauta* rites was, however, originally so slight, that it became necessary, in order to establish a direct connection with it, to add the twentieth book, which was compiled from the *Rigveda* for the purposes of the sacrificial ceremonial.

The conspicuous way in which *çrauta* works ignore the *Atharva* is therefore due to its being almost entirely unconnected with the subject-matter of the sacrifice, not to any pronounced disapproval or refusal to recognise its value in its own sphere. With the Gṛihya or Domestic Sūtras, which contain many elements of sorcery practice (*vidhāna*), we should expect the *Atharva* to betray a closer connection. This is, indeed, to some extent the case; for many verses quoted in these Sūtras are identical with or variants of those contained in the *Atharva*, even though the Domestic, like the Sacrificial, Sūtras endeavoured to borrow their verses as far as possible from the particular Veda to which they were attached. Otherwise, however, their references to the *Atharva* betray no greater regard for it than those in the Sacrificial Sūtras do. Such references to the fourth Veda are here, it is true, more frequent and formulaic; but this appears to mean nothing more than that the Gṛihya Sūtras belong to a later date.

In the sphere, too, of law (*dharma*), as dealing with popular usage and custom, the practices of the *Atharva* maintained a certain place; for the indispensable sciences of medicine and astrology were distinctively Atharvan, and the king's domestic chaplain (*purohita*), believed capable of rendering great services in the injury and overthrow of enemies by sorcery, seems usually to have been an Atharvan priest. At the same time it is only natural that we should first meet with censures of the practices of the *Atharva* in the legal literature, because such practices were thought to enable one man to harm another. The verdict of the law treatises on the whole is, that as incantations of various kinds are injurious, the *Atharva-veda* is inferior and its practices impure. This inferiority is directly expressed in the Dharma Sūtra of Āpastamba; and the later legal treatise (*smṛiti*) of Vishṇu classes the reciter of a deadly incantation from the *Atharva* among the seven kinds of assassins. Physicians and astrologers are pronounced impure; practices with roots are prohibited; sorceries and imprecations are punished with severe penances. In certain cases, however, the *Atharva-veda* is stated to be useful. Thus the Lawbook of Manu recommends it as the natural weapon of the Brahman against his enemies.

In the *Mahābhārata* we find the importance and the canonical character of the *Atharva* fully recognised.

The four Vedas are often mentioned, the gods Brahmā and Vishṇu being in several passages described as having created them. The *Atharva* is here often also referred to alone, and spoken of with approbation. Its practices are well known and seldom criticised adversely, magic and sorcery being, as a rule, regarded as good.

Finally, the Purāṇas not only regularly speak of the fourfold Veda, but assign to the *Atharva* the advanced position claimed for it by its own ritual literature. Thus the *Vishṇu Purāṇa* connects the *Atharva* with the fourth priest (the *brahman*) of the sacrificial ritual.

Nevertheless a certain prejudice has prevailed against the *Atharva* from the time of the Dharma Sūtras. This appears from the fact that, even at the present day, according to Burnell, the most influential Brahmans of Southern India still refuse to accept the authority of the fourth Veda, and deny its genuineness. A similar conclusion may be drawn from occasional statements in classical texts, and especially from the efforts of the later Atharvan writings themselves to vindicate the character of their Veda. These ritual texts not only never enumerate the Vedas without including the *Atharva*, but even sometimes place it at the head of the four Vedas. Under a sense of the exclusion of their Veda from the sphere of the sacrificial ritual, they lay claim to the fourth priest (the *brahman*), who in the Vedic religion was not attached to any of the three Vedas, but being required to have a knowledge of all three and of their sacrificial application, acted as superintendent or director of the sacrificial ceremonial. Ingeniously availing themselves of the fact that he was unconnected with any of the three Vedas, they put forward the claim of the fourth Veda as the special sphere of the fourth priest. That priest, moreover, was the most important as possessing a universal knowledge of religious lore (*brahma*), the comprehensive esoteric understanding of the nature of the gods and of the mystery of the sacrifice. Hence the *Gopatha Brāhmaṇa* exalts the *Atharva* as the highest religious lore (*brahma*), and calls it the *Brahmaveda*. The claim to the latter designation was doubtless helped by the word *brahma* often occurring in the *Atharva-veda* itself with the sense of "charm," and by the fact that the Veda contains a larger amount of theosophic matter (*brahmavidyā*) than any other Saṃhitā. The texts belonging to the other Vedas never suggest that the *Atharva* is the sphere of the fourth priest, some Brāhmaṇa passages expressly declaring that any one equipped with the requisite knowledge may be a *brahman*. The ritual texts of the *Atharva* further energetically urged that the *Purohita*, or domestic chaplain, should be a follower of the *Atharva-veda*. They appear to have finally succeeded in their claim to this office, doubtless because kings attached great value to a special knowledge of witchcraft.

The geographical data contained in the *Atharva* are but few, and furnish no certain evidence as to the region in which its hymns were composed. One hymn of its older portion (v. 22) makes mention of the Gandhāris, Mūjavats, Mahāvṛishas, and Balhikas (in the north-west), and the Magadhas and Angas (in the east); but they are referred to in such a way that no safe conclusions can be drawn as to the country in which the composer of the hymn in question lived.

The *Atharva* also contains a few astronomical data, the lunar mansions being enumerated in the nineteenth book. The names here given deviate considerably from those mentioned in the *Taittirīya Saṃhitā*, appearing mostly in a later form. The passage in which this list is found is, however, a late addition.

The language of the *Atharva* is, from a grammatical point of view, decidedly later than that of the *Rigveda*, but earlier than that of the Brāhmaṇas. In vocabulary it is chiefly remarkable for the large number of popular words which it contains, and which from lack of opportunity do not appear elsewhere.

It seems probable that the hymns of the *Atharva*, though some of them must be very old, were not edited till after the Brāhmaṇas of the *Rigveda* were composed.

On examining the contents of the *Atharva-veda* more in detail, we find that the hostile charms it contains are directed largely against various diseases or the demons which are supposed to cause them. There are spells to cure fever (*takman*), leprosy, jaundice, dropsy, scrofula, cough, ophthalmia, baldness, lack of vital power; fractures and wounds; the bite of snakes or injurious insects, and poison in general; mania and other ailments. These charms are accompanied by the employment of appropriate herbs. Hence the *Atharva* is the oldest literary monument of Indian medicine.

The following is a specimen of a charm against cough (vi. 105):—

Just as the soul with soul-desires
Swift to a distance flies away,
So even thou, O cough, fly forth
Along the soul's quick-darting course.

Just as the arrow, sharpened well,
Swift to a distance flies away,
So even thou, O cough, fly forth
Along the broad expanse of earth.

Just as the sun-god's shooting rays
Swift to a distance fly away,
So even thou, O cough, fly forth
Along the ocean's surging flood.

Here is a spell for the cure of leprosy by means of a dark-coloured plant :—

Born in the night art thou, O herb,
Dark-coloured, sable, black of hue :
Rich-tinted, tinge this leprosy,
And stain away its spots of grey! (i. 23, 1).

A large number of imprecations are directed against demons, sorcerers, and enemies. The following two stanzas deal with the latter two classes respectively :—

Bend round and pass us by, O curse,
Even as a burning fire a lake.
Here strike him down that curses us,
As heaven's lightning smites the tree (vi. 37, 2).

As, rising in the east, the sun
The stars' bright lustre takes away,
So both of women and of men,
My foes, the strength I take away (vii. 13, 1).

A considerable group of spells consists of imprecations directed against the oppressors of Brahmans and those who withhold from them their rightful rewards. The following is one of the threats held out against such evil-doers :—

Water with which they bathe the dead,
And that with which they wet his beard,
The gods assigned thee as thy share,
Oppressor of the Brahman priest (v. 19, 14).

Another group of charms is concerned with women, being intended to secure their love with the aid of various potent herbs. Some of them are of a hostile character, being meant to injure rivals. The following two stanzas belong to the former class :—

As round this heaven and earth the sun
Goes day by day, encircling them,
So do I go around thy mind,
That, woman, thou shalt love me well,
And shalt not turn away from me (vi. 8, 3).

'Tis winged with longing, barbed with love,
Its shaft is formed of fixed desire :
With this his arrow levelled well
Shall Kāma pierce thee to the heart (iii. 25, 2).

Among the auspicious charms of the *Atharva* there are many prayers for long life and health, for exemption from disease and death :—

If life in him declines or has departed,
If on the very brink of death he totters,
I snatch him from the lap of Dissolution,
I free him now to live a hundred autumns (iii. 11, 2).

Rise up from hence, O man, and straightway casting
Death's fetters from thy feet, depart not downward;
From life upon this earth be not yet sundered,
Nor from the sight of Agni and the sunlight (viii. 1, 4).

Another class of hymns includes prayers for protection from dangers and calamities, or for prosperity in the house or field, in cattle, trade, and even gambling. Here are two spells meant to secure luck at play :—

As at all times the lightning stroke
Smites irresistibly the tree :
So gamesters with the dice would I
Beat irresistibly to-day (vii. 5, 1).

O dice, give play that profit brings,
Like cows that yield abundant milk:
Attach me to a streak of gain,
As with a string the bow is bound (vii. 5, 9).

A certain number of hymns contain charms to secure harmony, to allay anger, strife, and discord, or to procure ascendency in the assembly. The following one is intended for the latter purpose :—

O assembly, we know thy name,
"Frolic"[1] *truly by name thou art:*
May all who meet and sit in thee
Be in their speech at one with me (vii. 12, 2).

A few hymns consist of formulas for the expiation of sins, such as offering imperfect sacrifices and marrying before an elder brother, or contain charms for removing the defilement caused by ominous birds, and for banishing evil dreams.

If waking, if asleep, I have
Committed sin, to sin inclined,
May what has been and what shall be
Loose me as from a wooden post (vi. 115, 2).

A short hymn (vi. 120), praying for the remission of sins, concludes with this stanza :—

In heaven, where our righteous friends are blessèd,
Having cast off diseases from their bodies,
From lameness free and not deformed in members,
There may we see our parents and our children.

Another group of hymns has the person of the king as its centre. They contain charms to be used at a royal election or consecration, for the restoration of an

[1] The word "frolic" alludes to the assembly-house (*sabhā*) being a place of social entertainment, especially of gambling.

exiled king, for the attainment of lustre and glory, and in particular for victory in battle. The following is a specimen of spells intended to strike terror into the enemy:—

Arise and arm, ye spectral forms,
Followed by meteoric flames;
Ye serpents, spirits of the deep,
Demons of night, pursue the foe! (xi. 10, 1).

Here is a stanza from a hymn (v. 21, 6) to the battle-drum meant to serve the same purpose:—

As birds start back affrighted at the eagle's cry,
As day and night they tremble at the lion's roar:
So thou, O drum, shout out against our enemies,
Scare them away in terror and confound their minds.

Among the cosmogonic and theosophic hymns the finest is a long one of sixty-three stanzas addressed to the earth (xii. 1). I translate a few lines to give some idea of its style and contents:—

The earth, on whom, with clamour loud,
Men that are mortal sing and dance,
On whom they fight in battle fierce:
This earth shall drive away from us our foemen,
And she shall make us free from all our rivals.

In secret places holding treasure manifold,
The earth shall riches give, and gems and gold to me:
Granting wealth lavishly, the kindly goddess
Shall goods abundantly bestow upon us.

The four hymns of Book XIII. are devoted to the praise of Rohita, the "Red" Sun, as a cosmogonic power. In another (xi. 5) the sun is glorified as a primeval principle under the guise of a Brahman disciple (*brahmachārin*). In others Prāṇa or Breath (xi. 4), Kāma or Love (ix. 2), and Kāla or Time (xix. 53–54), are personified as primordial powers. There is one hymn (xi. 7) in which even Ucchishṭa (the remnant of the sacrifice) is deified as the Supreme Being; except for its metrical form it belongs to the Brāhmaṇa type of literature.

In concluding this survey of the *Atharva-veda*, I would draw attention to a hymn to Varuṇa (iv. 16), which, though its last two stanzas are ordinary Atharvan spells for binding enemies with the fetters of that deity, in its remaining verses exalts divine omniscience in a strain unequalled in any other Vedic poem. The following three stanzas are perhaps the best:—

This earth is all King Varuṇa's dominion,
And that broad sky whose boundaries are distant.
The loins of Varuṇa are these two oceans,
Yet in this drop of water he is hidden.

He that should flee afar beyond the heaven
Would not escape King Varuṇa's attention:
His spies come hither, from the sky descending,
With all their thousand eyes the earth surveying.

King Varuṇa discerns all that's existent
Between the earth and sky, and all beyond them;
The winkings of men's eyes by him are counted;
As gamesters dice, so he lays down his statutes.

CHAPTER VIII

THE BRĀHMAṆAS

(*Circa* 800–500 B.C.)

THE period in which the poetry of the Vedic Saṃhitās arose was followed by one which produced a totally different literary type—the theological treatises called Brāhmaṇas. It is characteristic of the form of these works that they are composed in prose, and of their matter that they deal with the sacrificial ceremonial. Their main object being to explain the sacred significance of the ritual to those who are already familiar with the sacrifice, the descriptions they give of it are not exhaustive, much being stated only in outline or omitted altogether. They are ritual text-books, which, however, in no way aim at furnishing a complete survey of the sacrificial ceremonial to those who do not know it already. Their contents may be classified under the three heads of practical sacrificial directions (*vidhi*), explanations (*arthavāda*), exegetical, mythological, or polemical, and theological or philosophical speculations on the nature of things (*upanishad*). Even those which have been preserved form quite an extensive literature by themselves; yet many others must have been lost, as appears from the numerous names of and quotations from Brāhmaṇas unknown to us occurring in those which are extant. They reflect the spirit of an age in which all intellectual activity is concentrated on the sacrifice, describing its ceremonies, discussing its value, speculating on its origin and significance. It is only reasonable to suppose that an epoch like this, which produced no other literary monuments, lasted for a considerable time. For though the Brāhmaṇas are on the whole uniform in character, differences of age are traceable in them. Next to the prose portions of the *Yajurvedas*, the *Panchaviṃça* and the *Taittirīya* are proved by their syntax and vocabulary to be the most archaic of the regular Brāhmaṇas. This conclusion is confirmed by the fact that the latter is, and the former is known to have been, accented. A more recent group is formed by the *Jaiminīya*, the *Kaushītaki*, and the *Aitareya Brāhmaṇas*. The first of these is probably the oldest, while the third seems, on linguistic grounds at least, to be the latest of the three. The *Çatapatha Brāhmaṇa*, again, is posterior to these. For it shows a distinct advance in matter; its use of the narrative tenses is later than that of the *Aitareya;* and its style is decidedly developed in comparison with all the above-mentioned Brāhmaṇas. It is, indeed, accented, but in a way which differs entirely from the regular Vedic method. Latest of all are the *Gopatha Brāhmaṇa* of the *Atharva* and the short Brāhmaṇas of the *Sāmaveda*.

In language the Brāhmaṇas are considerably more limited in the use of forms than the *Rigveda*. The subjunctive is, however, still employed, as well as a good many of the old infinitives. Their syntax, indeed, represents the oldest Indian stage even better than the *Rigveda*, chiefly of course owing to the restrictions imposed by metre on the style of the latter. The Brāhmaṇas contain some metrical pieces (*gāthās*), which differ from the prose in which they are imbedded by certain peculiarities of their own and by a more archaic character. Allied to these is a remarkable poem of this period, the *Suparṇādhyāya*, an attempt, after the age of living Vedic poetry had come to an end, to compose in the style of the Vedic hymns. It contains many Vedic forms, and is accented, but it betrays its true character not only by its many modern forms, but by numerous monstrosities due to unsuccessful imitation of the Vedic language.

A further development are the Āraṇyakas or "Forest Treatises," the later age of which is indicated both by the position they occupy at the end of the Brāhmaṇas and by their theosophical character. These works are generally represented as meant for the use of pious men who have retired to the forest and no longer perform sacrifices. According to the view of Professor Oldenberg, they are, however, rather treatises which, owing to the superior mystic sanctity of their contents, were intended to be communicated to the pupil by his teacher in the solitude of the forest instead of in the village.

In tone and content the Āraṇyakas form a transition to the Upanishads, which are either imbedded in them, or more usually form their concluding portion. The word *upa-ni-shad* (literally "sitting down beside") having first doubtless meant "confidential session," came to signify "secret or esoteric doctrine," because these works were taught to select pupils (probably towards the end of their apprenticeship) in lectures from which the wider circle was excluded. Being entirely devoted to theological and philosophical speculations on the nature of things, the Upanishads mark the last stage of development in the Brāhmaṇa literature. As they generally come at the end of the Brāhmaṇas, they are also called *Vedānta* ("end of the Veda"), a term later interpreted to mean "final goal of the Veda." "Revelation" (*çruti*) was regarded as including them, while the Sūtras belonged to the sphere of tradition (*smṛiti*). The subject-matter of all the old Upanishads is essentially the same—the doctrine of the nature of the Ātman or Brahma (the supreme soul). This fundamental theme was expounded in various ways by the different Vedic schools, of which the Upanishads were originally the dogmatic text-books, just as the Brāhmaṇas were their ritual text-books.

The Āraṇyakas and Upanishads represent a phase of language which on the whole closely approaches to classical Sanskrit, the oldest Upanishads occupying a position linguistically midway between the Brāhmaṇas and the Sūtras.

Of the two Brāhmaṇas attached to the *Rigveda*, the more important is the *Aitareya*. The extant text consists of forty chapters (*adhyāya*) divided into eight books called *panchikās* or "pentads," because containing five chapters each. That its last ten chapters were a later addition appears likely both from internal evidence and from the fact that the closely related *Çānkhāyana Brāhmaṇa* contains nothing corresponding to their subject-matter, which is dealt with in the *Çānkhāyana Sūtra*. The last three books would further appear to have been composed at a later date than the first five, since the perfect in the former is used as a narrative tense, while in the latter it still has its original present force, as in the oldest Brāhmaṇas. The essential part of this Brāhmaṇa deals with the soma sacrifice. It treats first (1–16) of the soma rite called *Agnishṭoma*, which lasts one day, then (17–18) of that called *Gavāmayana*, which lasts 360 days, and thirdly (19–24) of the *Dvādaçāha* or "twelve days' rite." The next part (25–32), which is concerned with the *Agnihotra* or "fire sacrifice" and other matters, has the character of a supplement. The last portion (33–40), dealing with the ceremonies of the inauguration of the king and with the position of his domestic priest, bears similar signs of lateness.

The other Brāhmaṇa of the *Rigveda*, which goes by the name of *Kaushītaki* as well as *Çānkhāyana*, consists of thirty chapters. Its subject-matter is, on the whole, the same as that of the original part of the *Aitareya* (i.–v.), but is wider. For in its opening chapters it goes through the setting up of the sacred fire (*agni-ādhāna*), the daily morning and evening sacrifice (*agnihotra*), the new and full moon ritual, and the four-monthly sacrifices. The Soma sacrifice, however, occupies the chief position even here. The more definite and methodical treatment of the ritual in the *Kaushītaki* would seem to indicate that this Brāhmaṇa was composed at a later date than the first five books of the *Aitareya.* Such a conclusion is, however, not altogether borne out by a comparison of the linguistic data of these two works. Professor Weber argues from the occurrence in one passage of Īçāna and Mahādeva as designations of the god who was later exclusively called Çiva, that the *Kaushītaki Brāhmaṇa* was composed at about the same time as the latest books of the *White Yajurveda* and those parts of the *Atharva-veda* and of the *Çatapatha Brāhmaṇa* in which these appellations of the same god are found.

These Brāhmaṇas contain very few geographical data. From the way, however, in which the *Aitareya* mentions the Indian tribes, it may be safely inferred that this work had its origin in the country of the

Kuru-Panchālas, in which, as we have seen, the Vedic ritual must have been developed, and the hymns of the *Rigveda* were probably collected in the existing Saṃhitā. From the *Kaushītaki* we learn that the study of language was specially cultivated in the north of India, and that students who returned from there were regarded as authorities on linguistic questions.

The chief human interest of these Brāhmaṇas lies in the numerous myths and legends which they contain. The longest and most remarkable of those found in the *Aitareya* is the story of Çunaḥçepa (Dog's-Tail), which forms the third chapter of Book VII. The childless King Hariçchandra vowed, if he should have a son, to sacrifice him to Varuṇa. But when his son Rohita was born, he kept putting off the fulfilment of his promise. At length, when the boy was grown up, his father, pressed by Varuṇa, prepared to perform the sacrifice. Rohita, however, escaped to the forest, where he wandered for six years, while his father was afflicted with dropsy by Varuṇa. At last he fell in with a starving Brahman, who consented to sell to him for a hundred cows his son Çunaḥçepa as a substitute. Varuṇa agreed, saying, "A Brahman is worth more than a Kshatriya." Çunaḥçepa was accordingly bound to the stake, and the sacrifice was about to proceed, when the victim prayed to various gods in succession. As he repeated one verse after the other, the fetters of Varuṇa began to fall off and the dropsical swelling of the king to diminish, till finally Çunaḥçepa was released and Hariçchandra was restored to health again.

The style of the prose in which the *Aitareya* is composed is crude, clumsy, abrupt, and elliptical. The following quotation from the stanzas interspersed in the story of Çunaḥçepa may serve as a specimen of the *gāthās* found in the Brāhmaṇas. These verses are addressed by a sage named Nārada to King Hariçchandra on the importance of having a son :—

In him a father pays a debt
And reaches immortality,
When he beholds the countenance
Of a son born to him alive.

Than all the joy which living things
In waters feel, in earth and fire,
The happiness that in his son
A father feels is greater far.

At all times fathers by a son
Much darkness, too, have passed beyond:
In him the father's self is born,
He wafts him to the other shore.

Food is man's life and clothes afford protection,
Gold gives him beauty, marriages bring cattle;
His wife's a friend, his daughter causes pity:
A son is like a light in highest heaven.

To the *Aitareya Brāhmaṇa* belongs the *Aitareya Āraṇyaka.* It consists of eighteen chapters, distributed unequally among five books. The last two books are composed in the Sūtra style, and are really to be regarded as belonging to the Sūtra literature. Four parts can be clearly distinguished in the first three books. Book I. deals with various liturgies of the Soma sacrifice from a purely ritual point of view. The first three chapters of Book II., on the other hand, are theosophical in character, containing speculations about the world-soul under the names of Prāṇa and Purusha. It is allied in matter to the Upanishads, some of its more valuable thoughts recurring, occasionally even word for word, in the

Kaushītaki Upanishad. The third part consists of the remaining four sections of Book II., which form the regular *Aitareya Upanishad.* Finally, Book III. deals with the mystic and allegorical meaning of the three principal modes in which the Veda is recited in the *Saṃhitā*, *Pada* and *Krama Pāṭhas*, and of the various letters of the alphabet.

To the *Kaushītaki Brāhmaṇa* is attached the *Kaushītaki Āraṇyaka.* It consists of fifteen chapters. The first two of these correspond to Books I. and V. of the *Aitareya Āraṇyaka*, the seventh and eighth to Book III., while the intervening four chapters (3–6) form the *Kaushītaki Upanishad.* The latter is a long and very interesting Upanishad. It seems not improbably to have been added as an independent treatise to the completed Āraṇyaka, as it is not always found in the same part of the latter work in the manuscripts.

Brāhmaṇas belonging to two independent schools of the *Sāmaveda* have been preserved, those of the Tāṇḍins and of the Talavakāras or Jaiminīyas. Though several other works here claim the title of ritual text-books, only three are in reality Brāhmaṇas. The Brāhmaṇa of the Talavakāras, which for the most part is still unpublished, seems to consist of five books. The first three (unpublished) are mainly concerned with various parts of the sacrificial ceremonial. The fourth book, called the *Upanishad Brāhmaṇa* (probably "the Brāhmaṇa of mystic meanings"), besides all kinds of allegories of the Āraṇyaka order, two lists of teachers, a section about the origin of the vital airs (*prāṇa*) and about the *sāvitrī* stanza, contains the brief but important *Kena Upanishad.* Book V., entitled *Ārsheya-Brāhmaṇa*, is a short enumeration of the composers of the *Sāmaveda.*

To the school of the Tāṇḍins belongs the *Panchaviṃça* ("twenty-five fold"), also called *Tāṇḍya* or *Prauḍha, Brāhmaṇa*, which, as the first name implies, consists of twenty-five books. It is concerned with the Soma sacrifices in general, ranging from the minor offerings to those which lasted a hundred days, or even several years. Besides many legends, it contains a minute description of sacrifices performed on the Sarasvatī and Dṛishadvatī. Though Kurukshetra is known to it, other geographical data which it contains point to the home of this Brāhmaṇa having lain farther east. Noteworthy among its contents are the so-called *Vrātya-Stomas*, which are sacrifices meant to enable Aryan but non-Brahmanical Indians to enter the Brahmanical order. A point of interest in this Brāhmaṇa is the bitter hostility which it displays towards the school of the Kaushītakins. The *Shaḍviṃça Brāhmaṇa*, though nominally an independent work, is in reality a supplement to the *Panchaviṃça*, of which, as its name implies, it forms the twenty-sixth book. The last of its six chapters is called the *Adbhuta Brāhmaṇa*, which is intended to obviate the evil effects of various extraordinary events or portents. Among such phenomena are mentioned images of the gods when they laugh, cry, sing, dance, perspire, crack, and so forth.

The other Brāhmaṇa of this school, the *Chhāndogya Brāhmaṇa*, is only to a slight extent a ritual text-book. It does not deal with the Soma sacrifice at all, but only with ceremonies relating to birth and marriage or prayers addressed to divine beings. These are the contents of only the first two "lessons" of this Brāhmaṇa of the Sāma theologians. The remaining eight lessons constitute the *Chhāndogya Upanishad*.

There are four other short works which, though bearing the name, are not really Brāhmaṇas. These are the *Sāmavidhāna Brāhmaṇa*, a treatise on the employment of chants for all kinds of superstitious purposes; the *Devatādhyāya Brāhmaṇa*, containing some statements about the deities of the various chants of the *Sāmaveda;* the *Vaṃça Brāhmaṇa*, which furnishes a genealogy of the teachers of the *Sāmaveda;* and, finally, the *Saṃhitopanishad*, which, like the third book of the *Aitareya Āraṇyaka*, treats of the way in which the Veda should be recited.

The Brāhmaṇas of the *Sāmaveda* are distinguished by the exaggerated and fantastic character of their mystical speculations. A prominent feature in them is the constant identification of various kinds of *Sāmans* or chants with all kinds of terrestrial and celestial objects. At the same time they contain much matter that is interesting from a historical point of view.

In the *Black Yajurveda* the prose portions of the various Saṃhitās form the only Brāhmaṇas in the Kaṭha and the Maitrāyaṇīya schools. In the Taittirīya school they form the oldest and most important Brāhmaṇa. Here we have also the *Taittirīya Brāhmaṇa* as an independent work in three books. This, however, hardly differs in character from the *Taittirīya Saṃhitā*, being rather a continuation. It forms a supplement concerned with a few sacrifices omitted in the Saṃhitā, or handles, with greater fulness of detail, matters already dealt with. There is also a *Taittirīya Āraṇyaka*, which in its turn forms a supplement to the Brāhmaṇa. The last four of its ten sections constitute the two Upanishads of this school, vii.-ix. forming the *Taittirīya Upanishad*, and x. the *Mahā-Nārāyaṇa Upanishad*, also called the *Yājnikī Upanishad*. Excepting these four sections, the title of

Brāhmaṇa or Āraṇyaka does not indicate a difference of content as compared with the Saṃhitā, but is due to late and artificial imitation of the other Vedas.

The last three sections of Book III. of the Brāhmaṇa, as well as the first two books of the Āraṇyaka, originally belonged to the school of the Kaṭhas, though they have not been preserved as part of the tradition of that school. The different origin of these parts is indicated by the absence of the change of *y* and *v* to *iy* and *uv* respectively, which otherwise prevails in the *Taittirīya Brāhmaṇa* and *Āraṇyaka.* In one of these Kāṭhaka sections (*Taitt. Br.* iii. 11), by way of illustrating the significance of the particular fire called *nāchiketa*, the story is told of a boy, Nachiketas, who, on visiting the House of Death, was granted the fulfilment of three wishes by the god of the dead. On this story is based the *Kāṭhaka Upanishad.*

Though the *Maitrāyaṇī Saṃhitā* has no independent Brāhmaṇa, its fourth book, as consisting of explanations and supplements to the first three, is a kind of special Brāhmaṇa. Connected with this Saṃhitā, and in the manuscripts sometimes forming its second or its fifth book, is the *Maitrāyaṇa* (also called *Maitrāyaṇīya* and *Maitri*) *Upanishad.*

The ritual explanation of the *White Yajurveda* is to be found in extraordinary fulness in the *Çatapatha Brāhmaṇa*, the "Brāhmaṇa of the Hundred Paths," so called because it consists of one hundred lectures (*adhyāya*). This work is, next to the *Rigveda*, the most important production in the whole range of Vedic literature. Its text has come down in two recensions, those of the Mādhyaṃdina school, edited by Professor Weber, and of the Kāṇva school, which is in process of being edited by Professor Eggeling. The Mādhyaṃdina recension consists of fourteen books, while the Kāṇva has seventeen. The first nine of the former, corresponding to the original eighteen books of the *Vājasaneyi Saṃhitā*, doubtless form the oldest part. The fact that Book XII. is called *madhyama*, or "middle one," shows that the last five books (or possibly only X.–XIII.) were at one time regarded as a separate part of the Brāhmaṇa. Book X. treats of the mystery of the fire-altar (*agnirahasya*), XI. is a sort of recapitulation of the preceding ritual, while XII. and XIII. deal with various supplementary matters. The last book forms the Āraṇyaka, the six concluding chapters of which are the *Bṛihadāraṇyaka Upanishad.*

Books VI.–X. of the *Çatapatha Brāhmaṇa* occupy a peculiar position. Treating of the construction of the fire-altar, they recognise the teaching of Çāṇḍilya as their highest authority, Yājnavalkya not even being mentioned; while the peoples who are named, the Gāndhāras, Salvas, Kekayas, belong to the nòrth-west. In the other books Yājnavalkya is the highest authority, while hardly any but Eastern peoples, or those of the middle of Hindustan, the Kuru-Panchālas, Kosalas, Videhas, Sṛinjayas, are named. That the original authorship of the five Çāṇḍilya books was different from that of the others is indicated by a number of linguistic differences, which the hand of a later editor failed to remove. Thus the use of the perfect as a narrative tense is unknown to the Çāṇḍilya books (as well as to XIII.).

The geographical data of the *Çatapatha Brāhmaṇa* point to the land of the Kuru-Panchālas being still the centre of Brahmanical culture. Janamejaya is here celebrated as a king of the Kurus, and the most renowned Brahmanical teacher of the age, Āruṇi, is expressly stated to have been a Panchāla. Nevertheless, it is clear that the Brahmanical system had by this time spread to the countries to the east of Madhyadeça, to Kosala, with its capital, Ayodhyā (Oudh), and Videha (Tirhut or Northern Behar), with its capital, Mithilā. The court of King Janaka of Videha was thronged with Brahmans from the Kuru-Panchāla country. The tournaments of argument which were here held form a prominent feature in the later books of the *Çatapatha Brāhmaṇa.* The hero of these is Yājnavalkya, who, himself a pupil of Āruṇi, is regarded as the chief spiritual authority in the Brāhmaṇa (excepting Books VI.–X.). Certain passages of the Brāhmaṇa render it highly probable that Yājnavalkya was a native of Videha. The fact that its leading authority, who thus appears to have belonged to this Eastern country, is represented as vanquishing the most distinguished teachers of the West in argument, points to the redaction of the *White Yajurveda* having taken place in this eastern region.

The *Çatapatha Brāhmaṇa* contains reminiscences of the days when the country of Videha was not as yet Brahmanised. Thus Book I. relates a legend in which three stages in the eastward migration of the Aryans can be clearly distinguished. Māṭhava, the king of Videgha (the older form of Videha), whose family priest was Gotama Rāhūgaṇa, was at one time on the Sarasvatī. Agni Vaiçvānara (here typical of Brahmanical culture) thence went burning along this earth towards the east, followed by Māṭhava and his priest, till he came to the river Sadānīra (probably the modern Gandak, a tributary running into the Ganges near Patna), which flows from the northern mountain, and which he did not burn over. This river Brahmans did not cross in former times, thinking "it has not been burnt over by Agni Vaiçvānara." At that time the land to the eastward was very uncultivated and marshy, but now many Brahmans are there, and it is highly cultivated, for the Brahmans have caused Agni to taste it through sacrifices. Māṭhava the Videgha then said to Agni, "Where am I to abide?" "To the east of this river be thy abode," he replied. Even now, the writer adds, this river forms the boundary between the Kosalas (Oudh) and the Videhas (Tirhut).

The Vājasaneyi school of the *White Yajurveda* evidently felt a sense of the superiority of their sacrificial lore, which grew up in these eastern countries. Blame is frequently expressed in the *Çatapatha Brāhmaṇa* of the Adhvaryu priests of the Charaka school. The latter is meant as a comprehensive term embracing the three older schools of the *Black Yajurveda*, the Kaṭhas, the Kapishṭhalas, and the Maitrāyaṇīyas.

As Buddhism first obtained a firm footing in Kosala and Videha, it is interesting to inquire in what relation the *Çatapatha Brāhmaṇa* stands to the beginnings of that doctrine. In this connection it is to be noted that the words *Arhat*, *Çramana*, and *Pratibuddha* occur here for the first time, but as yet without the technical sense which they have in Buddhistic literature. Again, in the lists of teachers given in the Brāhmaṇa mention is made with special frequency of the Gautamas, a family name used by the Çākyas of Kapilavastu, among whom Buddha was born. Certain allusions are also suggestive of the beginnings of the Sānkhya doctrine; for mention is several times made of a teacher called Āsuri, and according to tradition Āsuri is the name of a leading authority for the Sānkhya system. If we inquire as to how far the legends of our Brāhmaṇa contain the germs of the later epic tales, we find that there is indeed some slight connection.

Janamejaya, the celebrated king of the Kurus in the *Mahābhārata*, is mentioned here for the first time. The Pāṇḍus, however, who proved victorious in the epic war, are not to be met with in this any more than in the other Brāhmaṇas; and Arjuna, the name of their chief, is still an appellation of Indra. But as the epic Arjuna is a son of Indra, his origin is doubtless to be traced to this epithet of Indra. Janaka, the famous king of Videha, is in all probability identical with the father of Sītā, the heroine of the *Rāmāyaṇa*.

Of two legends which furnished the classical poet Kālidāsa with the plots of two of his most famous dramas, one is told in detail, and the other is at least alluded to. The story of the love and separation of Purūravas and Urvaçī, already dimly shadowed forth in a hymn of the *Rigveda*, is here related with much more fulness; while Bharata, son of Duḥshanta and of the nymph Çakuntalā, also appears on the scene in this Brāhmaṇa.

A most interesting legend which reappears in the *Mahābhārata*, that of the Deluge, is here told for the first time in Indian literature, though it seems to be alluded to in the *Atharva-veda*, while it is known even to the Avesta. This myth is generally regarded as derived from a Semitic source. It tells how Manu once came into possession of a small fish, which asked him to rear it, and promised to save him from the coming flood. Having built a ship in accordance with the fish's advice, he entered it when the deluge arose, and was finally guided to the Northern Mountain by the fish, to whose horn he had tied his ship. Manu subsequently became the progenitor of mankind through his daughter.

The *Çatapatha Brāhmaṇa* is thus a mine of important data and noteworthy narratives. Internal evidence shows it to belong to a late period of the Brāhmaṇa age. Its style, as compared with the earlier works of the same class, displays some progress towards facility and clearness. Its treatment of the sacrificial ceremonial, which is essentially the same in the Brāhmaṇa portions of the *Black Yajurveda*, is throughout more lucid and systematic. On the theosophic side, too, we find the idea of the unity in the universe more fully developed than in any other Brāhmaṇa work, while its Upanishad is the finest product of Vedic philosophy.

To the *Atharva-veda* is attached the *Gopatha Brāhmaṇa*, though it has no particular connection with that Saṃhitā. This Brāhmaṇa consists of two books, the first containing five chapters, the second six. Both parts are very late, for they were composed after the *Vaitāna Sūtra* and practically without any Atharvan tradition. The matter of the former half, while not corresponding or following the order of the sacrifice in any ritual text, is to a considerable extent original, the rest being borrowed from Books XI. and XII. of the *Çatapatha Brāhmaṇa*, besides a few passages from the *Aitareya*. The main motive of this portion is the glorification of the *Atharva-veda* and of the fourth or *brahman* priest. The mention of the god Çiva points to its belonging to the post-Vedic rather than to the Brāhmaṇa period. Its presupposing the *Atharva-veda* in twenty books, and containing grammatical matters of a very advanced type, are other signs of lateness. The latter half bears more the stamp of a regular Brāhmaṇa, being a fairly connected account of the ritual in the sacrificial order of the *Vaitāna Çrauta Sūtra;* but it is for the most part a compilation. The ordinary historical relation of Brāhmaṇā and Sūtra is here reversed, the second book of the *Gopatha Brāhmaṇa* being based on the *Vaitāna Sūtra,* which stands to it practically in the relation of a Saṃhitā. About two-thirds of its matter have already been shown to be taken from older texts. The *Aitareya* and *Kaushītaki Brāhmaṇas* have been chiefly exploited, and to a less extent the *Maitrāyaṇī* and *Taittirīya Saṃhitās.* A few passages are derived from the *Çatapatha,* and even the *Panchaviṃça Brāhmaṇa.*

Though the Upanishads generally form a part of the Brāhmaṇas, being a continuation of their speculative side (*jnāna-kāṇḍa*), they really represent a new religion, which is in virtual opposition to the ritual or practical side (*karma-kāṇḍa*). Their aim is no longer the obtainment of earthly happiness and afterwards bliss in the abode of Yama by sacrificing correctly to the gods, but release from mundane existence by the absorption of the individual soul in the world-soul through correct knowledge. Here, therefore, the sacrificial ceremonial has become useless and speculative knowledge all-important.

The essential theme of the Upanishads is the nature of the world-soul. Their conception of it represents the final stage in the development from the world-man, Purusha, of the *Rigveda* to the world-soul, Ātman ; from the personal creator, Prajāpati, to the impersonal source of all being, Brahma. *Ātman* in the *Rigveda* means no more than "breath" ; wind, for instance, being spoken of as the *ātman* of Varuṇa. In the Brāhmaṇas it came to mean "soul" or "self." In one of their speculations the *prāṇas* or "vital airs," which are supposed to be based on the *ātman,* are identified with the gods, and so an *ātman* comes to be attributed to the universe.

In one of the later books of the *Çatapatha Brāhmaṇa* (X. vi. 3) this *ātman*, which has already arrived at a high degree of abstraction, is said to "pervade this universe." *Brahma* (neuter) in the *Rigveda* signified nothing more than "prayer" or "devotion." But even in the oldest Brāhmaṇas it has come to have the sense of "universal holiness," as manifested in prayer, priest, and sacrifice. In the Upanishads it is the holy principle which animates nature. Having a long subsequent history, this word is a very epitome of the evolution of religious thought in India. These two conceptions, Ātman and Brahma, are commonly treated as synonymous in the Upanishads. But, strictly speaking, Brahma, the older term, represents the cosmical principle which pervades the universe, Ātman the psychical principle manifested in man; and the latter, as the known, is used to explain the former as the unknown. The Ātman under the name of the Eternal (*aksharam*) is thus described in the *Bṛihadāraṇyaka Upanishad* (III. viii. 8, 11):—

"*It is not large, and not minute; not short, not long; without blood, without fat; without shadow, without darkness; without wind, without ether; not adhesive, not tangible; without smell, without taste; without eyes, ears, voice, or mind; without heat, breath, or mouth; without personal or family name; unaging, undying, without fear, immortal, dustless, not uncovered or covered; with nothing before, nothing behind, nothing within. It consumes no one and is consumed by no one. It is the unseen seer, the unheard hearer, the unthought thinker, the unknown knower. There is no other seer, no other hearer, no other thinker, no other knower. That is the Eternal in which space* (ākāça) *is woven and which is interwoven with it.*"

Here, for the first time in the history of human thought, we find the Absolute grasped and proclaimed.

A poetical account of the nature of the Ātman is given by the *Kāṭhaka Upanishad* in the following stanzas:—

That whence the sun's orb rises up,
And that in which it sinks again:
In it the gods are all contained,
Beyond it none can ever pass (iv. 9).

Its form can never be to sight apparent,
Not any one may with his eye behold it:
By heart and mind and soul alone they grasp it,
And those who know it thus become immortal (vi. 9).

Since not by speech and not by thought,
Not by the eye can it be reached:
How else may it be understood
But only when one says "it is"? (vi. 12).

The place of the more personal Prajāpati is taken in the Upanishads by the Ātman as a creative power. Thus the *Bṛihadāraṇyaka* (I. iv.) relates that in the beginning the Ātman or the Brahma was this universe. It was afraid in its loneliness and felt no pleasure. Desiring a second being, it became man and woman, whence the human race was produced. It then proceeded to produce male and female animals in a similar way; finally creating water, fire, the gods, and so forth. The author then proceeds in a more exalted strain:—

"*It* (*the Ātman*) *is here all-pervading down to the tips of the nails. One does not see it any more than a razor hidden in its case or fire in its receptacle. For it does not appear as a whole. When it breathes, it is called breath; when it speaks, voice; when it hears, ear; when it thinks, mind. These are merely the names of its activities. He who worships the one or the other of these, has not (correct) knowledge. . . . One should worship it as the Self. For in it all these (breath, etc.) become one.*"

In one of the later Upanishads, the *Çvetāçvatara* (iv. 10), the notion, so prominent in the later Vedānta system, that the material world is an illusion (*māyā*), is first met with. The world is here explained as an illusion produced by Brahma as a conjuror (*māyin*). This notion is, however, inherent even in the oldest Upanishads. It is virtually identical with the teaching of Plato that the things of experience are only the shadow of the real things, and with the teaching of Kant, that they are only phenomena of the thing in itself.

The great fundamental doctrine of the Upanishads is the identity of the individual *ātman* with the world *Ātman*. It is most forcibly expressed in a frequently repeated sentence of the *Chhāndogya Upanishad* (vi. 8–16): "*This whole world consists of it: that is the Real, that is the Soul, that art thou, O Çvetaketu.*" In that famous formula, "That art thou" (*tat tvam asi*), all the teachings of the Upanishads are summed up. The *Bṛihadāraṇyaka* (I. iv. 6) expresses the same doctrine thus: "*Whoever knows this, 'I am brahma'* (aham brahma asmi), *becomes the All. Even the gods are not able to prevent him from becoming it. For he becomes their Self* (ātman)."

This identity was already recognised in the *Çatapatha Brāhmaṇa* (X. vi. 3): "*Even as the smallest granule of millet, so is this golden Purusha in the heart. . . . That self of the spirit is my self: on passing from hence I shall obtain that Self.*"

We find everywhere in these treatises a restless striving to grasp the true nature of the pantheistic Self, now through one metaphor, now through another. Thus

(*Bṛih. Up.* II. iv.) the wise Yājnavalkya, about to renounce the world and retire to the forest, replies to the question of his wife, Maitreyī, with the words: "*As a lump of salt thrown into the water would dissolve and could not be taken out again, while the water, wherever tasted, would be salt, so is this great being endless, unlimited, simply compacted of cognition. Arising out of these elements, it disappears again in them. After death there is no consciousness;*" for, as he further explains, when the duality on which consciousness is based disappears, consciousness must necessarily cease.

In another passage of the same Upanishad (II. i. 20) we read: "*Just as the spider goes out of itself by means of its thread, as tiny sparks leap out of the fire, so from the Ātman issue all vital airs, all worlds, all gods, all beings.*"

Here, again, is a stanza from the *Muṇḍaka* (III. ii. 8):—

As rivers flow and disappear at last
In ocean's waters, name and form renouncing,
So, too, the sage, released from name and form,
Is merged in the divine and highest spirit.

In a passage of the *Bṛihadāraṇyaka* (III. vii.) Yājnavalkya describes the Ātman as the "inner guide" (*antaryāmin*): "*Who is in all beings, different from all beings, who guides all beings within, that is thy Self, the inward guide, immortal.*"

The same Upanishad contains an interesting conversation, in which King Ajātaçatru of Kāçi (Benares) instructs the Brahman, Bālāki Gārgya, that Brahma is not the spirit (*purusha*) which is in sun, moon, wind, and other natural phenomena, or even in the (waking) soul (*ātman*), but is either the dreaming soul, which is creative, assuming any form at pleasure, or, in the highest stage, the soul in dreamless sleep, for here all phenomena have disappeared. This is the first and the last condition of Brahma, in which no world exists, all material existence being only the phantasms of the dreaming world-soul.

Of somewhat similar purport is a passage of the *Chhāndogya* (viii. 7–12), where Prajāpati is represented as teaching the nature of the Ātman in three stages. The soul in the body as reflected in a mirror or water is first identified with Brahma, then the dreaming soul, and, lastly, the soul in dreamless sleep.

How generally accepted the pantheistic theory must have become by the time the disputations at the court of King Janaka took place, is indicated by the form in which questions are put. Thus two different sages in the *Bṛihadāraṇyaka* (iii. 4, 5) successively ask Yājnavalkya in the same words: "*Explain to us the Brahma which is manifest and not hidden, the Ātman that dwells in everything.*"

With the doctrine that true knowledge led to supreme bliss by the absorption of the individual soul in Brahma went hand in hand the theory of transmigration (*saṃsāra*). That theory is developed in the oldest Upanishads; it must have been firmly established by the time Buddhism arose, for Buddha accepted it without question. Its earliest form is found in the *Çatapatha Brāhmaṇa*, where the notion of being born again after death and dying repeatedly is coupled with that of retribution. Thus it is here said that those who have correct knowledge and perform a certain sacrifice are born again after death for immortality, while those who have not such knowledge and do not perform this sacrifice are reborn again and again, becoming the prey of Death. The notion here expressed does not go beyond repeated births and deaths in the next world. It is transformed to the doctrine of transmigration in the Upanishads by supposing rebirth to take place in this world. In the *Bṛihadāraṇyaka* we further meet with the beginnings of the doctrine of *karma*, or "action," which regulates the new birth, and makes it depend on a man's own deeds. When the body returns to the elements, nothing of the individuality is here said to remain but the *karma*, according to which a man becomes good or bad. This is, perhaps, the germ of the Buddhistic doctrine, which, though denying the existence of soul altogether, allows *karma* to continue after death and to determine the next birth.

The most important and detailed account of the theory of transmigration which we possess from Vedic times is supplied by the *Chhāndogya Upanishad.* The forest ascetic possessed of knowledge and faith, it is here said, after death enters the *devayāna*, the "path of the gods," which leads to absorption in Brahma, while the householder who has performed sacrifice and good works goes by the *pitṛiyāṇa* or "path of the Fathers" to the moon, where he remains till the consequences of his actions are exhausted. He then returns to earth, being first born again as a plant and afterwards as a man of one of the three highest castes. Here we have a double retribution, first in the next world, then by transmigration in this. The former is a survival of the old Vedic belief about the future life. The wicked are born again as outcasts (*chaṇḍālas*), dogs or swine.

The account of the *Bṛihadāraṇyaka* (VI. ii. 15–16) is similar. Those who have true knowledge and faith pass through the world of the gods and the sun to the world of Brahma, whence there is no return. Those who practise sacrifice and good works pass through the world of the Fathers to the moon, whence they return to earth, being born again as men. Others become birds, beasts, and reptiles.

The view of the *Kaushītaki Upanishad* (i. 2-3) is somewhat different. Here all who die go to the moon, whence some go by the "path of the Fathers" to Brahma, while others return to various forms of earthly existence, ranging from man to worm, according to the quality of their works and the degree of their knowledge.

The *Kāṭhaka*, one of the most remarkable and beautiful of the Upanishads, treats the question of life after death in the form of a legend. Nachiketas, a young Brahman, visits the realm of Yama, who offers him the choice of three boons. For the third he chooses the answer to the question, whether man exists after death or no. Death replies: "Even the gods have doubted about this; it is a subtle point; choose another boon." After vain efforts to evade the question by offering Nachiketas earthly power and riches, Yama at last yields to his persistence and reveals the secret. Life and death, he explains, are only different phases of development. True knowledge, which consists in recognising the identity of the individual soul with the world soul, raises its possessor beyond the reach of death :—

> *When every passion vanishes*
> *That nestles in the human heart,*
> *Then man gains immortality,*
> *Then Brahma is obtained by him* (vi. 14).

The story of the temptation of Nachiketas to choose the goods of this world in preference to the highest knowledge is probably the prototype of the legend of the temptation of Buddha by Māra or Death. Both by resisting the temptation obtain enlightenment.

It must not of course be supposed that the Upanishads, either as a whole or individually, offer a complete and consistent conception of the world logically developed. They are rather a mixture of half-poetical, half-philosophical fancies, of dialogues and disputations dealing tentatively with metaphysical questions. Their speculations were only later reduced to a system in the Vedānta philosophy. The earliest of them can hardly be dated later than about 600 B.C., since some important doctrines first met with in them are presupposed by Buddhism. They may be divided chronologically, on internal evidence, into four classes. The oldest group, consisting, in chronological order, of the *Bṛihadāraṇyaka*, *Chhāndogya*, *Taittirīya*, *Aitareya*, *Kaushītaki*, is written in prose which still suffers from the awkwardness of the Brāhmaṇa style. A transition is formed by the *Kena*, which is partly in verse and partly in prose, to a decidedly later class, the *Kāṭhaka*, *Īçā*, *Çvetāçvatara*, *Muṇḍaka*, *Mahānārāyaṇa*, which are metrical, and in which the Upanishad doctrine is no longer developing, but has become fixed. These are more attractive from the literary point of view. Even those of the older class acquire a peculiar charm from their liveliness, enthusiasm, and freedom from pedantry, while their language often rises to the level of eloquence. The third class, comprising the *Praçna*, *Maitrāyaṇīya*, and *Māṇḍūkya*, reverts to the use of prose, which is, however, of a much less archaic type than that of the first class, and approaches that of classical Sanskrit writers. The fourth class consists of the later Atharvan Upanishads, some of which are composed in prose, others in verse.

The *Aitareya*, one of the shortest of the Upanishads (extending to only about four octavo pages), consists of three chapters. The first represents the world as a creation of the Ātman (also called Brahma), and man as its highest manifestation. It is based on the Purusha hymn of the *Rigveda*, but the primeval man is in the Upanishad described as having been produced by the Ātman from the waters which it created. The Ātman is here said to occupy three abodes in man, the senses, mind, and heart, to which respectively correspond the three conditions of waking, dreaming, and deep sleep. The second chapter treats of the threefold birth of the Ātman. The end of transmigration is salvation, which is represented as an immortal existence in heaven. The last chapter dealing with the nature of the Ātman states that "consciousness (*prajnā*) is Brahma."

The *Kaushītaki Upanishad* is a treatise of considerable length divided into four chapters. The first deals with the two paths traversed by souls after death in connection with transmigration; the second with *Prāṇa* or life as a symbol of the Ātman. The last two, while discussing the doctrine of Brahma, contain a disquisition about the dependence of the objects of sense on the organs of sense, and of the latter on unconscious life (*prāṇa*) and conscious life (*prajnātmā*). Those who aim at redeeming knowledge are therefore admonished not to seek after objects or subjective faculties, but only the subject of cognition and action, which is described with much power as the highest god, and at the same time as the Ātman within us.

The Upanishads of the *Sāmaveda* start from the *sāman* or chant, just as those of the *Rigveda* from the *uktha* or hymn recited by the *Hotṛi* priest, in order, by interpreting it allegorically, to arrive at a knowledge of the Ātman or Brahma. The fact that the Upanishads have the same basis, which is, moreover, largely treated in a similar manner, leads to the conclusion that the various Vedic schools found a common body of oral tradition which they shaped into dogmatic texts-books or Upanishads in their own way.

Thus the *Chhāndogya*, which is equal in importance, and only slightly inferior in extent, to the *Bṛihadāraṇyaka*, bears clear traces, like the latter, of being made up of collections of floating materials. Each of its eight chapters forms an independent whole, followed by supplementary pieces often but slightly connected with the main subject-matter.

The first two chapters consist of mystical interpretations of the *sāman* and its chief part, called *Udgītha* ("loud song"). A supplement to the second chapter treats, among other subjects, of the origin of the syllable *om*, and of the three stages of religious life, those of the Brahman pupil, the householder, and the ascetic (to which later the religious mendicant was added as a fourth). The third chapter in the main deals with Brahma as the sun of the universe, the natural sun being its manifestation. The infinite Brahma is further described as dwelling, whole and undivided, in the heart of man. The way in which Brahma is to be attained is then described, and the great fundamental dogma of the identity of Brahma with the Ātman (or, as we might say, of God and Soul) is declared. The chapter concludes with a myth which forms a connecting link between the cosmogonic conceptions of the *Rigveda* and those of the law-book of Manu. The fourth chapter, containing discussions about wind, breath, and other phenomena connected with Brahma, also teaches how the soul makes its way to Brahma after death.

The first half of chapter v. is almost identical with the beginning of chapter vi. of the *Bṛihadāraṇyaka*. It is chiefly noteworthy for the theory of transmigration which it contains. The second half of the chapter is important as the earliest statement of the doctrine that the manifold world is unreal. The *sat* by desire produced from itself the three primary elements, heat, water, food (the later number being five—ether, air, fire, water, earth). As individual soul (*jīva-ātman*) it entered into these, which, by certain partial combinations called "triplication," became various products (*vikāra*) or phenomena. But the latter are a mere name. *Sat* is the only reality, it is the Ātman: "Thou art that." Chapter vii. enumerates sixteen forms in which Brahma may be adored, rising by gradation from *nāman*, "name," to *bhūman*, "infinity," which is the all-in-all and the Ātman within us. The first half of the last chapter discusses the Ātman in the heart and the universe, as well as how to attain it. The concluding portion of the chapter distinguishes the false from the true Ātman, illustrated by the three stages in which it appears—in the material body, in dreaming, and in sound sleep. In the latter stage we have the true Ātman, in which the distinction between subject and object has disappeared.

To the *Sāmaveda* also belongs a very short treatise which was long called the *Talavakāra Upanishad*, from the school to which it was attached, but later, when it became separated from that school, received the name of *Kena*, from its initial word. It consists of two distinct parts. The second, composed in prose and much older, describes the relation of the Vedic gods to Brahma, representing them as deriving their power from and entirely dependent on the latter. The first part, which is metrical and belongs to the period of fully developed Vedānta doctrine, distinguishes from the qualified Brahma, which is an object of worship, the unqualified Brahma, which is unknowable :—

To it no eye can penetrate,
Nor speech nor thought can ever reach:
It rests unknown; we cannot see
How any one may teach it us.

The various Upanishads of the *Black Yajurveda* all bear the stamp of lateness. The *Maitrāyaṇa* is a prose work of considerable extent, in which occasional stanzas are interspersed. It consists of seven chapters, the seventh and the concluding eight sections of the sixth forming a supplement. The fact that it retains the orthographical and euphonic peculiarities of the Maitrāyaṇa school, gives this Upanishad an archaic appearance. But its many quotations from other Upanishads, the occurrence of several late words, the developed Sānkhya doctrine presupposed by it, distinct references to anti-Vedic heretical schools, all combine to render the late character of this work undoubted. It is, in fact, a summing up of the old Upanishad doctrines with an admixture of ideas derived from the Sānkhya system and from Buddhism. The main body of the treatise expounds the nature of the Ātman, communicated to King Bṛihadratha of the race of Ikshvāku (probably identical with the king of that name mentioned in the *Rāmāyaṇa*), who declaims at some length on the misery and transitoriness of earthly existence. Though pessimism is not unknown to the old Upanishads, it is much more pronounced here, doubtless in consequence of Sānkhya and Buddhistic influence.

The subject is treated in the form of three questions.

The answer to the first, how the Ātman enters the body, is that Prajāpati enters in the form of the five vital airs in order to animate the lifeless bodies created by him. The second question is, How does the supreme soul become the individual soul (*bhūtātman*)? This is answered rather in accordance with the Sānkhya than the Vedānta doctrine. Overcome by the three qualities of matter (*prakṛiti*), the Ātman, forgetting its real nature, becomes involved in self-consciousness and transmigration. The third question is, How is deliverance from this state of misery possible? This is answered in conformity with neither Vedānta nor Sānkhya doctrine, but in a reactionary spirit. Only those who observe the old requirements of Brahmanism, the rules of caste and the religious orders (*āçramas*), are declared capable of attaining salvation by knowledge, penance, and meditation on Brahma. The chief gods, that is to say, the triad of the Brāhmaṇa period, Fire, Wind, Sun, the three abstractions, Time, Breath, Food, and the three popular gods, Brahmā, Rudra (*i.e.* Çiva), and Vishṇu are explained as manifestations of Brahma.

The remainder of this Upanishad is supplementary, but contains several passages of considerable interest. We have here a cosmogonic myth, like those of the Brāhmaṇas, in which the three qualities of matter, *Tamas*, *Rajas*, *Sattva*, are connected with Rudra, Brahmā, and Vishṇu, and which is in other respects very remarkable as a connecting link between the philosophy of the *Rigveda* and the later Sānkhya system. The sun is further represented as the external, and *prāṇa* (breath) as the internal, symbol of the Ātman, their worship being recommended by means of the sacred syllable *om*, the three "utterances" (*vyāhṛitis*) *bhūr*, *bhuvaḥ*, *svar*, and the famous *Sāvitrī* stanza. As a means of attaining Brahma we find a recommendation of *Yoga* or the ascetic practices leading to a state of mental concentration and bordering on trance. The information we here receive of these practices is still undeveloped compared with the later system. In addition to the three conditions of Brahma, waking, dreaming, and deep sleep, mention is made of a fourth (*turīya*) and highest stage. The Upanishad concludes with the declaration that the Ātman entered the world of duality because it wished to taste both truth and illusion.

Older than the *Maitrāyaṇa*, which borrows from them, are two other Upanishads of the *Black Yajurveda*, the *Kāṭhaka* and the *Çvetāçvatara*. The former contains some 120 and the latter some 110 stanzas.

The *Kāṭhaka* deals with the legend of Nachiketas, which is told in the Kāṭhaka portion of the *Taittirīya Brāhmaṇa*, and a knowledge of which it presupposes. This is indicated by the fact that it begins with the same words as the Brāhmaṇa story. The treatise appears to have consisted originally of the first only of its two chapters. For the second, with its more developed notions about *Yoga* and its much more pronounced view as to the unreality of phenomena, looks like a later addition. The first contains an introductory narrative, an account of the Ātman, of its embodiment and final return by means of *Yoga*. The second chapter, though less well arranged, on the whole corresponds in matter with the first. Its fourth section, while discussing the nature of the Ātman, identifies both soul (*purusha*) and matter (*prakṛiti*) with it. The fifth section deals with the manifestation of the Ātman in the world, and especially in man. The way in which it at the same time remains outside them in its full integrity and is not affected by the suffering of living beings, is strikingly illustrated by the analogy of both light and air, which pervade space and yet embrace every object, and of the sun, the eye of the universe, which remains free from the blemishes of all other eyes outside of it. In the last section *Yoga* is taught to be the means of attaining the highest goal. The gradation of mental faculties here described is of great interest for the history of the Sānkhya and Yoga system. An unconscious contradiction runs through this discussion, inasmuch as though the Ātman is regarded as the all-in-all, a sharp contrast is drawn between soul and matter. It is the contradiction between the later Vedānta and the Sānkhya-Yoga systems of philosphy.

According to its own statement, the *Çvetāçvatara Upanishad* derives its name from an individual author, and the tradition which attributes it to one of the schools of the *Black Yajurveda* hardly seems to have a sufficient foundation. Its confused arrangement, the irregularities and arbitrary changes of its metres, the number of interpolated quotations which it contains, make the assumption likely that the work in its present form is not the work of a single author. In its present form it is certainly later than the *Kāṭhaka*, since it contains several passages which must be referred to that work, besides many stanzas borrowed from it with or without variation. Its lateness is further indicated by the developed theory of *Yoga* which it contains, besides the more or less definite form in which it exhibits various Vedānta doctrines either unknown to or only foreshadowed in the earlier Upanishads. Among these may be mentioned the destruction of the world by Brahma at the end of a cosmic age (*kalpa*), as well as its periodic renewal out of Brahma, and especially the explanation of the world as an illusion (*māyā*) produced by Brahma. At the same time the author shows a strange predilection for the personified forms of Brahma as Savitṛi, Īçāna, or Rudra. Though Çiva has not yet become the name of Rudra, its frequent use as an adjective connected with the latter shows that it is in course of becoming fixed as the proper name of the highest god. In this Upanishad we meet with a number of the terms and fundamental notions of the Sānkhya, though the point of view is thoroughly Vedāntist; matter (*prakṛiti*), for instance, being represented as an illusion produced by Brahma.

To the *White Yajurveda* is attached the longest, and, beside the *Chhāndogya*, the most important of the Upanishads. It bears even clearer traces than that work of being a conglomerate of what must originally have been separate treatises. It is divided into three parts, each containing two chapters. The last part is designated, even in the tradition of the commentaries, as a supplement (*Khila-kāṇḍa*), a statement fully borne out by the contents. That the first and second parts were also originally independent of each other is sufficiently proved by both containing the legend of Yājnavalkya and his two wives in almost identical words throughout. To each of these parts (aș well as to Book x. of the *Çatapatha Brāhmaṇa*) a successive list (*vaṃça*) of teachers is attached. A comparison of these lists seems to justify the conclusion that the first part (called *Madhukāṇḍa*) and the second (*Yājnavalkya-kāṇḍa*) existed during nine generations as independent Upanishads within the school of the *White Yajurveda*, and were then combined by a teacher named Āgniveçya; the third part, which consists of all kinds of supplementary matter, being subsequently added. These lists further make the conclusion probable that the leading teachers of the ritual tradition (Brāhmaṇas) were different from those of the philosophical tradition (Upanishads).

Beginning with an allegorical interpretation of the most important sacrifice, the *Açvamedha* (horse-sacrifice), as the universe, the first chapter proceeds to deal with *prāṇa* (breath) as a symbol of soul, and then with the creation of the world out of the Ātman or Brahma, insisting on the dependence of all existence on the Supreme Soul, which appears in every individual as his self. The polemical attitude adopted against the worship of the gods is characteristic, showing that the passage belongs to an early period, in which the doctrine of the superiority of the Ātman to the gods was still asserting itself. The next chapter deals with the nature of the Ātman and its manifestations, *purusha* and *prāṇa*.

The second part of the Upanishad consists of four philosophical discussions, in which Yājnavalkya is the chief speaker. The first (iii. 1–9) is a great disputation, in which the sage proves his superiority to nine successive interlocutors. One of the most interesting conclusions here arrived at is that Brahma is theoretically unknowable, but can be comprehended practically. The second discourse is a dialogue between King Janaka and Yājnavalkya, in which the latter shows the untenableness of six definitions set up by other teachers as to the nature of Brahma; for instance, that it is identical with Breath or Mind. He finally declares that the Ātman can only be described negatively, being intangible, indestructible, independent, immovable.

The third discourse (iv. 3-4) is another dialogue between Janaka and Yājnavalkya. It presents a picture of the soul in the conditions of waking, dreaming, deep sleep, dying, transmigration, and salvation. For wealth of illustration, fervour of conviction, beauty and elevation of thought, this piece is unequalled in the Upanishads or any other work of Indian literature. Its literary effect is heightened by the numerous stanzas with which it is interspersed. These are, however, doubtless later additions. The dreaming soul is thus described :—

Leaving its lower nest in breath's protection,
And upward from that nest, immortal, soaring,
Where'er it lists it roves about immortal,
The golden-pinioned only swan of spirit (IV. iii. 13).

It roves in dream condition up and downward,
Divinely many shapes and forms assuming (ib. 14).

Then follows an account of the dreamless state of the soul :—

As a falcon or an eagle, having flown about in the air, exhausted folds together its wings and prepares to alight, so the spirit hastes to that condition in which, asleep, it feels no desire and sees no dream (19).

This is its essential form, in which it rises above desire, is free from evil and without fear. For as one embraced by a beloved woman wots not of anything without or within, so also the soul embraced by the cognitional Self wots not of anything without or within (21).

With regard to the souls of those who are not saved, the view of the writer appears to be that after death they enter a new body immediately and without any intervening retribution in the other world, in exact accordance with their intellectual and moral quality.

As a caterpillar, when it has reached the point of a leaf, makes a new beginning and draws itself across, so the soul, after casting off the body and letting go ignorance, makes a new beginning and draws itself across (IV. iv. 3).

As a goldsmith takes the material of an image and hammers out of it another newer and more beautiful form, so also the soul after casting off the body and letting go ignorance, creates for itself another newer and more beautiful form, either that of the Fathers or the Gāndharvas or the Gods, or Prajāpati or Brahma, or other beings (IV. iv. 4).

But the vital airs of him who is saved, who knows himself to be identical with Brahma, do not depart, for he is absorbed in Brahma and is Brahma.

As a serpent's skin, dead and cast off, lies upon an ant-hill, so his body then lies; but that which is bodiless and immortal, the life, is pure Brahma, is pure light (IV. iv. 7).

The fourth discourse is a dialogue between Yājnavalkya and his wife Maitreyī, before the former, about to renounce the world, retires to the solitude of the forest. There are several indications that it is a secondary recension of the same conversation occurring in a previous chapter (II. iv.).

The first chapter of the third or supplementary part consists of fifteen sections, which are often quite short, are mostly unconnected in matter, and appear to be of very different age. The second chapter, however, forms a long and important treatise (identical with that found in the *Chhāndogya*) on the doctrine of transmigration. The views here expressed are so much at variance with those of Yājnavalkya that this text must have originated in another Vedic school, and have been loosely attached to this Upanishad owing to the peculiar importance of its contents. The preceding and following section, which are connected with it, and are also found in the *Chhāndogya*, must have been added at the same time.

Not only is the longest Upanishad attached to the *White Yajurveda*, but also one of the very shortest, consisting of only eighteen stanzas. This is the *Īçā*, which is so called from its initial word. Though forming the last chapter of the *Vājasaneyi Saṃhitā*, it belongs to a rather late period. It is about contemporaneous with the latest parts of the *Brihadāraṇyaka*, is more developed in many points than the *Kāṭhaka*, but seems to be older than the *Çvetāçvatara*. Its leading motive is to contrast him who knows himself to be the same as the Ātman with him who does not possess true knowledge. It affords an excellent survey of the fundamental doctrines of the Vedānta philosophy.

A large and indefinite number of Upanishads is attributed to the *Atharva-veda*, but the most authoritative list recognises twenty-seven altogether. They are for the most part of very late origin, being post-Vedic, and, all but three, contemporaneous with the Purāṇas. One of them is actually a Muhammadan treatise entitled the *Alla Upanishad!* The older Upanishads which belong to the first three Vedas were, with a few exceptions like the *Çvetāçvatara*, the dogmatic text-books of actual Vedic schools, and received their names from those schools, being connected with and supplementary to the ritual Brāhmaṇas. The Upanishads of the *Atharva-veda*, on the other hand, are with few exceptions like the *Māṇḍūkya* and the *Jābāla*, no longer connected with Vedic schools, but derive their names from their subject-matter or some other circumstance. They appear for the most part to represent the views of theosophic, mystic, ascetic, or sectarian associations, who wished to have an Upanishad of their own in imitation of the old Vedic schools. They became attached to the *Atharva-veda* not from any internal connection, but partly because the followers of the *Atharva-veda* desired to become possessed of dogmatic text-books of their own, and partly because the fourth Veda was not protected from the intrusion of foreign elements by the watchfulness of religious guilds like the old Vedic schools.

The fundamental doctrine common to all the Upanishads of the *Atharva-veda* is developed by most of them in various special directions. They may accordingly be divided into four categories which run chronologically parallel with one another, each containing relatively old and late productions. The first group, as directly investigating the nature of the Ātman, has a scope similar to that of the Upanishads of the other Vedas, and goes no further than the latter in developing its main thesis. The next group, taking the fundamental doctrine for granted, treats of absorption in the Ātman through ascetic meditation (*yoga*) based on the component parts of the sacred syllable *om*. These Upanishads are almost without exception composed in verse and are quite short, consisting on the average of about twenty stanzas. In the third category the life of the religious mendicant (*sannyāsin*), as a practical consequence of the Upanishad doctrine, is recommended and described. These Upanishads, too, are short, but are written in prose, though with an admixture of verse. The last group is sectarian in character, interpreting the popular gods Çiva (under various names, such as Īçāna, Maheçvara, Mahādeva) and Vishṇu (as Nārāyaṇa and Nṛisiṃha or "Man-lion") as personifications of the Ātman. The different Avatārs of Vishṇu are here regarded as human manifestations of the Ātman.

The oldest and most important of these Atharvan Upanishads, as representing the Vedānta doctrine most faithfully, are the *Muṇḍaka*, the *Praçna*, and to a less degree the *Māṇḍūkya.* The first two come nearest to the Upanishads of the older Vedas, and are much quoted by Bādarāyaṇa and Çankara, the great authorities of the later Vedānta philosophy. They are the only original and legitimate Upanishads of the *Atharva.* The *Muṇḍaka* derives its name from being the Upanishad of the tonsured (*muṇḍa*), an association of ascetics who shaved their heads, as the Buddhist monks did later. It is one of the most popular of the Upanishads, not owing to the originality of its contents, which are for the most part derived from older texts, but owing to the purity with which it reproduces the old Vedānta doctrine, and the beauty of the stanzas in which it is composed. It presupposes, above all, the *Chhāndogya Upanishad,* and in all probability the *Bṛihadāraṇyaka*, the *Taittirīya*, and the *Kāṭhaka.* Having several important passages in common with the *Çvetāçvatara* and the *Bṛihannārāyaṇa* of the *Black Yajurveda*, it probably belongs to the same epoch, coming between the two in order of time. It consists of three parts, which, speaking generally, deal respectively with the preparations for the knowledge of Brahma, the doctrine of Brahma, and the way to Brahma.

The *Praçna Upanishad,* written in prose and apparently belonging to the Pippalāda recension of the *Atharva-veda*, is so called because it treats, in the form of questions (*praçna*) addressed by six students of Brahma to the sage PIPPALĀDA, six main points of the

Vedānta doctrine. These questions concern the origin of matter and life (*prāṇa*) from Prajāpati; the superiority of life (*prāṇa*) above the other vital powers; the nature and divisions of the vital powers; dreaming and dreamless sleep; meditation on the syllable *om;* and the sixteen parts of man.

The *Māṇḍūkya* is a very short prose Upanishad, which would hardly fill two pages of the present book. Though bearing the name of a half-forgotten school of the *Rigveda*, it is reckoned among the Upanishads of the *Atharva-veda.* It must date from a considerably later time than the prose Upanishads of the three older Vedas, with the unmethodical treatment and prolixity of which its precision and conciseness are in marked contrast. It has many points of contact with the *Maitrāyaṇa Upanishad*, to which it seems to be posterior. It appears, however, to be older than the rest of the treatises which form the fourth class of the Upanishads of the *Atharva-veda.* Thus it distinguishes only three *morae* in the syllable *om*, and not yet three and a half. The fundamental idea of this Upanishad is that the sacred syllable is an expression of the universe. It is somewhat remarkable that this work is not quoted by Çankara; nevertheless, it not only exercised a great influence on several Upanishads of the *Atharva-veda*, but was used more than any other Upanishad by the author of the well-known later epitome of the Vedānta doctrine, the *Vedānta-sāra.*

It is, however, chiefly important as having given rise to one of the most remarkable products of Indian philosophy, the *Kārikā* of Gauḍapāda. This work consists of more than 200 stanzas divided into four parts, the first of which includes the *Māṇḍūkya Upanishad.*

The esteem in which the *Kārikā* was held is indicated by the fact that its parts are reckoned as four Upanishads. There is much probability in the assumption that its author is identical with Gauḍapāda, the teacher of Govinda, whose pupil was the great Vedāntist commentator, ÇANKARA (800 A.D.). The point of view of the latter is the same essentially as that of the author of the *Kārikā*, and many of the thoughts and figures which begin to appear in the earlier work are in common use in Çankara's commentaries. Çankara may, in fact, be said to have reduced the doctrines of Gauḍapāda to a system, as did Plato those of Parmenides. Indeed, the two leading ideas which pervade the Indian poem, viz., that there is no duality (*advaita*) and no becoming (*ajāti*), are, as Professor Deussen points out, identical with those of the Greek philosopher.

The first part of the *Kārikā* is practically a metrical paraphrase of the *Māṇḍūkya Upanishad*. Peculiar to it is the statement that the world is not an illusion or a development in any sense, but the very nature or essence (*svabhāva*) of Brahma, just as the rays, which are all the same (*i.e.* light), are not different from the sun. The remainder of the poem is independent of the Upanishad and goes far beyond its doctrines. The second part has the special title of *Vaitathya* or the "Falseness" of the doctrine of reality. Just as a rope is in the dark mistaken for a snake, so the Ātman in the darkness of ignorance is mistaken for the world. Every attempt to imagine the Ātman under empirical forms is futile, for every one's idea of it is dependent on his experience of the world.

The third part is entitled *Advaita*, "Non-duality." The identity of the Supreme Soul (*Ātman*) with the individual soul (*jīva*) is illustrated by comparison with space, and that part of it which is contained in a jar. Arguing against the theory of genesis and plurality, the poet lays down the axiom that nothing can become different from its own nature. The production of the existent (*sato janma*) is impossible, for that would be produced which already exists. The production of the non-existent (*asato janma*) is also impossible, for the non-existent is never produced, any more than the son of a barren woman. The last part is entitled *Alāta-çānti*, or "Extinction of the firebrand (circle)," so called from an ingenious comparison made to explain how plurality and genesis seem to exist in the world. If a stick which is glowing at one end is waved about, fiery lines or circles are produced without anything being added to or issuing from the single burning point. The fiery line or circle exists only in the consciousness (*vijnāna*). So, too, the many phenomena of the world are merely the vibrations of the consciousness, which is one.

CHAPTER IX

THE SŪTRAS

(*Circa* 500–200 B.C.)

As the Upanishads were a development of the speculative side of the Brāhmaṇas and constituted the textbooks of Vedic dogma, so the Çrauta Sūtras form the continuation of their ritual side, though they are not, like the Upanishads, regarded as a part of revelation. A sacred character was never attributed to them, probably because they were felt to be treatises compiled, with the help of oral priestly tradition, from the contents of the Brāhmaṇas solely to meet practical needs. The oldest of them seem to go back to about the time when Buddhism came into being. Indeed it is quite possible that the rise of the rival religion gave the first impetus to the composition of systematic manuals of Brahmanic worship. The Buddhists in their turn must have come to regard Sūtras as the type of treatise best adapted for the expression of religious doctrine, for the earliest Pāli texts are works of this character. The term Kalpa Sūtra is used to designate the whole body of Sūtras concerned with religion which belonged to a particular Vedic school. Where such a complete collection has been preserved, the Çrauta Sūtra forms its first and most extensive portion.

To the *Rigveda* belong the Çrauta manuals of two

Sūtra schools (*charaṇas*), the Çānkhāyanas and the Āçvalāyanas, the former of whom were in later times settled in Northern Gujarat, the latter in the South between the Godāvarī and the Kṛishṇā. The ritual is described in much the same order by both, but the account of the great royal sacrifices is much more detailed in the *Çānkhāyana Çrauta Sūtra.* The latter, which is closely connected with the *Çānkhāyana Brāhmaṇa*, seems to be the older of the two, on the ground both of its matter and of its style, which in many parts resembles that of the Brāhmaṇas. It consists of eighteen books, the last two of which were added later, and correspond to the first two books of the *Kaushītaki Āraṇyaka.* The Çrauta Sūtra of ĀÇVALĀYANA, which consists of twelve books, is related to the *Aitareya Brāhmaṇa.* Āçvalāyana is also known as the author of the fourth book of the *Aitareya Āraṇyaka*, and was according to tradition the pupil of Çaunaka.

Three Çrauta Sūtras to the *Sāmaveda* have been preserved. The oldest, that of MAÇAKA, also called *Ārsheya-kalpa*, is nothing more than an enumeration of the prayers belonging to the various ceremonies of the Soma sacrifice in the order of the *Panchaviṃça Brāhmaṇa.* The Çrauta Sūtra composed by LĀṬYĀYANA, became the accepted manual of the Kauthuma school. This Sūtra, like that of Maçaka, which it quotes, is closely connected with the *Panchaviṃça Brāhmaṇa.* The Çrauta Sūtra of DRĀHYĀYAṆA, which differs but little from that of Lāṭyāyana, belongs to the Rāṇāyanīya branch of the *Sāma-veda.*

To the *White Yajurveda* belongs the Çrauta Sūtra of KĀTYĀYANA. This manual, which consists of twenty-six chapters, on the whole strictly follows the sacrificial order of the *Çatapatha Brāhmaṇa.* Three of its chapters (xxii.–xxiv.), however, relate to the ceremonial of the *Sāmaveda.* Owing to the enigmatical character of its style, it appears to be one of the later productions of the Sūtra period.

No less than six Çrauta Sūtras belonging to the *Black Yajurveda* have been preserved, but only two of them have as yet been published. Four of these form a very closely connected group, being part of the Kalpa Sūtras of four subdivisions of the Taittirīya Çākhā, which represented the later sūtra schools (*charaṇas*) not claiming a special revelation of Veda or Brāhmaṇa. The Çrauta Sūtra of ĀPASTAMBA forms the first twenty-four of the thirty chapters (*praçnas*) into which his Kalpa Sūtra is divided; and that of HIRAṆYAKEÇIN, an offshoot of the Āpastambas, the first eighteen of the twenty-nine chapters of his Kalpa Sūtra. The Sūtra of BAUDHĀYANA, who is older than Āpastamba, as well as that of BHĀRADVĀJA, has not yet been published.

Connected with the *Maitrāyaṇī Saṃhitā* is the *Mānava Çrauta Sūtra.* It belongs to the Mānavas, who were a subdivision of the Maitrāyaṇīyas, and to whom the law-book of Manu probably traces its origin. It seems to be one of the oldest. It has a descriptive character, resembling the Brāhmaṇa parts of the *Yajurveda,* and differing from them only in simply describing the course of the sacrifice, to the exclusion of legends, speculations, or discussions of any kind. There is also a *Vaikhānasa Çrauta Sūtra* attached to the *Black Yajurveda,* but it is known only in a few MSS.

The Çrauta Sūtra of the *Atharva-veda* is the *Vaitāna Sūtra.* It is neither old nor original, but was undoubtedly compiled in order to supply the *Atharva,* like the other Vedas, with a Sūtra of its own. It probably received its name from the word with which it begins, since the term *vaitāna* ("relating to the three sacrificial fires") is equally applicable to all Çrauta Sūtras. It agrees to a considerable extent with the *Gopatha Brāhmaṇa*, though it distinctly follows the Sūtra of Kātyāyana to the *White Yajurveda*. One indication of its lateness is the fact that whereas in other cases a Gṛihya regularly presupposes the Çrauta Sūtra, the *Vaitāna* is dependent on the domestic sūtra of the *Atharva-veda*.

Though the Çrauta Sūtras are indispensable for the right understanding of the sacrificial ritual, they are, from any other point of view, a most unattractive form of literature. It will, therefore, suffice to mention in briefest outline the ceremonies with which they deal. It is important to remember, in the first place, that these rites are never congregational, but are always performed on behalf of a single individual, the so-called *Yajamāna* or sacrificer, who takes but little part in them. The officiators are Brahman priests, whose number varies from one to sixteen, according to the nature of the ceremony. In all these rites an important part is played by the three sacred fires which surround the *vedi*, a slightly excavated spot covered with a litter of grass for the reception of offerings to the gods. The first ceremony of all is the setting up of the sacred fires (*agni-ādheya*), which are kindled by the sacrificer and his wife with the firesticks, and are thereafter to be regularly maintained.

The Çrauta rites, fourteen in number, are divided into the two main groups of seven oblation (*havis*) sacrifices and seven soma sacrifices. Different forms of the animal sacrifice are classed with each group. The *havis* sacrifices consist of offerings of milk, ghee, porridge, grain, cakes, and so forth. The commonest is the *Agnihotra*, the daily morning and evening oblation of milk to the three fires. The most important of the others are the new and full moon sacrifices (*darçapūrṇa-māsa*) and those offered at the beginning of the three seasons (*chāturmāsya*). Besides some other recurrent sacrifices, there are very many which are to be offered on some particular occasion, or for the attainment of some special object.

The various kinds of Soma sacrifices were much more complicated. Even the simplest and fundamental form, the *Agnishṭoma* ("praise of Agni") required the ministrations of sixteen priests. This rite occupied only one day, with three pressings of soma, at morning, noon, and evening; but this day was preceded by very detailed preparatory ceremonies, one of which was the initiation (*dīkshā*) of the sacrificer and his wife. Other soma sacrifices lasted for several days up to twelve; while another class, called *sattras* or "sessions," extended to a year or more.

A very sacred ceremony that can be connected with the soma sacrifice is the *Agnichayana*, or "Piling of the fire-altar," which lasts for a year. It begins with a sacrifice of five animals. Then a long time is occupied in preparing the earthenware vessel, called *ukhā*, in which fire is to be maintained for a year. Very elaborate rules are given both as to the ingredients, such as the hair of a black antelope, with which the clay is to be mixed, and as to how it is to be shaped, and finally burnt. Then the bricks, which have different and particular sizes, have to be built up in prescribed order. The lowest of the five strata must have 1950, all of them together, a total of 10,800 bricks. Many of these have their special name and significance. Thus the altar is gradually built up, as its bricks are placed in position, to the accompaniment of appropriate rites and verses, by a formidable array of priests. These are but some of the main points in the ceremony; but they will probably give some faint idea of the enormous complexity and the vast mass of detail, where the smallest of minutiæ are of importance, in the Brahman ritual. No other religion has ever known its like.

As the domestic ritual is almost entirely excluded from the Brāhmaṇas, the authors of the Gṛihya Sūtras had only the authority of popular tradition to rely on when they systematised the observances of daily life. As a type, the Gṛihya manuals must be somewhat later than the Çrauta, for they regularly presuppose a knowledge of the latter.

To the *Rigveda* belongs in the first place the *Çānkhāyana Gṛihya Sūtra.* It consists of six books, but only the first four form the original portion of the work, and even these contain interpolations. Closely connected with this work is the *Çāmbavya Gṛihya*, which also belongs to the school of the Kaushītakins, and is as yet known only in manuscript. Though borrowing largely from Çānkhāyana, it is not identical with that work. It knows nothing of the last two books, nor even a number of ceremonies described in the third and fourth, while having a book of its own concerning the sacrifice to the Manes. Connected with the *Aitareya Brāhmaṇa* is the Gṛihya Sūtra of Āçvalāyana, which its author in the first aphorism gives us to understand is a continuation of his Çrauta Sūtra. It consists of four books, and, like the latter work, ends with the words "adoration to Çaunaka."

The chief Gṛihya Sūtra of the *Sāmaveda* is that of GOBHILA, which is one of the oldest, completest, and most interesting works of this class. Its seems to have been used by both the schools of its Veda. Besides the text of the *Sāmaveda* it presupposes the *Mantra Brāhmaṇa.* The latter is a collection, in the ritual order, of the *mantras* (except those occurring in the *Sāmaveda* itself), which are quoted by Gobhila in an abbreviated form. The Gṛihya Sūtra of KHĀDIRA, belonging to the Drāhyāyaṇa school and used by the Rāṇāyanīya branch of the *Sāmaveda,* is little more than Gobhila remodelled in a more succinct form.

The Gṛihya Sūtra of the *White Yajurveda* is that of PĀRASKARA, also called the *Kātīya* or *Vājasaneya Gṛihya Sūtra.* It is so closely connected with the Çrauta Sūtra of Kātyāyana, that it is often quoted under the name of that author. The later law-book of Yājnavalkya bears evidence of the influence of Pāraskara's work.

Of the seven Gṛihya Sūtras of the *Black Yajurveda* only three have as yet been published. The Gṛihya of Āpastamba forms two books (26–27) of his Kalpa Sūtra. The first of these two books is the *Mantrapāṭha,* which is a collection of the formulas accompanying the ceremonies. The Gṛihya Sūtra, in the strict sense, is the second book, which presupposes the *Mantrapāṭha.* Books XIX. and XX. of Hiraṇyakeçin's Kalpa Sūtra form his Gṛihya Sūtra. About Baudhāyana's Gṛihya not much is known, still less about that of Bhāradvāja. The *Mānava Gṛihya Sūtra* is closely connected with the Çrauta, repeating many of the statements of the latter verbally. It is interesting as containing a ceremony unknown to other Gṛihya Sūtras, the worship of the Vināyakas. The passage reappears in a versified form in Yājnavalkya's law-book, where the four Vināyakas are transformed into the one Vināyaka, the god Gaṇeça. With the *Mānava* is clearly connected the *Kāṭhaka Gṛihya Sūtra*, not only in the principle of its arrangement, but even in the wording of many passages. It is nearly related to the law-book of Vishṇu. The *Vaikhānasa Gṛihya Sūtra* is an extensive work bearing traces of a late origin, and partly treating of subjects otherwise relegated to works of a supplementary character.

To the *Atharva-veda* belongs the important *Kauçika Sūtra*. It is not a mere Gṛihya Sūtra, for besides giving the more important rules of the domestic ritual, it deals with the magical and other practices specially connected with its Veda. By its extensive references to these subjects it supplies much material unknown to other Vedic schools. It is a composite work, apparently made up of four or five different treatises. In combination with the *Atharva-veda* it supplies an almost complete picture of the ordinary life of the Vedic Indian.

The Gṛihya Sūtras give the rules for the numerous ceremonies applicable to the domestic life of a man and his family from birth to the grave. For the performance of their ritual only the domestic (*āvasathya* or *vaivāhika*) fire was required, as contrasted with the three sacrificial fires of the Çrauta Sūtras. They describe forty consecrations or sacraments (*saṃskāras*) which are performed at various important epochs in the life of the individual. The first eighteen, extending from conception to marriage, are called "bodily sacraments." The remaining twenty-two are sacrifices. Eight of these, the five daily sacrifices (*mahāyajna*) and some other "baked offerings" (*pākayajna*), form part of the Gṛihya ceremonies, the rest belonging to the Çrauta ritual.

The first of the sacraments is the *puṃsavana* or ceremony aiming at the obtainment of a son. The most common expedient prescribed is the pounded shoot of a banyan tree placed in the wife's right nostril. After the birth-rites (*jāta-karma*), the ceremony of giving the child its names (*nāma-karaṇa*) takes place, generally on the tenth day after birth. Two are given, one being the "secret name," known only to the parents, as a protection against witchcraft, the other for common use. Minute directions are given as to the quality of the name; for instance, that it should contain an even number of syllables, begin with a soft letter, and have a semi-vowel in the middle; that for a Brahman it should end in *-çarman*, for a Kshatriya in *-varman*, and a Vaiçya in *-gupta*. Generally in the third year takes place the ceremony of tonsure (*chūḍā-karaṇa*), when the boy's hair was cut, one or more tufts being left on the top, so that his hair might be worn after the fashion prevailing in his family. In the sixteenth year the rite of shaving the beard was performed. Its name, *go-dāna*, or "gift of cows," is due to the fee usually having been a couple of cattle.

By far the most important ceremony of boyhood was that of apprenticeship to a teacher or initiation (*upanayana*), which in the case of a Brahman may take place between the eighth and sixteenth year, but a few years later in the case of the Kshatriya and the Vaiçya. On this occasion the youth receives a staff, a garment, a girdle, and a cord worn over one shoulder and under the other arm. The first is made of different wood, the others of different materials according to caste. The sacred cord is the outward token of the *Ārya* or member of one of the three highest castes, and by investiture with it he attains his second birth, being thenceforward a "twice-born" man (*dvi-ja*). The spiritual significance of this initiation is the right to study the Veda, and especially to recite the most sacred of prayers, the *Sāvitrī*. In this ceremony the teacher (*āchārya*) who initiates the young Brahman is regarded as his spiritual father, and the *Sāvitrī* as his mother.

The rite of *upanayana* is still practised in India. It is based on a very old custom. The Avestan ceremony of investing the boy of fifteen with a sacred cord upon his admission into the Zoroastrian community shows that it goes back to Indo-Iranian times. The prevalence among primitive races all over the world of a rite of initiation, regarded as a second birth, upon the attainment of manhood, indicates that it was a still older custom, which in the Brahman system became transformed into a ceremony of admission to Vedic study.

Besides his studies, the course of which is regulated by detailed rules, the constant duties of the pupil are the collection of fuel, the performance of devotions at morning and evening twilight, begging food, sleeping on the ground, and obedience to his teacher.

At the conclusion of religious studentship (*brahmacharya*), which lasted for twelve years, or till the pupil had mastered his Veda, he performs the rite of return (*samāvartana*), the principal part of which is a bath, with which he symbolically washes off his apprenticeship. He is now a *snātaka* ("one who has bathed"), and soon proceeds to the most important sacrament of his life, marriage. The main elements of this ceremony doubtless go back to the Indo-European period, and belong rather to the sphere of witchcraft than of the sacrificial cult. The taking of her hand placed the bride in the power of her husband. The stone on which she stepped was to give her firmness. The seven steps which she took with her husband, and the sacrificial food which she shared with him, were to inaugurate friendship and community. Future abundance and male offspring were prognosticated when she had been conducted to her husband's house, by seating her on the hide of a red bull and placing upon her lap the son of a woman who had only borne living male children. The god most closely connected with the rite was Agni; for the husband led his bride three times round the nuptial fire—whence the Sanskrit name for wedding, *pari-ṇaya*, "leading round"—and the newly kindled domestic fire was to accompany the couple throughout life. Offerings are made to it and Vedic formulas pronounced. After sunset the husband leads out his bride, and as he points to the pole-star and the star Arundhatī, they exhort each other to be constant and undivided for ever. These wedding ceremonies, preserved much as they are described in the Sūtras, are still widely prevalent in the India of to-day.

All the above-mentioned sacraments are exclusively meant for males, the only one in which girls had a share being marriage (*vivāha*). About twelve of these *Saṃskāras* are still practised in India, investiture being still the most important next to marriage. Some of the ceremonies only survive in a symbolical form, as those connected with religious studentship.

Among the most important duties of the new householder is the regular daily offering of the five great sacrifices (*mahā-yajna*), which are the sacrifice to the Veda (*brahma-yajna*), or Vedic recitation; the offering to the gods (*deva-yajna*) of melted butter in fire (*homa*); the libation (*tarpaṇa*) to the Manes (*pitṛi-yajna*); offerings (called *bali*) deposited in various places on the ground to demons and all beings (*bhūta-yajna*); and the sacrifice to men (*manushya-yajna*), consisting in hospitality, especially to Brahman mendicants. The first is regarded as by far the highest; the recitation of the *sāvitrī*, in particular, at morning and evening worship, is as meritorious as having studied the Veda. All these five daily sacrifices are still in partial use among orthodox Brahmans.

There are other sacrifices which occur periodically. Such are the new and full moon sacrifices, in which, according to the Gṛihya ritual, a baked offering (*pāka-yajna*) is made, while, according to the Çrauta ceremony, cakes (*puroḍāça*) are offered. There is, further, at the beginning of the rains an offering made to serpents, when the use of a raised bed is enjoined, owing to the danger from snakes at that time. Various ceremonies are connected with the building and entering of a new house. Detailed rules are given about the site as well as the construction. A door on the west is, for instance, forbidden. On the completion of the house, which is built of wood and bamboo, an animal is sacrificed. Other ceremonies are concerned with cattle; for instance, the release of a young bull for the benefit of the community. Then there are agricultural ceremonies, such as the offering of the first-fruits and rites connected with ploughing. Mention is also made of offerings to monuments (*chaityas*) erected to the memory of teachers. There are, moreover, directions as to what is to be done in case of evil dreams, bad omens, and disease.

Finally, one of the most interesting subjects with which the Gṛihya Sūtras deal is that of funeral rites (*antyeshṭi*) and the worship of the Manes. All but children under two years of age are to be cremated. The dead man's hair and beard are cut off and his nails trimmed, the body being anointed with nard and a wreath being placed on the head. Before being burnt the corpse is laid on a black antelope skin. In the case of a Kshatriya, his bow (in that of a Brahman his staff, of a Vaiçya his goad) is taken from his hand, broken, and cast on the pyre, while a cow or a goat is burnt with the corpse. Afterwards a purifying ablution is performed by all relations to the seventh or tenth degree. They then sit down on a grassy spot and listen to old stories or a sermon on the transitoriness of life till the stars appear. At last, without looking round, they return in procession to their homes, where various observances are gone through. A death is followed by a period of impurity, generally lasting three days, during which the relatives are required, among other things, to sleep on the ground and refrain from eating flesh. On the night after the death a cake is offered to the deceased, and a libation of water is poured out; a vessel with milk and water is also placed in the open air, and the dead man is called upon to bathe in it. Generally after the tenth day the bones are collected and placed in an urn, which is buried to the accompaniment of the Rigvedic verse, "Approach thy mother earth" (x. 18, 10).

The soul is supposed to remain separated from the

Manes for a time as a *preta* or "ghost." A *çrāddha*, or "offering given with faith" (*çraddhā*), of which it is the special object (*ekoddishṭa*), is presented to it in this state, the idea being that it would otherwise return and disquiet the relatives. Before the expiry of a year he is admitted to the circle of the Manes by a rite which makes him their *sapiṇḍa* ("united by the funeral cake"). After the lapse of a year or more another elaborate ceremony (called *pitṛi-medha*) takes place in connection with the erection of a monument, when the bones are taken out of the urn and buried in a suitable place. There are further various general offerings to the Manes, or *çrāddhas*, which take place at fixed periods, such as that on the day of new moon (*pārvaṇa çrāddha*), while others are only occasional and optional. These rites still play an important part in India, well-to-do families in Bengal spending not less than 5000 to 6000 rupees on their first *çrāddha*.

From all these offerings of the Gṛihya ritual are to be distinguished the two regular sacrifices of the Çrauta ritual, the one called *Piṇḍa-pitṛi-yajna* immediately preceding the new-moon sacrifice, the other being connected with the third of the four-monthly sacrifices.

The ceremonial of ancestor-worship was especially elaborated, and developed a special literature of its own, extending from the Vedic period to the legal Compendia of the Middle Ages. The *Çrāddha-kalpa* of Hemādri comprises upwards of 1700 pages in the edition of the *Bibliotheca Indica*.

The above is the briefest possible sketch of the abundant material of the Gṛihya Sūtras, illustrating the daily domestic life of ancient India. Perhaps, however, enough has been said to show that they have much human interest, and that they occupy an important place in the history of civilisation.

The second branch of the Sūtra literature, based on tradition or *Smṛiti*, are the Dharma Sūtras, which deal with the customs of everyday life (*sāmayāchārika*). They are the earliest Indian works on law, treating fully of its religious, but only partially and briefly of its secular, aspect. The term Dharma Sūtra is, strictly speaking, applied to those collections of legal aphorisms which form part of the body of Sūtras belonging to a particular branch (*çākhā*) of the Veda. In this sense only three have been preserved, all of them attached to the Taittirīya division of the *Black Yajurveda*. But there is good reason to suppose that other works of the same kind which have been preserved, or are known to have existed, were originally also attached to individual Vedic schools. That Sūtras on Dharma were composed at a very early period is shown by the fact that Yāska, who dates from near the beginning of the Sūtra age, quotes legal rules in the Sūtra style. Indeed, one or two of those extant must go back to about his time.

The Dharma Sūtra which has been best preserved, and has remained free from the influence of sectarians or modern editors, is that of the Āpastambas. It forms two (28–29) of the thirty sections of the great *Āpastamba Kalpa Sūtra*, or body of aphorisms concerning the performance of sacrifices and the duties of the three upper classes. It deals chiefly with the duties of the Vedic student and of the householder, with forbidden food, purifications, and penances, while, on the secular side, it touches upon the law of marriage, inheritance, and crime only. From the disapprobation which the author expresses for a certain practice of the people of the North, it may be inferred that he belonged to the South, where his school is known to have been settled in later times. Owing to the pre-Pāṇinean character of its language and other criteria, Bühler has assigned this Dharma Sūtra to about 400 B.C.

Very closely connected with this work is the Dharma Sūtra of Hiraṇyakeçin; for the differences between the two do not go much beyond varieties of reading. In keeping with this relationship is the tradition that Hiraṇyakeçin branched off from the Āpastambas and founded a new school in the Konkan country on the south-west (about Goa). The lower limit for this separation from the Āpastambas is about 500 A.D., when a Hiraṇyakeçin Brahman is mentioned in an inscription. The main importance of this Sūtra lies in its confirming, by the parallelism of its text, the genuineness of by far the greatest part of Āpastamba's work. It forms two (26–27) of the twenty-nine chapters of the Kalpa Sūtra belonging to the school of Hiraṇyakeçin.

The third Dharma Sūtra, generally styled a *dharma-çāstra* in the MSS., is that of Baudhāyana. Its position, however, within the Kalpa Sūtra of its school is not so fixed as in the two previous cases. Its subject-matter, when compared with that of Āpastamba's Dharma Sūtra, indicates that it is the older of the two, just as the more archaic and awkward style of Baudhāyana's Gṛihya Sūtra shows the latter to be earlier than the corresponding work of Āpastamba. The Baudhāyana school cannot be traced at the present day, but it appears to have belonged to Southern India, where the famous Vedic commentator Sāyaṇa was a member of it in the fourteenth century. The subjects dealt with in their Dharma Sūtra are multifarious, including the duties of the four religious orders, the mixed castes, various kinds of sacrifice, purification, penance, auspicious ceremonies, duties of kings, criminal justice, examination of witnesses, law of inheritance and marriage, the position of women. The fourth section, which is almost entirely composed in *çlokas*, is probably a modern addition, and even the third is of somewhat doubtful age.

With the above works must be classed the well-preserved law-book of GAUTAMA. Though it does not form part of a Kalpa Sūtra, it must at one time have been connected with a Vedic school; for the Gautamas are mentioned as a subdivision of the Rāṇāyanīya branch of the *Sāmaveda*, and Kumārila's statement that Gautama's treatise originally belonged to that Veda is confirmed by the fact that its twenty-sixth section is taken word for word from the *Sāmavidhāna Brāhmaṇa*. Though entitled a Dharma Çāstra, it is in style and character a regular Dharma Sūtra. It is composed entirely in prose aphorisms, without any admixture of verse, as in the other works of this class. Its varied contents resemble and are treated much in the same way as those of the Dharma Sūtra of Baudhāyana. The latter has indeed been shown to contain passages based on or borrowed from Gautama's work, which is therefore the oldest Dharma Sūtra that has been preserved, or at least published, and can hardly date from later than about 500 B.C.

Another work of the Sūtra type, and belonging to the Vedic period, is the Dharma Çāstra of VASISHṬHA. It has survived only in inferior MSS., and without the preserving influence of a commentary. It contains thirty chapters (*adhyāyas*), of which the last five appear to consist for the most part of late additions. Many of the Sūtras, not only here, but even in the older portions, are hopelessly corrupt. The prose aphorisms of the work are intermingled with verse, the archaic *trishṭubh* metre being frequently employed instead of the later *çlokas* of Manu and others. The contents, which bear the Dharma Sūtra stamp, produce the impression of antiquity in various respects. Thus here, as in the Dharma Sūtra of Āpastamba, only six forms of marriage are recognised, instead of the orthodox eight. Kumārila states that in his time Vasishṭha's law-book, while acknowledged to have general authority, was studied by followers of the *Rigveda* only. That he meant the present work and no other, is proved by the quotations from it which he gives, and which are found in the published text. As Vasishṭha, in citing Vedic Saṃhitās and Sūtras, shows a predilection for works belonging to the North of India, it is to be inferred that he or his school belonged to that part. Vasishṭha gives a quotation from Gautama which appears to refer to a passage in the extant text of the latter. His various quotations from Manu are derived, not from the later famous law-book, but evidently from a legal Sūtra related to our Manu. On the other hand, the extant text of Manu contains a quotation from Vasishṭha which actually occurs in the published edition of the latter. Hence Vasishṭha's work must be later than that of Gautama, and earlier than that of Manu. It is further probable that the original part of the Sūtra of a school connected with the *Rigveda* and belonging to the North dates from a period some centuries before our era.

Some Dharma Sūtras are known from quotations only, the oldest being those mentioned in other Dharma

Sūtras. Particular interest attaches to one of these, the Sūtra of Manu, or the Mānavas, because of its relationship to the famous *Mānava dharma-çāstra.* Of the numerous quotations from it in Vasishṭha, six are found unaltered or but slightly modified in our text of Manu. One passage cited in Vasishṭha is composed partly in prose and partly in verse, the latter portion recurring in Manu. The metrical quotations show a mixture of *trishṭubh* and *çloka* verses, like other Dharma Sūtras. These quoted fragments probably represent a *Mānava dharma-sūtra* which supplied the basis of our *Mānava dharma-çāstra* or *Code of Manu.*

Fragments of a legal treatise in prose and verse, attributed to the brothers Çankha and Likhita, who became proverbial for justice, have been similarly preserved. This work, which must have been extensive, and dealt with all branches of law, is already quoted as authoritative by Parāçara. The statement of Kumārila (700 A.D.) that it was connected with the Vājasaneyin school of the *White Yajurveda* is borne out by the quotations from it which have survived.

Sūtras need not necessarily go back to the oldest period of Indian law, as this style of composition was never entirely superseded by the use of metre. Thus there is a *Vaikhānasa dharma-sūtra* in four *praçnas*, which, as internal evidence shows, cannot be earlier than the third century A.D. It refers to the cult of Nārāyaṇa (Vishṇu), and mentions Wednesday by the name of *budha-vāra*, "day of Mercury." It is not a regular Dharma Sūtra, for it contains nothing connected with law in the strict sense, but is only a treatise on domestic law (*grihya-dharma*). It deals with the religious duties of the four orders (*āçramas*), especially with those of the forest hermit. For it is with the latter order that the Vaikhānasas, or followers of Vikhanas, are specially connected. They seem to have been one of the youngest offshoots of the Taittirīya school.

Looking back on the vast mass of ritual and usage regulated by the Sūtras, we are tempted to conclude that it was entirely the conscious work of an idle priesthood, invented to enslave and maintain in spiritual servitude the minds of the Hindu people. But the progress of research tends to show that the basis even of the sacerdotal ritual of the Brahmans was popular religious observances. Otherwise it would be hard to understand how Brahmanism acquired and retained such a hold on the population of India. The originality of the Brahmans consisted in elaborating and systematising observances which they already found in existence. This they certainly succeeded in doing to an extent unknown elsewhere.

Comparative studies have shown that many ritual practices go back to the period when the Indians and Persians were still one people. Thus the sacrifice was even then the centre of a developed ceremonial, and was tended by a priestly class. Many terms of the Vedic ritual already existed then, especially *soma*, which was pressed, purified through a sieve, mixed with milk, and offered as the main libation. Investiture with a sacred cord was, as we have seen, also known, and was in its turn based on the still older ceremony of the initiation of youths on entering manhood. The offering of gifts to the gods in fire is Indo-European, as is shown by the agreement of the Greeks, Romans, and Indians. Indo-European also is that part of the marriage ritual in which the newly wedded couple walk round the nuptial fire, the bridegroom presenting a burnt offering and the bride an offering of grain; for among the Romans also the young pair walked round the altar from left to right before offering bread (*far*) in the fire. Indo-European, too, must be the practice of scattering rice or grain (as a symbol of fertility) over the bride and bridegroom, as prescribed in the Sūtras; for it is widely diffused among peoples who cannot have borrowed it. Still older is the Indian ceremony of producing the sacrificial fire by the friction of two pieces of wood. Similarly the practice in the construction of the Indian fire-altar of walling up in the lowest layer of bricks the heads of five different victims, including that of a man, goes back to an ancient belief that a building can only be firmly erected when a man or an animal is buried with its foundations.

Finally, we have as a division of the Sūtras, concerned with religious practice, the Çulva Sūtras. The thirtieth and last *praçna* of the great Kalpa Sūtra of Āpastamba is a treatise of this class. These are practical manuals giving the measurements necessary for the construction of the *vedi*, of the altars, and so forth. They show quite an advanced knowledge of geometry, and constitute the oldest Indian mathematical works.

The whole body of Vedic works composed in the Sūtra style, is according to the Indian traditional view, divided into six classes called Vedāngas ("members of the Veda"). These are *çikshā*, or phonetics; *chhandas*, or metre; *vyākaraṇa*, or grammar; *nirukta*, or etymology; *kalpa*, or religious practice; and *jyotisha*, or astronomy. The first four were meant as aids to the correct reciting and understanding of the sacred texts; the last two deal with religious rites or duties, and their proper seasons. They all have their origin in the exigencies of religion, and the last four furnish the beginnings or (in one case) the full development of five branches of science that flourished in the post-Vedic period. In the fourth and sixth group the name of the class has been applied to designate a particular work representing it.

Of *kalpa* we have already treated at length above. No work representing astronomy has survived from the Vedic period; for the Vedic calendar, called *jyotisha*, the two recensions of which profess to belong to the *Rigveda* and *Yajurveda* respectively, dates from far on in the post-Vedic age.

The *Taittirīya Āraṇyaka* (vii. 1) already mentions *çikshā*, or phonetics, a subject which even then appears to have dealt with letters, accents, quantity, pronunciation, and euphonic rules. Several works bearing the title of *çikshā* have been preserved, but they are only late supplements of Vedic literature. They are short manuals containing directions for Vedic recitation and correct pronunciation. The earliest surviving results of phonetic studies are of course the Saṃhitā texts of the various Vedas, which were edited in accordance with euphonic rules. A further advance was made by the constitution of the *pada-pāṭha*, or word-text of the Vedas, which, by resolving the euphonic combinations and giving each word (even the parts of compounds) separately, in its original form unmodified by phonetic rules, furnished a basis for all subsequent studies. Yāska, Pāṇini, and other grammarians do not always accept the analyses of the *Padapāṭhas* when they think they understand a Vedic form better. Patanjali even directly contests their authoritativeness. The treatises really representative of Vedic phonetics are the Prātiçākhyas, which are directly connected with the *Saṃhitā* and

Padapāṭha. It is their object to determine the relation of these to each other. In so doing they furnish a systematic account of Vedic euphonic combination, besides adding phonetic discussions to secure the correct recitation of the sacred texts. They are generally regarded as anterior to Pāṇini, who shows unmistakable points of contact with them. It is perhaps more correct to suppose that Pāṇini used the present Prātiçākhyas in an older form, as, whenever he touches on Vedic *sandhi*, he is always less complete in his statements than they are, while the Prātiçākhyas, especially that of the *Atharva-veda*, are dependent on the terminology of the grammarians. Four of these treatises have been preserved and published. One belongs to the *Rigveda*, another to the *Atharva-*, and two to the *Yajur-veda*, being attached to the *Vājasaneyi* and the *Taittirīya Saṃhitā* respectively. They are so called because intended for the use of each respective branch (*çākhā*) of the Vedas.

The *Prātiçākhya Sūtra* of the *Rigveda* is an extensive metrical work in three books, traditionally attributed to Çaunaka, the teacher of Āçvalāyana; it may, however, in its present form only be a production of the school of Çaunaka. This Prātiçākhya was later epitomised, with the addition of some supplementary matter, in a short treatise entitled *Upalekha.* The *Taittirīya Prātiçākhya* is particularly interesting owing to the various peculiar names of teachers occurring among the twenty which it mentions. The *Vājasaneyi Prātiçākhya*, in eight chapters, names Kātyāyana as its author, and mentions Çaunaka among other predecessors. The *Atharva-veda Prātiçākhya*, in four chapters, belonging to the school of the Çaunakas, is more grammatical than the other works of this class.

Metre, to which there are many scattered references in the Brāhmaṇas, is separately treated in a section of the *Çānkhāyana Çrauta Sūtra* (7, 27), in the last three sections (*paṭalas*) of the *Rigveda Prātiçākhya*, and especially in the *Nidāna Sūtra*, which belongs to the *Sāmaveda*. A part of the *Chhandaḥ Sūtra* of Pingala also deals with Vedic metres; but though it claims to be a Vedānga, it is in reality a late supplement, dealing chiefly with post-Vedic prosody, on which, indeed, it is the standard authority.

Finally, Kātyāyana's two Anukramaṇīs or indices, mentioned below, each contains a section, varying but slightly from the other, on Vedic metres. These sections are, however, almost identical in matter with the sixteenth *paṭala* of the *Rigveda Prātiçākhya*, and may possibly be older than the corresponding passage in the *Prātiçākhya*, though the latter work as a whole is doubtless anterior to the *Anukramaṇī*.

The *Padapāṭhas* show that their authors had not only made investigations as to pronunciation and *Sandhi*, but already knew a good deal about the grammatical analysis of words; for they separate both the parts of compounds and the prefixes of verbs, as well as certain suffixes and terminations of nouns. They had doubtless already distinguished the four parts of speech (*padajātāni*), though these are first mentioned by Yāska as *nāman*, or "noun" (including *sarva-nāman*, "representing all nouns" or "pronouns"), *ākhyāta*, "predicate," *i.e.* "verb"; *upasarga*, "supplement," *i.e.* "preposition"; *nipāta*, "incidental addition," *i.e.* "particle." It is perhaps to the separation of these categories that the name for grammar, *vyākaraṇa*, originally referred, rather than to the analysis of words. Even the Brāhmaṇas bear evidence of linguistic investigations, for they mention various grammatical terms, such as "letter" (*varṇa*), "masculine" (*vṛishan*), "number" (*vachana*), "case-form" (*vibhakti*). Still more such references are to be found in the Āraṇyakas, the Upanishads, and the Sūtras. But the most important information we have of pre-Pāṇinean grammar is that found in Yāska's work.

Grammatical studies must have been cultivated to a considerable extent before Yāska's time, for he distinguishes a Northern and an Eastern school, besides mentioning nearly twenty predecessors, among whom Çākaṭāyana, Gārgya, and Çākalya are the most important. By the time of Yāska grammarians had learned to distinguish clearly between the stem and the formative elements of words; recognising the personal terminations and the tense affixes of the verb on the one hand, and primary (*kṛit*) or secondary (*taddhita*) nominal suffixes on the other. Yāska has an interesting discussion on the theory of Çākaṭāyana, which he himself follows, that nouns are derived from verbs. Gārgya and some other grammarians, he shows, admit this theory in a general way, but deny that it is applicable to all nouns. He criticises their objections, and finally dismisses them as untenable. On Çākaṭāyana's theory of the verbal origin of nouns the whole system of Pāṇini is founded. The sūtra of that grammarian contains hundreds of rules dealing with Vedic forms; but these are of the nature of exceptions to the main body of his rules, which are meant to describe the Sanskrit language. His work almost entirely dominates the subsequent literature. Though belonging to the middle of the Sūtra period, it must be regarded as the definite starting-point of the post-Vedic age. Coming to be regarded as an infallible authority, Pāṇini superseded all his predecessors, whose works have consequently perished. Yāska alone survives, and that only because he was not directly a grammarian; for his work represents, and alone represents, the Vedānga "etymology."

Yāska's *Nirukta* is in reality a Vedic commentary, and is older by some centuries than any other exegetical work preserved in Sanskrit. Its bases are the *Nighaṇṭus*, collections of rare or obscure Vedic words, arranged for the use of teachers. Yāska had before him five such collections. The first three contain groups of synonyms, the fourth specially difficult words, and the fifth a classification of the Vedic gods. These Yāska explained for the most part in the twelve books of his commentary (to which two others were added later). In so doing he adduces as examples a large number of verses, chiefly from the *Rigveda*, which he interprets with many etymological remarks.

The first book is an introduction, dealing with the principles of grammar and exegesis. The second and third elucidate certain points in the synonymous *nighaṇṭus;* Books IV.–VI. comment on the fourth section, and VII.–XII. on the fifth. The *Nirukta*, besides being very important from the point of view of exegesis and grammar, is highly interesting as the earliest specimen of Sanskrit prose of the classical type, considerably earlier than Pāṇini himself. Yāska already uses essentially the same grammatical terminology as Pāṇini, employing, for instance, the same words for root (*dhātu*), primary, and secondary suffixes. But he must have lived a long time before Pāṇini; for a considerable number of important grammarians' names are mentioned between them. Yāska must, therefore, go back to the fifth century, and undoubtedly belongs to the beginning of the Sūtra period.

One point of very great importance proved by the *Nirukta* is that the *Rigveda* had a very fixed form in Yāska's time, and was essentially identical with our text. His deviations are very insignificant. Thus in one passage (X. 29. 1) he reads *vāyó* as one word, against *vā yó* as two words in Çākalya's Pada text. Yāska's paraphrases show that he also occasionally differed from the Saṃhitā text, though the quotations themselves from the *Rigveda* have been corrected so as to agree absolutely with the traditional text. But these slight variations are probably due to mistakes in the *Nirukta* rather than to varieties of reading in the *Rigveda*. There are a few insignificant deviations of this kind even in Sāyaṇa, but they are always manifestly oversights on the part of the commentator.

To the Sūtras is attached a very extensive literature of *Pariçishṭas* or "supplements," which seem to have existed in all the Vedic schools. They contain details on matters only touched upon in the Sūtras, or supplementary information about subjects not dealt with at all by them. Thus, there is the *Āçvalāyana Gṛihya-pariçishṭa*, in four chapters, connected with the *Rigveda*. The *Gobhila saṃgraha-pariçishṭa* is a compendium of Gṛihya practices in general, with a special leaning towards magical rites, which came to be attached to the *Sāmaveda*. Closely related to, and probably later than this work, is the *Karma-pradīpa* ("lamp of rites"), also variously called *sāma-gṛihya-* or *chhāndogyagṛihya-pariçishṭa*, *chhandoga-pariçishṭa*, *Gobhila-smṛiti*, attributed to the Kātyāyana of the *White Yajurveda* or to Gobhila. It deals with the same subjects, though independently, as the *Gṛihya saṃgraha*, with which it occasionally agrees in whole *çlokas*.

Of great importance for the understanding of the sacrificial ceremonial are the Prayogas ("Manuals") and Paddhatis ("Guides"), of which a vast number exist in manuscript. These works represent both the Çrauta and the Gṛihya ritual according to the various schools. The Prayogas describe the course of each sacrifice and the functions of the different groups of priests, solely from the point of view of practical performance, while the Paddhatis rather follow the systematic accounts of the Sūtras and sketch their contents. There are also versified accounts of the ritual called *Kārikās*, which are directly attached to Sūtras or to Paddhatis. The oldest of them appears to be the *Kārikā* of Kumārila (c. 700 A.D.).

Of a supplementary character are also the class of writings called Anukramaṇīs or Vedic Indices, which give lists of the hymns, the authors, the metres, and the deities in the order in which they occur in the various Saṃhitās. To the *Rigveda* belonged seven of these works, all attributed to Çaunaka, and composed in the mixture of the *çloka* and *trishṭubh* metre, which is also found in Çaunaka's *Rigveda Prātiçākhya*. There is also a General Index or *Sarvānukramaṇī* which is attributed to Kātyāyana, and epitomises in the Sūtra style the contents of the metrical indices. Of the metrical indices five have been preserved. The *Ārshānukramaṇī*, containing rather less than 300 *çlokas*, gives a list of the Rishis or authors of the *Rigveda*. Its present text represents a modernised form of that which was known to the commentator Shaḍguruçishya in the twelfth century. The *Chhandonukramaṇī*, which is of almost exactly the same length, enumerates the metres in which the hymns of the *Rigveda* are composed. It also states for each book the number of verses in each metre as well as the aggregate in all metres. The *Anuvākānukramaṇī* is a short index containing only about forty verses. It states the initial words of each of the eighty-five *anuvākas* or lessons into which the *Rigveda* is divided, and the number of hymns contained in these *anuvākas*. It further states that the *Rigveda* contains 1017 hymns (or 1025 according to the Vāshkala recension), 10,580½ verses, 153,826 words, 432,000 syllables, besides some other statistical details. The number of verses given does not exactly tally with various calculations that have recently been made, but the differences are only slight, and may be due to the way in which certain repeated verses were counted by the author of the index.

There is another short index, known as yet only in two MSS., called the *Pādānukramaṇī*, or "index of lines" (*pādas*), and composed in the same mixed metre as the others. The *Sūktānukramaṇī*, which has not survived, and is only known by name, probably consisted only of the initial words (*pratīkas*) of the hymns. It probably perished because the *Sarvānukramaṇī* would have rendered such a work superfluous. No MS. of the *Devatānukramaṇī* or "Index of gods" exists, but ten quotations from it have been preserved by the commentator Shaḍguruçishya. It must have been superseded by the *Bṛihaddevatā*, an index of the "many gods," a much more extensive work than any of the other Anukramaṇīs, as it contains about 1200 *çlokas* interspersed with occasional *trishṭubhs*. It is divided into eight *adhyāyas* corresponding to the *ashṭakas* of the *Rigveda*. Following the order of the *Rigveda*, its main object is to state the deity for each verse. But as it contains a large number of illustrative myths and legends, it is of great value as an early collection of stories. It is to a considerable extent based on Yāska's *Nirukta*. Besides Yāska himself and other teachers named by that scholar, it also mentions Bhāguri and Āçvalāyana as well as the *Nidāna Sūtra*. A peculiarity of this work is that it refers to a number of supplementary hymns (*khilas*) which do not form part of the canonical text of the *Rigveda*.

Later, at least, than the original form of these metrical Anukramaṇīs, is the *Sarvānukramaṇī* of KĀTYĀYANA, which combines the data contained in them within the compass of a single work. Composed in the Sūtra style, it is of considerable length, occupying about forty-six pages in the printed edition. For every hymn in the *Rigveda* it states the initial word or words, the number of its verses, as well as the author, the deity, and the metre, even for single verses. There is an introduction in twelve sections, nine of which form a short treatise on Vedic metres corresponding to the last three sections of the *Rigveda Prātiçākhya*. The author begins with the statement that he is going to supply an index of the *pratīkas* and so forth of the *Rigveda* according to the authorities (*yathopadeçam*), because without such knowledge the Çrauta and Smārta rites cannot be accomplished. These authorities are doubtless the metrical indices described above. For the text of the *Sarvānukramaṇī*, which is composed in a concise Sūtra style, not only contains some metrical lines (*pādas*), but also a number of passages either directly taken from the *Ārshānukramaṇī* and the *Bṛihaddevatā*, or with their metrical wording but slightly altered. Another metrical work attributed to Çaunaka is the *Ṛigvidhāna*, which describes the magical effects produced by the recitation of hymns or single verses of the *Rigveda*.

To the Pariçishṭas of the *Sāmaveda* belong the two indices called *Ārsha* and *Daivata*, enumerating respectively the Rishis and deities of the text of the Naigeya branch of the *Sāmaveda*. They quote Yāska, Çaunaka, and Āçvalāyana among others. There are also two Anukramaṇīs attached to the *Black Yajurveda*. That of the Ātreya school consists of two parts, the first of which is in prose, and the second in *çlokas*. It contains little more than an enumeration of names referring to the contents of its Saṃhitā. The Anukramaṇī of the Chārāyaṇīya school of the *Kāṭhaka* is an index of the authors of the various sections and verses. Its statements regarding passages derived from the *Rigveda* differ much from those of the *Sarvānukramaṇī* of the *Rigveda*, giving a number of totally new names. It claims to be the work of Atri, who communicated it to Laugākshi. The *Anukramaṇī* of the *White Yajurveda* in the Mādhyaṃdina recension, attributed to Kātyāyana, consists of five sections. The first four are an index of authors, deities, and metres. The authors of verses taken from the *Rigveda* generally agree with those in the *Sarvānukramaṇī*. There are, however, a good many exceptions, several new names belonging to a later period, some even to that of the *Çatapatha Brāhmaṇa*. The fifth section gives a summary account of the metres occurring in the text. It is identical with the corresponding portion of the introduction to the *Sarvānukramaṇī*, which was probably the original position of the section. There are many other Pariçishṭas of the *White Yajurveda*, all attributed to Kātyāyana. Only three of these need be mentioned here. The *Nigama-pariçishṭa*, a glossary of synonymous words occurring in the *White Yajurveda*, has a lexicographical interest. The *Pravarādhyāya*, or "Chapter on Ancestors," is a list of Brahman families drawn up for the purpose of determining the forbidden degrees of relationship in marriage, and of indicating the priests suitable for the performance of sacrifice. The *Charaṇa-vyūha*, or "Exposition of the Schools" of the various Vedas, is a very late work of little importance, giving a far less complete enumeration of the Vedic schools than certain sections of the *Vishṇu-* and the *Vāyu-Purāṇa*. There is also a *Charaṇa-vyūha* among the Pariçishṭas of the *Atharva-veda*, which number upwards of seventy. This work makes the statement that the *Atharva* contains 2000 hymns and 12,380 verses.

In concluding this account of Vedic literature, I cannot omit to say a few words about SĀYAṆA, the great mediæval Vedic scholar, to whom or to whose initiation we owe a number of valuable commentaries on the *Rig-veda*, the *Aitareya Brāhmaṇa* and *Āraṇyaka*, as well as the *Taittirīya Saṃhitā*, *Brāhmaṇa*, and *Āraṇyaka*, besides a number of other works. His comments on the two Saṃhitās would appear to have been only partially composed by himself and to have been completed by his pupils. He died in 1387, having written his works under Bukka I. (1350–79), whose teacher and minister he calls himself, and his successor, Harihara (1379–99). These princes belonged to a family which, throwing off the Muhammadan yoke in the earlier half of the fourteenth century, founded the dynasty of Vijayanagara ("city of victory"), now Hampi, on the Tungabhadrā, in the Bellary district. Sāyaṇa's elder brother, Mādhava, was minister of King

Bukka, and died as abbot of the monastery of Çṛingeri, under the name of Vidyāraṇyasvāmin. Not only did he too produce works of his own, but Sāyaṇa's commentaries, as composed under his patronage, were dedicated to him as *mādhavīya*, or ("influenced by Mādhava"). By an interesting coincidence Professor Max Müller's second edition of the *Rigveda*, with the commentary of Sāyaṇa, was brought out under the auspices of a Mahārāja of Vijayanagara. The latter city has, however, nothing to do with that from which King Bukka derived his title.

CHAPTER X

THE EPICS

(*Circa* 500–50 B.C.)

In turning from the Vedic to the Sanskrit period, we are confronted with a literature which is essentially different from that of the earlier age in matter, spirit, and form. Vedic literature is essentially religious; Sanskrit literature, abundantly developed in every other direction, is profane. But, doubtless as a result of the speculative tendencies of the Upanishads, a moralising spirit at the same time breathes through it as a whole. The religion itself which now prevails is very different from that of the Vedic age. For in the new period the three great gods, Brahmā, Vishṇu, and Çiva are the chief objects of worship. The important deities of the Veda have sunk to a subordinate position, though Indra is still relatively prominent as the chief of a warrior's heaven. Some new gods of lesser rank have arisen, such as Kubera, god of wealth; Gaṇeça, god of learning; Kārttikeya, god of war; Çrī or Lakshmī, goddess of beauty and fortune; Durgā or Pārvatī, the terrible spouse of Çiva; besides the serpent deities and several classes of demigods and demons.

While the spirit of Vedic literature, at least in its earlier phase, is optimistic, Sanskrit poetry is pervaded by *Weltschmerz*, resulting from the now universally accepted doctrine of transmigration. To that doctrine, according to which beings pass by gradations from Brahmā through men and animals to the lowest forms of existence, is doubtless also largely due the fantastic element characteristic of this later poetry. Here, for instance, we read of Vishṇu coming down to earth in the shape of animals, of sages and saints wandering between heaven and earth, of human kings visiting Indra in heaven.

Hand in hand with this fondness for introducing the marvellous and supernatural into the description of human events goes a tendency to exaggeration. Thus King Viçvāmitra, we are told, practised penance for thousands of years in succession; and the power of asceticism is described as so great as to cause even the worlds and the gods to tremble. The very bulk of the *Mahābhārata*, consisting as it does of more than 200,000 lines, is a concrete illustration of this defective sense of proportion.

As regards the form in which it is presented to us, Sanskrit literature contrasts with that of both the earlier and the later Vedic period. While prose was employed in the Yajurvedas and the Brāhmaṇas, and finally attained to a certain degree of development, it almost disappears in Sanskrit, nearly every branch of literature being treated in verse, often much to the detriment of the subject, as in the case of law. The only departments almost entirely restricted to the use of prose are grammar and philosophy, but the cramped and enigmatical style in which these subjects are treated hardly deserves the name of prose at all. Literary prose is found only in fables, fairy tales, romances, and partially in the drama. In consequence of this neglect, the prose of the later period compares unfavourably with that of the Brāhmaṇas. Even the style of the romances or prose *kāvyas*, subject as it is to the strict rules of poetics, is as clumsy as that of the grammatical commentaries; for the use of immense compounds, like those of the Sūtras, is one of its essential characteristics.

Sanskrit literature, then, resembles that of the earlier Vedic age in being almost entirely metrical. But the metres in which it is written, though nearly all based on those of the Veda, are different. The bulk of the literature is composed in the *çloka*, a development of the Vedic *anushṭubh* stanza of four octosyllabic lines; but while all four lines ended iambically in the prototype, the first and third line have in the *çloka* acquired a trochaic rhythm. The numerous other metres employed in the classical poetry have become much more elaborate than their Vedic originals by having the quantity of every syllable in the line strictly determined.

The style, too, excepting the two old epics, is in Sanskrit poetry made more artificial by the frequent use of long compounds, as well as by the application of the elaborate rules of poetics, while the language is regulated by the grammar of Pāṇini. Thus classical Sanskrit literature, teeming as it does with fantastic and exaggerated ideas, while bound by the strictest rules of form, is like a tropical garden full of luxuriant and rank growth, in which, however, many a fair flower of true poetry may be culled.

It is impossible even for the Sanskrit scholar who has not lived in India to appreciate fully the merits of this later poetry, much more so for those who can only become acquainted with it in translations. For, in the first place, the metres, artificial and elaborate though they are, have a beauty of their own which cannot be reproduced in other languages. Again, to understand it thoroughly, the reader must have seen the tropical plains and forests of Hindustan steeped in intense sunshine or bathed in brilliant moonlight; he must have viewed the silent ascetic seated at the foot of the sacred fig-tree; he must have experienced the feelings inspired by the approach of the monsoon; he must have watched beast and bird disporting themselves in tank and river; he must know the varying aspects of Nature in the different seasons; in short, he must be acquainted with all the sights and sounds of an Indian landscape, the mere allusion to one of which may call up some familiar scene or touch some chord of sentiment. Otherwise, for instance, the mango-tree, the red Açoka, the orange Kadamba, the various creepers, the different kinds of lotus, the mention of each of which should convey a vivid picture, are but empty names. Without a knowledge, moreover, of the habits, modes of thought, and traditions of the people, much must remain meaningless. But those who are properly equipped can see many beauties in classical Sanskrit poetry which are entirely lost to others. Thus a distinguished scholar known to the present writer has entered so fully into the spirit of that poetry, that he is unable to derive pleasure from any other.

It would be a mistake to suppose that Sanskrit literature came into being only at the close of the Vedic period, or that it merely forms its continuation and development. As a profane literature, it must, in its earliest phases, which are lost, have been contemporaneous with the religious literature of the Vedas. Beside the productions of the latest Vedic period, that of the Upanishads and Sūtras, there grew up, on the one hand, the rich

Pāli literature of Buddhism, and, on the other, the earliest form of Sanskrit poetry in the shape of epic tales. We have seen that even the *Rigveda* contains some hymns of a narrative character. Later we find in the Brāhmaṇas a number of short legends, mostly in prose, but sometimes partly metrical, as the story of Çunaḥçepa in the *Aitareya*. Again, the *Nirukta*, which must date from the fifth century B.C., contains many prose tales, and the oldest existing collection of Vedic legend, the metrical *Bṛihaddevatā*, cannot belong to a much later time.

Sanskrit epic poetry falls into two main classes. That which comprises old stories goes by the name of *Itihāsa*, "legend," *Ākhyāna*, "narrative," or *Purāṇa*, "ancient tale," while the other is called *Kāvya* or artificial epic. The *Mahābhārata* is the chief and oldest representative of the former group, the *Rāmāyaṇa* of the latter. Both these great epics are composed in the same form of the *çloka* metre as that employed in classical Sanskrit poetry. The *Mahābhārata*, however, also contains, as remnants of an older phase, archaic verses in the *upajāti* and *vaṃçastha* (developments of the Vedic *trishṭubh* and *jagatī*) metres, besides preserving some old prose stories in what is otherwise an entirely metrical work. It further differs from the sister epic in introducing speeches with words, such as "Bṛihadaçva spake," which do not form part of the verse, and which may be survivals of prose narrative connecting old epic songs. The *Rāmāyaṇa*, again, is, in the main, the work of a single poet, homogeneous in plan and execution, composed in the east of India. The *Mahābhārata*, arising in the western half of the country, is a congeries of parts, the only unity about which is the connectedness of the epic cycle with which they deal; its epic kernel, moreover, which forms only about one-fifth of the whole work, has become so overgrown with didactic matter, that in its final shape it is not an epic at all, but an encyclopædia of moral teaching.

The *Mahābhārata*, which in its present form consists of over 100,000 *çlokas*, equal to about eight times as much as the Iliad and Odyssey put together, is by far the longest poem known to literary history. It is a conglomerate of epic and didactic matter divided into eighteen books called *parvan*, with a nineteenth, the *Harivaṃça*, as a supplement. The books vary very considerably in length, the twelfth being the longest, with nearly 14,000, the seventeenth the shortest, with only 312 *çlokas*. All the eighteen books, excepting the eighth and the last three, are divided into subordinate *parvans*; each book is also cut up into chapters (*adhyāyas*).

No European edition of the whole epic has yet been undertaken. This remains one of the great tasks reserved for the future of Sanskrit philology, and can only be accomplished by the collaboration of several scholars. There are complete MSS. of the *Mahābhārata* in London, Oxford, Paris, and Berlin, besides many others in different parts of India; while the number of MSS. containing only parts of the poem can hardly be counted.

Three main editions of the epic have appeared in India. The *editio princeps*, including the *Harivaṃça*, but without any commentary, was published in four volumes at Calcutta in 1834–39. Another and better edition, which has subsequently been reproduced several times, was printed at Bombay in 1863. This edition, though not including the supplementary book, contains the commentary of Nīlakaṇṭha. These two editions do not on the whole differ considerably. Being derived from a common source, they represent one and the same recension. The Bombay edition, however, generally has the better readings. It contains about 200 *çlokas* more than the Calcutta edition, but these additions are of no importance.

A third edition, printed in Telugu characters, was published in four volumes at Madras in 1855–60. It includes the *Harivaṃça* and extracts from Nīlakaṇṭha's commentary. This edition represents a distinct South Indian recension, which seems to differ from that of the North about as much as the three recensions of the *Rāmāyaṇa* do from one another. Both recensions are of about equal length, omissions in the first being compensated by others in the second. Sometimes one has the better text, sometimes the other.

The epic kernel of the *Mahābhārata*, or the "Great Battle of the descendants of Bharata," consisting of about 20,000 *çlokas*, describes the eighteen days' fight between Duryodhana, leader of the Kurus, and Yudhishṭhira, chief of the Pāṇḍus, who were cousins, both descended from King Bharata, son of Çakuntalā. Within this narrative frame has come to be included a vast number of old legends about gods, kings, and sages; accounts of cosmogony and theogony; disquisitions on philosophy, law, religion, and the duties of the military caste. These lengthy and heterogeneous interpolations render it very difficult to follow the thread of the narrative. Entire works are sometimes inserted to illustrate a particular statement. Thus, while the two armies are drawn up prepared for battle, a whole philosophical poem, in eighteen cantos, the *Bhagavad-*

gītā, is recited to the hero Arjuna, who hesitates to advance and fight against his kin. Hence the *Mahābhārata* claims to be not only a heroic poem (*kāvya*), but a compendium teaching, in accordance with the Veda, the fourfold end of human existence (spiritual merit, wealth, pleasure, and salvation), a *smṛiti* or work of sacred tradition, which expounds the whole duty of man, and is intended for the religious instruction of all Hindus. Thus, in one (I. lxii. 35) of many similar passages, it makes the statement about itself that "this collection of all sacred texts, in which the greatness of cows and Brahmans is exalted, must be listened to by virtuous-minded men." Its title, *Kārshṇa Veda*, or "Veda of Kṛishṇa" (a form of Vishṇu), the occurrence of a famous invocation of Nārāyaṇa and Nara (names of Vishṇu) and Sarasvatī (Vishṇu's wife) at the beginning of each of its larger sections, and the prevalence of Vishnuite doctrines throughout the work, prove it to have been a *smṛiti* of the ancient Vishnuite sect of the Bhāgavatas.

Thus it is clear that the *Mahābhārata* in its present shape contains an epic nucleus, that it favours the worship of Vishṇu, and that it has become a comprehensive didactic work. We further find in Book I. the direct statements that the poem at one time contained 24,000 *çlokas* before the episodes (*upākhyāna*) were added, that it originally consisted of only 8800 *çlokas*, and that it has three beginnings. These data render it probable that the epic underwent three stages of development from the time it first assumed definite shape; and this conclusion is corroborated by various internal and external arguments.

There can be little doubt that the original kernel of

the epic has as a historical background an ancient conflict between the two neighbouring tribes of the Kurus and Panchālas, who finally coalesced into a single people. In the Yajurvedas these two tribes already appear united, and in the *Kāṭhaka* King Dhṛitarāshṭra Vaichitravīrya, one of the chief figures of the *Mahābhārata*, is mentioned as a well-known person. Hence the historical germ of the great epic is to be traced to a very early period, which cannot well be later than the tenth century B.C. Old songs about the ancient feud and the heroes who played a part in it, must have been handed down by word of mouth and recited in popular assemblies or at great public sacrifices.

These disconnected battle-songs were, we must assume, worked up by some poetic genius into a comparatively short epic, describing the tragic fate of the Kuru race, who, with justice and virtue on their side, perished through the treachery of the victorious sons of Pāṇḍu, with Kṛishṇa at their head. To the period of this original epic doubtless belong the traces the *Mahābhārata* has preserved unchanged of the heroic spirit and the customs of ancient times, so different from the later state of things which the *Mahābhārata* as a whole reflects. To this period also belongs the figure of Brahmā as the highest god. The evidence of Pāli literature shows that Brahmā already occupied that position in Buddha's time. We may, then, perhaps assume that the original form of our epic came into being about the fifth century B.C. The oldest evidence we have for the existence of the *Mahābhārata* in some shape or other is to be found in Āçvalāyana's Gṛihya Sūtra, where a *Bhārata* and *Mahābhārata* are mentioned. This would also point to about the fifth century B.C.

To the next stage, in which the epic, handed down by rhapsodists, swelled to a length of about 20,000 *çlokas*, belongs the representation of the victorious Pāṇḍus in a favourable light, and the introduction on a level with Brahmā of the two other great gods, Çiva, and especially Vishṇu, of whom Kṛishṇa appears as an incarnation.

We gather from the account of Megasthenes that about 300 B.C., these two gods were already prominent, and the people were divided into Çivaites and Vishnuites. Moreover, the Yavanas or Greeks are mentioned in the *Mahābhārata* as allies of the Kurus, and even the Çakas (Scythians) and Pahlavas (Parthians) are named along with them; Hindu temples are also referred to as well as Buddhist relic mounds. Thus an extension of the original epic must have taken place after 300 B.C. and by the beginning of our era.

The Brahmans knew how to utilise the great influence of the old epic tradition by gradually incorporating didactic matter calculated to impress upon the people, and especially on kings, the doctrines of the priestly caste. It thus at last assumed the character of a vast treatise on duty (*dharma*), in which the divine origin and immutability of Brahman institutions, the eternity of the caste system, and the subordination of all to the priests, are laid down. When the *Mahābhārata* attributes its origin to Vyāsa, it implies a belief in a final redaction, for the name simply means "Arranger." Dahlmann has recently put forward the theory that the great epic was a didactic work from the very outset; this view, however, appears to be quite irreconcilable with the data of the poem, and is not likely to find any support among scholars.

What evidence have we as to when the *Mahābhārata* attained to the form in which we possess it? There is an inscription in a land grant dating from 462 A.D. or at the latest 532 A.D., which proves incontrovertibly that the epic about 500 A.D. was practically of exactly the same length as it is stated to have in the survey of contents (*anukramaṇikā*) given in Book I., and as it actually has now; for it contains the following words: "It has been declared in the *Mahābhārata*, the compilation embracing 100,000 verses, by the highest sage, Vyāsa, the Vyāsa of the Vedas, the son of Parāçara." This quotation at the same time proves that the epic at that date included the very long 12th and 13th, as well as the extensive supplementary book, the *Harivaṃça*, without any one of which it would have been impossible to speak even approximately of 100,000 verses. There are also several land grants, dated between 450 and 500 A.D., and found in various parts of India, which quote the *Mahābhārata* as an authority teaching the rewards of pious donors and the punishments of impious despoilers. This shows that in the middle of the fifth century it already possessed the same character as at present, that of a Smṛiti or Dharmaçāstra. It is only reasonable to suppose that it had acquired this character at least a century earlier, or by about 350 A.D. Further research in the writings of the Northern Buddhists and their dated Chinese translations will probably enable us to put this date back by some centuries. We are already justified in considering it likely that the great epic had become a didactic compendium before the beginning of our era. In any case, the present state of our knowledge entirely disproves the suggestions put forward by Prof. Holtzmann in his work on the *Mahābhārata*, that the epic was turned into a Dharmaçāstra by the Brahmans after 900 A.D., and that whole books were added at this late period.

The literary evidence of Sanskrit authors from about 600 to 1100 A.D. supplies us with a considerable amount of information as to the state of the great epic during those five centuries. An examination of the works of Bāṇa, and of his predecessor Subandhu, shows that these authors, who belong to the beginning of the seventh century, not only studied and made use of legends from every one of the eighteen books of the *Mahābhārata* for the poetical embellishment of their works, but were even acquainted with the *Harivaṃça*. We also know that in Bāṇa's time the *Bhagavadgītā* was included in the great epic. The same writer mentions that the *Mahābhārata* was recited in the temple of Mahākāla at Ujjain. That such recitation was already a widespread practice at that time is corroborated by an inscription of about 600 A.D. from the remote Indian colony of Kamboja, which states that copies of the *Mahābhārata*, as well as of the *Rāmāyaṇa* and of an unnamed Purāṇa, were presented to a temple there, and that the donor had made arrangements to ensure their daily recitation in perpetuity. This evidence shows that the *Mahābhārata* cannot have been a mere heroic poem, but must have borne the character of a Smṛiti work of long-established authority. Even at the present day both public and private recitations of the Epics and Purāṇas are common in India, and are always instituted for the edification and religious instruction of worshippers in temples or of members of the family. As a rule, the Sanskrit texts are not only declaimed, but also explained in the vernacular tongue for the benefit both of women, and of such males as belong to classes unacquainted with the learned language of the Brahmans.

We next come to the eminent Mīmāṃsā philosopher KUMĀRILA, who has been proved to have flourished in the first half of the eighth century A.D. In the small portion of his great commentary, entitled *Tantra-vārttika*, which has been examined, no fewer than ten of the eighteen books of the *Mahābhārata* are named, quoted, or referred to. It is clear that the epic as known to him not only included the first book (*ādiparvan*), but that that book in his time closely resembled the form of its text which we possess. It even appears to have contained the first section, called *anukramaṇikā* or "Survey of contents," and the second, entitled *parva-saṃgraha* or "Synopsis of sections." Kumārila also knew Books XII. and XIII., which have frequently been pronounced to be of late origin, as well as XIX. It is evident from his treatment of the epic that he regarded it as a work of sacred tradition and of great antiquity, intended from the beginning for the instruction of all the four castes. To him it is not an account of the great war between the Kauravas and Pāṇḍus; the descriptions of battles were only used for the purpose of rousing the martial instincts of the warrior caste.

The great Vedāntist philosopher Çankarāchārya, who wrote his commentary in 804 A.D., often quotes the *Mahābhārata* as a Smṛiti, and in discussing a verse from Book XII. expressly states that the *Mahābhārata* was intended for the religious instruction of those classes who by their position are debarred from studying the Vedas and the Vedānta.

From the middle of the eleventh century A.D. we have the oldest known abstract of the *Mahābhārata*, the work of the Kashmirian poet KSHEMENDRA, entitled *Bhārata-Manjarī*. This condensation is specially important, because it enables the scholar to determine the state of the text in detail at that time. Professor Bühler's careful comparison of the MSS. of this work with the great epic has led him to the conclusion that Kshemendra's original did not differ from the *Mahābhārata* as we have it at present in any other way than two classes of MSS. differ from each other. This poetical epitome shows several omissions, but these are on the whole of such a nature as is to be expected in any similar abridgment. It is, however, likely that twelve chapters (342–353) of Book XII., treating of Nārāyaṇa, which the abbreviator passes over, did not exist in the original known to him. There can, moreover, be no doubt that the forms of several proper names found in the *Manjarī* are better and older than those given by the editions of the *Mahābhārata*. Though the division of the original into eighteen books is found in the abridgment also, it is made up by turning the third section (*gadā-parvan*) of Book IX. (*çalya-parvan*) into a separate book, while combining Books XII. and XIII. into a single one. This variation probably represents an old division, as it occurs in many MSS. of the *Mahābhārata*.

Another work of importance in determining the state of the *Mahābhārata* is a Javanese translation of the epic, also dating from the eleventh century.

The best-known commentator of the *Mahābhārata* is NĪLAKAṆṬHA, who lived at Kūrpara, to the west of the Godāvarī, in Mahārāshṭra, and, according to Burnell, belongs to the sixteenth century. Older than Nīlakaṇṭha, who quotes him, is ARJUNA MIÇRA, whose commentary, along with that of Nīlakaṇṭha, appears in an edition of the *Mahābhārata* begun at Calcutta in 1875. The earliest extant commentator of the great epic is SARVAJNA NĀRĀYAṆA, large fragments of whose notes have been preserved, and who cannot have written later than in the second half of the fourteenth century, but may be somewhat older.

The main story of the *Mahābhārata* in the briefest possible outline is as follows: In the country of the Bharatas, which, from the name of the ruling race, had come to be called Kurukshetra, or "Land of the Kurus," there lived at Hastināpura, fifty-seven miles north-east of the modern Delhi, two princes named Dhṛitarāshṭra and Pāṇḍu. The elder of these brothers being blind, Pāṇḍu succeeded to the throne and reigned gloriously. He had five sons called Pāṇḍavas, the chief of whom were Yudhishṭhira, Bhīma, and Arjuna. Dhṛitarāshṭra had a hundred sons, usually called Kauravas, or Kuru princes, the most prominent of whom was Duryodhana. On the premature death of Pāṇḍu, Dhṛitarāshṭra took over the reins of government, and receiving his five nephews into his palace, had them brought up with his own sons. As the Pāṇḍus distinguished themselves greatly in feats of arms and helped him to victory, the king appointed his eldest nephew, Yudhishṭhira, to be heir-apparent. The Pāṇḍu princes, however, soon found it necessary to escape from the plots their cousins now began to set on foot against them. They made their way to the king of Panchāla, whose daughter Draupadī was won, in a contest between many kings and heroes, by Arjuna, who alone was able to bend the king's great bow and to hit a certain mark. In order to avoid strife, Draupadī consented to become the common wife of the five princes. At Draupadī's *svayaṃvara* (public choice of a husband) the Pāṇḍus made acquaintance with Kṛishṇa, the hero of the Yādavas, who from this time onward became their fast friend and adviser. Dhṛitarāshṭra, thinking it best to conciliate the Pāṇḍavas in view of their double alliance with the Panchālas and Yādavas, now divided his kingdom, giving Hastināpura to his sons, and to his nephews a district where they built the city of Indraprastha, the modern Delhi (i.).

Here the Pāṇḍavas ruled wisely and prospered greatly. Duryodhana's jealousy being aroused, he resolved to ruin his cousins, with the aid of his uncle Çakuni, a skilful gamester. Dhṛitarāshṭra was accordingly induced to invite the Pāṇḍus to Hastināpura. Here Yudhishṭhira, accepting the challenge to play at dice with Duryodhana, lost everything, his kingdom, his wealth, his army, his brothers, and finally Draupadī. In the end a compromise was made by which the Pāṇḍavas agreed to go into banishment for twelve years, and to remain incognito for a thirteenth, after which they might return and regain their kingdom (ii.).

With Draupadī they accordingly departed to the Kāmyaka forest on the Sarasvatī. The account of their twelve years' life here, and the many legends told to console them in their exile, constitute the *vana-parvan* or "Forest book," one of the longest in the poem (iii.).

The thirteenth year they spent in disguise as servants of Virāṭa, king of the Matsyas. At this time the Kurus, in alliance with another king, invaded the country of the Matsyas, causing much distress. Then the Pāṇḍus arose, put the enemy to flight, and restored the king. They now made themselves known, and entered into an alliance with the king (iv.).

Their message demanding back their possessions

receiving no answer, they prepared for war. The rival armies met in the sacred region of Kurukshetra, with numerous allies on both sides. Joined with the Kurus were, among others, the people of Kosala, Videha, Anga, Banga (Bengal), Kalinga on the east, and those of Sindhu, Gandhāra, Bahlīka (Balk), together with the Çakas and Yavanas on the west. The Pāṇḍus, on the other hand, were aided by the Panchālas, the Matsyas, part of the Yādavas under Kṛishṇa, besides the kings of Kāçi (Benares), Chedi, Magadha, and others (v.).

The battle raged for eighteen days, till all the Kurus were destroyed, and only the Pāṇḍavas and Kṛishṇa with his charioteer escaped alive. The account of it extends over five books (vi.–x.). Then follows a description of the obsequies of the dead (xi.). In the next two books, Bhīma, the leader of the Kurus, on his deathbed, instructs Yudhishṭhira for about 20,000 *çlokas* on the duties of kings and other topics.

The Pāṇḍus having been reconciled to the old king Dhṛitarāshṭra, Yudhishṭhira was crowned king in Hastināpura, and instituted a great horse-sacrifice (xiv.). Dhṛitarāshṭra having remained at Hastināpura for fifteen years, at length retired, with his wife Gāndhārī, to the jungle, where they perished in a forest conflagration (xv.). Among the Yādavas, who had taken different sides in the great war, an internecine conflict broke out, which resulted in the annihilation of this people. Kṛishṇa sadly withdrew to the wilderness, where he was accidentally shot dead by a hunter (xvi.).

The Pāṇḍus themselves, at last weary of life, leaving the young prince Parīkshit, grandson of Arjuna, to rule over Hastināpura, retired to the forest, and dying as they wandered towards Meru, the mountain of the gods (xvii.), ascended to heaven with their faithful spouse (xviii.).

Here the framework of the great epic, which begins at the commencement of the first book, comes to an end. King Parīkshit having died of snake-bite, his son Janamejaya instituted a great sacrifice to the serpents. At that sacrifice the epic was recited by Vaiçampāyana, who had learnt it from Vyāsa. The latter, we are told, after arranging the four Vedas, composed the *Mahābhārata*, which treats of the excellence of the Pāṇḍus, the greatness of Kṛishṇa, and the wickedness of the sons of Dhṛitarāshṭra.

The supplementary book, the *Harivaṃça*, or "Family of Vishṇu," is concerned only with Kṛishṇa. It contains more than 16,000 *çlokas*, and is divided into three sections. The first of these describes the history of Kṛishṇa's ancestors down to the time of Vishṇu's incarnation in him; the second gives an account of Kṛishṇa's exploits; the third treats of the future corruptions of the *Kali*, or fourth age of the world.

The episodes of the *Mahābhārata* are numerous and often very extensive, constituting, as we have seen, about four-fifths of the whole poem. Many of them are interesting for various reasons, and some are distinguished by considerable poetic beauty. One of them, the story of Çakuntalā (occurring in Book I.), supplied Kālidāsa with the subject of his famous play. Episodes are specially plentiful in Book III., being related to while away the time of the exiled Pāṇḍus. Here is found the *Matsyopākhyāna*, or "Episode of the fish," being the story of the flood, narrated with more diffuseness than the simple story told in the *Çatapatha Brāhmaṇa*. The fish here declares itself to be Brahmā, Lord of creatures, and not yet Vishṇu, as in the *Bhāgavata Purāṇa.* Manu no longer appears as the progenitor of mankind, but as a creator who produces all beings and worlds anew by means of his ascetic power.

Another episode is the history of Rāma, interesting in its relation to Vālmīki's *Rāmāyaṇa,* which deals with the same subject at much greater length. The myth of the descent of the Ganges from heaven to earth, here narrated, is told in the *Rāmāyaṇa* also.

Another legend is that of the sage Ṛiçya-çṛinga, who having produced rain in the country of Lomapāda, king of the Angas, was rewarded with the hand of the princess Çāntā, and performed that sacrifice for King Daçaratha which brought about the birth of Rāma. This episode is peculiarly important from a critical point of view, as the legend recurs not only in the *Rāmāyaṇa,* but also in the *Padma Purāṇa,* the *Skanda Purāṇa,* and a number of other sources.

Of special interest is the story of King Uçīnara, son of Çibi, who sacrificed his life to save a pigeon from a hawk. It is told again in another part of Book III. about Çibi himself, as well as in Book XIII. about Vṛishadarbha, son of Çibi. Distinctly Buddhistic in origin and character, the story is famous in Pāli as well as Sanskrit literature, and spread beyond the limits of India.

The story of the abduction of Draupadī forms an episode of her life while she dwelt with the Pāṇḍus in the Kāmyaka forest. Accidentally seen when alone by King Jayadratha of Sindhu, who was passing with a great army, and fell in love with her at first sight, she was forcibly carried off, and only rescued after a terrible fight, in which the Pāṇḍus annihilated Jayadratha's host.

20

Interesting as an illustration of the mythological ideas of the age is the episode which describes the journey of Arjuna to Indra's heaven. Here we see the mighty warrior-god of the Vedas transformed into a glorified king of later times, living a life of ease amid the splendours of his celestial court, where the ear is lulled by strains of music, while the eye is ravished by the graceful dancing and exquisite beauty of heavenly nymphs.

In the story of Sāvitrī we have one of the finest of the many ideal female characters which the older epic poetry of India has created. Sāvitrī, daughter of Açvapati, king of Madra, chooses as her husband Satyavat, the handsome and noble son of a blind and exiled king, who dwells in a forest hermitage. Though warned by the sage Nārada that the prince is fated to live but a single year, she persists in her choice, and after the wedding departs with her husband to his father's forest retreat. Here she lives happily till she begins to be tortured with anxiety on the approach of the fatal day. When it arrives, she follows her husband on his way to cut wood in the forest. After a time he lies down exhausted. Yama, the god of death, appears, and taking his soul, departs. As Sāvitrī persistently follows him, Yama grants her various boons, always excepting the life of her husband; but yielding at last to her importunities, he restores the soul to the lifeless body. Satyavat recovers, and lives happily for many years with his faithful Sāvitrī.

One of the oldest and most beautiful stories inserted in the *Mahābhārata* is the *Nalopākhyāna*, or "Episode of Nala." It is one of the least corrupted of the episodes, its great popularity having prevented the transforming hand of an editor from introducing Çiva and Vishṇu, or from effacing the simplicity of the manners it depicts—the prince, for instance, cooks his own food—or from changing the character of Indra, and other old traits. The poem is pervaded by a high tone of morality, manifested above all in the heroic devotion and fidelity of Damayantī, its leading character. It also contains many passages distinguished by tender pathos.

The story is told by the wise Bṛihadaçva to the exiled Yudhishṭhira, in order to console him for the loss of the kingdom he has forfeited at play. Nala, prince of Nishada, chosen from among many competitors for her hand by Damayantī, princess of Vidarbha, passes several years of happy married life with her. Then, possessed by the demon Kali, and indulging in gambling, he loses his kingdom and all his possessions. Wandering half naked in the forest with Damayantī, he abandons her in his frenzy. Very pathetic is the scene describing how he repeatedly returns to the spot where his wife lies asleep on the ground before he finally deserts her. Equally touching are the accounts of her terror on awaking to find herself alone in the forest, and of her lamentations as she roams in search of her husband, and calls out to him—

Hero, valiant, knowing duty,
To honour faithful, lord of earth,
If thou art within this forest,
Then show thee in thy proper form.
Shall I hear the voice of Nala,
Sweet as the draught of Amṛita,
With its deep and gentle accent,
Like rumble of the thunder-cloud,
Saying "Daughter of Vidarbha!"
To me with clear and blessèd sound,
Rich, like Vedas murmured flowing,
At once destroying all my grief?

There are graphic descriptions of the beauties and terrors of the tropical forest in which Damayantī wanders. At last she finds her way back to her father's court at Kuṇḍina. Many and striking are the similes with which the poet dwells on the grief and wasted form of the princess in her separation from her husband. She is

Like the young moon's slender crescent
Obscured by black clouds in the sky;
Like the lotus-flower uprooted,
All parched and withered by the sun;
Like the pallid night, when Rāhu
Has swallowed up the darkened moon.

Nala, meanwhile, transformed into a dwarf, has become charioteer to the king of Oudh. Damayantī at last hears news leading her to suspect her husband's whereabouts. She accordingly holds out hopes of her hand to the king of Oudh, on condition of his driving the distance of 500 miles to Kuṇḍina in a single day. Nala, acting as his charioteer, accomplishes the feat, and is rewarded by the king with the secret of the highest skill in dicing. Recognised by his wife in spite of his disguise, he regains his true form. He plays again, and wins back his lost kingdom. Thus after years of adventure, sorrow, and humiliation he is at last reunited with Damayantī, with whom he spends the rest of his days in happiness.

Though several supernatural and miraculous features like those which occur in fairy tales are found in the episode of Nala, they are not sufficient to mar the spirit of true poetry which pervades the story as a whole.

The Purāṇas.

Closely connected with the *Mahāonārata* is a distinct class of eighteen epic works, didactic in character and sectarian in purpose, going by the name of Purāṇa. The term *purāṇa* is already found in the Brāhmaṇas designating cosmogonic inquiries generally. It is also used in the *Mahābhārata* somewhat vaguely to express "ancient legendary lore," implying didactic as well as narrative matter, and pointing to an old collection of epic stories. One passage of the epic (I. v. 1) describes *purāṇa* as containing stories of the gods and genealogies of the sages. In Book XVIII., as well as in the *Harivaṃça*, mention is even made of eighteen Purāṇas, which, however, have not been preserved; for those known to us are all, on the whole, later than the *Mahābhārata*, and for the most part derive their legends of ancient days from the great epic itself. Nevertheless they contain much that is old; and it is not always possible to assume that the passages they have in common with the *Mahābhārata* and *Manu* have been borrowed from those works. They are connected by many threads with the old law-books (*smṛitis*) and the Vedas, representing probably a development of older works of the same class. In that part of their contents which is peculiar to them, the Purāṇas agree so closely, being often verbally identical for pages, that they must be derived from some older collection as a common source. Most of them are introduced in exactly the same way as the *Mahābhārata*, Ugraçravas, the son of Lomaharshaṇa, being represented as relating their contents to Çaunaka on the occasion of a sacrifice in the Naimisha forest. The object of most of these legendary compilations is to recommend the sectarian cult of Vishṇu, though some of them favour the worship of Çiva.

Besides cosmogony, they deal with mythical descriptions of the earth, the doctrine of the cosmic ages, the exploits of ancient gods, saints, and heroes, accounts of the Avatārs of Vishṇu, the genealogies of the Solar and Lunar race of kings, and enumerations of the thousand names of Vishṇu or of Çiva. They also contain rules about the worship of the gods by means of prayers, fastings, votive offerings, festivals, and pilgrimages.

The *Garuḍa*, as well as the late and unimportant *Agni Purāṇa*, practically constitute abstracts of the *Mahābhārata* and the *Harivaṃça*.

The *Vāyu*, which appears to be one of the oldest, coincides in part of its matter with the *Mahābhārata*, but is more closely connected with the *Harivaṃça*, the passage which deals with the creation of the world often agreeing verbatim with the corresponding part of the latter poem.

The relationship of the *Matsya Purāṇa* to the great epic and its supplementary book as sources is similarly intimate. It is introduced with the story of Manu and the Fish (*Matsya*). The *Kūrma*, besides giving an account of the various Avatārs of Vishṇu (of which the tortoise or *kūrma* is one), of the genealogies of gods and kings, as well as other matters, contains an extensive account of the world in accordance with the accepted cosmological notions of the *Mahābhārata* and of the Purāṇas in general. The world is here represented as consisting of seven concentric islands separated by different oceans. The central island, with Mount Meru in the middle, is *Jambu-dvīpa*, of which *Bhārata-varsha*, the "kingdom of the Bharatas," or India, is the main division.

The *Mārkaṇḍeya*, which expressly recognises the priority of the *Mahābhārata*, is so called because it is related by the sage Mārkaṇḍeya to explain difficulties suggested by the epic, such as, How could Kṛishṇa become a man? Its leading feature is narrative and it is the least sectarian of the Purāṇas.

The extensive *Padma Purāṇa*, which contains a great many stories agreeing with those of the *Mahābhārata*, is, on the other hand, strongly Vishnuite in tone. Yet this, as well as the *Mārkaṇḍeya*, expressly states the doctrine of the *Tri-mūrti* or Trinity, that Brahmā, Vishṇu, and Çiva are only one being. This doctrine, already to be found in the *Harivaṃça*, is not so prominent in post-Vedic literature as is commonly supposed. It is interesting to note that the story of Rāma, as told in the *Padma Purāṇa*, follows not only the *Rāmāyaṇa* but also Kālidāsa's account in the *Raghuvaṃça*, with which it often agrees literally. Again, the story of Çakuntalā is related, not in accordance with the *Mahābhārata*, but with Kālidāsa's drama.

The *Brahma-vaivarta Purāṇa* is also strongly sectarian in favour of Vishṇu in the form of Kṛishṇa. It is to be noted that both here and in the *Padma Purāṇa* an important part is played by Kṛishṇa's mistress Rādhā, who is unknown to the *Harivaṃça*, the *Vishṇu*, and even the *Bhāgavata Purāṇa*.

The *Vishṇu Purāṇa*, which very often agrees with the *Mahābhārata* in its subject-matter, corresponds most closely to the Indian definition of a Purāṇa, as treating of the five topics of primary creation, secondary creation, genealogies of gods and patriarchs, reigns of various Manus, and the history of the old dynasties of kings.

The *Bhāgavata Purāṇa,* which consists of about 18,000 *çlokas,* derives its name from being dedicated to the glorification of Bhāgavata or Vishṇu. It is later than the *Vishṇu,* which it presupposes, probably dating from the thirteenth century. It exercises a more powerful influence in India than any other Purāṇa. The most popular part is the tenth book, which narrates in detail the history of Kṛishṇa, and has been translated into perhaps every one of the vernacular languages of India.

Other Vishnuite Purāṇas of a late date are the *Brahma,* the *Nāradīya,* the *Vāmana,* and the *Varāha,* the latter two called after the Dwarf and the Boar incarnations of Vishṇu.

Those which specially favour the cult of Çiva are the *Skanda,* the *Çiva,* the *Linga,* and the *Bhavishya* or *Bhavishyat Purāṇas.* The latter two contain little narrative matter, being rather ritual in character. A *Bhavishyat Purāṇa* is already mentioned in the *Āpastamba Dharma Sūtra.*

Besides these eighteen Purāṇas there is also an equal number of secondary works of the same class called *Upa-purāṇas,* in which the epic matter has become entirely subordinate to the ritual element.

THE RĀMĀYAṆA.

Though there is, as we shall see, good reason for supposing that the original part of the *Rāmāyaṇa* assumed shape at a time when the *Mahābhārata* was still in a state of flux, we have deferred describing it on account of its connection with the subsequent development of epic poetry in Sanskrit literature.

In its present form the *Rāmāyaṇa* consists of about 24,000 *çlokas*, and is divided into seven books. It has been preserved in three distinct recensions, the West Indian (A), the Bengal (B), and the Bombay (C). About one-third of the *çlokas* in each recension occurs in neither of the other two. The Bombay recension has in most cases preserved the oldest form of the text; for, as the other two arose in the centres of classical Sanskrit literature, where the *Gauḍa* and the *Vaidarbha* styles of composition respectively flourished, the irregularities of the epic language have been removed in them. The *Rāmāyaṇa* was here treated as a regular *kāvya* or artificial epic, a fate which the *Mahābhārata* escaped because it early lost its original character, and came to be regarded as a didactic work. These two later recensions must not, however, be looked upon as mere revisions of the Bombay text. The variations of all three are of such a kind that they can for the most part be accounted for only by the fluctuations of oral tradition among the professional reciters of the epic, at the time when the three recensions assumed definite shape in different parts of the country by being committed to writing. After having been thus fixed, the fate of each of these recensions was of course similar to that of any other text. They appear to go back to comparatively early times. For quotations from the *Rāmāyaṇa* occurring in works that belong to the eighth and ninth centuries A.D. show that a recension allied to the present C, and probably another allied to the present A, existed at that period. Moreover, Kshemendra's poetical abstract of the epic, the *Rāmāyaṇa-kathāsāra-manjarī*, which follows the contents of the original step by step, proves that its author used A, and perhaps B also, in the middle of the eleventh century.

Bhoja, the composer of another epitome, the *Rāmāyaṇa-champū*, probably used C in the same century.

The careful investigations of Professor JACOBI have shown that the *Rāmāyaṇa* originally consisted of five books only (ii.–vi.). The seventh is undoubtedly a later addition, for the conclusion of the sixth was evidently at one time the end of the whole poem. Again, the first book has several passages which conflict with statements in the later books. It further contains two tables of contents (in cantos i. and iii.) which were clearly made at different times; for one of them takes no notice of the first and last books, and must, therefore, have been made before these were added. What was obviously a part of the commencement of the original poem has been separated from its continuation at the opening of Book II., and now forms the beginning of the fifth canto of Book I. Some cantos have also been interpolated in the genuine books. As Professor Jacobi shows, all these additions to the original body of the epic have been for the most part so loosely attached that the junctures are easy to recognise. They are, however, pervaded by the same spirit as the older part. There is, therefore, no reason for the supposition that they are due to a Brahman revision intended to transform a poem originally meant for the warrior caste. They seem rather to owe their origin simply to the desire of professional rhapsodists to meet the demands of the popular taste. We are told in the *Rāmāyaṇa* itself that the poem was either recited by professional minstrels or sung to the accompaniment of a stringed instrument, being handed down orally, in the first place by Rāma's two sons Kuça and Lava. These names are nothing more than the inventions of popular etymology meant to explain the Sanskrit word *kuçīlava*, "bard" or "actor." The new parts were incorporated before the three recensions which have come down to us arose, but a considerable time must have elapsed between the composition of the original poem and that of the additions. For the tribal hero of the former has in the latter been transformed into a national hero, the moral ideal of the people; and the human hero (like Kṛishṇa in the *Mahābhārata*) of the five genuine books (excepting a few interpolations) has in the first and last become deified and identified with the god Vishṇu, his divine nature in these additions being always present to the minds of their authors. Here, too, VĀLMĪKI, the composer of the *Rāmāyaṇa*, appears as a contemporary of Rāma, and is already regarded as a seer. A long interval of time must have been necessary for such transformations as these.

As to the place of its origin, there is good reason for believing that the *Rāmāyaṇa* arose in Kosala, the country ruled by the race of Ikshvāku in Ayodhyā (Oudh). For we are told in the seventh book (canto 45) that the hermitage of Vālmīki lay on the south bank of the Ganges; the poet must further have been connected with the royal house of Ayodhyā, as the banished Sītā took refuge in his hermitage, where her twin sons were born, brought up, and later learnt the epic from his lips; and lastly, the statement is made in the first book (canto 5) that the *Rāmāyaṇa* arose in the family of the Ikshvākus. In Ayodhyā, then, there must have been current among the court bards (*sūta*) a number of epic tales narrating the fortunes of the Ikshvāku hero Rāma. Such legends, we may assume, Vālmīki worked up into a single homogeneous production, which, as the earliest epic of importance conforming to the rules of poetics, justly received the name of *ādi-kāvya*, or "first artificial poem," from its author's successors. This work was then learnt by professional rhapsodists (*kuçīlava*) and recited by them in public as they wandered about the country.

The original part of the *Rāmāyaṇa* appears to have been completed at a time when the epic kernel of the *Mahābhārata* had not as yet assumed definite shape. For while the heroes of the latter are not mentioned in the *Rāmāyaṇa*, the story of Rāma is often referred to in the longer epic. Again, in a passage of Book VII. of the *Mahābhārata*, which cannot be regarded as a later addition, two lines are quoted as Vālmīki's that occur unaltered in Book VI. of the *Rāmāyaṇa*. The poem of Vālmīki must, therefore, have been generally known as an old work before the *Mahābhārata* assumed a coherent form. In Book III. (cantos 277–291) of the latter epic, moreover, there is a *Rāmopākhyāna* or "Episode of Rāma," which seems to be based on the *Rāmāyaṇa*, as it contains several verses agreeing more or less with Vālmīki's lines, and its author presupposes on the part of his audience a knowledge of the *Rāmāyaṇa* as represented by the Bombay recension.

A further question of importance in determining the age of the *Rāmāyaṇa* is its relation to Buddhistic literature. Now, the story of Rāma is found in a somewhat altered form in one of the Pāli Birth-Stories, the *Daçaratha Jātaka*. As this version confines itself to the first part of Rāma's adventures, his sojourn in the forest, it might at first sight seem to be the older of the two. There is, however, at least an indication that the second part of the story, the expedition to Lankā, was also known to the author of the *Jātaka;* for while Vālmīki's poem concludes with the reunion of Rāma and Sītā, the

Jātaka is made to end with the marriage of the couple after the manner of fairy tales, there being at the same time traces that they were wedded all along in the original source of the legend. Moreover, a verse from the old part of the *Rāmāyaṇa* (vi. 128) actually occurs in a Pāli form embedded in the prose of this *Jātaka*.

It might, indeed, be inferred from the greater freedom with which they handle the *çloka* metre that the canonical Buddhistic writings are older than the *Rāmāyaṇa*, in which the *çloka* is of the classical Sanskrit type. But, as a matter of fact, these Pāli works on the whole observe the laws of the classical *çloka*, their metrical irregularities being most probably caused by the recent application of Pāli to literary purposes as well as by the inferior preservation of Pāli works. On the other hand, Buddhistic literature early made use of the *Āryā* metre, which, though so popular in classical Sanskrit poetry, is not yet to be found in the Sanskrit epics.

The only mention of Buddha in the *Rāmāyaṇa* occurs in a passage which is evidently interpolated. Hence the balance of the evidence in relation to Buddhism seems to favour the pre-Buddhistic origin of the genuine *Rāmāyaṇa*.

The question whether the Greeks were known to the author of our epic is, of course, also of chronological moment. An examination of the poem shows that the Yavanas (Greeks) are only mentioned twice, once in Book I. and once in a canto of Book IV., which Professor Jacobi shows to be an interpolation. The only conclusion to be drawn from this is that the additions to the original poem were made some time after 300 B.C. Professor Weber's assumption of Greek influence in the story of the *Rāmāyaṇa* seems to lack foundation.

For the tale of the abduction of Sītā and the expedition to Lankā for her recovery has no real correspondence with that of the rape of Helen and the Trojan war. Nor is there any sufficient reason to suppose that the account of Rāma bending a powerful bow in order to win Sītā was borrowed from the adventures of Ulysses. Stories of similar feats of strength for a like object are to be found in the poetry of other nations besides the Greeks, and could easily have arisen independently.

The political aspect of Eastern India as revealed by the *Rāmāyaṇa* sheds some additional light on the age of the epic. In the first place, no mention is made of the city of Pāṭaliputra (Patna), which was founded by King Kālāçoka (under whom the second Buddhist council was held at Vaiçālī about 380 B.C.), and which by the time of Megasthenes (300 B.C.) had become the capital of India. Yet Rāma is in Book I. (canto 35) described as passing the very spot where that city stood, and the poet makes a point (in cantos 32–33) of referring to the foundation of a number of cities in Eastern Hindustan, such as Kauçāmbī, Kānyakubja, and Kāmpilya, in order to show how far the fame of the *Rāmāyaṇa* spread beyond the confines of Kosala, the land of its origin. Had Pāṭaliputra existed at the time, it could not have failed to be mentioned.

It is further a noteworthy fact that the capital of Kosala is in the original *Rāmāyaṇa* regularly called Ayodhyā, while the Buddhists, Jains, Greeks, and Patanjali always give it the name of Sāketa. Now in the last book of the *Rāmāyaṇa* we are told that Rāma's son, Lava, fixed the seat of his government at Çrāvastī, a city not mentioned at all in the old part of the epic; and in Buddha's time King Prasenajit of Kosala is known to have reigned at Çrāvastī. All this points to the conclusion that the original *Rāmāyaṇa* was composed when the ancient Ayodhyā had not yet been deserted, but was still the chief city of Kosala, when its new name of Sāketa was still unknown, and before the seat of government was transferred to Çrāvastī.

Again, in the old part of Book I., Mithilā and Viçālā are spoken of as twin cities under separate rulers, while we know that by Buddha's time they had coalesced to the famous city of Vaiçālī, which was then ruled by an oligarchy.

The political conditions described in the *Rāmāyaṇa* indicate the patriarchal rule of kings possessing only a small territory, and never point to the existence of more complex states; while the references of the poets of the *Mahābhārata* to the dominions in Eastern India ruled by a powerful king, Jarāsandha, and embracing many lands besides Magadha, reflect the political conditions of the fourth century B.C. The cumulative evidence of the above arguments makes it difficult to avoid the conclusion that the kernel of the *Rāmāyaṇa* was composed before 500 B.C., while the more recent portions were probably not added till the second century B.C. and later.

This conclusion does not at first sight seem to be borne out by the linguistic evidence of the *Rāmāyaṇa*. For the epic (*ārsha*) dialect of the Bombay recension, which is practically the same as that of the *Mahābhārata*, both betrays a stage of development decidedly later than that of Pāṇini, and is taken no notice of by that grammarian. But it is, for all that, not necessarily later in date. For Pāṇini deals only with the refined Sanskrit of the cultured (*çishṭa*), that is to say, of the Brahmans, which would be more archaic than the popular dialect of wandering rhapsodists; and he would naturally have ignored the latter. Now at the time of the Açoka inscriptions, or hardly more than half a century later than Pāṇini, Prākrit was the language of the people in the part of India where the *Rāmāyaṇa* was composed. It is, therefore, not at all likely that the *Rāmāyaṇa*, which aimed at popularity, should have been composed as late as the time of Pāṇini, when it could not have been generally understood. If the language of the epic is later than Pāṇini, it is difficult to see how it escaped the dominating influence of his grammar. It is more likely that the popular Sanskrit of the epics received general currency at a much earlier date by the composition of a poem like that of Vālmīki. A searching comparative investigation of the classical Kāvyas will probably show that they are linguistically more closely connected with the old epic poetry, and that they deviate more from the Pāṇinean standard than is usually supposed.

In style the *Rāmāyaṇa* is already far removed from the naïve popular epic, in which the story is the chief thing, and not its form. Vālmīki is rich in similes, which he often cumulates; he not infrequently uses the cognate figure called *rūpaka* or "identification" (*e.g.* "foot-lotus") with much skill, and also occasionally employs other ornaments familiar to the classical poets, besides approximating to them in the style of his descriptions. The *Rāmāyaṇa*, in fact, represents the dawn of the later artificial poetry (*kāvya*), which was in all probability the direct continuation and development of the art handed down by the rhapsodists who recited Vālmīki's work. Such a relationship is distinctly recognised by the authors of the great classical epics (*mahākavis*) when they refer to him as the *ādi-kavi* or "first poet."

The story of the *Rāmāyaṇa*, as narrated in the five genuine books, consists of two distinct parts. The first describes the events at the court of King Daçaratha at Ayodhyā and their consequences. Here we have a purely human and natural account of the intrigues of a queen to set her son upon the throne. There is nothing fantastic in the narrative, nor has it any mythological background. If the epic ended with the return of Rāma's brother, Bharata, to the capital, after the old king's death, it might pass for a historical saga. For Ikshvāku, Daçaratha, and Rāma are the names of celebrated and mighty kings, mentioned even in the *Rigveda*, though not there connected with one another in any way.

The character of the second part is entirely different. Based on a foundation of myths, it is full of the marvellous and fantastic. The oldest theory as to the significance of the story was that of Lassen, who held that it was intended to represent allegorically the first attempt of the Aryans to conquer the South. But Rāma is nowhere described as founding an Aryan realm in the Dekhan, nor is any such intention on his part indicated anywhere in the epic. Weber subsequently expressed the same view in a somewhat modified form. According to him, the *Rāmāyaṇa* was meant to account for the spread of Aryan culture to the South and to Ceylon. But this form of the allegorical theory also lacks any confirmation from the statements of the epic itself; for Rāma's expedition is nowhere represented as producing any change or improvement in the civilisation of the South. The poet knows nothing about the Dekhan beyond the fact that Brahman hermitages are to be found there. Otherwise it is a region haunted by the monsters and fabulous beings with which an Indian imagination would people an unknown land.

There is much more probability in the opinion of Jacobi, that the *Rāmāyaṇa* contains no allegory at all, but is based on Indian mythology. The foundation of the second part would thus be a celestial myth of the Veda transformed into a narrative of earthly adventures according to a not uncommon development. Sītā can be traced to the *Rigveda*, where she appears as the Furrow personified and invoked as a goddess. In some of the Gṛihya Sūtras she again appears as a genius of the ploughed field, is praised as a being of great beauty, and is accounted the wife of Indra or Parjanya, the rain-god. There are traces of this origin in the *Rāmāyaṇa* itself. For Sītā is represented (i. 66) as having emerged from the earth when her father Janaka was once ploughing, and at last she disappears underground in the arms of the goddess Earth (vii. 97). Her husband, Rāma, would be no other than Indra, and his conflict with Rāvaṇa, chief of the demons, would represent the Indra-Vṛitra myth of the *Rigveda*. This identification is confirmed by the name of Rāvaṇa's son being Indrajit, "Conqueror of Indra," or Indraçatru, "Foe of Indra," the latter being actually an epithet of Vṛitra in the *Rigveda*. Rāvaṇa's most notable feat, the rape of Sītā, has its prototype in the stealing of the cows recovered by Indra. Hanumat, the chief of the monkeys and Rāma's ally in the recovery of Sītā, is the son of the wind-god, with the patronymic Māruti, and is described as flying hundreds of leagues through the air to find Sītā. Hence in his figure perhaps survives a reminiscence of Indra's alliance with the Maruts in his conflict with Vṛitra, and of the dog Saramā, who, as Indra's messenger, crosses the waters of the Rasā and tracks the cows. Saramā recurs as the name of a demoness who consoles Sītā in her captivity. The name of Hanumat being Sanskrit, the character is probably not borrowed from the aborigines. As Hanumat is at the present day the tutelary deity of village settlements all over India, Prof. Jacobi's surmise that he must have been connected with agriculture, and may have been a genius of the monsoon, has some probability.

The main story of the *Rāmāyaṇa* begins with an account of the city of Ayodhyā under the rule of the mighty King Daçaratha, the sons of whose three wives, Kauçalyā, Kaikeyī, and Sumitrā, are Rāma, Bharata, and Lakshmaṇa respectively. Rāma is married to Sītā, daughter of Janaka, king of Videha. Daçaratha, feeling the approach of old age, one day announces in a great assembly that he desires to make Rāma heir-apparent, an announcement received with general rejoicing because of Rāma's great popularity. Kaikeyī, meanwhile, wishing her son Bharata to succeed, reminds the king that he had once offered her the choice of two boons, of which she had as yet not availed herself. When Daçaratha at last promises to fulfil whatever she may desire, Kaikeyī requests him to appoint Bharata his successor, and to banish Rāma for fourteen years. The king, having in vain implored her to retract, passes a sleepless night. Next day, when the solemn consecration of Rāma is to take place, Daçaratha sends for his son and informs him of his fate. Rāma receives the news calmly and prepares to obey his father's command as his highest duty. Sītā and Lakshmaṇa resolve on sharing his fortunes, and accompany him in his exile.

The aged king, overcome with grief at parting from his son, withdraws from Kaikeyī, and passing the remainder of his days with Rāma's mother, Kauçalyā, finally dies lamenting for his banished son. Rāma has meanwhile lived peacefully and happily with Sītā and his brother in the wild forest of Daṇḍaka. On the death of the old king, Bharata, who in the interval has lived with the parents of his mother, is summoned to the throne. Refusing the succession with noble indignation, he sets out for the forest in order to bring Rāma back to Ayodhyā. Rāma, though much moved by his brother's request, declines to return because he must fulfil his vow of exile. Taking off his gold-embroidered shoes, he gives them to Bharata as a sign that he hands over his inheritance to him. Bharata returning to Ayodhyā, places Rāma's shoes on the throne, and keeping the royal umbrella over them, holds council and dispenses justice by their side.

Rāma now sets about the task of combating the formidable giants that infest the Daṇḍaka forest and are a terror to the pious hermits settled there. Having, by the advice of the sage Agastya, procured the weapons of Indra, he begins a successful conflict, in which he slays many thousands of demons. Their chief, Rāvaṇa, enraged and determined on revenge, turns one of his followers into a golden deer, which appears to Sītā. While Rāma and Lakshmaṇa are engaged, at her request, in pursuit of it, Rāvaṇa in the guise of an ascetic approaches Sītā, carries her off by force, and wounds the vulture Jaṭāyu, which guards her abode. Rāma on his return is seized with grief and despair; but, as he is burning the remains of the vulture, a voice from the pyre proclaims to him how he can conquer his foes and recover his wife. He now proceeds to conclude a solemn alliance with the chiefs of the monkeys, Hanumat and Sugrīva. With the help of the latter, Rāma slays the terrible giant Bali. Hanumat meanwhile crosses from the mainland to the island of Lankā, the abode of Rāvaṇa, in search of Sītā. Here he finds her wandering sadly in a grove and announces to her that deliverance is at hand. After slaying a number of demons, he returns and reports his discovery to Rāma. A plan of campaign is now arranged. The monkeys having miraculously built a bridge from the continent to Lankā with the aid of the god of the sea, Rāma leads his army across, slays Rāvaṇa, and wins back Sītā. After she has purified herself from the suspicion of infidelity by the ordeal of fire, Rāma joyfully returns with her to Ayodhyā, where he reigns gloriously in association with his faithful brother Bharata, and gladdens his subjects with a new golden age.

Such in bare outline is the main story of the *Rāmāyaṇa*. By the addition of the first and last books Vālmīki's epic has in the following way been transformed into a poem meant to glorify the god Vishṇu. Rāvaṇa, having obtained from Brahmā the boon of being invulnerable to gods, demigods, and demons, abuses his immunity in so terrible a manner that the gods are reduced to despair. Bethinking themselves at last that Rāvaṇa had in his arrogance forgotten to ask that he should not be wounded by men, they implore Vishṇu to allow himself to be born as a man for the destruction of the demon. Vishṇu, consenting, is born as Rāma, and accomplishes the task. At the end of the seventh book Brahmā and the other gods come to Rāma, pay homage to him, and proclaim that he is really Vishṇu, "the glorious lord of the discus." The belief here expressed that Rāma is an incarnation of Vishṇu, the highest god, has secured to the hero of our epic the worship of the Hindus down to the present day. That belief, forming the fundamental doctrine of the religious system of Rāmānuja in the twelfth and of Rāmānanda in the fourteenth century, has done much to counteract the spread of the degrading superstitions and impurities of Çivaism both in the South and in the North of India.

The *Rāmāyaṇa* contains several interesting episodes, though, of course, far fewer than the *Mahābhārata*. One of them, a thoroughly Indian story, full of exaggerations and impossibilities, is the legend, told in Book I., of the descent of the Ganges. It relates how the sacred river was brought down from heaven to earth in order to purify the remains of the 60,000 sons of King Sagara, who were reduced to ashes by the sage Kapila when his devotions were disturbed by them.

Another episode (i. 52–65) is that of Viçvāmitra, a powerful king, who comes into conflict with the great sage Vasishṭha by endeavouring to take away his miraculous cow by force. Viçvāmitra then engages in mighty penances, in which he resists the seductions of beautiful nymphs, and which extend over thousands of years, till he finally attains Brahmanhood, and is reconciled with his rival, Vasishṭha.

The short episode which relates the origin of the *çloka* metre is one of the most attractive and poetical. Vālmīki in his forest hermitage is preparing to describe worthily the fortunes of Rāma. While he is watching a fond pair of birds on the bank of the river, the male is suddenly shot by a hunter, and falls dead on the ground, weltering in his blood. Vālmīki, deeply touched by the grief of the bereaved female, involuntarily utters words lamenting the death of her mate and threatening vengeance on the wicked murderer. But, strange to tell, his utterance is no ordinary speech and flows in a melodious stream. As he wanders, lost in thought, towards his hut, Brahmā appears and announces to the poet that he has unconsciously created the rhythm of the *çloka* metre. The deity then bids him compose in this measure the divine poem on the life and deeds of Rāma. This story may have a historical significance, for it indicates with some probability that the classical form of the *çloka* was first fixed by Vālmīki, the author of the original part of the *Rāmāyaṇa.*

The epic contains the following verse foretelling its everlasting fame :—

As long as mountain ranges stand
And rivers flow upon the earth :
So long will this Rāmāyaṇa
Survive upon the lips of men.

This prophecy has been perhaps even more abundantly fulfilled than the well-known prediction of Horace. No product of Sanskrit literature has enjoyed a greater popularity in India down to the present day than the *Rāmāyaṇa.* Its story furnishes the subject of many other Sanskrit poems as well as plays, and still delights, from the lips of reciters, the hearts of myriads of the Indian people, as at the great annual Rāma festival held at Benares. It has been translated into many Indian vernaculars. Above all, it inspired the greatest poet of mediæval Hindustan, Tulsī Dās, to compose in Hindī his version of the epic entitled *Rām Charit Mānas,* which, with its ideal standard of virtue and purity, is a kind of bible to a hundred millions of the people of Northern India.

CHAPTER XI

KĀVYA OR COURT EPIC

(*Circa* 200 B.C.–1100 A.D.)

THE real history of the Kāvya, or artificial epic poetry of India, does not begin till the first half of the seventh century A.D., with the reign of King Harsha-vardhana of Thāneçar and Kanauj (606–648), who ruled over the whole of Northern India, and under whose patronage Bāṇa wrote his historical romance, *Harsha-charita*, and other works. The date of no Kāvya before this landmark has as yet been fixed with certainty. One work, however, which is dominated by the Kāvya style, the *Bṛihatsaṃhitā* of the astronomer Varāhamihira, can without hesitation be assigned to the middle of the sixth century. But as to the date of the most famous classical poets, Kālidāsa, Subandhu, Bhāravi, Guṇāḍhya, and others, we have no historical authority. The most definite statement that can be made about them is that their fame was widely diffused by about 600 A.D., as is attested by the way in which their names are mentioned in Bāṇa and in an inscription of 634 A.D. Some of them, moreover, like Guṇāḍhya, to whose work Subandhu repeatedly alludes, must certainly belong to a much earlier time. The scanty materials supplied by the poets themselves, which might help to determine their dates, are difficult to utilise, because the history of India, both political and social, during the first five centuries of our era, is still involved in obscurity.

With regard to the age of court poetry in general, we have the important literary evidence of the quotations in Patanjali's *Mahābhāshya,* which show that Kāvya flourished in his day, and must have been developed before the beginning of our era. Several of these quoted verses are composed in the artificial metres of the classical poetry, while the heroic *anushṭubh çlokas* agree in matter as well as form, not with the popular, but with the court epics.

We further know that Açvaghosha's *Buddha-charita,* or "Doings of Buddha," was translated into Chinese between 414 and 421 A.D. This work not only calls itself a *mahākāvya,* or "great court epic," but is actually written in the Kāvya style. AÇVAGHOSHA was, according to the Buddhist tradition, a contemporary of King Kanishka, and would thus belong to the first century A.D. In any case, it is evident that his poem could not have been composed later than between 350 and 400 A.D. The mere fact, too, that a Buddhist monk thus early conceived the plan of writing the legend of Buddha according to the rules of the classical Sanskrit epic shows how popular the Brahmanical artificial poetry must have become, at any rate by the fourth century A.D., and probably long before.

The progress of epigraphic research during the last quarter of a century has begun to shed considerable light on the history of court poetry during the dark age embracing the first five centuries of our era. Mr. Fleet's third volume of the *Corpus Inscriptionum Indicarum* contains no fewer than eighteen inscriptions of importance in this respect. These are written mostly in verse, but partly also in elevated prose. They cover a period of two centuries, from about 350 to 550 A.D. Most of them employ the Gupta era, beginning A.D. 319, and first used by Chandragupta II., named Vikramāditya, whose inscriptions and coins range from A.D. 400 to 413. A few of them employ the Mālava era, the earlier name of the Vikrama era, which dates from 57 B.C. Several of these inscriptions are *praçastis* or panegyrics on kings. An examination of them proves that the poetical style prevailing in the fourth, fifth, and sixth centuries did not differ from that of the classical Kāvyas which have been preserved. Samudragupta, the second of the Gupta line, who belongs to the second half of the fourth century, was, we learn, himself a poet, as well as a supporter of poets. Among the latter was at least one, by name Harisheṇa, who in his panegyric on his royal patron, which consists of some thirty lines (nine stanzas) of poetry and about an equal number of lines of prose, shows a mastery of style rivalling that of Kālidāsa and Daṇḍin. In agreement with the rule of all the Sanskrit treatises on poetics, his prose is full of inordinately long compounds, one of them containing more than 120 syllables. In his poetry he, like Kālidāsa and others, follows the Vidarbha style, in which the avoidance of long compounds is a leading characteristic. In this style, which must have been fully developed by A.D. 300, is also written an inscription by Vīrasena, the minister of Chandragupta II., Samudragupta's successor.

A very important inscription dates from the year 529 of the Mālava (Vikrama) era, or A.D. 473. It consists of a poem of no fewer than forty-four stanzas (containing 150 metrical lines), composed by a poet named Vatsabhaṭṭi, to commemorate the consecration of a temple of the sun at Daçapura (now Mandasor). A detailed examination of this inscription not only leads to the conclusion that in the fifth century a rich Kāvya literature must have existed, but in particular shows that the poem has several affinities with Kālidāsa's writings. The latter fact renders it probable that Vatsabhaṭṭi, a man of inferior poetic talent, who professes to have produced his work with effort, knew and utilised the poems of Kālidāsa. The reign of Chandragupta Vikramāditya II., at the beginning of the fifth century A.D., therefore seems in the meantime the most probable approximate date for India's greatest poet.

Besides the epigraphic evidence of the Gupta period, we have two important literary prose inscriptions of considerable length, one from Girnār and the other from Nāsik, both belonging to the second century A.D. They show that even then there existed a prose Kāvya style which, in general character and in many details, resembled that of the classical tales and romances. For they not only employ long and frequent compounds, but also the ornaments of alliteration and various kinds of simile and metaphor. Their use of poetical figures is, however, much less frequent and elaborate, occasionally not going beyond the simplicity of the popular epic. They are altogether less artificial than the prose parts of Harisheṇa's Kāvya, and *à fortiori* than the works of Daṇḍin, Subandhu, and Bāṇa. From the Girnār inscription it appears that its author must have been acquainted with a theory of poetics, that metrical Kāvyas conforming to the rules of the Vidarbha style were composed in his day, and that poetry of this kind was cultivated at the courts of princes then as in later times. It cannot be supposed that Kāvya literature was a new invention of the second century; it must, on the contrary, have passed through a lengthened development before that time. Thus epigraphy not merely confirms the evidence of the *Mahābhāshya* that artificial court poetry originated before the commencement of our era, but shows that that poetry continued to be cultivated throughout the succeeding centuries.

These results of the researches of the late Professor Bühler and of Mr. Fleet render untenable Professor Max Müller's well-known theory of the renaissance of Sanskrit literature in the sixth century, which was set forth by that scholar with his usual brilliance in *India, what can it Teach us?* and which held the field for several years.

Professor Max Müller's preliminary assertion that the Indians, in consequence of the incursions of the Çakas (Scythians) and other foreigners, ceased from literary activity during the first two centuries A.D., is refuted by the evidence of the last two inscriptions mentioned above. Any such interruption of intellectual life during that period is, even apart from epigraphical testimony, rendered highly improbable by other considerations. The Scythians, in the first place, permanently subjugated only about one-fifth of India; for their dominion, which does not appear to have extended farther east than Mathurā (Muttra), was limited to the Panjāb, Sindh, Gujarat, Rājputana, and the Central Indian Agency. The conquerors, moreover, rapidly became Hinduised. Most of them already had Indian names in the second generation. One of them, Ushabhadāta (the Sanskrit Ṛishabhadatta), described his exploits in an inscription composed in a mixture of Sanskrit and Prākrit. Kanishka himself (78 A.D.), as well as his successors, was a patron of Buddhism; and national Indian architecture and sculpture attained a high development at Mathurā under these rulers. When the invaders thus rapidly acquired the civilisation of the comparatively small portion of India they conquered, there is no reason to assume the suppression of literary activity in that part of the country, much less in India as a whole.

The main thesis of Professor Max Müller is, that in the middle of the sixth century A.D. the reign of a King Vikramāditya of Ujjain, with whom tradition connected the names of Kālidāsa and other distinguished authors, was the golden age of Indian court poetry. This renaissance theory is based on Fergusson's ingenious chronological hypothesis that a supposed King Vikrama of Ujjain, having expelled the Scythians from India, in commemoration of his victory founded the Vikrama era in 544 A.D., dating its commencement back 600 years to 57 B.C. The epigraphical researches of Mr. Fleet have destroyed Fergusson's hypothesis. From these researches it results that the Vikrama era of 57 B.C., far from having been founded in 544 A.D., had already been in use for more than a century previously under the name of the Mālava era (which came to be called the Vikrama era about 800 A.D.). It further appears that no Çakas (Scythians) could have been driven out of Western India in the middle of the sixth century, because that country had already been conquered by the Guptas more than a hundred years before. Lastly, it turns out that, though other foreign conquerors, the Hūnas, were actually expelled from Western India in the first half of the sixth century, they were driven out, not by a Vikramāditya, but by a king named Yaçodharman Vishṇuvardhana.

Thus the great King Vikramāditya vanishes from

the historical ground of the sixth century into the realm of myth. With Vikramāditya an often-quoted but ill-authenticated verse occurring in a work of the sixteenth century associates Dhanvantari, Kshapaṇaka, Amarasiṃha, Varāhamihira, and Vararuchi as among the "nine gems" of his court. With the disappearance of Vikrama from the sixth century A.D. this verse has lost all chronological validity with reference to the date of the authors it enumerates; it is even inadmissible to conclude from such legendary testimony that they were contemporaries. Even though one of them, Varāhamihira, actually does belong to the sixth century, each of them can now only be placed in the sixth century separately and by other arguments. Apart from the mythical Vikramāditya, there is now no reason to suppose that court poetry attained a special development in that century, for Harisheṇa's paneygyric, and some other epigraphic poems of the Gupta period, show that it flourished greatly at least two hundred years earlier.

None of the other arguments by which it has been attempted to place KĀLIDĀSA separately in the sixth century have any cogency. One of the chief of these is derived from the explanation given by the fourteenth-century commentator, Mallinātha, of the word *dignāga*, "world-elephant," occurring in the 14th stanza of Kālidāsa's *Meghadūta*. He sees in it a punning allusion to Dignāga, a hated rival of the poet. This explanation, to begin with, is extremely dubious in itself. Then it is uncertain whether Mallinātha means the Buddhist teacher Dignāga. Thirdly, little weight can be attached to the Buddhistic tradition that Dignāga was a pupil of Vasubandhu, for this statement is not found till the sixteenth century. Fourthly, the assertion that Vasubandhu belongs to the sixth century depends chiefly on the Vikramāditya theory, and is opposed to Chinese evidence, which indicates that works of Vasubandhu were translated in A.D. 404. Thus every link in the chain of this argument is very weak.

The other main argument is that Kālidāsa must have lived after Āryabhaṭa (A.D. 499), because he shows a knowledge of the scientific astronomy borrowed from the Greeks. But it has been shown by Dr. Thibaut that an Indian astronomical treatise, undoubtedly written under Greek influence, the *Romaka Siddhānta*, is older than Āryabhaṭa, and cannot be placed later than A.D. 400. It may be added that a passage of Kālidāsa's *Raghuvaṃça* (xiv. 40) has been erroneously adduced in support of the astronomical argument, as implying that eclipses of the moon are due to the shadow of the earth: it really refers only to the spots in the moon as caused, in accordance with the doctrine of the Purāṇas, by a reflection of the earth.

Thus there is, in the present state of our knowledge, good reason to suppose that Kālidāsa lived not in the sixth, but in the beginning of the fifth century A.D. The question of his age, however, is not likely to be definitely solved till the language, the style, and the poetical technique of each of his works have been minutely investigated, in comparison with datable epigraphic documents, as well as with the rules given by the oldest Sanskrit treatises on poetics.

As the popular epic poetry of the *Mahābhārata* was the chief source of the Purāṇas, so the *Rāmāyaṇa* the earliest artificial epic, was succeeded, though after a long interval of time, by a number of Kāvyas ranging from the fifth to the twelfth century. While in the old epic poetry form is subordinated to matter, it is of primary importance in the Kāvyas, the matter becoming more and more merely a means for the display of tricks of style. The later the author of a Kāvya is, the more he seeks to win the admiration of his audience by the cleverness of his conceits and the ingenuity of his diction, appealing always to the head rather than the heart. Even the very best of the Kāvyas were composed in more strict conformity with fixed rules than the poetry of any other country. For not only is the language dominated by the grammatical rules of Pāṇini, but the style is regulated by the elaborate laws about various forms of alliteration and figures of speech laid down in the treatises on poetics.

The two most important Kāvyas are Kālidāsa's *Raghuvaṃça* and *Kumāra-sambhava*, both distinguished by independence of treatment as well as considerable poetical beauty. They have several stanzas in common, many others which offer but slight variations, and a large number of passages which, though differing in expression, are strikingly analogous in thought. In both poems, too, the same metre is employed to describe the same situation. In both poems each canto is, as a rule, composed in one metre, but changes with the beginning of the new canto. The prevailing metres are the classical form of the *anushṭubh* and the *upajāti*, a development of the Vedic *trishṭubh*.

The *Raghuvaṃça*, or "Race of Raghu," which consists of nineteen cantos, describes the life of Rāma together with an account of his forefathers and successors. The first nine cantos deal with his nearest four ancestors, beginning with Dilīpa and his son Raghu. The story of Rāma occupies the next six (x.–xv.), and agrees pretty closely with that in the *Rāmāyaṇa* of Vālmīki, whom Kālidāsa here (xv. 41) speaks of as "the first poet." The following two cantos are concerned with the three nearest descendants of Rāma, while the last two run through the remainder of twenty-four kings who reigned in Ayodhyā as his descendants, ending rather abruptly with the death of the voluptuous King Agnivarṇa. The names of these successors of Rāma agree closely with those in the list given in the *Vishṇu-purāṇa.*

The narrative in the *Raghuvaṃça* moves with some rapidity, not being too much impeded by long descriptions. It abounds with apt and striking similes and contains much genuine poetry, while the style, for a Kāvya, is simple, though many passages are undoubtedly too artificial for the European taste. The following stanza, sung by a bard whose duty it is to waken the king in the morning (v. 75), may serve as a specimen—

The flow'rs to thee presented droop and fade,
The lamps have lost the wreath of rays they shed,
Thy sweet-voiced parrot, in his cage confined,
Repeats the call we sound to waken thee.

More than twenty commentaries on the *Raghuvaṃça* are known. The most famous is the *Saṃjīvanī* of MALLINĀTHA, who explains every word of the text, and who has the great merit of endeavouring to find out and preserve the readings of the poet himself. He knew a number of earlier commentaries, among which he names with approval those of Dakshiṇāvarta and Nātha. The latter no longer exist. Among the other extant commentaries may be mentioned the *Subodhinī*, composed by Dinakara Miçra in 1385, and the *Çiçuhitaishiṇī*, by a Jain named Chāritravardhana, of which Dinakara's work appears to be an epitome.

The *Kumāra-sambhava*, or the "Birth of the War-god," consists, when complete, of seventeen cantos. The first seven are entirely devoted to the courtship and wedding of the god Çiva and of Pārvatī, daughter of Himālaya, the parents of the youthful god. This fact in itself indicates that description is the prevailing characteristic of the poem. It abounds in that poetical miniature painting in which lies the chief literary strength of the Indian. Affording the poet free scope for the indulgence of his rich and original imaginative powers, it is conspicuous for wealth of illustration. The following rendering of a stanza in the *Viyoginī* metre (in which lines of ten and eleven syllables ending iambically alternate) may serve as a specimen. The poet shows how the duty of a wife following her husband in death is exemplified even by objects in Nature poetically conceived as spouses—

After the Lord of Night the moonlight goes,
Along with the cloud the lightning is dissolved:
Wives ever follow in their husbands' path;
Even things bereft of sense obey this law.

Usually the first seven cantos only are to be found in the printed editions, owing to the excessively erotic character of the remaining ten. The poem concludes with an account of the destruction of the demon Tāraka, the object for which the god of war was born.

More than twenty commentaries on the *Kumāra-sambhava* have been preserved. Several of them are by the same authors, notably Mallinātha, as those on the *Raghuvaṃça*.

The subject-matter of the later Kāvyas, which is derived from the two great epics, becomes more and more mixed up with lyric, erotic, and didactic elements. It is increasingly regarded as a means for the display of elaborate conceits, till at last nothing remains but bombast and verbal jugglery. The *Bhaṭṭi-kāvya*, written in Valabhī under King Çrīdharasena, probably in the seventh century, and ascribed by various commentators to the poet and grammarian Bhartṛihari (died 651 A.D.), deals in 22 cantos with the story of Rāma, but only with the object of illustrating the forms of Sanskrit grammar.

The *Kirātārjunīya* describes, in eighteen cantos, the combat, first narrated in the *Mahābhārata*, between Çiva, in the guise of a *Kirāta* or mountaineer, and Arjuna. It cannot have been composed later than the sixth century, as its author, BHĀRAVI, is mentioned in an inscription of 634 A.D. The fifteenth canto of this poem contains a number of stanzas illustrating all kinds of verbal tricks like those described in Daṇḍin's *Kāvyādarça*. Thus one stanza (14) contains no consonant but *n* (excepting a *t* at the end);[1] while each half-line in a subsequent one (25), if its syllables be read backwards, is identical with the other half.[2]

The *Çiçupāla-vadha*, or "Death of Çiçupāla," describes, in twenty cantos, how that prince, son of a king of Chedi, and cousin of Kṛishṇa, was slain by Vishṇu. Having been composed by the poet MĀGHA, it also goes by the name of *Māgha-kāvya*. It probably dates from the ninth, and must undoubtedly have been composed before the end of the tenth century. The nineteenth canto is full

[1] *Na nonanunno nunnono nānā nānānanā nanu*
Nunno 'nunno nanunneno nānenā nunnanunnanut.

[2] *Devākānini kāvāde*, &c.

of metrical puzzles, some of a highly complex character (*e.g.* 29). It contains an example of a stanza (34) which, if read backwards, is identical with the preceding one read in the ordinary way. At the same time this Kāvya is, as a whole, by no means lacking in poetical beauties and striking thoughts.

The *Naishadhīya* (also called *Naishadha-charita*), in twenty-two cantos, deals with the story of Nala, king of Nishada, the well-known episode of the *Mahābhārata*. It was composed by ÇRĪHARSHA, who belongs to the latter half of the twelfth century.

These six artificial epics are recognised as *Mahākāvyas*, or "Great Poems," and have all been commented on by Mallinātha. The characteristics of this higher class are set forth by Daṇḍin in his *Kāvyādarça*, or "Mirror of Poetry" (i. 14–19). Their subjects must be derived from epic story (*itihāsa*), they should be extensive, and ought to be embellished with descriptions of cities, seas, mountains, seasons, sunrise, weddings, battles fought by the hero, and so forth.

An extensive Mahākāvya, in fifty cantos, is the *Haravijaya*, or "Victory of Çiva," by a Kashmirian poet named RATNĀKARA, who belongs to the ninth century.

Another late epic, narrating the fortunes of the same hero as the *Naishadhīya*, is the *Nalodaya*, or "Rise of Nala," which describes the restoration to power of King Nala after he had lost his all. Though attributed to Kālidāsa, it is unmistakably the product of a much later age. The chief aim of the author is to show off his skill in the manipulation of the most varied and artificial metres, as well as all the elaborate tricks of style exhibited in the latest Kāvyas. Rhyme even is introduced, and that, too, not only at the end of, but within metrical lines.

The really epic material is but scantily treated, narrative making way for long descriptions and lyrical effusions. Thus the second and longest of the four cantos of the poem is purely lyrical, describing only the bliss of the newly-wedded pair, with all kinds of irrelevant additions.

The culmination of artificiality is attained by the *Rāghava-pāṇḍavīya*, a poem composed by KAVIRĀJA, who perhaps flourished about A.D. 800. It celebrates simultaneously the actions of Rāghava or Rāma and of the Pāṇḍava princes. The composition is so arranged that by the use of ambiguous words and phrases the story of the *Rāmāyaṇa* and the *Mahābhārata* is told at one and the same time. The same words, according to the sense in which they are understood, narrate the events of each epic. A *tour de force* of this kind is doubtless unique in the literatures of the world. Kavirāja has, however, found imitators in India itself.

A Mahākāvya which is as yet only known in MS. is the *Navasāhasānka-charita*, a poem celebrating the doings of Navasāhasānka, otherwise Sindhurāja, a king of Mālava, and composed by a poet named PADMAGUPTA, who lived about 1000 A.D. It consists of eighteen cantos, containing over 1500 stanzas in nineteen different metres. The poet refrains from the employment of metrical tricks; but he greatly impedes the progress of the narrative by introducing interminable speeches and long-winded descriptions.

We may mention, in conclusion, that there is also an epic in Prākrit which is attributed to Kālidāsa. This is the *Setu-bandha*, "Building of the Bridge," or *Rāvaṇa-vadha*, "Death of Rāvaṇa," which relates the story of Rāma. It is supposed to have been composed by the poet to commemorate the building of a bridge of boats across the Vitastā (Jhelum) by King Pravarasena of Kashmir.

There are a few prose romances dating from the sixth and seventh centuries, which being classed as Kāvyas by the Sanskrit writers on poetics, may be mentioned in this place. The abundant use of immense compounds, which of course makes them very difficult reading, is an essential characteristic of the style of these works. As to their matter, they contain but little action, consisting largely of scenes which are strung together by a meagre thread of narrative, and are made the occasion of lengthy descriptions full of long strings of comparisons and often teeming with puns. In spite, however, of their highly artificial and involved style, many really poetical thoughts may be found embedded in what to the European taste is an unattractive setting.

The *Daça-kumāra-charita*, or "Adventures of the Ten Princes," contains stories of common life and reflects a corrupt state of society. It is by DAṆḌIN, and probably dates from the sixth century A.D. *Vāsavadattā*, by SUBANDHU, relates the popular story of the heroine Vāsavadattā, princess of Ujjayinī, and Udayana, king of Vatsa. It was probably written quite at the beginning of the seventh century. Slightly later is BĀṆA'S *Kādambarī*, a poetical romance narrating the fortunes of a princess of that name. Another work of a somewhat similar character by the same author is the *Harsha-charita*, a romance in eight chapters, in which Bāṇa attempts to give some account of the life of King Harshavardhana of Kanauj. There is, however, but little narrative. Thus in twenty-five pages of the eighth chapter there are to be found five long descriptions, extending on the average to two pages, to say nothing of shorter ones. There is, for instance, a long disquisition, covering four pages, and full of strings of comparisons, about the miseries of servitude. A servant, "like a painted bow, is for ever bent in the one act of distending a string of imaginary virtues, but there is no force in him; like a heap of dust-sweepings gathered by a broom, he carries off toilet-leavings; like the meal offered to the Divine Mothers, he is cast out into space even at night; like a pumping machine, he has left all weight behind him and bends even for water," and so on. Soon after comes a description, covering two pages, of the trees in a forest. This is immediately followed by another page enumerating the various kinds of students thronging the wood in order to avail themselves of the teaching of a great Buddhist sage; they even include monkeys busily engaged in ritual ceremonies, devout parrots expounding a Buddhist dictionary, owls lecturing on the various births of Buddha, and tigers who have given up eating flesh under the calming influence of Buddhist teaching. Next comes a page describing the sage himself. "He was clad in a very soft red cloth, as if he were the eastern quarter of the sky bathed in the morning sunshine, teaching the other quarters to assume the red Buddhist attire, while they were flushed with the pure red glow of his body like a ruby freshly cut." Soon after comes a long account, bristling with puns, of a disconsolate princess lying prostrate in the wood—"lost in the forest and in thought, bent upon death and the root of a tree, fallen upon calamity and her nurse's bosom, parted from her husband and happiness, burned with the fierce sunshine and the woes of widowhood, her mouth closed with silence as well as by her hand, and held fast by her companions as well as by grief. I saw her with her kindred and her graces all gone, her ears and her soul left bare, her ornaments and her aims abandoned, her bracelets and her hopes broken, her companions and the needle-like grass-spears clinging round her feet, her eye and her beloved fixed within her bosom, her sighs and her hair long, her limbs and her merits exhausted, her aged attendants and her streaming tears falling down at her feet," and so forth.

CHAPTER XII

LYRIC POETRY

(*Circa* 400–1100 A.D.)

SANSKRIT lyrical poetry has not produced many works of any considerable length. But among these are included two of the most perfect creations of Kālidāsa, a writer distinguished no less in this field than as an epic and a dramatic author. His lyrical talent is, indeed, also sufficiently prominent in his plays.

Kālidāsa's *Meghadūta*, or "Cloud Messenger," is a lyrical gem which won the admiration of Goethe. It consists of 115 stanzas composed in the *Mandākrānta* metre of four lines of seventeen syllables. The theme is a message which an exile sends by a cloud to his wife dwelling far away. The idea is applied by Schiller in his *Maria Stuart*, where the captive Queen of Scots calls on the clouds as they fly southwards to greet the land of her youth (act iii. sc. 1). The exile is a Yaksha or attendant of Kubera, the god of wealth, who for neglect of his duty has been banished to the groves on the slopes of Rāmagiri in Central India. Emaciated and melancholy, he sees, at the approach of the rainy season, a dark cloud moving northwards. The sight fills his heart with yearning, and impels him to address to the cloud a request to convey a message of hope to his wife in the remote Himālaya. In the first half of the poem the Yaksha describes with much power and beauty the various scenes the cloud must traverse on its northward course :

Mount Āmrakūṭa, on whose peak it will rest after quenching with showers the forest fires; the Narmadā, winding at the foot of the Vindhya hills; the town of Vidiçā (Bhilsa), and the stream of the Vetravatī (Betwah); the city of Ujjayinī (Ujjain) in the land of Avanti; the sacred region of Kurukshetra; the Ganges and the mountains from which she sprang, white with snowfields, till Alakā on Mount Kailāsa is finally reached.

In the second half of the poem the Yaksha first describes the beauties of this city and his own dwelling there. Going on to paint in glowing colours the charms of his wife, her surroundings, and her occupations, he imagines her tossing on her couch, sleepless and emaciated, through the watches of the night. Then, when her eye rests on the window, the cloud shall proclaim to her with thunder-sound her husband's message, that he is still alive and ever longs to behold her:—

In creepers I discern thy form, in eyes of startled hinds thy glances,
And in the moon thy lovely face, in peacocks' plumes thy shining tresses;
The sportive frown upon thy brow in flowing waters' tiny ripples:
But never in one place combined can I, alas! behold thy likeness.

But courage, he says; our sorrow will end at last—we shall be re-united—

And then we will our hearts' desire, grown more intense by separation,
Enjoy in nights all glorious and bright, with full-orbed autumn moonlight.

Then begging the cloud, after delivering his message, to return with reassuring news, the exile finally dismisses him with the hope that he may never, even for a moment, be divided from his lightning spouse.

Besides the expression of emotion, the descriptive element is very prominent in this fine poem. This is still more true of Kālidāsa's *Ṛitusaṃhāra*, or "Cycle of the Seasons." That little work, which consists of 153 stanzas in six cantos, and is composed in various metres, is a highly poetical description of the six seasons into which classical Sanskrit poets usually divide the Indian year. With glowing descriptions of the beauties of Nature, in which erotic scenes are interspersed, the poet adroitly interweaves the expression of human emotions. Perhaps no other work of Kālidāsa's manifests so strikingly the poet's deep sympathy with Nature, his keen powers of observation, and his skill in depicting an Indian landscape in vivid colours.

The poem opens with an account of summer. If the glow of the sun is then too great during the day, the moonlit nights are all the more delightful to lovers. The moon, beholding the face of beauteous maidens, is beside itself with jealousy; then, too, it is that the heart of the wanderer is burnt by the fire of separation. Next follows a brilliant description of the effects of the heat: the thirst or lethargy it produces in serpent, lion, elephant, buffalo, boar, gazelle, peacock, crane, frogs, and fishes; the devastation caused by the forest fire which devours trees and shrubs, and drives before it crowds of terror-stricken beasts.

The close heat is succeeded by the rains, which are announced by the approach of the dark heavy clouds with their banner of lightning and drum of thunder. Slowly they move accompanied by *chātaka* birds, fabled to live exclusively on raindrops, till at length they discharge their water. The wild streams, like wanton girls, grasp in a trice the tottering trees upon their banks, as they rush onwards to the sea. The earth becomes covered with young blades of grass, and the forests clothe themselves with golden buds—

The mountains fill the soul with yearning thoughts of love,
When rain-charged clouds bend down to kiss the tow'ring rocks,
When all around upon their slopes the streams gush down,
And throngs of peacocks that begin to dance are seen.

Next comes the autumn, beauteous as a newly-wedded bride, with face of full-blown lotuses, with robe of sugar-cane and ripening rice, with the cry of flamingoes representing the tinkling of her anklets. The graceful creepers vie with the arms of lovely women, and the jasmine, showing through the crimson *açoka* blossoms, rivals the dazzling teeth and red lips of smiling maidens.

Winter follows, when the rice ripens, while the lotus fades and the fields in the morning are covered with rime—

Then the Priyangu creeper, reaching ripeness,
Buffeted constantly by chilling breezes,
Grows, O Beloved, ever pale and paler,
Like lonely maiden from her lover parted.

This is the time dear to lovers, whose joys the poet describes in glowing colours.

In the cold season a fire and the mild rays of the sun are pleasant. The night does not attract lovers now, for the moonbeams are cold and the light of the stars is pale.

The poet dwells longest on the delights of spring, the last of the six seasons. It is then that maidens, with *karṇikāra* flowers on their ears, with red *açoka* blossoms and sprays of jasmine in their locks, go to meet their lovers. Then the hum of intoxicated bees is heard, and the note of the Indian cuckoo; then the blossoms of the mango-tree are seen: these are the sharp arrows wherewith the god of the flowery bow enflames the hearts of maidens to love.

A lyric poem of a very artificial character, and consisting of only twenty-two stanzas, is the *Ghaṭa-karpara*, or "Potsherd," called after the author's name, which is worked into the last verse. The date of the poet is unknown. He is mentioned as one of the "nine gems" at the court of the mythical Vikramāditya in the verse already mentioned.

The *Chaura-panchāçikā*, or "Fifty Stanzas of the Thief," is a lyrical poem which contains many beauties. Its author was the Kashmirian Bilhaṇa, who belongs to the later half of the eleventh century. According to the romantic tradition, this poet secretly enjoyed the love of a princess, and when found out was condemned to death. He thereupon composed fifty stanzas, each beginning with the words "Even now I remember," in which he describes with glowing enthusiasm the joys of love he had experienced. Their effect on the king was so great that he forgave the poet and bestowed on him the hand of his daughter.

The main bulk of the lyrical creations of mediæval India are not connected poems of considerable length, but consist of that miniature painting which, as with a few strokes, depicts an amatory situation or sentiment in a single stanza of four lines. These lyrics are in many respects cognate to the sententious poetry which the Indians cultivated with such eminent success. Bearing evidence of great wealth of observation and depth of feeling, they are often drawn by a master-hand. Many of them are in matter and form gems of perfect beauty. Some of their charm is, however, lost in translation owing to the impossibility of reproducing the elaborate metres employed in the original. Several Sanskrit poets composed collections of these miniature lyrics.

The most eminent of these authors is BHARTṚIHARI, grammarian, philosopher, and poet in one. Only the literary training of India could make such a combination possible, and even there it has hardly a parallel. Bhartṛihari lived in the first half of the seventh century. The Chinese traveller I Tsing, who spent more than twenty years in India at the end of that century, records that, having turned Buddhist monk, the poet again became a layman, and fluctuated altogether seven times between the monastery and the world. Bhartṛihari blamed himself for, but could not overcome, his inconstancy. He wrote three centuries of detached stanzas. Of the first and last, which are sententious in character, there will be occasion to say something later. Only the second, entitled *Çṛingāra-çataka*, or "Century of Love," deals with erotic sentiment. Here Bhartṛihari, in graceful and meditative verse, shows himself to be well acquainted both with the charms of women and with the arts by which they captivate the hearts of men. Who, he asks in one of these miniature poems, is not filled with yearning thoughts of love in spring, when the air swoons with the scent of the mango blossom and is filled with the hum of bees intoxicated with honey? In another he avers that none can resist the charms of lotus-eyed maidens, not even learned men, whose utterances about renouncing love are mere idle words. The poet himself laments that, when his beloved is away, the brightness goes out of his life—

Beside the lamp, the flaming hearth,
In light of sun or moon and stars,
Without my dear one's lustrous eyes
This world is wholly dark to me.

At the same time he warns the unwary against reflecting over-much on female beauty—

Let not thy thoughts, O Wanderer,
Roam in that forest, woman's form:
For there a robber ever lurks,
Ready to strike—the God of Love.

In another stanza the Indian Cupid appears as a fisherman, who, casting on the ocean of this world a hook called woman, quickly catches men as fishes eager for the bait of ruddy lips, and bakes them in the fire of love.

Strange are the contradictions in which the poet finds himself involved by loving a maiden—

Remembered she but causes pain;
At sight of her my madness grows;
When touched, she makes my senses reel:
How, pray, can such an one be loved?

So towards the end of the Century the poet's heart begins to turn from the allurements of love. "Cease, maiden," he exclaims, "to cast thy glances on me: thy trouble is in vain. I am an altered man; youth has gone by and my thoughts are bent on the forest; my infatuation is over, and the whole world I now account but as a wisp of straw." Thus Bhartṛihari prepares the way for his third collection, the "Century of Renunciation."

A short but charming treasury of detached erotic verses is the *Çṛingāra-tilaka,* which tradition attributes to Kālidāsa. In its twenty-three stanzas occur some highly imaginative analogies, worked out with much originality. In one of them, for instance, the poet asks how it comes that a maiden, whose features and limbs resemble various tender flowers, should have a heart of stone. In another he compares his mistress to a hunter—

> *This maiden like a huntsman is;*
> *Her brow is like the bow he bends;*
> *Her sidelong glances are his darts;*
> *My heart's the antelope she slays.*

The most important lyrical work of this kind is the *Amaru-çataka*, or "Hundred stanzas of Amaru." The author is a master in the art of painting lovers in all their moods, bliss and dejection, anger and devotion. He is especially skilful in depicting the various stages of estrangement and reconciliation. It is remarkable how, with a subject so limited, in situations and emotions so similar, the poet succeeds in arresting the attention with surprising turns of thought, and with subtle touches which are ever new. The love which Amaru as well as other Indian lyrists portrays is not of the romantic and ideal, but rather of the sensuous type. Nevertheless his work often shows delicacy of feeling and refinement of thought. Such, for instance, is the case when he describes a wife watching in the gloaming for the return of her absent husband.

Many lyrical gems are to be found preserved in the Sanskrit treatises on poetics. One such is a stanza on the red *açoka*. In this the poet asks the tree to say whither his mistress has gone; it need not shake its head in the wind, as if to say it did not know; for how could it be flowering so brilliantly had it not been touched by the foot of his beloved?[1]

In all this lyrical poetry the plant and animal world plays an important part and is treated with much charm. Of flowers, the lotus is the most conspicuous. One of these stanzas, for example, describes the day-lotuses as closing their calyx-eyes in the evening, because unwilling to see the sun, their spouse and benefactor, sink down bereft of his rays. Another describes with pathetic beauty the dream of a bee: "The night will pass, the fair dawn will come, the sun will rise, the lotuses will laugh;" while a bee thus mused within the calyx, an elephant, alas! tore up the lotus plant.

Various birds to which poetical myths are attached are frequently introduced as furnishing analogies to human life and love. The *chātaka*, which would rather die of thirst than drink aught but the raindrops from the cloud, affords an illustration of pride. The *chakora*, supposed to imbibe the rays of the moon, affords a parallel to the lover who with his eyes drinks in the beams of his beloved's face. The *chakravāka*, which, fabled to be condemned to nocturnal separation from his mate, calls to her with plaintive cry during the watches of the night, serves as an emblem of conjugal fidelity.

In all this lyric poetry the bright eyes and beauty of Indian girls find a setting in scenes brilliant with blossoming trees, fragrant with flowers, gay with the plumage and vocal with the song of birds, diversified with lotus ponds steeped in tropical sunshine and with large-eyed gazelles reclining in the shade. Some of its gems are well worthy of having inspired the genius of

[1] Referring to the poetical belief that the *açoka* only blossoms when struck by the foot of a beautiful girl.

Heine to produce such lyrics as *Die Lotosblume* and *Auf Flügeln des Gesanges.*

A considerable amount of lyrical poetry of the same type has also been produced in Prākrit, especially in the extensive anthology entitled *Saptaçataka*, or "Seven Centuries," of the poet Hāla, who probably lived before A.D. 1000. It contains many beauties, and is altogether a rich treasury of popular Indian lyrical poetry. It must suffice here to refer to but one of the stanzas contained in this collection. In this little poem the moon is described as a white swan sailing on the pure nocturnal lake of the heavens, studded with starry lotuses.

The transitional stage between pure lyric and pure drama is represented by the *Gītagovinda*, or "Cowherd in Song," a lyrical drama, which, though dating from the twelfth century, is the earliest literary specimen of a primitive type of play that still survives in Bengal, and must have preceded the regular dramas. The poem contains no dialogue in the proper sense, for its three characters only engage in a kind of lyrical monologue, of which one of the other two is supposed to be an auditor, sometimes even no one at all. The subject of the poem is the love of Kṛishṇa for the beautiful cowherdess Rādhā, the estrangement of the lovers, and their final reconciliation. It is taken from that episode of Kṛishṇa's life in which he himself was a herdsman (*go-vinda*), living on the banks of the Yamunā, and enjoying to the full the love of the cowherdesses. The only three characters of the poem are Kṛishṇa, Rādhā, and a confidante of the latter.

Its author, Jayadeva, was probably a native of Bengal, having been a contemporary of a Bengal king named Lakshmaṇasena. It is probable that he took as his model popular plays representing incidents from the life of Kṛishṇa, as the modern *yātrās* in Bengal still do. The latter festival plays even now consist chiefly of lyrical stanzas, partly recited and partly sung, the dialogue being but scanty, and to a considerable extent left to improvisation. On such a basis Jayadeva created his highly artificial poem. The great perfection of form he has here attained, by combining grace of diction with ease in handling the most difficult metres, has not failed to win the admiration of all who are capable of reading the original Sanskrit. Making abundant use of alliteration and the most complex rhymes occurring, as in the *Nalodaya*, not only at the end, but in the middle of metrical lines,[1] the poet has adapted the most varied and melodious measures to the expression of exuberant erotic emotions, with a skill which could not be surpassed. It seems impossible to reproduce Jayadeva's verse adequately in an English garb. The German poet Rückert, has, however, come as near to the highly artificial beauty of the original, both in form and matter, as is feasible in any translation.

It is somewhat strange that a poem which describes the transports of sensual love with all the exuberance of an Oriental fancy should, in the present instance, and not for the first time, have received an allegorical explanation in a mystical religious sense. According to Indian interpreters, the separation of Kṛishṇa and Rādhā, their seeking for each other, and their final reconciliation represent the relation of the supreme deity to the human soul. This may possibly have been the intention of Jayadeva, though only as a leading idea, not to be followed out in detail.

[1] E.g. *amala-kamala-dala-lochana bhava-mochana.*

CHAPTER XIII

THE DRAMA

(*Circa* 400–1000 A.D.)

TO the European mind the history of the Indian drama cannot but be a source of abundant interest; for here we have an important branch of literature which has had a full and varied national development, quite independent of Western influence, and which throws much light on Hindu social customs during the five or six centuries preceding the Muhammadan conquest.

The earliest forms of dramatic literature in India are represented by those hymns of the *Rigveda* which contain dialogues, such as those of Saramā and the Paṇis, Yama and Yamī, Purūravas and Urvaçī, the latter, indeed, being the foundation of a regular play composed much more than a thousand years later by the greatest dramatist of India. The origin of the acted drama is, however, wrapt in obscurity. Nevertheless, the evidence of tradition and of language suffice to direct us with considerable probability to its source.

The words for actor (*naṭa*) and play (*nāṭaka*) are derived from the verb *naṭ*, the Prākrit or vernacular form of the Sanskrit *nṛit*, "to dance." The name is familiar to English ears in the form of *nautch*, the Indian dancing of the present day. The latter, indeed, probably represents the beginnings of the Indian drama. It must at first have consisted only of rude pantomime, in which the dancing movements of the body were accompanied by mute mimicking gestures of hand and face. Songs, doubtless, also early formed an ingredient in such performances. Thus Bharata, the name of the mythical inventor of the drama, which in Sanskrit also means "actor," in several of the vernaculars signifies "singer," as in the Gujaratī *Bharot*. The addition of dialogue was the last step in the development, which was thus much the same in India and in Greece. This primitive stage is represented by the Bengal *yātrās* and the *Gītagovinda*. These form the transition to the fully-developed Sanskrit play in which lyrics and dialogue are blended.

The earliest references to the acted drama are to be found in the *Mahābhāshya*, which mentions representations of the *Kaṃsavadha*, the "Slaying of Kaṃsa," and the *Balibandha*, or "Binding of Bali," episodes in the history of Kṛishṇa. Indian tradition describes Bharata as having caused to be acted before the gods a play representing the *svayaṃvara* of Lakshmī, wife of Vishṇu. Tradition further makes Kṛishṇa and his cowherdesses the starting-point of the *saṃgīta*, a representation consisting of a mixture of song, music, and dancing. The *Gītagovinda* is concerned with Kṛishṇa, and the modern *yātrās* generally represent scenes from the life of that deity. From all this it seems likely that the Indian drama was developed in connection with the cult of Vishṇu-Kṛishṇa, and that the earliest acted representations were therefore, like the mysteries of the Christian Middle Ages, a kind of religious plays, in which scenes from the legend of the god were enacted mainly with the aid of song and dance, supplemented with prose dialogue improvised by the performers.

The drama has had a rich and varied development in India, as is shown not only by the numerous plays that have been preserved, but by the native treatises on poetics which contain elaborate rules for the construction and style of plays. Thus the *Sāhitya-darpaṇa*, or "Mirror of Rhetoric," divides Sanskrit dramas into two main classes, a higher (*rūpaka*) and a lower (*uparūpaka*), and distinguishes no fewer than ten species of the former and eighteen of the latter.

The characteristic features of the Indian drama which strike the Western student are the entire absence of tragedy, the interchange of lyrical stanzas with prose dialogue, and the use of Sanskrit for some characters and of Prākrit for others.

The Sanskrit drama is a mixed composition, in which joy is mingled with sorrow, in which the jester usually plays a prominent part, while the hero and heroine are often in the depths of despair. But it never has a sad ending. The emotions of terror, grief, or pity, with which the audience are inspired, are therefore always tranquillised by the happy termination of the story. Nor may any deeply tragic incident take place in the course of the play; for death is never allowed to be represented on the stage. Indeed nothing considered indecorous, whether of a serious or comic character, is allowed to be enacted in the sight or hearing of the spectators, such as the utterance of a curse, degradation, banishment, national calamity, biting, scratching, kissing, eating, or sleeping.

Sanskrit plays are full of lyrical passages describing scenes or persons presented to view, or containing reflections suggested by the incidents that occur. They usually consist of four-line stanzas. *Çakuntalā* contains nearly two hundred such, representing something like one half of the whole play. These lyrical passages are composed in a great many different metres. Thus the first thirty-four stanzas of *Çakuntalā* exhibit no fewer than eleven varieties of verse. It is not possible, as in the case of the simple Vedic metres, to imitate in English the almost infinite resources of the complicated and entirely quantitative classical Sanskrit measures. The spirit of the lyrical passages is, therefore, probably best reproduced by using blank verse as the familiar metre of our drama. The prose of the dialogue in the plays is often very commonplace, serving only as an introduction to the lofty sentiment of the poetry that follows.

In accordance with their social position, the various characters in a Sanskrit play speak different dialects. Sanskrit is employed only by heroes, kings, Brahmans, and men of high rank; Prākrit by all women and by men of the lower orders. Distinctions are further made in the use of Prākrit itself. Thus women of high position employ Mahārāshṭrī in lyrical passages, but otherwise they, as well as children and the better class of servants, speak Çaurasenī. Māgadhī is used, for instance, by attendants in the royal palace, Avantī by rogues or gamblers, Abhīrī by cowherds, Paiçāchī by charcoal-burners, and Apabhramça by the lowest and most despised people as well as barbarians.

The Sanskrit dramatists show considerable skill in weaving the incidents of the plot and in the portrayal of individual character, but do not show much fertility of invention, commonly borrowing the story of their plays from history or epic legend. Love is the subject of most Indian dramas. The hero, usually a king, already the husband of one or more wives, is smitten at first sight with the charms of some fair maiden. The heroine, equally susceptible, at once reciprocates his affection, but concealing her passion, keeps her lover in agonies of suspense. Harassed by doubts, obstacles, and delays, both are reduced to a melancholy and emaciated condition. The somewhat doleful effect produced by their plight is relieved by the animated doings of the heroine's confidantes, but especially by the proceedings of the court-jester (*vidūshaka*), the constant companion of the hero. He excites ridicule by his bodily defects no less than his clumsy interference with the course of the hero's affairs. His attempts at wit are, however, not of a high order. It is somewhat strange that a character occupying the position of a universal butt should always be a Brahman.

While the Indian drama shows some affinities with Greek comedy, it affords more striking points of resemblance to the productions of the Elizabethan playwrights, and in particular of Shakespeare. The aim of the Indian dramatists is not to portray types of character, but individual persons; nor do they observe the rule of unity of time or place. They are given to introducing romantic and fabulous elements; they mix prose with verse; they blend the comic with the serious, and introduce puns and comic distortions of words. The character of the *vidūshaka*, too, is a close parallel to the fool in Shakespeare. Common to both are also several contrivances intended to further the action of the drama, such as the writing of letters, the introduction of a play within a play, the restoration of the dead to life, and the use of intoxication on the stage as a humorous device. Such a series of coincidences, in a case where influence or borrowing is absolutely out of the question, is an instructive instance of how similar developments can arise independently.

Every Sanskrit play begins with a prologue or introduction, which regularly opens with a prayer or benediction (*nāndī*) invoking the national deity in favour of the audience. Then generally follows a dialogue between the stage-manager and one or two actors, which refers to the play and its author, seeks to win public favour by paying a complimentary tribute to the critical acumen of the spectators, mentions past events and present circumstances elucidating the plot, and invariably ends by adroitly introducing one of the characters of the actual play. A Sanskrit drama is divided into scenes and acts. The former are marked by the entrance of one character and the exit of another. The stage is never left vacant till the end of the act, nor does any change of locality take place till then. Before a new act an interlude (called *vishkambha* or *praveçaka*), consisting of a monologue or dialogue, is often introduced. In this scene allusion is made to events supposed to have occurred in the interval, and the audience are prepared for what is about to take place. The whole piece closes with a prayer for national prosperity, which is addressed to the favourite deity and is spoken by one of the principal characters.

The number of acts in a play varies from one to ten ; but, while fluctuating somewhat, is determined by the character of the drama. Thus the species called *nāṭikā* has four acts and the farcical *prahasana* only one.

The duration of the events is supposed to be identical with the time occupied in performing them on the stage, or, at most, a day; and a night is assumed to elapse between each act and that which follows. Occasionally, however, the interval is much longer. Thus in Kālidāsa's *Çakuntalā* and *Urvaçī* several years pass between the first and the last act; while in Bhavabhūti's *Uttara-rāmacharita* no less than twelve years elapse between the first and the second act.

Nor is unity of place observed; for the scene may be transferred from one part of the earth to another, or even to the aërial regions. Change of locality sometimes occurs even within the same act; as when a journey is supposed to be performed through the air in a celestial car. It is somewhat curious that while there are many and minute stage directions about dress and decorations no less than about the actions of the players, nothing is said in this way as to change of scene. As regards the number of characters appearing in a play, no limit of any kind is imposed.

There were no special theatres in the Indian Middle Ages, and plays seem to have been performed in the concert-room (*saṃgīta-çālā*) of royal palaces. A curtain divided in the middle was a necessary part of the stage arrangement; it did not, however, separate the audience from the stage, as in the Roman theatre, but formed the background of the stage. Behind the curtain was the tiring-room (*nepathya*), whence the actors came on the stage. When they were intended to enter hurriedly, they were directed to do so "with a toss of the curtain." The stage scenery and decorations were of a very simple order, much being left to the imagination of the spectator, as in the Shakespearian drama. Weapons, seats, thrones, and chariots appeared on the stage; but it is highly improbable that the latter were drawn by the living animals supposed to be attached to them. Owing to the very frequent intercourse between the inhabitants of heaven and earth, there may have been some kind of aërial contrivance to represent celestial chariots; but owing to the repeated occurrence of the stage direction "gesticulating" (*nāṭayitvā*) in this connection, it is to be supposed that the impression of motion and speed was produced on the audience simply by the gestures of the actors.

The best productions of the Indian drama are nearly a dozen in number, and date from a period embracing something like four hundred years, from about the beginning of the fifth to the end of the eighth century A.D. These plays are the compositions of the great dramatists Kālidāsa and Bhavabhūti, or have come down under the names of the royal patrons Çūdraka and Çrīharsha, to whom their real authors attributed them.

The greatest of all is KĀLIDĀSA, already known to us as the author of several of the best Kāvyas. Three of his plays have been preserved, *Çakuntalā*, *Vikramorvaçī*, and *Mālavikāgnimitra*. The richness of creative fancy which he displays in these, and his skill in the expression of tender feeling, assign him a high place among the dramatists of the world. The harmony of the poetic sentiment is nowhere disturbed by anything violent or terrifying. Every passion is softened without being enfeebled. The ardour of love never goes beyond æsthetic bounds; it never maddens to wild jealousy or hate. The torments of sorrow are toned down to a profound and touching melancholy. It was here at last that the Indian genius found the law of moderation in poetry, which it hardly knew elsewhere, and thus produced works of enduring beauty. Hence it was that *Çakuntalā* exercised so great a fascination on the calm intellect of Goethe, who at the same time was so strongly repelled by the extravagances of Hindu mythological art.

In comparison with the Greek and the modern drama, Nature occupies a much more important place in Sanskrit plays. The characters are surrounded by Nature, with which they are in constant communion. The mango and other trees, creepers, lotuses, and pale-red trumpet-flowers, gazelles, flamingoes, bright-hued parrots, and Indian cuckoos, in the midst of which they move, are often addressed by them and form an essential part of their lives. Hence the influence of Nature on the minds of lovers is much dwelt on. Prominent everywhere in classical Sanskrit poetry, these elements of Nature luxuriate most of all in the drama.

The finest of Kālidāsa's works are, it cannot be denied, defective as stage-plays. The very delicacy of the sentiment, combined with a certain want of action, renders them incapable of producing a powerful effect on an audience. The best representatives of the romantic drama of India are *Çakuntalā* and *Vikramorvaçī*. Dealing with the love adventures of two famous kings of ancient epic legend, they represent scenes far removed from reality, in which heaven and earth are not separated, and men, demigods, nymphs, and saints are intermingled. *Mālavikāgnimitra*, on the other hand, not concerned with the heroic or divine, is a palace-and-harem drama, a story of contemporary love and intrigue.

The plot of *Çakuntalā* is derived from the first book of the *Mahābhārata*. The hero is Dushyanta, a celebrated king of ancient days, the heroine, Çakuntalā, the daughter of a celestial nymph, Menakā, and of the sage Viçvāmitra; while their son, Bharata, became the founder of a famous race. The piece consists of seven acts, and belongs to the class of drama by native writers on poetics styled *nāṭaka*, or "*the* play." In this the plot must be taken from mythology or history, the characters must be heroic or divine; it should be written in elaborate style, and full of noble sentiments, with five acts at least, and not more than ten.

After the prelude, in which an actress sings a charming lyric on the beauties of summer-time, King Dushyanta appears pursuing a gazelle in the sacred grove of the sage Kaṇva. Here he catches sight of Çakuntalā, who, accompanied by her two maiden friends, is engaged in watering her favourite trees. Struck by her beauty, he exclaims—

Her lip is ruddy as an opening bud,
Her graceful arms resemble tender shoots:
Attractive as the bloom upon the tree,
The glow of youth is spread on all her limbs.

Seizing an opportunity of addressing her, he soon feels that it is impossible for him to return to his capital—

My limbs move forward, while my heart flies back,
Like silken standard borne against the breeze.

In the second act the comic element is introduced with the jester Māṭhavya, who is as much disgusted with his master's love-lorn condition as with his fondness for the chase. In the third act, the love-sick Çakuntalā is discovered lying on a bed of flowers in an arbour. The king overhears her conversation with her two friends, shows himself, and offers to wed the heroine. An interlude explains how a choleric ascetic, named Durvāsa, enraged at not being greeted by Çakuntalā with due courtesy, owing to her pre-occupied state, had pronounced a curse which should cause her to be entirely forgotten by her lover, who could recognise her only by means of a ring.

The king having meanwhile married Çakuntalā and returned home, the sage Kaṇva has resolved to send her to her husband. The way in which Çakuntalā takes leave of the sacred grove in which she has been brought up, of her flowers, her gazelles, and her friends, is charmingly described in the fourth act. This is the act which contains the most obvious beauties; for here the poet displays to the full the richness of his fancy, his abundant sympathy with Nature, and a profound knowledge of the human heart.

A young Brahman pupil thus describes the dawning of the day on which Çakuntalā is to leave the forest hermitage—

On yonder side the moon, the Lord of Plants,
Sinks down behind the western mountain's crest;
On this, the sun preceded by the dawn
Appears: the setting and the rise at once
Of these two orbs the symbols are of man's
Own fluctuating fortunes in the world.

Then he continues—

The moon has gone; the lilies on the lake,
Whose beauty lingers in the memory,
No more delight my gaze: they droop and fade;
Deep is their sorrow for their absent lord.

The aged hermit of the grove thus expresses his feelings at the approaching loss of Çakuntalā—

My heart is touched with sadness at the thought
"Çakuntalā must go to-day"; my throat
Is choked with flow of tears repressed; my sight
Is dimmed with pensiveness; but if the grief

Of an old forest hermit is so great,
How keen must be the pang a father feels
When freshly parted from a cherished child!

Then calling on the trees to give her a kindly farewell, he exclaims—

The trees, the kinsmen of her forest home,
Now to Çakuntalā give leave to go:
They with the Kokila's melodious cry
Their answer make.

Thereupon the following good wishes are uttered by voices in the air—

Thy journey be auspicious; may the breeze,
Gentle and soothing, fan thy cheek; may lakes
All bright with lily cups delight thine eye;
The sunbeams' heat be cooled by shady trees;
The dust beneath thy feet the pollen be
Of lotuses.

The fifth act, in which Çakuntalā appears before her husband, is deeply moving. The king fails to recognise her, and, though treating her not unkindly, refuses to acknowledge her as his wife. As a last resource, Çakuntalā bethinks herself of the ring given her by her husband, but on discovering that it is lost, abandons hope. She is then borne off to heaven by celestial agency.

In the following interlude we see a fisherman dragged along by constables for having in his possession the royal signet-ring, which he professes to have found inside a fish. The king, however, causes him to be set free, rewarding him handsomely for his find. Recollection of his former love now returns to Dushyanta. While he is indulging in sorrow at his repudiation of Çakuntalā, Mātali, Indra's charioteer, appears on the scene to ask the king's aid in vanquishing the demons.

In the last act Dushyanta is seen driving in Indra's car to Hemakūṭa, the mountain of the Gandharvas. Here he sees a young boy playing with a lion cub. Taking his hand, without knowing him to be his own son, he exclaims—

If now the touch of but a stranger's child
Thus sends a thrill of joy through all my limbs,
What transports must he waken in the soul
Of that blest father from whose loins he sprang!

Soon after he finds and recognises Çakuntalā, with whom he is at length happily reunited.

Kālidāsa's play has come down to us in two main recensions. The so-called Devanāgarī one, shorter and more concise, is probably the older and better. The more diffuse Bengal recension became known first through the translation of Sir William Jones.

Vikramorvaçī, or "Urvaçī won by Valour," is a play in five acts, belonging to the class called *Troṭaka*, which is described as representing events partly terrestrial and partly celestial, and as consisting of five, seven, eight, or nine acts. Its plot is briefly as follows. King Purūravas, hearing from nymphs that their companion, Urvaçī, has been carried off by demons, goes to the rescue and brings her back on his car. He is enraptured by the beauty of the nymph, no less than she is captivated by her deliverer. Urvaçī being summoned before the throne of Indra, the lovers are soon obliged to part.

In the second act Urvaçī appears for a short time to the king as he disconsolately wanders in the garden. A letter, in which she had written a confession of her love, is discovered by the queen, who refuses to be pacified.

In the third act we learn that Urvaçī had been acting before Indra in a play representing the betrothal of Lakshmī, and had, when asked on whom her heart was set, named Purūravas instead of Purushottama (*i.e.* Vishṇu). She is consequently cursed by her teacher, Bharata, but is forgiven by Indra, who allows her to be united with Purūravas till the latter sees his offspring.

The fourth act is peculiar in being almost entirely lyrical. The lovers are wandering near Kailāsa, the divine mountain, when Urvaçī, in a fit of jealousy, enters the grove of Kumāra, god of war, which is forbidden to all females. In consequence of Bharata's curse, she is instantly transformed into a creeper. The king, beside himself with grief at her loss, seeks her everywhere. He apostrophises various insects, birds, beasts, and even a mountain peak, to tell him where she is. At last he thinks he sees her in the mountain stream :—

The rippling wave is like her frown; the row
Of tossing birds her girdle; streaks of foam
Her flutt'ring garment as she speeds along;
The current, her devious and stumbling gait:
'Tis she turned in her wrath into a stream.

Finally, under the influence of a magic stone, which has come into his possession, he clasps a creeper, which is transformed into Urvaçī in his arms.

Between the fourth and fifth acts several years elapse. Then Purūravas, by accident, discovers his son Āyus, whom Urvaçī had secretly borne, and had caused to be brought up in a hermitage. Urvaçī must therefore return to heaven. Indra, however, in return for Purūravas' services against the demons, makes a new concession, and allows the nymph to remain with the king for good.

There are two recensions of this play also, one of them belonging to Southern India.

The doubts long entertained, on the ground of its

inferiority and different character, as to whether *Mālavikāgnimitra*, or "Mālavikā and Agnimitra," is really the work of Kālidāsa, who is mentioned in the prologue as the author, are hardly justified. The piece has been shown by Weber to agree pretty closely in thought and diction with the two other plays of the poet; and though certainly not equal to the latter in poetic merit, it possesses many beauties. The subject is not heroic or divine, the plot being derived from the ordinary palace life of Indian princes, and thus supplying a peculiarly good picture of the social conditions of the times. The hero is a historical king of the dynasty of the Çungas, who reigned at Vidiçā (Bhilsa) in the second century B.C. The play describes the loves of this king Agnimitra and of Mālavikā, one of the attendants of the queen, who jealously keeps her out of the king's sight on account of her great beauty. The various endeavours of the king to see and converse with Mālavikā give rise to numerous little intrigues. In the course of these Agnimitra nowhere appears as a despot, but acts with much delicate consideration for the feelings of his spouses. It finally turns out that Mālavikā is by birth a princess, who had only come to be an attendant at Agnimitra's court through having fallen into the hands of robbers. There being now no objection to her union with the king, all ends happily.

While Kālidāsa stands highest in poetical refinement, in tenderness, and depth of feeling, the author of the *Mṛicchakaṭikā*, or "Clay Cart," is pre-eminent among Indian playwrights for the distinctively dramatic qualities of vigour, life, and action, no less than sharpness of characterisation, being thus allied in genius to Shakespeare. This play is also marked by originality and good sense. Attributed to a king named Çūdraka, who is panegyrised in the prologue, it is probably the work of a poet patronised by him, perhaps Daṇḍin, as Professor Pischel thinks. In any case, it not improbably belongs to the sixth century. It is divided into ten acts, and belongs to the dramatic class called *prakaraṇa.* The name has little to do with the play, being derived from an unimportant episode of the sixth act. The scene is laid in Ujjayinī and its neighbourhood. The number of characters appearing on the stage is very considerable. The chief among them are Chārudatta, a Brahman merchant who has lost all his property by excessive liberality, and Vasantasenā, a rich courtesan who loves the poor but noble Chārudatta, and ultimately becomes his wife. The third act contains a humorous account of a burglary, in which stealing is treated as a fine art. In the fourth act there is a detailed description of the splendours of Vasantasenā's palace. Though containing much exaggeration, it furnishes an interesting picture of the kind of luxury that prevailed in those days. Altogether this play abounds in comic situations, besides containing many serious scenes, some of which even border on the tragic.

To the first half of the seventh century belong the two dramas attributed to the famous King Çrīharsha or Harshadeva, a patron of poets, whom we already know as Harshavardhana of Thāneçar and Kanauj. *Ratnāvalī*, or "The Pearl Necklace," reflecting the court and harem life of the age, has many points of similarity with Kālidāsa's *Mālavikāgnimitra*, by which, indeed, its plot was probably suggested. It is the story of the loves of Udayana, king of Vatsa, and of Sāgarikā, an attendant of his queen Vāsavadattā. The heroine ultimately turns out to be Ratnāvalī, princess of Ceylon, who had found her way to

Udayana's court after suffering shipwreck. The plot is unconnected with mythology, but is based on an historical or epic tradition, which recurs in a somewhat different form in Somadeva's *Kathāsaritsāgara.* As concerned with the second marriage of the king, it forms a sequel to the popular love-story of Vāsavadattā. It is impossible to say whether the poet modified the main outlines of the traditional story, but the character of the magician who conjures up a vision of the gods and a conflagration, is his invention, as well as the incidents, which are of an entirely domestic nature. The real author was doubtless some poet resident at Çrīharsha's court, possibly Bāṇa, who also wrote a play entitled *Pārvatīpariṇaya.*

Altogether, *Ratnāvalī* is an agreeable play, with well-drawn characters and many poetical beauties. Of the latter the following lines, in which the king describes the pale light in the east heralding the rise of the moon, may serve as a specimen :—

> *Our minds intent upon the festival,*
> *We saw not that the twilight passed away:*
> *Behold, the east proclaims the lord of night*
> *Still hidden by the mountain where he rises,*
> *Even as a maiden by her pale face shows*
> *That in her inmost heart a lover dwells.*

Another play of considerable merit attributed to Çrīharsha is *Nāgānanda.* It is a sensational piece with a Buddhistic colouring, the hero being a Buddhist and Buddha being praised in the introductory benediction. For this reason its author was probably different from that of *Ratnāvalī*, and may have been Dhāvaka, who, like Bāṇa, is known to have lived at the court of Çrīharsha.

The dramatist BHAVABHŪTI was a Brahman of the Taittirīya school of the *Yajurveda* and belonged, as we learn from his prologues, to Vidarbha (now Berar) in Southern India. He knew the city of Ujjayinī well, and probably spent at least a part of his life there. His patron was King Yaçovarman of Kānyakubja (Kanauj), who ruled during the first half of the eighth century.

Three plays by this poet, all abounding in poetic beauties, have come down to us. They contrast in two or three respects with the works of the earlier dramatists. The absence of the character of the jester is characteristic of them, the comic and witty element entering into them only to a slight extent. While other Indian poets dwell on the delicate and mild beauties of Nature, Bhavabhūti loves to depict her grand and sublime aspects, doubtless owing to the influence on his mind of the southern mountains of his native land. He is, moreover, skilful not only in drawing characters inspired by tender and noble sentiment, but in giving effective expression to depth and force of passion.

The best known and most popular of Bhavabhūti's plays is *Mālatī-mādhava*, a *prakaraṇa* in ten acts. The scene is laid in Ujjayinī, and the subject is the love-story of Mālatī, daughter of a minister of the country, and Mādhava, a young scholar studying in the city, and son of the minister of another state. Skilfully interwoven with this main story are the fortunes of Makaranda, a friend of Mādhava, and Madayantikā, a sister of the king's favourite. Mālatī and Mādhava meet and fall in love; but the king has determined that the heroine shall marry his favourite, whom she detests. This plan is frustrated by Makaranda, who, personating Mālatī, goes through the wedding ceremony with the bridegroom. The lovers, aided in their projects by two amiable Buddhist nuns, are finally united. The piece is a sort of

Indian *Romeo and Juliet* with a happy ending, the part played by the nun Kāmandakī being analogous to that of Friar Laurence in Shakespeare's drama. The contrast produced by scenes of tender love, and the horrible doings of the priestess of the dread goddess Durgā, is certainly effective, but perhaps too violent. The use made of swoons, from which the recovery is, however, very rapid, is rather too common in this play.

The ninth act contains several fine passages describing the scenery of the Vindhya range. The following is a translation of one of them :—

This mountain with its towering rocks delights
The eye : its peaks grow dark with gathering clouds ;
Its groves are thronged with peacocks eloquent
In joy ; the trees upon its slopes are bright
With birds that flit about their nests ; the caves
Reverberate the growl of bears ; the scent
Of incense-trees is wafted, sharp and cool,
From branches broken off by elephants.

The other two dramas of Bhavabhūti represent the fortunes of the same national hero, Rāma. The plot of the *Mahāvīra-charita*, or "The Fortunes of the Great Hero," varies but slightly from the story told in the *Rāmāyaṇa*. The play, which is divided into seven acts and is crowded with characters, concludes with the coronation of Rāma. The last act illustrates well how much is left to the imagination of the spectator. It represents the journey of Rāma in an aërial car from Ceylon all the way to Ayodhyā (Oudh) in Northern India, the scenes traversed being described by one of the company.

The *Uttara-rāma-charita*, or "The Later Fortunes of Rāma," is a romantic piece containing many fine passages. Owing to lack of action, however, it is rather a dramatic poem than a play. The description of the tender love of Rāma and Sītā, purified by sorrow, exhibits more genuine pathos than appears perhaps in any other Indian drama. The play begins with the banishment of Sītā and ends with her restoration, after twelve years of grievous solitude, to the throne of Ayodhyā amid popular acclamations. Her two sons, born after her banishment and reared in the wilderness by the sage Vālmīki, without any knowledge of their royal descent, furnish a striking parallel to the two princes Guiderius and Arviragus who are brought up by the hermit Belarius in Shakespeare's *Cymbeline.* The scene in which their meeting with their father Rāma is described reaches a high degree of poetic merit.

Among the works of other dramatists, VIÇĀKHADATTA'S *Mudrā-rākshasa,* or "Rākshasa and the Seal," deserves special mention because of its unique character. For, unlike all the other dramas hitherto described, it is a play of political intrigue, composed, moreover, with much dramatic talent, being full of life, action, and sustained interest. Nothing more definite can be said as to its date than that it was probably written not later than about 800 A.D. The action of the piece takes place in the time of Chandragupta, who, soon after Alexander's invasion of India, founded a new dynasty at Pāṭaliputra by deposing the last king of the Nanda line. Rākshasa, the minister of the latter, refusing to recognise the usurper, endeavours to be avenged on him for the ruin of his late master. The plot turns on the efforts of the Brahman Chāṇakya, the minister of Chandragupta, to win over the noble Rākshasa to his master's cause. In this he is ultimately successful.

BHAṬṬA NĀRĀYAṆA'S *Veṇīsaṃhāra,* or "Binding of the

braid of hair," is a play in six acts, deriving its plot from the *Mahābhārata*. Its action turns on the incident of Draupadī being dragged by the hair of her head into the assembly by one of the brothers of Duryodhana. Its age is known from its author having been the grantee of a copperplate dated 840 A.D. Though not conspicuous for poetic merit, it has long been a great favourite in India owing to its express partiality for the cult of Kṛishṇa.

To about 900 A.D. belongs the poet RĀJAÇEKHARA, the distinguishing feature of whose dramas are lightness and grace of diction. Four of his plays have survived, and are entitled *Viddha-çālabhanjikā*, *Karpūra-manjarī*, *Bāla-rāmāyaṇa*, and *Prachaṇḍa-pāṇḍava* or *Bāla-bhārata*.

The poet KSHEMĪÇVARA, who probably lived in the tenth century A.D. at Kānyakubja under King Mahīpāla, is the author of a play named *Chaṇḍakauçika*, or "The Angry Kauçika."

In the eleventh century DĀMODARA MIÇRA composed the *Hanuman-nāṭaka*, "The Play of Hanumat," also called *Mahā-nāṭaka*, or "The Great Play." According to tradition, he lived at the court of Bhoja, king of Mālava, who resided at Dhārā (now Dhār) and Ujjayinī (Ujjain) in the early part of the eleventh century. It is a piece of little merit, dealing with the story of Rāma in connection with his ally Hanumat, the monkey chief. It consists of fourteen acts, lacking coherence, and producing the impression of fragments patched together.

KṚISHṆA MIÇRA'S *Prabodha-chandrodaya*, or "Rise of the Moon of Knowledge," a play in six acts, dating from about the end of the eleventh century, deserves special attention as one of the most remarkable products of Indian literature. Though an allegorical piece of theologico-philosophical purport, in which practically only abstract notions and symbolical figures act as persons, it is remarkable for dramatic life and vigour. It aims at glorifying orthodox Brahmanism in the Vishnuite sense, just as the allegorical plays of the Spanish poet Calderon were intended to exalt the Catholic faith. The Indian poet has succeeded in the difficult task of creating an attractive play with abstractions like Revelation, Will, Reason, Religion, by transforming them into living beings of flesh and blood. The evil King Error appears on the scene as ruler of Benares, surrounded by his faithful adherents, the Follies and Vices, while Religion and the noble King Reason, accompanied by all the Virtues, have been banished. There is, however, a prophecy that Reason will some day be re-united with Revelation; the fruit of the union will be True Knowledge, which will destroy the reign of Error. The struggle for this union and its consummation, followed by the final triumph of the good party, forms the plot of the piece.

A large number of Sanskrit plays have been written since the twelfth century[1] down to modern times, their plots being generally derived from the *Mahābhārata* and the *Rāmāyaṇa*. Besides these, there are farces in one or more acts, mostly of a coarse type, in which various vices, such as hypocrisy, are satirised. These later productions reach a much lower level of art than the works of the early Indian dramatists.

[1] It is interesting to note that two Sanskrit plays, composed in the twelfth century, and not as yet known in manuscript form, have been partially preserved in inscriptions found at Ajmere (see Kielhorn, in Appendix to *Epigraphia Indica*, vol. v. p. 20, No. 134. Calcutta, 1899).

CHAPTER XIV

FAIRY TALES AND FABLES

(*Circa* 400–1100 A.D.)

THE didactic and sententious note which prevails in classical Sanskrit literature cannot fail to strike the student. It is, however, specially pronounced in the fairy tales and fables, where the abundant introduction of ethical reflections and proverbial philosophy is characteristic. The apologue with its moral is peculiarly subject to this method of treatment.

A distinguishing feature of the Sanskrit collections of fairy tales and fables, which are to a considerable extent found mixed together, is the insertion of a number of different stories within the framework of a single narrative. The characters of the main story in turn relate various tales to edify one another or to prove the correctness of their own special views. As within the limits of a minor story a second one can be similarly introduced and the process further repeated, the construction of the whole work comes to resemble that of a set of Chinese boxes. This style of narration was borrowed from India by the neighbouring Oriental peoples of Persia and Arabia, who employed it in composing independent works. The most notable instance is, of course, the *Arabian Nights.*

The *Panchatantra*, so called because it is divided

into five books, is, from the literary point of view, the most important and interesting work in this branch of Indian literature. It consists for the most part of fables, which are written in prose with an admixture of illustrative aphoristic verse. At what time this collection first assumed definite shape, it is impossible to say. We know, however, that it existed in the first half of the sixth century A.D., since it was translated by order of King Khosru Anushīrvan (531–79) into Pehlevi, the literary language of Persia at that time. We may, indeed, assume that it was known in the fifth century; for a considerable time must have elapsed before it became so famous that a foreign king desired its translation.

If not actually a Buddhistic work, the *Panchatantra* must be derived from Buddhistic sources. This follows from the fact that a number of its fables can be traced to Buddhistic writings, and from the internal evidence of the book itself. Apologues and fables were current among the Buddhists from the earliest times. They were ascribed to Buddha, and their sanctity increased by identifying the best character in any story with Buddha himself in a previous birth. Hence such tales were called *Jātakas*, or "Birth Stories." There is evidence that a collection of stories under that name existed as early as the Council of Vesālī, about 380 B.C.; and in the fifth century A.D. they assumed the shape they now have in the Pāli *Sutta-piṭaka*. Moreover, two Chinese encylopædias, the older of which was completed in 668 A.D., contain a large number of Indian fables translated into Chinese, and cite no fewer than 202 Buddhist works as their sources. In its present form, however, the *Panchatantra* is the production of Brahmans, who, though they transformed or omitted such parts as betrayed animus against Brahmanism, have nevertheless left uneffaced many traces of the Buddhistic origin of the collection. Though now divided into only five books, it is shown by the evidence of the oldest translation to have at one time embraced twelve. What its original name was we cannot say, but it may not improbably have been called after the two jackals, Karaṭaka and Damanaka, who play a prominent part in the first book; for the title of the old Syriac version is *Kalilag and Damnag*, and that of the Arabic translation *Kalīlah and Dimnah*.

Originally the *Panchatantra* was probably intended to be a manual for the instruction of the sons of kings in the principles of conduct (*nīti*), a kind of "Mirror of Princes." For it is introduced with the story of King Amaraçakti of Mahilāropya, a city of the south, who wishes to discover a scholar capable of training his three stupid and idle sons. He at last finds a Brahman who undertakes to teach the princes in six months enough to make them surpass all others in knowledge of moral science. This object he duly accomplishes by composing the *Panchatantra* and reciting it to the young princes.

The framework of the first book, entitled "Separation of Friends," is the story of a bull and a lion, who are introduced to one another in the forest by two jackals and become fast friends. One of the jackals, feeling himself neglected, starts an intrigue by telling both the lion and the bull that each is plotting against the other. As a result the bull is killed in battle with the lion, and the jackal, as prime minister of the latter, enjoys the fruits of his machinations. The main story of the second book, which is called "Acquisition of Friends," deals with the adventures of a tortoise, a deer, a crow, and a mouse. It is meant to illustrate the advantages of judicious friendships. The third book, or "The War of the Crows and the Owls," points out the danger of friendship concluded between those who are old enemies. The fourth book, entitled "Loss of what has been Acquired," illustrates, by the main story of the monkey and the crocodile, how fools can be made by flattery to part with their possessions. The fifth book, entitled "Inconsiderate Action," contains a number of stories connected with the experiences of a barber, who came to grief through failing to take all the circumstances of the case into consideration.

The book is pervaded by a quaint humour which transfers to the animal kingdom all sorts of human action. Thus animals devote themselves to the study of the Vedàs and to the practice of religious rites; they engage in disquisitions about gods, saints, and heroes; or exchange views regarding subtle rules of ethics; but suddenly their fierce animal nature breaks out. A pious cat, for instance, called upon to act as umpire in a dispute between a sparrow and a monkey, inspires such confidence in the litigants, by a long discourse on the vanity of life and the supreme importance of virtue, that they come close up in order to hear better the words of wisdom. In an instant he seizes one of the disputants with his claws, the other with his teeth, and devours them both. Very humorous is the story of the conceited musical donkey. Trespassing one moonlight night in a cucumber field, he feels impelled to sing, and answers the objections of his friend the jackal by a lecture on the charms of music. He then begins to bray, arouses the watchmen, and receives a sound drubbing.

With abundant irony and satire the most various human vices are exposed, among others the hypocrisy and avarice of Brahmans, the intriguing character of courtiers, and the faithlessness of women. A vigorous popular spirit of reaction against Brahman pretensions here finds expression, and altogether a sound and healthy view of life prevails, forming a refreshing contrast to the exaggeration found in many branches of Indian literature.

The following translation of a short fable from the first book may serve as a specimen of the style of the *Panchatantra*.

"There was in a certain forest region a herd of monkeys. Once in the winter season, when their bodies were shivering from contact with the cold wind, and were buffeted with torrents of rain, they could find no rest. So some of the monkeys, collecting *gũnja* berries, which are like sparks, stood round blowing in order to obtain a fire. Now a bird named Needlebeak, seeing this vain endeavour of theirs, exclaimed, 'Ho, you are all great fools; these are not sparks of fire, they are *gunja* berries. Why, therefore, this vain endeavour? You will never protect yourselves against the cold in this way. You had better look for a spot in the forest which is sheltered from the wind, or a cave, or a cleft in the mountains. Even now mighty rain clouds are appearing.' Thereupon an old monkey among them said, 'Ho, what business of yours is this? Be off. There is a saying—

A man of judgment who desires
His own success should not accost
One constantly disturbed in work
Or gamblers who have lost at play.

And another—

Who joins in conversation with
A hunter who has chased in vain,
Or with a fool who has become
Involved in ruin, comes to grief.

"The bird, however, without paying any attention to him, continually said to the monkeys, 'Ho, why this vain endeavour?' So, as he did not for a moment cease to chatter, one of the monkeys, enraged at their futile efforts, seized him by the wings and dashed him against a stone. And so he (de)ceased.

"Hence I say—

Unbending wood cannot be bent,
A razor cannot cut a stone:
Mark this, O Needlebeak! Try not
To lecture him who will not learn."

A similar collection of fables is the celebrated *Hitopadeça*, or "Salutary Advice," which, owing to its intrinsic merit, is one of the best known and most popular works of Sanskrit literature in India, and which, because of its suitability for teaching purposes, is read by nearly all beginners of Sanskrit in England. It is based chiefly on the *Panchatantra*, in which twenty-five of its forty-three fables are found. The first three books of the older collection have been, in the main, drawn upon; for there is but one story, that of the ass in the tiger's skin, taken from Book IV., and only three from Book V. The introduction is similar to that of the *Panchatantra*, but the father of the ignorant and vicious princes is here called Sudarçana of Pāṭaliputra (Patna). The *Hitopadeça* is divided into four books. The framework and titles of the first two agree with the first two of the *Panchatantra*, but in inverted order. The third and fourth books are called "War" and "Peace" respectively, the main story describing the conflict and reconciliation of the Geese and the Peacocks.

The sententious element is here much more prominent than in the *Panchatantra*, and the number of verses introduced is often so great as to seriously impede the progress of the prose narrative. These verses, however, abound in wise maxims and fine thoughts. The stanzas dealing with the transitoriness of human life near the end of Book IV. have a peculiarly pensive beauty of their own. The following two may serve as specimens:—

As on the mighty ocean's waves
Two floating logs together come,
And, having met, for ever part:
So briefly joined are living things.

As streams of rivers onward flow,
And never more return again:
So day and night still bear away
The life oj every mortal man.

It is uncertain who was the author of the *Hitopadeça;* nor can anything more definite be said about the date of this compilation than that it is more than 500 years old, as the earliest known MS. of it was written in 1373 A.D.

As both the *Panchatantra* and the *Hitopadeça* were originally intended as manuals for the instruction of kings in domestic and foreign policy, they belong to the class of literature which the Hindus call *nīti-çāstra*, or "Science of Political Ethics." A purely metrical treatise, dealing directly with the principles of policy, is the *Nīti-sāra*, or "Essence of Conduct," of Kāmandaka, which is one of the sources of the maxims introduced by the author of the *Hitopadeça.*

A collection of pretty and ingenious fairy tales, with a highly Oriental colouring, is the *Vetāla-panchaviṃçati*, or "Twenty-five Tales of the Vetāla" (a demon supposed to occupy corpses). The framework of this collection is briefly as follows. King Vikrama of Ujjayinī is directed by an ascetic (*yogin*) to take down from a tree and convey a corpse, without uttering a single word, to a spot in a graveyard where certain rites for the attainment of high magical powers are to take place. As the king is carrying the corpse along on his shoulders, a Vetāla, which has entered it, begins to speak and tells him a fairy tale. On the king inadvertently replying to a question, the corpse at once disappears and is found hanging on the tree again. The king goes back to fetch it, and the same process is repeated till the Vetāla has told twenty-five tales. Each of these is so constructed as to end in a subtle problem, on which the king is asked to express his opinion. The stories contained in this work are known to many English readers under the title of *Vikram and the Vampire.*

Another collection of fairy tales is the *Siṃhāsana-dvātriṃçikā*, or "Thirty-two Stories of the Lion-seat" (*i.e.* throne), which also goes by the name of *Vikrama-charita*, or "Adventures of Vikrama." Here it is the throne of King Vikrama that tells the tales. Both this and the preceding collection are of Buddhistic origin.

A third work of the same kind is the *Çuka-saptati*, or "Seventy Stories of a Parrot." Here a wife, whose husband is travelling abroad, and who is inclined to run after other men, turns to her husband's clever parrot for advice. The bird, while seeming to approve of her plans, warns her of the risks she runs, and makes her promise not to go and meet any paramour unless she can extricate herself from difficulties as So-and-so did. Requested to tell the story, he does so, but only as far as the dilemma, when he asks the woman what course the person concerned should take. As she cannot guess, the parrot promises to tell her if she stays at home that night. Seventy days pass in the same way, till the husband returns.

These three collections of fairy tales are all written in prose and are comparatively short. There is, however, another of special importance, which is composed in verse and is of very considerable length. For it contains no less than 22,000 *çlokas*, equal to nearly one-fourth of the *Mahābhārata*, or to almost twice as much as the Iliad and Odyssey put together. This is the *Kathā-sarit-sāgara*, or "Ocean of Rivers of Stories." It is divided into 124 chapters, called *tarangas*, or "waves," to be in keeping with the title of the work. Independent of these is another division into eighteen books called *lambakas*.

The author was SOMADEVA, a Kashmirian poet, who composed his work about 1070 A.D. Though he himself was a Brahman, his work contains not only many traces of the Buddhistic character of his sources, but even direct allusions to Buddhist Birth Stories. He states the real basis of his work to have been the *Bṛihat-kathā*, or "Great Narration," which Bāṇa mentions, by the poet Guṇādhya, who is quoted by Daṇḍin. This original must, in the opinion of Bühler, go back to the first or second century A.D.

A somewhat earlier recast of this work was made about A.D. 1037 by a contemporary of Somadeva's named KSHEMENDRA VYĀSADĀSA. It is entitled *Bṛihat-kathā-manjarī*, and is only about one-third as long as the *Kathā-*

sarit-sāgara. Kshemendra and Somadeva worked independently of each other, and both state that the original from which they translated was written in the *paiçāchī bhāshā* or "Goblin language," a term applied to a number of Low Prākrit dialects spoken by the most ignorant and degraded classes. The *Kathā-sarit-sāgara* also contains (*Tarangas* 60–64) a recast of the first three books of the *Panchatantra,* which books, it is interesting to find, had the same form in Somadeva's time as when they were translated into Pehlevi (about 570 A.D.).

Somadeva's work contains many most entertaining stories; for instance, that of the king who, through ignorance of the phonetic rules of Sanskrit grammar, misunderstood a remark made by his wife, and overcome with shame, determined to become a good Sanskrit scholar or die in the attempt. One of the most famous tales it contains is that of King Çibi, who offered up his life to save a pigeon from a hawk. It is a *Jātaka,* and is often represented on Buddhist sculptures; for example, on the tope of Amarāvatī, which dates from about the beginning of our era. It also occurs in a Chinese as well as a Muhammadan form.

ETHICAL POETRY.

The proneness of the Indian mind to reflection not only produced important results in religion, philosophy, and science; it also found a more abundant expression in poetry than the literature of any other nation can boast. Scattered throughout the most various departments of Sanskrit literature are innumerable apophthegms in which wise and noble, striking and original thoughts often appear in a highly finished and poetical garb.

These are plentiful in the law-books; in the epic and the drama they are frequently on the lips of heroes, sages, and gods; and in fables are constantly uttered by tigers, jackals, cats, and other animals. Above all, the *Mahābhārata*, which, to the pious Hindu, constitutes a moral encyclopædia, is an inexhaustible mine of proverbial philosophy. It is, however, natural that ethical maxims should be introduced in greatest abundance into works which, like the *Panchatantra* and *Hitopadeça*, were intended to be handbooks of practical moral philosophy.

Owing to the universality of this mode of expression in Sanskrit literature, there are but few works consisting exclusively of poetical aphorisms. The most important are the two collections by the highly-gifted Bhartṛihari, entitled respectively *Nītiçataka*, or "Century of Conduct," and *Vairāgya-çataka*, or "Century of Renunciation." Others are the *Çānti-çataka*, or "Century of Tranquillity," by a Kashmirian poet named Çilhaṇa; the *Moha-mudgara*, or "Hammer of Folly," a short poem commending the relinquishment of worldly desires, and wrongly attributed to Çankarāchārya; and the *Chāṇakya-çataka*, the "Centuries of Chāṇakya," the reputed author of which was famous in India as a master of diplomacy, and is the leading character in the political drama *Mudrārākshasa*. The *Nīti-manjarī*, or "Cluster of Blossoms of Conduct," which has not yet been published, is a collection of a peculiar kind. The moral maxims which it contains are illustrated by stories, and these are taken exclusively from the *Rigveda*. It consists of about 200 *çlokas*, and was composed by an author named Dyā Dviveda who accompanied his work with a commentary. In the latter he quotes largely from the *Bṛihaddevatā*, Sāyaṇa on the *Rigveda*, and other authors.

There are also some modern anthologies of Sanskrit gnomic poetry. One of these is Çrīdharadāsa's *Sadukti-karṇāmṛita*, or "Ear-nectar of Good Maxims," containing quotations from 446 poets, mostly of Bengal, and compiled in 1205 A.D. The *Çārngadhara-paddhati*, or "Anthology of Çārngadhara," dating from the fourteenth century, comprises about 6000 stanzas culled from 264 authors. The *Subhāshitāvalī*, or "Series of Fine Sayings," compiled by Vallabhadeva, contains some 3500 stanzas taken from about 350 poets. All that is best in Sanskrit sententious poetry has been collected by Dr. Böhtlingk, the Nestor of Indianists, in his *Indische Sprüche*. This work contains the text, critically edited and accompanied by a prose German translation, of nearly 8000 stanzas, which are culled from the whole field of classical Sanskrit literature and arranged according to the alphabetical order of the initial word.

Though composed in Pāli, the *Dhammapada* may perhaps be mentioned here. It is a collection of aphorisms representing the most beautiful, profound, and poetical thoughts in Buddhist literature.

The keynote prevailing in all this poetry is the doctrine of the vanity of human life, which was developed before the rise of Buddhism in the sixth century B.C., and has dominated Indian thought ever since. There is no true happiness, we are here taught, but in the abandonment of desire and retirement from the world. The poet sees the luxuriant beauties of nature spread before his eyes, and feels their charm; but he turns from them sad and disappointed to seek mental calm and lasting happiness in the solitude of the forest. Hence the picture of a pious anchorite living in contemplation is often painted with enthusiasm. Free from all desires, he is as happy as a king, when the earth is his couch, his arms his pillow, the sky his tent, the moon his lamp, when renunciation is his spouse, and the cardinal points are the maidens that fan him with winds. No Indian poet inculcates renunciation more forcibly than Bhartṛihari; the humorous and ironical touches which he occasionally introduces are doubtless due to the character of this remarkable man, who wavered between the spiritual and the worldly life throughout his career.

Renunciation is not, however, the only goal to which the transitoriness of worldly goods leads the gnomic poets of India. The necessity of pursuing virtue is the practical lesson which they also draw from the vanity of mundane existence, and which finds expression in many noble admonitions :—

Transient indeed is human life,
Like the moon's disc in waters seen:
Knowing how true this is, a man
Should ever practise what is good (*Hit.* iv. 133).

It is often said that when a man dies and leaves all his loved ones behind, his good works alone can accompany him on his journey to his next life. Nor should sin ever be committed in this life when there is none to see, for it is always witnessed by the "old hermit dwelling in the heart," as the conscience is picturesquely called.

That spirit of universal tolerance and love of mankind which enabled Buddhism to overstep the bounds not only of caste but of nationality, and thus to become the earliest world-religion, breathes throughout this poetry. Even the *Mahābhārata*, though a work of the Brahmans, contains such liberal sentiments as this :—

Men of high rank win no esteem
If lacking in good qualities;
A Çūdra even deserves respect
Who knows and does his duty well (xiii. 2610).

The following stanza shows how cosmopolitan Bhartṛihari was in his views :—

" This man's our own, a stranger that" :
Thus narrow-minded people think.
However, noble-minded men
Regard the whole world as their kin.

But these poets go even beyond the limits of humanity and inculcate sympathy with the joys and sorrows of all creatures :—

To harm no living thing in deed,
In thought or word, to exercise
Benevolence and charity :
Virtue's eternal law is this (*Mahābh.* xii. 5997).

Gentleness and forbearance towards good and bad alike are thus recommended in the *Hitopadeça* :—

Even to beings destitute
Of virtue good men pity show :
The moon does not her light withdraw
Even from the pariah's abode (i. 63).

The *Panchatantra*, again, dissuades thus from thoughts of revenge :—

Devise no ill at any time
To injure those that do thee harm :
They of themselves will some day fall,
Like trees that grow on river banks.

The good qualities of the virtuous are often described and contrasted with the characteristics of evil-doers.

This, for instance, is how Bhartṛihari illustrates the humility of the benevolent :—

The trees bend downward with the burden of their fruit,
The clouds bow low, heavy with waters they will shed:
The noble hold not high their heads through pride of wealth;
Thus those behave who are on others' good intent (i. 71).

Many fine thoughts about true friendship and the value of intercourse with good men are found here, often exemplified in a truly poetical spirit. This, for instance, is from the *Panchatantra* :—

Who is not made a better man
By contact with a noble friend?
A water-drop on lotus-leaves
Assumes the splendour of a pearl (iii. 61).

It is perhaps natural that poetry with a strong pessimistic colouring should contain many bitter sayings about women and their character. Here is an example of how they are often described :—

The love of women but a moment lasts,
Like colours of the dawn or evening red;
Their aims are crooked like a river's course;
Inconstant are they as the lightning flash;
Like serpents, they deserve no confidence (*Kathās.* xxxvii. 143).

At the same time there are several passages in which female character is represented in a more favourable light, and others sing the praise of faithful wives.

Here, too, we meet with many pithy sayings about the misery of poverty and the degradation of servitude; while the power of money to invest the worthless man with the appearance of every talent and virtue is described with bitter irony and scathing sarcasm.

As might be expected, true knowledge receives frequent and high appreciation in Sanskrit ethical poetry. It is compared with a rich treasure which cannot be divided among relations, which no thief can steal, and which is never diminished by being imparted to others. Contempt, on the other hand, is poured on pedantry and spurious learning. Those who have read many books, without understanding their sense, are likened to an ass laden with sandal wood, who feels only the weight, but knows nothing of the value of his burden.

As the belief in transmigration has cast its shadow over Indian thought from pre-Buddhistic times, it is only natural that the conception of fate should be prominent in Sanskrit moral poetry. Here, indeed, we often read that no one can escape from the operation of destiny, but at the same time we find constant admonitions not to let this fact paralyse human effort. For, as is shown in the *Hitopadeça* and elsewhere, fate is nothing else than the result of action done in a former birth. Hence every man can by right conduct shape his future fate, just as a potter can mould a lump of clay into whatever form he desires. Human action is thus a necessary complement to fate; the latter cannot proceed without the former any more than a cart, as the *Hitopadeça* expresses it, can move with only one wheel. This doctrine is inculcated with many apt illustrations. Thus in one stanza of the *Hitopadeça* it is pointed out that "antelopes do not enter into the mouth of the sleeping lion"; in another the question is asked, "Who without work could obtain oil from sesamum seeds?" Or, as the *Mahābhārata* once puts it, fate without human action cannot be fulfilled, just as seed sown outside the field bears no fruit.

For those who are suffering from the assaults of

adverse fate there are many exhortations to firmness and constancy. The following is a stanza of this kind from the *Panchatantra*:—

> *In fortune and calamity*
> *The great ever remain the same:*
> *The sun is at its rising red,*
> *Red also when about to set.*

Collected in the ethico-didactic works which have been described in this chapter, and scattered throughout the rest of the literature, the notions held by the Brahmans in the sphere of moral philosophy have never received a methodical treatment, as in the Pāli literature of Buddhism. In the orthodox systems of Hindu philosophy, to which we now turn, they find no place.

CHAPTER XV

PHILOSOPHY

THE beginnings of Indian philosophy, which are to be found in the latest hymns of the *Rigveda* and in the *Atharvaveda*, are concerned with speculations on the origin of the world and on the eternal principle by which it is created and maintained. The *Yajurveda* further contains fantastic cosmogonic legends describing how the Creator produces all things by means of the omnipotent sacrifice. With these Vedic ideas are intimately connected, and indeed largely identical, those of the earlier Upanishads. This philosophy is essentially pantheistic and idealistic. By the side of it grew up an atheistic and empirical school of thought, which in the sixth century B.C. furnished the foundation of the two great unorthodox religious systems of Buddhism and Jainism.

The Upanishad philosophy is in a chaotic condition, but the speculations of this and of other schools of thought were gradually reduced to order and systematised in manuals from about the first century of our era onwards. Altogether nine systems may be distinguished, some of which must in their origin go back to the beginning of the sixth century B.C. at least. Of the six systems which are accounted orthodox no less than four were originally atheistic, and one remained so throughout. The strangeness of this fact disappears when we reflect that the only conditions of orthodoxy in India were the recognition of the class privileges of the Brahman caste and a nominal acknowledgment of the infallibility of the Veda, neither full agreement with Vedic doctrines nor the confession of a belief in the existence of God being required. With these two limitations the utmost freedom of thought prevailed in Brahmanism. Hence the boldest philosophical speculation and conformity with the popular religion went hand and hand, to a degree which has never been equalled in any other country. Of the orthodox systems, by far the most important are the pantheistic Vedānta, which, as continuing the doctrines of the Upanishads, has been the dominant philosophy of Brahmanism since the end of the Vedic period, and the atheistic Sānkhya, which, for the first time in the history of the world, asserted the complete independence of the human mind and attempted to solve its problems solely by the aid of reason.

On the Sānkhya were based the two heterodox religious systems of Buddhism and Jainism, which denied the authority of the Veda, and opposed the Brahman caste system and ceremonial. Still more heterodox was the Materialist philosophy of Chārvāka, which went further and denied even the fundamental doctrines common to all other schools of Indian thought, orthodox and unorthodox, the belief in transmigration dependent on retribution, and the belief in salvation or release from transmigration.

The theory that every individual passes after death into a series of new existences in heavens or hells, or in the bodies of men and animals, or in plants on earth, where it is rewarded or punished for all deeds committed in a former life, was already so firmly established in the sixth century B.C., that Buddha received it without question into his religious system; and it has dominated the belief of the Indian people from those early times down to the present day. There is, perhaps, no more remarkable fact in the history of the human mind than that this strange doctrine, never philosophically demonstrated, should have been regarded as self-evident for 2500 years by every philosophical school or religious sect in India, excepting only the Materialists. By the acceptance ot this doctrine the Vedic optimism, which looked forward to a life of eternal happiness in heaven, was transformed into the gloomy prospect of an interminable series of miserable existences leading from one death to another. The transition to the developed view of the Upanishads is to be found in the *Çatapatha Brāhmaṇa* (above, p. 223).

How is the origin of the momentous doctrine which produced this change to be accounted for? The *Rigveda* contains no traces of it beyond a couple of passages in the last book which speak of the soul of a dead man as going to the waters or plants. It seems hardly likely that so far-reaching a theory should have been developed from the stray fancies of one or two later Vedic poets. It seems more probable that the Aryan settlers received the first impulse in this direction from the aboriginal inhabitants of India. As is well known, there is among half-savage tribes a wide-spread belief that the soul after death passes into the trunks of trees and the bodies of animals. Thus the Sonthals of India are said even at the present day to hold that the souls of the good enter into fruit-bearing trees. But among such races the notion of transmigration does not go beyond a belief in the continuance of human existence in animals and trees. If, therefore, the Aryan Indians borrowed the idea from the aborigines, they certainly deserve the credit of having elaborated out of it the theory of an unbroken chain of existences, intimately connected with the moral principle of requital. The immovable hold it acquired on Indian thought is doubtless due to the satisfactory explanation it offered of the misfortune or prosperity which is often clearly caused by no action done in this life. Indeed, the Indian doctrine of transmigration, fantastic though it may appear to us, has the twofold merit of satisfying the requirement of justice in the moral government of the world, and at the same time inculcating a valuable ethical principle which makes every man the architect of his own fate. For, as every bad deed done in this existence must be expiated, so every good deed will be rewarded in the next existence. From the enjoyment of the fruits of actions already done there is no escape; for, in the words of the *Mahābhārata*, "as among a thousand cows a calf finds its mother, so the deed previously done follows after the doer."

The cycle of existences (*saṃsāra*) is regarded as having no beginning, for as every event of the present life is the result of an action done in a past one, the same must hold true of each preceding existence *ad infinitum.* The subsequent effectiveness of guilt and of merit, commonly called *adṛishṭa* or "the unseen," but often also simply *karma*, "deed or work," is believed to regulate not only the life of the individual, but the origin and development of everything in the world; for whatever takes place cannot but affect some creature, and must therefore, by the law of retribution, be due to some previous act of that creature. In other words, the operations of nature are also the results of the good or bad deeds of living beings. There is thus no room for independent divine rule by the side of the power of *karma*, which governs everything with iron necessity. Hence, even the systems which acknowledge a God can only assign to him the function of guiding the world and the life of creatures in strict accordance with the law of retribution, which even he cannot break. The periodic destruction and renewal of the universe, an application of the theory on a grand scale, forms part of the doctrine of *saṃsāra* or cycle of existence.

Common to all the systems of philosophy, and as old as that of transmigration, is the doctrine of salvation, which puts an end to transmigration. All action is brought about by desire, which, in its turn is based on *avidyā*, a sort of "ignorance," that mistakes the true nature of things, and is the ultimate source of transmigration. Originally having only the negative sense of non-knowledge (*a-vidyā*), the word here came to have the positive sense of "false knowledge." Such ignorance is dispelled by saving knowledge, which, according to every philosophical school of India, consists in some special form of cognition. This universal knowledge, which is not the result of merit, but breaks into life independently, destroys the subsequent effect of works which would otherwise bear fruit in future existences, and thus puts an end to transmigration. It cannot, however, influence those works the fruit of which has already begun to ripen. Hence, the present life continues from the moment of enlightenment till definite salvation at death, just as the potter's wheel goes on revolving for a time after the completion of the pot. But no merit or demerit results from acts done after enlightenment (or "conversion" as we should say), because all desire for the objects of the world is at an end.

The popular beliefs about heavens and hells, gods, demi-gods, and demons, were retained in Buddhism and Jainism, as well as in the orthodox systems. But these higher and more fortunate beings were considered to be also subject to the law of transmigration, and, unless they obtained saving knowledge, to be on a lower level than the man who had obtained such knowledge.

The monistic theory of the early Upanishads, which identified the individual soul with Brahma, aroused the opposition of the rationalistic founder of the Sānkhya system, KAPILA, who, according to Buddhist legends, was pre-Buddhistic, and whose doctrines Buddha followed and elaborated. His teaching is entirely dualistic, admitting only two things, both without beginning and end, but essentially different, matter on the one hand, and an infinite plurality of individual souls on the other. An account of the nature and the mutual relation of these two, forms the main content of the system. Kapila was, indeed, the first who drew a sharp line of demarcation between the two domains of matter and soul. The saving knowledge which delivers from the misery of transmigration consists, according to the Sānkhya system, in recognising the absolute distinction between soul and matter.

The existence of a supreme god who creates and rules the universe is denied, and would be irreconcilable with the system. For according to its doctrine the unconscious matter of Nature originally contains within itself the power of evolution (in the interest of souls, which are entirely passive during the process), while *karma* alone determines the course of that evolution.

The adherents of the system defend their atheism by maintaining that the origin of misery presents an insoluble problem to the theist, for a god who has created and rules the world could not possibly escape from the reproach of cruelty and partiality. Much stress is laid by this school in general on the absence of any cogent proof for the existence of God.

The world is maintained to be real, and that from all eternity; for the existent can only be produced from the existent. The reality of an object is regarded as resulting simply from perception, always supposing the senses of the perceiver to be sound. The world is described as developing according to certain laws out of primitive matter (*prakṛiti* or *pradhāna*). The genuine philosophic spirit of its method of rising from the known elements of experience to the unknown by logical demonstration till the ultimate cause is reached, must give this system a special interest in the eyes of evolutionists whose views are founded on the results of modern physical science.

The evolution and diversity of the world are explained by primæval matter, although uniform and indivisible, consisting of three different substances called *guṇas* or constituents (originally "strands" of a rope). By the combination of these in varying proportions the diverse material products were supposed to have arisen. The constituent, called *sattva*, distinguished by the qualities of luminousness and lightness in the object, and by virtue, benevolence, and other pleasing attributes in the subject, is associated with the feeling of joy; *rajas*, distinguished by activity and various hurtful qualities, is associated with pain; and *tamas*, distinguished by heaviness, rigidity, and darkness on the one hand, and fear, unconsciousness, and so forth, on the other, is associated with apathy. At the end of a cosmic period all things are supposed to be dissolved into primitive matter, the alternations of evolution, existence, and dissolution having neither beginning nor end.

The psychology of the Sānkhya system is specially important. Peculiarly interesting is its doctrine that all mental operations, such as perception, thinking, willing, are not performed by the soul, but are merely mechanical processes of the internal organs, that is to say, of matter. The soul itself possesses no attributes or qualities, and can only be described negatively. There being no qualitative difference between souls, the principle of personality and identity is supplied by the subtile or internal body, which, chiefly formed of the inner organs and the senses, surrounds and is made conscious by the soul. This internal body, being the vehicle of merit and demerit, which are the basis of transmigration, accompanies the soul on its wanderings from one gross body to another, whether the latter be that of a god, a man, an animal, or a tree. Conscious life is bondage to pain, in which pleasure is included by this peculiarly pessimistic system. When salvation, which is the absolute cessation of pain, is obtained, the internal body is dissolved into its material elements, and the soul, becoming finally isolated, continues to exist individually, but in absolute unconsciousness.

The name of the system, which only begins to be mentioned in the later Upanishads, and more frequently in the *Mahābhārata*, is derived from *saṃkhyā*, "number." There is, however, some doubt as to whether it originally meant "enumeration," from the twenty-five *tattvas* or principles which it sets forth, or "inferential or discriminative" doctrine, from the method which it pursues.

Kapila, the founder of the system, whose teaching is presupposed by Buddhism, and whom Buddhistic legend connects with Kapila-vastu, the birthplace of Buddha, must have lived before the middle of the sixth century. No work of his, if he ever committed his system to writing, has been preserved. Indeed, the very existence of such a person as Kapila has been doubted, in spite of the unanimity with which Indian tradition designates a man of this name as the founder of the system. The second leading authority of the Sānkhya philosophy was Panchaçikha, who may have lived about the beginning of our era. The oldest systematic manual which has been preserved is the *Sānkhya-kārikā* of ĪÇVARA-KṚISHṆA. As it was translated into Chinese between 557 and 583 A.D., it cannot belong to a later century than the fifth, and may be still older. This work deals very concisely and methodically with the doctrines of the Sānkhya in sixty-nine stanzas (composed in the complicated *Āryā* metre), to which three others were subsequently added. It appears to have superseded the Sūtras of Panchaçikha, who is mentioned in it as the chief disseminator of the system. There are two excellent commentaries on the *Sānkhya-kārikā*, the one composed about 700 A.D. by Gauḍapāda, and the other soon after 1100 A.D. by Vāchaspati Miçra.

The *Sānkhya Sūtras*, long regarded as the oldest manual of the system, and attributed to Kapila, were probably not composed till about 1400 A.D. The author of this work, which also goes by the name of *Sānkhya-pravachana*, endeavours in vain to show that there is no difference between the doctrines of the Sānkhya and of the Upanishads. He is also much influenced by the ideas of the Yoga as well as the Vedānta system. In the oldest commentary on this work, that of Aniruddha, composed about 1500 A.D., the objectiveness of the treatment is particularly useful. Much more detailed, but far less objective, is the commentary of Vijnāna-bhikshu, entitled *Sānkhya-pravachana-bhāshya*, and written in the second half of the sixteenth century. The author's point of view being theistic, he effaces the characteristic features of the different systems in the endeavour to show that all the six orthodox systems contain the absolute truth in their main doctrines.

From the beginning of our era down to recent times the Sānkhya doctrines have exercised considerable influence on the religious and philosophical life of India, though to a much less extent than the Vedānta. Some of its individual teachings, such as that of the three *guṇas*, have become the common property of the whole of Sanskrit literature. At the time of the great Vedāntist, Çankara (800 A.D.), the Sānkhya system was held in high honour. The law book of Manu followed this doctrine, though with an admixture of the theistic notions of the Mīmāṃsā and Vedānta systems as well as of popular mythology. The *Mahābhārata*, especially Book XII., is full of Sānkhya doctrines; indeed almost every detail of the teachings of this system is to be found somewhere in the great epic. Its numerous deviations from the regular Sānkhya text-books are only secondary, as Professor Garbe thinks, even though the *Mahābhārata* is our oldest actual source for the system. Nearly half the Purāṇas follow the cosmogony of the Sānkhya, and even those which are Vedāntic are largely influenced by its doctrines. The purity of the Sānkhya notions are, however, everywhere in the Purāṇas obscured by Vedānta doctrines, especially that of cosmical illusion. A peculiarity of the Purāṇic Sānkhya is the conception of Spirit or *Purusha* as the male, and Matter or *Prakṛiti* as the female, principle in creation.

On the Sānkhya system are based the two philosophical religions of Buddhism and Jainism in all their main outlines. Their fundamental doctrine is that life is nothing but suffering. The cause of suffering is the desire, based on ignorance, to live and enjoy the world. The aim of both is to redeem mankind from the misery of mundane existence by the annihilation of desire, with the aid of renunciation of the world and the practice of unbounded kindness towards all creatures. These two pessimistic religions are so extremely similar that the Jainas, or adherents of Jina, were long looked upon as a Buddhist sect. Research has, however, led to the discovery that the founders of both systems were contemporaries, the most eminent of the many teachers who in the sixth century opposed the Brahman ceremonial and caste pretensions in Northern Central India. Both religions, while acknowledging the lower and ephemeral gods of Brahmanism, deny, like the Sānkhya, the existence of an eternal supreme Deity. As they developed, they diverged in various respects from the system to which they owed their philosophical notions. Hence it came about that Sānkhya writers stoutly opposed some of their teachings, particularly the Buddhist denial of soul, the doctrine that all things have only a momentary existence, and that salvation is an annihilation of self. Here, however, it should be noted that Buddha himself refused to decide the question whether *nirvāṇa* is complete extinction or an unending state of unconscious bliss.

The latter view was doubtless a concession to the Vedāntic conception of Brahma, in which the individual soul is merged on attaining salvation.

The importance of these systems lies not in their metaphysical speculations, which occupy but a subordinate position, but in their high development of moral principles, which are almost entirely neglected in the orthodox systems of Indian philosophy. The fate of the two religions has been strangely different. Jainism has survived as an insignificant sect in India alone; Buddhism has long since vanished from the land of its birth, but has become a world religion counting more adherents than any other faith.

The Sānkhya philosophy, with the addition of a peculiar form of mental asceticism as the most effective means of acquiring saving knowledge, appears to have assumed definite shape in a manual at an earlier period than any of the other orthodox systems. This is the Yoga philosophy founded by PATANJALI and expounded in the *Yoga Sūtras.* The priority of this textbook is rendered highly probable by the fact that it is the only philosophical Sūtra work which contains no polemics against the others. There seems, moreover, to be no sufficient ground to doubt the correctness of the native tradition identifying the founder of the Yoga system with the grammarian Patanjali. The *Yoga Sūtras* therefore probably date from the second century B.C. This work also goes by the name of *Sānkhya-pravachana,* the same as that given to the later *Sānkhya Sūtras,* a sufficiently clear proof of its close connection with Kapila's philosophy. In the *Mahābhārata* the two systems are actually spoken of as one and the same.

In order to make his system more acceptable, Patanjali introduced into it the doctrine of a personal god, but in so loose a way as not to affect the system as a whole. Indeed, the parts of the Sūtras dealing with the person of God are not only unconnected with the other parts of the treatise, but even contradict the foundations of the system. For the final aim of man is here represented as the absolute isolation (*kaivalya*) of the soul from matter, just as in the Sānkhya system, and not union with or absorption in God. Nor are the individual souls here derived from the "special soul" or God, but are like the latter without a beginning.

The really distinctive part of the system is the establishment of the views prevailing in Patanjali's time with regard to asceticism and the mysterious powers to be acquired by its practice. *Yoga*, or "yoking" the mind, means mental concentration on a particular object. The belief that fasting and other penances produce supernatural powers goes back to remote prehistoric times, and still prevails among savage races. Bodily asceticism of this kind is known to the Vedas under the name of *tapas*. From this, with the advance of intellectual life in India, was developed the practice of mental asceticism called *yoga*, which must have been known and practised several centuries before Patanjali's time. For recent investigations have shown that Buddhism started not only from the theoretical Sānkhya but from the practical Yoga doctrine; and the condition of ecstatic abstraction was from the beginning held in high esteem among the Buddhists. Patanjali only elaborated the doctrine, describing at length the means of attaining concentration and carrying it to the highest pitch. In his system the methodical practice of Yoga acquired a special importance; for, in addition to conferring supernatural powers, it here becomes the chief means of salvation. His Sūtras consist of four chapters dealing with deep meditation (*samādhi*), the means for obtaining it (*sādhana*), the miraculous powers (*vibhūti*) it confers, and the isolation (*kaivalya*) of the redeemed soul. The oldest and best commentary on this work is that of Vyāsa, dating from the seventh century A.D.

Many of the later Upanishads are largely concerned with the Yoga doctrine. The lawbook of Manu in Book VI. refers to various details of Yoga practice. Indeed, it seems likely, owing to the theistic point of view of that work, that its Sānkhya notions were derived from the Yoga system. The *Mahābhārata* treats of Yoga in considerable detail, especially in Book XII. It is particularly prominent in the *Bhagavadgītā*, which is even designated a *yoga-çāstra*. Belief in the efficacy of Yoga still prevails in India, and its practice survives. But its adherents, the Yogīs, are at the present day often nothing more than conjurers and jugglers.

The exercises of mental concentration are in the later commentaries distinguished by the name of *rāja-yoga* or "chief Yoga." The external expedients are called *kriyā-yoga*, or "practical Yoga." The more intense form of the latter, in later works called *haṭha-yoga*, or "forcible Yoga," and dealing for the most part with suppression of the breath, is very often contrasted with *rāja-yoga*.

Among the eight branches of Yoga practice the sitting posture (*āsana*), as not only conducive to concentration, but of therapeutic value, is considered important. In describing its various forms later writers positively revelled, eighty-four being frequently stated to be their normal number. In the *haṭha-yoga* there are also a number of other postures and contortions of the limbs designated *mudrā*. The best-known *mudrā*, called *khecharī*, consists in turning the tongue back towards the throat and keeping the gaze fixed on a point between the eyebrows. Such practices, in conjunction with the suppression of breath, were capable of producing a condition of trance. There is at least the one well-authenticated case of a Yogī named Haridās who in the thirties wandered about in Rājputāna and Lahore, allowing himself to be buried for money when in the cataleptic condition. The burial of the Master of Ballantrae by the Indian Secundra Dass in Stevenson's novel was doubtless suggested by an account of this ascetic.

In contrast with the two older and intimately connected dualistic schools of the Sānkhya and Yoga, there arose about the beginning of our era the only two, even of the six orthodox systems of philosophy, which were theistic from the outset. One of them, being based on the Vedas and the Brāhmaṇas, is concerned with the practical side of Vedic religion; while the other, alone among the philosophical systems, represents a methodical development of the fundamental non-dualistic speculations of the Upanishads. The former, which has only been accounted a philosophical system at all because of its close connection with the latter, is the *Pūrva-mīmāṃsā* or "First Inquiry," also called *Karma-mīmāṃsā* or "Inquiry concerning Works," but usually simply *Mīmāṃsā*. Founded by JAIMINI, and set forth in the *Karma-mīmāṃsā Sūtras*, this system discusses the sacred ceremonies and the rewards resulting from their performance. Holding the Veda to be uncreated and existent from all eternity, it lays special stress on the proposition that articulate sounds are eternal, and on the consequent doctrine that the connection of a word with its sense is not due to convention, but is by nature inherent in the word itself. Owing to its lack of philosophical interest, this system has not as yet much occupied the attention of European scholars.

The oldest commentary in existence on the *Mīmāṃsā Sūtras* is the *bhāshya* of Çabara Svāmin, which in its turn was commented on about 700 A.D. by the great Mīmāṃsist KUMĀRILA in his *Tantra-vārttika* and in his *Çloka-vārttika,* the latter a metrical paraphrase of Çabara's exposition of the first aphorism of Patanjali. Among the later commentaries on the *Mīmāṃsā Sūtras* the most important is the *Jaiminīya-nyāya-mālā-vistara* of Mādhava (fourteenth century).

Far more deserving of attention is the theoretical system of the *Uttara-mīmāṃsā,* or "Second Inquiry." For it not only systematises the doctrines of the Upanishads—therefore usually termed *Vedānta,* or "End of the Veda"—but also represents the philosophical views of the Indian thinkers of to-day. In the words of Professor Deussen, its relation to the earlier Upanishads resembles that of Christian dogmatics to the New Testament. Its fundamental doctrine, expressed in the famous formula *tat tvam asi,* "thou art that," is the identity of the individual soul with God (*brahma*). Hence it is also called the *Brahma-* or *Çārīraka-mīmāṃsā,* "Inquiry concerning Brahma or the embodied soul." The eternal and infinite Brahma not being made up of parts or liable to change, the individual soul, it is here laid down, cannot be a part or emanation of it, but is the whole indivisible Brahma. As there is no other existence but Brahma, the Vedānta is styled the *advaita-vāda*, or "doctrine of non-duality," being, in other words, an idealistic monism. The evidence of experience, which shows a multiplicity of phenomena, and the statements of the Veda, which teach a multiplicity of souls, are brushed aside as the phantasms of a dream which are only true till waking takes place.

The ultimate cause of all such false impressions is *avidyā* or innate ignorance, which this, like the other systems, simply postulates, but does not in any way seek to account for. It is this ignorance which prevents the soul from recognising that the empirical world is mere *māyā* or illusion. Thus to the Vedāntist the universe is like a mirage, which the soul under the influence of desire (*tṛishṇā* or "thirst") fancies it perceives, just as the panting hart sees before it sheets of water in the *fata morgana* (picturesquely called *mṛiga-tṛishṇā* or "deer-thirst" in Sanskrit). The illusion vanishes as if by magic, when the scales fall from the eyes, on the acquisition of true knowledge. Then the semblance of any distinction between the soul and God disappears, and salvation (*moksha*), the chief end of man, is attained.

Saving knowledge cannot of course be acquired by worldly experience, but is revealed in the theoretical part (*jnāna-kāṇḍa*) of the Vedas, that is to say, in the Upanishads. By this correct knowledge the illusion of the multiplicity of phenomena is dispelled, just as the illusion of a snake when there is only a rope. Two forms of knowledge are, however, distinguished in the Vedānta, a higher (*parā*) and a lower (*aparā*). The former is concerned with the higher and impersonal Brahma (neuter), which is without form or attributes, while the latter deals with the lower and personal Brahmā (masculine), who is the soul of the universe, the Lord (*içvara*) who has created the world and grants salvation. The contradiction resulting from one and the same thing having form and no form, attributes and no attributes, is solved by the explanation that the lower Brahmā has no reality, but is merely an illusory form of the higher and only Brahma, produced by ignorance.

The doctrines of the Vedānta are laid down in the *Brahma-sūtras* of Bādarāyaṇa. This text-book, the meaning of which is not intelligible without the aid of a commentary, was expounded in his *bhāshya* by the famous Vedāntist philosopher ÇANKARA, whose name is intimately connected with the revival of Brahmanism. He was born in 788 A.D., became an ascetic in 820, and probably lived to an advanced age. There is every likelihood that his expositions agree in all essentials with the meaning of the *Brahma-sūtras*. The full elaboration of the doctrine of *Māyā*, or cosmic illusion, is, however, due to him. An excellent epitome of the teachings of the Vedānta, as set forth by Çankara, is the *Vedānta-sāra* of Sadānanda Yogīndra. Its author departs from Çankara's views only in a few particulars, which show an admixture of Sānkhya doctrine.

Among the many commentaries on the *Brahma-sūtras* subsequent to Çankara, the most important is that of Rāmānuja, who lived in the earlier half of the twelfth century. This writer gives expression to the views of the Pāncharātras or Bhāgavatas, an old Vishnuite sect, whose doctrine, closely allied to Christian ideas, is expounded in the *Bhagavadgītā* and the *Bhāgavata-purāṇa*, as well as in the special text-books of the sect. The tenets of the Bhāgavatas, as set forth by Rāmānuja, diverge considerably from those of the *Brahma-sūtras* on which he is commenting. For, according to him, individual souls are not identical with God; they suffer from innate unbelief, not ignorance, while belief or the love of God (*bhakti*), not knowledge, is the means of salvation or union with God.

The last two orthodox systems of philosophy, the Vaiçeshika and the Nyāya, form a closely-connected pair, since a strict classification of ideas, as well as the explanation of the origin of the world from atoms, is common to both. Much the older of the two is the Vaiçeshika, which is already assailed in the *Brahma-sūtras.* It is there described as undeserving of attention, because it had no adherents. This was certainly not the case in later times, when this system became very popular. It received its name from the category of "particularity" (*viçesha*) on which great stress is laid in its theory of atoms. The memory of its founder is only preserved in his nickname Kaṇāda (also Kaṇabhuj or Kaṇa-bhaksha), which means "atom-eater."

The main importance of the system lies in the logical categories which it set up and under which it classed all phenomena. The six which it originally set up are substance, quality, motion, generality, particularity, and inherence. They are rigorously defined and further subdivided. The most interesting is that of inherence or inseparable connection (*samavāya*), which, being clearly distinguished from that of accident or separable connection (*saṃyoga*), is described as the relation between a thing and its properties, the whole and its parts, genus and species, motion and the object in motion. Later was added a seventh, that of non-existence (*abhāva*), which, by affording special facilities for the display of subtlety, has had a momentous influence on Indian logic. This category was further subdivided into prior and posterior non-existence (which we should respectively call future and past existence), mutual non-existence (as between a jar and cloth), and absolute non-existence (as fire in water).

Though largely concerned with these categories, the Vaiçeshika system aimed at attaining a comprehensive philosophic view in connection with them. Thus while dealing with the category of "substance," it develops its theory of the origin of the world from atoms. The consideration of the category of "quality" similarly leads to its treatment of psychology, which is remarkable and has analogies with that of the Sānkhya. Soul is here regarded as without beginning or end, and all-pervading, subject to the limitations of neither time nor space. Intimately connected with soul is "mind" (*manas*), the internal organ of thought, which alone enables the soul to know not only external objects but its own qualities. As this organ is, in contrast with soul, an atom, it can only comprehend a single object at any given moment. This is the explanation why the soul cannot be conscious of all objects simultaneously.

The Nyāya system is only a development and complement of that of Kaṇāda, its metaphysics and psychology being the same. Its specific character consists in its being a very detailed and acute exposition of formal logic. As such it has remained the foundation of philosophical studies in India down to the present day. Besides dealing fully with the means of knowledge, which it states to be perception, inference, analogy, and trustworthy evidence, it treats exhaustively of syllogisms and fallacies. It is interesting to note that the Indian mind here independently arrived at an exposition of the syllogism as the form of deductive reasoning. The text-book of this system is the *Nyāya-sūtra* of Gotama. The importance here attached to logic appears from the very first aphorism, which enumerates sixteen logical notions with the remark that salvation depends on a correct knowledge of their nature.

Neither the *Vaiçeshika* nor the *Nyāya-sūtras* originally accepted the existence of God; and though both schools later became theistic, they never went so far as to assume a creator of matter. Their theology is first found developed in Udayanāchārya's *Kusumānjali*, which was written about 1200 A.D., and in works which deal with the two systems conjointly. Here God is regarded as a "special" soul, which differs from all other individual eternal souls by exemption from all qualities connected with transmigration, and by the possession of the power and knowledge qualifying him to be a regulator of the universe.

Of the eclectic movement combining Sānkhya, Yoga, and Vedānta doctrines, the oldest literary representative is the *Çvetāçvatara Upanishad.* More famous is the *Bhagavadgītā*, in which the Supreme Being incarnate as Kṛishṇa expounds to Arjuna his doctrines in this sense. The burden of his teaching is that the zealous performance of his duty is a man's most important task, to whatever caste he may belong. The beauty and the power of the language in which this doctrine is inculcated, is unsurpassed in any other work of Indian literature.

By the side of the orthodox systems and the two non-Brahmanical religions, flourished the *lokāyata* ("directed to the world of sense"), or materialistic school, usually called that of the Chārvākas from the name of the founder of the doctrine. It was regarded as peculiarly heretical, for it not only rejected the authority of the

Vedas and Brahmanic ceremonial, but denied the doctrines of transmigration and salvation accepted by all other systems. Materialistic teachings may be traced even before the time of Buddha, and they have had many secret followers in India down to the present day. The system, however, seems never to have had more than one text-book, the lost Sūtras of Bṛihaspati, its mythical founder. Our knowledge of it is derived partly from the polemics of other schools, but especially from the *Sarva-darçana-saṃgraha*, or "Compendium of all the Philosophical Systems," composed in the fourteenth century by the well-known Vedāntist Mādhavāchārya, brother of Sāyaṇa. The strong scepticism of the Chārvākas showed itself in the rejection of all the means of knowledge accepted by other schools, excepting perception. To them matter was the only reality. Soul they regarded as nothing but the body with the attribute of intelligence. They held it to be created when the body is formed by the combination of elements, just as the power of intoxication arises from the mixture of certain ingredients. Hence with the annihilation of the body the soul also is annihilated. Not transmigration, they affirm, but the true nature of things, is the cause from which phenomena proceed. The existence of all that transcends the senses they deny, sometimes with an admixture of irony. Thus the highest being, they say, is the king of the land, whose existence is proved by the perception of the whole world; hell is earthly pain produced by earthly causes; and salvation is the dissolution of the body. Even in the attribution of their text-book to Bṛihaspati, the name of the preceptor of the gods, a touch of irony is to be detected. The religion of the Brahmans receives a severe handling. The Vedas, say the Chārvākas, are only the incoherent rhapsodies of knaves, and are tainted with the three blemishes of falsehood, self-contradiction, and tautology; Vedic teachers are impostors, whose doctrines are mutually destructive; and the ritual of the Brahmans is useful only as a means of livelihood. "If," they ask, "an animal sacrificed reaches heaven, why does the sacrificer not rather offer his own father?"

On the moral side the system is pure hedonism. For the only end of man is here stated to be sensual pleasure, which is to be enjoyed by neglecting as far as possible the pains connected with it, just as a man who desires fish takes the scales and bones into the bargain. "While life remains, let a man live happily, let him feed on ghee even though he run into debt; when once the body becomes ashes, how can it ever return again?"

The author of the *Sarvadarçana-saṃgraha*, placing himself with remarkable mental detachment in the position of an adherent in each case, describes altogether sixteen systems. The six which have not been sketched above, besides being of little importance, are not purely philosophic. Five of these are sectarian, one Vishnuite and four Çivite, all of them being strongly tinctured with Sānkhya and Vedānta doctrines. The sixth, the system of Pāṇini, is classed by Mādhava among the philosophies, simply because the Indian grammarians accepted the Mīmāṃsā dogma of the eternity of sound, and philosophically developed the Yoga theory of the *sphuṭa*, or the imperceptible and eternal element inherent in every word as the vehicle of its sense.

CHAPTER XVI

SANSKRIT LITERATURE AND THE WEST

WANT of space makes it impossible for me to give even the briefest account of the numerous and, in many cases, important legal and scientific works written in Sanskrit. But I cannot conclude this survey of Sanskrit literature as an embodiment of Indian culture without sketching rapidly the influence which it has received from and exercised upon the nations of the West. An adequate treatment of this highly interesting theme could only be presented in a special volume.

The oldest trace of contact between the Indians and the peoples of the West is to be found in the history of Indian writing, which, as we have already seen (p. 16) was derived from a Semitic source, probably as early as 800 B.C.

The Aryans having conquered Hindustan in prehistoric times, began themselves to fall under foreign domination from an early period. The extreme northwest became subject to Persian sway from about 500 to 331 B.C. under the Achæmenid dynasty. Cyrus the First made tributary the Indian tribes of the Gandhāras and Açvakas. The old Persian inscriptions of Behistun and Persepolis show that his successor, Darius Hystaspis, ruled over not only the Gandharians, but also the people of the Indus. Herodotus also states that this monarch had subjected the "Northern Indians." At the command of the same Darius, a Greek named Skylax is said to have travelled in India, and to have navigated the Indus in 509 B.C. From his account various Greek writers, among them Herodotus, derived their information about India. In the army which Xerxes led against Greece in 480 B.C. there were divisions of Gandharians and Indians, whose dress and equipment are described by Herodotus. That historian also makes the statement that the satrapy of India furnished the heaviest tribute in the Persian empire, adding that the gold with which it was paid was brought from a desert in the east, where it was dug up by ants larger than foxes.

At the beginning of the fourth century B.C., the Greek physician Ktesias, who resided at the court of Artaxerxes II., learnt much from the Persians about India, and was personally acquainted with wise Indians. Little useful information can, however, be derived from the account of India which he wrote after his return in 398 B.C., as it has been very imperfectly preserved, and his reputation for veracity did not stand high among his countrymen.

The destruction of the Persian empire by Alexander the Great led to a new invasion of India, which fixes the first absolutely certain date in Indian history. In 327 B.C. Alexander passed over the Hindu Kush with an army of 120,000 infantry and 30,000 cavalry. After taking the town of Pushkalavatī (the Greek Peukelaotis) at the confluence of the Kabul and Indus, and subduing the Açvakas (variously called Assakanoi, Aspasioi, Hippasioi, by Greek writers) on the north and the Gandhāras on the south of the Kabul River, he crossed the Indus early in 326. At Takshaçilā (Greek Taxiles), between the Indus and the Jhelum (Hydaspes), the Greeks for the first time saw Brahman Yogīs, or "the wise men of the Indians," as they called them, and were astonished at their asceticism and strange doctrines.

Between the Jhelum and the Chenab (Akesines) lay the kingdom of the Pauravas or Pauras, whose prince, called Porus by the Greeks from the name of his people, led out an army of 50,000 infantry, 4000 cavalry, 200 elephants, and 400 chariots to check the advance of the invader. Then on the banks of the Jhelum was fought the great historic battle, in which Alexander, after a severe struggle, finally won the day by superior numbers and force of genius. He continued his victorious march eastwards till he reached the Sutlej (Greek Zadadres). But here his further progress towards the Ganges was arrested by the opposition of his Macedonians, intimidated by the accounts they heard of the great power of the king of the Prasioi (Sanskrit Prāchyas, or "Easterns"). Hence, after appointing satraps of the Panjāb and of Sindh, he sailed down to the mouths of the Indus and returned to Persia by Gedrosia. Of the writings of those who accompanied Alexander, nothing has been preserved except statements from them in later authors.

After Alexander's death the assassination of the old king Porus by Eudemus, the satrap of the Panjāb, led to a rebellion in which the Indians cast off the Greek yoke under the leadership of a young adventurer named Chandragupta (the Sandrakottos or Sandrokyptos of the Greeks). Having gained possession of the Indus territory in 317, and dethroned the king of Pāṭaliputra in 315 B.C., he became master of the whole Ganges Valley as well. The Maurya dynasty, which he thus founded, lasted for 137 years (315–178 B.C.). His empire was the largest hitherto known in India, as it embraced the whole territory between the Himālaya and the Vindhya from the mouths of the Ganges to the Indus, including Gujarat.

Seleucus, who had founded a kingdom in Media and Persia, feeling himself unable to vanquish Chandragupta, sent a Greek named Megasthenes to reside at his court at Pāṭaliputra. This ambassador thus lived for several years in the heart of India between 311 and 302 B.C., and wrote a work entitled *Ta Indika*, which is particularly valuable as the earliest direct record of his visit by a foreigner who knew the country himself. Megasthenes furnishes particulars about the strength of Chandragupta's army and the administration of the state. He mentions forest ascetics (*Hylobioi*), and distinguishes *Brachmānes* and *Sarmanai* as two classes of philosophers, meaning, doubtless, Brahmans and Buddhists (*çramaṇas*). He tells us that the Indians worshipped the rain-bringing Zeus (Indra) as well as the Ganges, which must, therefore, have already been a sacred river. By his description of the god Dionysus, whom they worshipped in the mountains, Çiva must be intended, and by Herakles, adored in the plains, especially among the Çūrasenas on the Yamunā and in the city of Methora, no other can be meant than Vishṇu and his incarnation Kṛishṇa, the chief city of whose tribe of Yādavas was Mathurā (Muttra). These statements seem to justify the conclusion that Çiva and Vishṇu were already prominent as highest gods, the former in the mountains, the latter in the Ganges Valley. Kṛishṇa would also seem to have been regarded as an Avatār of Vishṇu, though it is to be noted that Kṛishṇa is not yet mentioned in the old Buddhist Sūtras. We also learn from Megasthenes that the doctrine of the four ages of the world (*yugas*) was fully developed in India by his time.

Chandragupta's grandson, the famous Açoka, not only maintained his national Indian empire, but extended it in every direction. Having adopted Buddhism as the state religion, he did much to spread its doctrines, especially to Ceylon, which since then has remained the most faithful guardian of Buddhist tradition.

After Açoka's death the Græco-Bactrian princes began about 200 B.C. to conquer Western India, and ruled there for about eighty years. Euthydemos extended his dominions to the Jhelum. His son Demetrios (early in the second century B.C.) appears to have held sway over the Lower Indus, Mālava, Gujarat, and probably also Kashmir. He is called "King of the Indians," and was the first to introduce a bilingual coinage by adding an Indian inscription in *Kharoshṭhī* characters on the reverse to the Greek on the obverse. Eukratides (190–160 B.C.), who rebelled against Demetrios, subjected the Panjāb as far east as the Beäs. After the reign of Heliokles (160–120 B.C.), the Greek princes in India ceased to be connected with Bactria. The most prominent among these Græco-Indians was Menander (*c.* 150 B.C.), who, under the name of Milinda, is well known in Buddhist writings. The last vestige of Greek domination in India disappeared about 20 B.C., having lasted nearly two centuries. It is a remarkable fact that no Greek monumental inscriptions have ever been found in India.

With the beginning of the Græco-Indian period also commenced the incursions of the Scythic tribes, who are called Indo-Scythians by the Greeks, and by the Indians Çakas, the Persian designation of Scythians in general. Of these so-called Scythians the Jāts of the Panjāb are supposed to be the descendants. The rule of these Çaka kings, the earliest of whom is Maues or Moa (*c.* 120 B.C.), endured down to 178 A.D., or about three centuries. Their memory is preserved in India by the Çaka era, which is still in use, and dates from 78 A.D., the inaugural year of Kanishka, the only famous king of this race. His dominions, which included Kānyakubja (Kanauj) on the Ganges, extended beyond the confines of India to parts of Central Asia. A zealous adherent of Buddhism, he made Gandhāra and Kashmir the chief seat of that religion, and held the fourth Buddhist council in the latter country.

About 20 B.C. the Çakas were followed into India by the Kushanas, who were one of the five tribes of the Yueh-chi from Central Asia, and who subsequently conquered the whole of Northern India.

After having been again united into a single empire almost as great as that of Chandragupta under the national dynasty of the Guptas, from 319 to 480 A.D., Northern India, partly owing to the attacks of the Hūṇas, was split up into several kingdoms, some under the later Guptas, till 606 A.D., when Harshavardhana of Kanauj gained paramount power over the whole of Northern India. During his reign the poet Bāṇa flourished, and the celebrated Chinese pilgrim Hiouen Thsang visited India.

With the Muhammadan conquest about 1000 A.D. the country again fell under a foreign yoke. As after Alexander's invasion, we have the good fortune to possess in Albērūnī's *India* (*c.* 1030 A.D.) the valuable work of a cultivated foreigner, giving a detailed account of the civilisation of India at this new era in its history.

This repeated contact of the Indians with foreign invaders from the West naturally led to mutual influences in various branches of literature.

With regard to the Epics, we find the statement of the Greek rhetorician Dio Chrysostomos (50–117 A.D.) that the Indians sang in their own language the poetry of Homer, the sorrows of Priam, the laments of Andromache and Hecuba, the valour of Achilles and Hector. The similarity of some of the leading characters of the *Mahābhārata*, to which the Greek writer evidently alludes, caused him to suppose that the Indian epic was a translation of the *Iliad*. There is, however, no connection of of any kind between the two poems. Nor does Professor Weber's assumption of Greek influence on the *Rāmāyaṇa* appear to have any sufficient basis (p. 307).

The view has been held that the worship of Kṛishṇa, who, as we have seen, plays an important part in the *Mahābhārata*, arose under the influence of Christianity, with which it certainly has some rather striking points of resemblance. This theory is, however, rendered improbable, at least as far as the origin of the cult of Kṛishṇa is concerned, by the conclusions at which we have arrived regarding the age of the *Mahābhārata* (pp. 286–287), as well as by the statements of Megasthenes, which indicate that Kṛishṇa was deified and worshipped some centuries before the beginning of our era. We know, moreover, from the *Mahābhāshya* that the story of Kṛishṇa was the subject of dramatic representations in the second or, at latest, the first century before the birth of Christ.

It is an interesting question whether the Indian drama has any genetic connection with that of Greece. It must be admitted that opportunities for such a connection may have existed during the first three centuries preceding our era. On his expedition to India, Alexander was accompanied by numerous artists, among whom there may have been actors. Seleucus gave his daughter in marriage to Chandragupta, and both that ruler and Ptolemy II. maintained relations with the court of Pāṭaliputra by means of ambassadors. Greek dynasties ruled in Western India for nearly two centuries. Alexandria was connected by a lively commerce with the town called by the Greeks Barygaza (now Broach), at the mouth of the Narmadā (Nerbudda) in Gujarat; with the latter town was united by a trade route the city of Ujjayinī (Greek Ozēnē), which in consequence reached a high pitch of prosperity. Philostratus (second century A.D.), not it is true a very trustworthy authority, states in his Life of Apollonius of Tyana, who visited India about 50 A.D., that Greek literature was held in high esteem by the Brahmans. Indian inscriptions mention Yavana or Greek girls sent to India as tribute, and Sanskrit authors, especially Kālidāsa, describe Indian princes as waited on by them. Professor Weber has even conjectured that the Indian god of love, Kāma, bears a dolphin (*makara*) in his banner, like the Greek Erōs, through the influence of Greek courtesans.

The existence of such conditions has induced Professor Weber to believe that the representations of Greek plays, which must have taken place at the courts of Greek princes in Bactria, in the Panjāb, and in Gujarat, suggested the drama to the Indians as a subject for imitation. This theory is supported by the fact that the curtain of the Indian stage is called *yavanikā* or the "Greek partition." Weber at the same time admits that there is no internal connection between the Indian and the Greek drama.

Professor Windisch, however, went further, and maintained such internal connection. It was, indeed, impossible for him to point out any affinity to the Greek tragedy, but he thought he could trace in the *Mṛiccha-kaṭikā* the influence of the new Attic comedy, which reached its zenith with Menander about 300 B.C. The points in which that play resembles this later Greek comedy are fewer and slighter in other Sanskrit dramas, and can easily be explained as independently developed in India. The improbability of the theory is emphasised by the still greater affinity of the Indian drama to that of Shakespeare. It is doubtful whether Greek plays were ever actually performed in India; at any rate, no references to such performances have been preserved. The earliest Sanskrit plays extant are, moreover, separated from the Greek period by at least four hundred years. The Indian drama has had a thoroughly national development, and even its origin, though obscure, easily admits of an indigenous explanation. The name of the curtain, *yavanikā*, may, indeed, be a reminiscence of Greek plays actually seen in India; but it is uncertain whether the Greek theatre had a curtain at all; in any case, it did not form the background of the stage.

It is a fact worth noting, that the beginning of one of the most famous of modern European dramas has been modelled on that of a celebrated Sanskrit play. The prelude of *Çakuntalā* suggested to Goethe the plan of the prologue on the stage in *Faust*, where the stage-manager, the merryandrew, and the poet converse regarding the play about to be performed (*cf.* p. 351). Forster's German translation of Kālidāsa's masterpiece appeared in 1791, and the profound impression it produced on Goethe is proved by the well-known epigram he composed on *Çakuntalā* in the same year. The impression was a lasting one; for the theatre prologue of *Faust* was not written till 1797, and as late as 1830 the poet thought of adapting the Indian play for the Weimar stage.

If in epic and dramatic poetry hardly any definite influences can be traced between India and the West, how different is the case in the domain of fables and fairy tales! The story of the migration of these from India certainly forms the most romantic chapter in the literary history of the world.

We know that in the sixth century A.D. there existed in India a Buddhist collection of fables, in which animals play the part of human beings (*cf.* p. 369). By the command of the Sassanian king, Khosru Anūshīrvān (531–579), this work was translated by a Persian physician named Barzoi into Pehlevī. Both this version and the unmodified original have been lost, but two early and notable translations from the Pehlevī have been preserved. The Syriac one was made about 570 A.D., and called *Kalīlag and Damnag*. A manuscript of it was found by chance in 1870, and, becoming known to scholars by a wonderful chapter of lucky accidents, was published in 1876. The Arabic translation from the Pehlevī, entitled *Kalīlah and Dimnah*, or "Fables of Pilpay," was made in the eighth century by a Persian convert to Islam, who died about 760 A.D. In this translation a wicked king is represented to be reclaimed to virtue by a Brahman philosopher named *Bidbah*, a word which has been satisfactorily traced through Pehlevī to the Sanskrit *vidyāpati*, "master of sciences," "chief scholar." From this *bidbah* is derived the modern Bidpai or Pilpay, which is thus not a proper name at all.

This Arabic version is of great importance, as the

source of other versions which exercised very great influence in shaping the literature of the Middle Ages in Europe. These versions of it were the later Syriac (*c.* 1000 A.D.), the Greek (1180), the Persian (*c.* 1130), recast later (*c.* 1494) under the title of *Anvār-i-Suhailī*, or "Lights of Canopus," the old Spanish (1251), and the Hebrew one made about 1250.

The fourth stratum of translation is represented by John of Capua's rendering of the Hebrew version into Latin (*c.* 1270), entitled *Directorium Humanæ Vitæ*, which was printed about 1480.

From John of Capua's work was made, at the instance of Duke Eberhardt of Wurtemberg, the famous German version, *Das Buch der Byspel der alten Wysen*, or "Book of Apologues of the Ancient Sages," first printed about 1481. The fact that four dated editions appeared at Ulm between 1483 and 1485, and thirteen more down to 1592, is a sufficiently eloquent proof of the importance of this work as a means of instruction and amusement during the fifteenth and sixteenth centuries. The *Directorium* was also the source of the Italian version, printed at Venice in 1552, from which came the English translation of Sir Thomas North (1570). The latter was thus separated from the Indian original by five intervening translations and a thousand years of time.

It is interesting to note the changes which tales undergo in the course of such wanderings. In the second edition of his Fables (1678), La Fontaine acknowledges his indebtedness for a large part of his work to the Indian sage Pilpay. A well-known story in the French writer is that of the milkmaid, who, while carrying a pail of milk on her head to market, and building all kinds of castles in the air with the future proceeds of the sale of the milk, suddenly gives a jump of joy at the prospect of her approaching fortune, and thereby shatters the pail to pieces on the ground. This is only a transformation of a story still preserved in the *Panchatantra*. Here it is a Brahman who, having filled an alms-bowl with the remnants of some rice-pap he has begged, hangs it up on a nail in the wall above his bed. He dreams of the money he will procure by selling the rice when a famine breaks out. Then he will gradually acquire cattle, buy a fine house, and marry a beautiful girl with a rich dowry. One day when he calls to his wife to take away his son who is playing about, and she does not hear, he will rise up to give her a kick. As this thought passes through his mind, his foot shatters the alms-bowl, the contents of which are spilt all over him.

Another *Panchatantra* story recurring in La Fontaine is that of the too avaricious jackal. Finding the dead bodies of a boar and a hunter, besides the bow of the latter, he resolves on devouring the bowstring first. As soon as he begins to gnaw, the bow starts asunder, pierces his head, and kills him. In La Fontaine the jackal has become a wolf, and the latter is killed by the arrow shot off as he touches the bow.

Nothing, perhaps, in the history of the migration of Indian tales is more remarkable than the story of *Barlaam and Josaphat*. At the court of Khalif Almansur (753–774), under whom *Kalīlah and Dimnah* was translated into Arabic, there lived a Christian known as John of Damascus, who wrote in Greek the story of *Barlaam and Josaphat* as a manual of Christian theology. This became one of the most popular books of the Middle Ages, being translated into many Oriental as well as European languages. It is enlivened by a number of fables and parables, most of which have been traced to Indian sources. The very hero of the story, Prince Josaphat, has an Indian origin, being, in fact, no other than Buddha. The name has been shown to be a corruption of *Bodhisattva*, a well-known designation of the Indian reformer. Josaphat rose to the rank of a saint both in the Greek and the Roman Church, his day in the former being August 26, in the latter November 27. That the founder of an atheistic Oriental religion should have developed into a Christian saint is one of the most astounding facts in religious history.

Though Europe was thus undoubtedly indebted to India for its mediæval literature of fairy tales and fables, the Indian claim to priority of origin in ancient times is somewhat dubious. A certain number of apologues found in the collections of Æsop and Babrius are distinctly related to Indian fables. The Indian claim is supported by the argument that the relation of the jackal to the lion is a natural one in the Indian fable, while the connection of the fox and the lion in Greece has no basis in fact. On the other side it has been urged that animals and birds which are peculiar to India play but a minor part in Indian fables, while there exists a Greek representation of the Æsopian fable of the fox and the raven, dating from the sixth century B.C. Weber and Benfey both conclude that the Indians borrowed a few fables from the Greeks, admitting at the same time that the Indians had independent fables of their own before. Rudimentary fables are found even in the *Chhāndogya Upanishad*, and the transmigration theory would have favoured the development of this form of tale; indeed Buddha himself in the old *Jātaka* stories appears in the form of various animals.

Contemporaneously with the fable literature, the most intellectual game the world has known began its westward migration from India. Chess in Sanskrit is called *chatur-anga*, or the "four-limbed army," because it represents a *kriegspiel*, in which two armies, consisting of infantry, cavalry, chariots, and elephants, each led by a king and his councillor, are opposed. The earliest direct mention of the game in Sanskrit literature is found in the works of Bāṇa, and the *Kāvyālaṃkāra* of Rudraṭa, a Kashmirian poet of the ninth century, contains a metrical puzzle illustrating the moves of the chariot, the elephant, and the horse. Introduced into Persia in the sixth century, chess was brought by the Arabs to Europe, where it was generally known by 1100 A.D. It has left its mark on mediæval poetry, on the idioms of European languages (*e.g.* "check," from the Persian *shah*, "king"), on the science of arithmetic in the calculation of progressions with the chessboard, and even in heraldry, where the "rook" often figures in coats of arms. Beside the fable literature of India, this Indian game served to while away the tedious life of myriads during the Middle Ages in Europe.

Turning to Philosophical Literature, we find that the early Greek and Indian philosophers have many points in common. Some of the leading doctrines of the Eleatics, that God and the universe are one, that everything existing in multiplicity has no reality, that thinking and being are identical, are all to be found in the philosophy of the Upanishads and the Vedānta system, which is its outcome. Again, the doctrine of Empedocles, that nothing can arise which has not existed before, and that nothing existing can be annihilated, has its exact parallel in the characteristic doctrine of the Sānkhya system about the eternity and indestructibility of matter. According to Greek tradition, Thales, Empedocles, Anaxagoras, Democritus, and others undertook journeys to Oriental countries in order to study philosophy. Hence there is at least the historical possibility of the Greeks having been influenced by Indian thought through Persia.

Whatever may be the truth in the cases just mentioned, the dependence of Pythagoras on Indian philosophy and science certainly seems to have a high degree of probability. Almost all the doctrines ascribed to him, religious, philosophical, mathematical, were known in India in the sixth century B.C. The coincidences are so numerous that their cumulative force becomes considerable. The transmigration theory, the assumption of five elements, the Pythagorean theorem in geometry, the prohibition as to eating beans, the religio-philosophical character of the Pythagorean fraternity, and the mystical speculations of the Pythagorean school, all have their close parallels in ancient India. The doctrine of metempsychosis in the case of Pythagoras appears without any connection or explanatory background, and was regarded by the Greeks as of foreign origin. He could not have derived it from Egypt, as it was not known to the ancient Egyptians. In spite, however, of the later tradition, it seems impossible that Pythagoras should have made his way to India at so early a date, but he could quite well have met Indians in Persia.

Coming to later centuries, we find indications that the Neo-Platonist philosophy may have been influenced by the Sānkhya system, which flourished in the first centuries of our era, and could easily have become known at Alexandria owing to the lively intercourse between that city and India at the time. From this source Plotinus (204–269 A.D.), chief of the Neo-Platonists, may have derived his doctrine that soul is free from suffering, which belongs only to matter, his identification of soul with light, and his illustrative use of the mirror, in which the reflections of objects appear, for the purpose of explaining the phenomena of consciousness. The influence of the Yoga system on Plotinus is suggested by his requirement that man should renounce the world of sense and strive after truth by contemplation. Connection with Sānkhya ideas is still more likely in the case of Plotinus's most eminent pupil, Porphyry (232–304 A.D.), who lays particular stress on the difference between soul and matter, on the omnipresence of soul when freed from the bonds of matter, and on the doctrine that the world has no beginning. It is also noteworthy that he rejects sacrifice and prohibits the killing of animals.

The influence of Indian philosophy on Christian Gnosticism in the second and third centuries seems at any rate undoubted. The Gnostic doctrine of the opposition between soul and matter, of the personal existence of intellect, will, and so forth, the identification of soul and light, are derived from the Sānkhya system. The division, peculiar to several Gnostics, of men into the three classes of *pneumatikoi*, *psychikoi*, and *hylikoi*, is also based on the Sānkhya doctrine of the three *guṇas*. Again, Bardesanes, a Gnostic of the Syrian school, who obtained information about India from Indian philosophers, assumed the existence of a subtle ethereal body which is identical with the *linga-çarīra* of the Sānkhya system. Finally, the many heavens of the Gnostics are evidently derived from the fantastic cosmogony of later Buddhism.

With regard to the present century, the influence of Indian thought on the pessimistic philosophy of Schopenhauer and Von Hartmann is well known. How great an impression the Upanishads produced on the former, even in a second-hand Latin translation, may be inferred from his writing that they were his consolation in life and would be so in death.

In Science, too, the debt of Europe to India has been considerable. There is, in the first place, the great fact that the Indians invented the numerical figures used all over the world. The influence which the decimal system of reckoning dependent on those figures has had not only on mathematics, but on the progress of civilisation in general, can hardly be over-estimated. During the eighth and ninth centuries the Indians became the teachers in arithmetic and algebra of the Arabs, and through them of the nations of the West. Thus, though we call the latter science by an Arabic name, it is a gift we owe to India.

In Geometry the points of contact between the Çulva Sūtras and the work of the Greeks are so considerable, that, according to Cantor, the historian of mathematics, borrowing must have taken place on one side or the other. In the opinion of that authority, the Çulva Sūtras were influenced by the Alexandrian geometry of Hero (215 B.C.), which, he thinks, came to India after 100 B.C. The Çulva Sūtras are, however, probably far earlier than that date, for they form an integral portion of the Çrauta Sūtras, and their geometry is a part of the Brahmanical theology, having taken its rise in India from practical motives as much as the science of grammar. The prose parts of the Yajurvedas and the Brāhmaṇas constantly speak of the arrangement of the sacrificial ground and the construction of altars according to very strict rules, the slightest deviation from which might cause the greatest disaster. It is not likely that the exclusive Brahmans should have been willing to borrow anything closely connected with their religion from foreigners.

Of Astronomy the ancient Indians had but slight independent knowledge. It is probable that they derived their early acquaintance with the twenty-eight divisions of the moon's orbit from the Chaldeans through their commercial relations with the Phœnicians. Indian astronomy did not really begin to flourish till it was affected by that of Greece; it is indeed the one science in which undoubtedly strong Greek influence can be proved. The debt which the native astronomers always acknowledge they owe to the Yavanas is sufficiently obvious from the numerous Greek terms in Indian astronomical writings. Thus, in Varāha Mihira's *Horā-çāstra* the signs of the zodiac are enumerated either by Sanskrit names translated from the Greek or by the original Greek names, as *Āra* for *Ares*, *Heli* for *Hēlios*, *Jyau* for *Zeus*. Many technical terms were directly borrowed from Greek works, as *kendra* for *kentron*, *jāmitra* for *diametron*. Some of the very names of the oldest astronomical treatises of the Indians indicate their Western origin. Thus the *Romaka-siddhānta* means the "Roman manual." The title of Varāha Mihira's *Horā-çāstra* contains the Greek word *hōrā*.

In a few respects, however, the Indians independently advanced astronomical science further than the Greeks themselves, and at a later period they in their turn influenced the West even in astronomy. For in the eighth and ninth centuries they became the teachers of the Arabs in this science also. The *siddhāntas* (Arabic *Sind Hind*), the writings of Āryabhaṭa (called Arjehīr), and the *Ahargaṇa* (*Arkand*), attributed to Brahmagupta, were translated or adapted by the Arabs, and Khalifs of Bagdad repeatedly summoned Indian astronomers to their court to supervise this work. Through the Arabs, Indian astronomy then migrated to Europe, which in this case only received back in a roundabout way what it had given long before. Thus the Sanskrit word *uchcha*, "apex of a planet's orbit," was borrowed in the form of *aux* (gen. *aug-is*) in Latin translations of Arabic astronomers.

After Bhāskara (twelfth century), Hindu astronomy, ceasing to make further progress, became once more merged in the astrology from which it had sprung. It was now the turn of the Arabs, and, by a strange inversion of things, an Arabic writer of the ninth century who had written on Indian astronomy and arithmetic, in this period became an object of study to the Hindus. The old Greek terms remained, but new Arabic ones were added as the necessity for them arose.

The question as to whether Indian Medical Science in its earlier period was affected by that of the Greeks cannot yet be answered with certainty, the two systems not having hitherto been compared with sufficient care. Recently, however, some close parallels have been discovered between the works of Hippocrates and Charaka (according to a Chinese authority, the official physician of King Kanishka), which render Greek influence before the beginning of our era likely.

On the other hand, the effect of Hindu medical

science upon the Arabs after about 700 A.D. was considerable, for the Khalifs of Bagdad caused several books on the subject to be translated. The works of Charaka and Suçruta (probably not later than the fourth century A.D.) were rendered into Arabic at the close of the eighth century, and are quoted as authorities by the celebrated Arabic physician Al-Razi, who died in 932 A.D. Arabic medicine in its turn became the chief authority, down to the seventeenth century, of European physicians. By the latter Indian medical authors must have been thought highly of, for Charaka is repeatedly mentioned in the Latin translations of the Arab writers Avicenna (Ibn Sīnā), Rhazes (Al-Razi), and Serapion (Ibn Sarāfyūn). In modern days European surgery has borrowed the operation of rhinoplasty, or the formation of artificial noses, from India, where Englishmen became acquainted with the art in the last century.

We have already seen that the discovery of the Sanskrit language and literature led, in the present century, to the foundation of the two new sciences of Comparative Mythology and Comparative Philology. Through the latter it has even affected the practical school-teaching of the classical languages in Europe. The interest in Buddhism has already produced an immense literature in Europe. Some of the finest lyrics of Heine, and works like Sir Edwin Arnold's *Light of Asia*, to mention only a few instances, have drawn their inspiration from Sanskrit poetry. The intellectual debt of Europe to Sanskrit literature has thus been undeniably great; it may perhaps become greater still in the years that are to come.

APPENDIX ON TECHNICAL LITERATURE

LAW.

ON Sanskrit legal literature in general, consult the very valuable work of Jolly, *Recht und Sitte*, in Bühler's *Encyclopædia*, 1896 (complete bibliography). There are several secondary Dharma Sūtras of the post-Vedic period. The most important of these is the *Vaishṇava Dharma Çāstra* or *Vishṇu Smṛiti* (closely connected with the *Kāṭhaka Gṛihya Sūtra*), not earlier than 200 A.D. in its final redaction (ed. by Jolly, Calcutta, 1881, trans. by him in the *Sacred Books of the East*, Oxford, 1880). The regular post-Vedic lawbooks are metrical (mostly in *çlokas*). They are much wider in scope than the Dharma Sūtras, which are limited to matters connected with religion. The most important and earliest of the metrical Smṛitis is the *Mānava Dharma Çāstra*, or *Code of Manu*, not improbably based on a *Mānava Dharma Sūtra*. It is closely connected with the *Mahābhārata*, of which three books alone (iii., xii., xvi.) contain as many as 260 of its 2684 *çlokas*. It probably assumed its present shape not much later than 200 A.D. It was ed. by Jolly, London, 1887; trans. by Bühler, with valuable introd., in the *Sacred Books*, Oxford, 1886; also trans. by Burnell (ed. by Hopkins), London, 1884; text ed., with seven comm., by Mandlik, Bombay, 1886; text, with Kullūka's comm., Bombay, 1888, better than Nirn. Sāg. Pr., ed. 1887. Next comes the *Yājnavalkya Dharma Çāstra*, which is much more concise (1009 *çlokas*). It was probably based on a Dharma Sūtra of the *White*

Yajurveda; its third section resembles the *Pāraskara Gṛihya Sūtra*, but it is unmistakably connected with the *Mānava Grihya Sūtra* of the *Black Yajurveda.* Its approximate date seems to be about 350 A.D. Its author probably belonged to Mithilā, capital of Videha (Tirhut). *Yājnavalkya*, ed. and trans. by Stenzler, Berlin, 1849; with comm. *Mitāksharā*, 3rd ed., Bombay, 1892. The *Nārada Smṛiti* is the first to limit *dharma* to law in the strict sense. It contains more than 12,000 *çlokas*, and appears to have been founded chiefly on *Manu.* Bāṇa mentions a *Nāradīya Dharma Çāstra*, and Nārada was annotated by one of the earliest legal commentators in the eighth century. His date is probably about 500 A.D. *Nārada*, ed. by Jolly, Calcutta, 1885, trans. by him in *Sacred Books*, vol. xxxiii. 1889. A late lawbook is the *Parāçara Smṛiti* (anterior to 1300 A.D.), ed. in Bombay Sansk. Series, 1893; trans. *Bibl. Ind.*, 1887. The second stage of post-Vedic legal literature is formed by the commentaries. The oldest one preserved is that of Medhātithi on *Manu;* he dates from about 900 A.D. The most famous comm. on *Manu* is that of Kullūka-bhaṭṭa, composed at Benares in the fifteenth century, but it is nothing more than a plagiarism of Govindarāja, a commentator of the twelfth century. The most celebrated comm. on *Yājnavalkya* is the *Mitākshara* of Vijnāneçvara, composed about 1100 A.D. It early attained to the position of a standard work, not only in the Dekhan, but even in Benares and a great part of Northern India. In the present century it acquired the greatest importance in the practice of the Anglo-Indian law-courts through Colebrooke's translation of the section which it contains on the law of inheritance. From about 1000 A.D. onwards, an innumerable multitude of legal compendia, called *Dharma-nibandhas*, was produced in India. The most imposing of them is the voluminous work in five parts entitled *Chaturvarga-chintāmaṇi*, composed by Hemādri about 1300 A.D. It hardly treats of law at all, but is a perfect mine of interesting quotations from the Smṛitis and the Purāṇas; it has been edited in the *Bibl. Ind.* The *Dharmaratna* of Jīmūtavāhana (probably fifteenth century) may here be mentioned, because part of it is the famous treatise on the law of inheritance entitled *Dāyabhāga*, which is the chief work of the Bengal School on the subject, and was translated by Colebrooke. It should be noted that the Indian Smṛitis are not on the same footing as the lawbooks of other nations, but are works of private individuals; they were also written by Brahmans for Brahmans, whose caste pretensions they consequently exaggerate. It is therefore important to check their statements by outside evidence.

History.

No work of a directly historical character is met with in Sanskrit literature till after the Muhammadan conquest. This is the *Rājatarangiṇī*, or "River of Kings," a chronicle of the kings of Kashmir, begun by its author, Kalhaṇa, in 1148 A.D. It contains nearly 8000 *çlokas*. The early part of the work is legendary in character. The poet does not become historical till he approaches his own times. This work (ed. M. A. Stein, Bombay, 1892; trans. by Y. C. Datta, Calc., 1898) is of considerable value for the archæology and chronology of Kashmir.

Grammar.

On the native grammatical literature see especially Wackernagel, *Altindische Grammatik*, vol. i. p. lix. *sqq.* The oldest grammar preserved is that of Pāṇini, who, however, mentions no fewer than sixty-four predecessors. He belonged to the extreme north-west of India, and probably flourished about 300 B.C. His work consists of nearly 4000 sūtras divided into eight chapters; text with German trans., ed. by Böhtlingk, Leipsic, 1887. Pāṇini had before him a list of irregularly formed words, which survives, in a somewhat modified form, as the *Uṇādi Sūtra* (ed. by Aufrecht, with Ujjvaladatta's comm., Bonn, 1859). There are also two appendixes to which Pāṇini refers: one is the *Dhātupāṭha*, "List of Verbal Roots," containing some 2000 roots, of which only about 800 have been found in Sanskrit literature, and from which about fifty Vedic verbs are omitted; the second is the *Gaṇapāṭha*, or "List of Word-Groups," to which certain rules apply. These *gaṇas* were metrically arranged in the *Gaṇaratna-mahodadhi*, composed by Vardhamāna in 1140 A.D. (ed. by Eggeling, London, 1879). Among the earliest attempts to explain Pāṇini was the formulation of rules of interpretation or *paribhāshās*; a collection of these was made in the last century by Nāgojibhaṭṭa in his *Paribhāshenduçekhara* (ed. by Kielhorn, Bombay Sansk. Ser., 1868 and 1871). Next we have the *Vārttikas* or "Notes" of Kātyāyana (probably third century B.C.) on 1245 of Pāṇini's rules, and, somewhat later, numerous grammatical *Kārikās* or comments in metrical form: all this critical work was collected by Patanjali in his *Mahābhāshya* or "Great Commentary," with supplementary comments of his own (ed. Kielhorn, 3 vols., Bombay). He deals with 1713 rules of Pāṇini. He probably lived in the later half of the second century B.C., and in any case not later than the beginning of our era. The *Mahābhāshya* was commented on in the seventh century by Bhartṛihari in his *Vākyapadīya* (ed. in Benares Sansk. Ser.), which is concerned with the philosophy of grammar, and by Kaiyaṭa (probably thirteenth century). About 650 A.D. was composed the first complete comm. on Pāṇini, the *Kāçikā Vṛitti* or "Benares Commentary," by Jayāditya and Vāmana (2nd ed. Benares, 1898). In the fifteenth century Rāmachandra, in his *Prakriyā-kaumudī*, or "Moonlight of Method," endeavoured to make Pāṇini's grammar easier by a more practical arrangement of its matter. Bhaṭṭoji's *Siddhānta-kaumudī* (seventeenth century) has a similar aim (ed. Nirṇaya Sāgara Press, Bombay, 1894); an abridgment of this work, the *Laghu-kaumudī*, by Varadarāja (ed. Ballantyne, with English trans., 4th ed., Benares, 1891), is commonly used as an introduction to the native system of grammar. Among non-Pāṇinean grammarians may be mentioned Chandra (about 600 A.D.), the pseudo-Çākaṭāyana (later than the *Kāçikā*), and, the most important, Hemachandra (12th cent.), author of a Prākrit grammar (ed. and trans. by Pischel, two vols., Halle, 1877–80), and of the *Uṇādigaṇa Sūtra* (ed. Kirste, Vienna, 1895). The *Kātantra* of Çarvavarman (ed. Eggeling, *Bibl. Ind.*) seems to have been the most influential of the later grammars. Vararuchi's *Prākṛita-prakāça* is a Prākrit grammar (ed. by Cowell, 2nd ed., 1868). The *Mugdhabodha* (13th cent.) of Vopadeva is the Sanskrit grammar chiefly used in Bengal. The *Phiṭ Sūtra* (later than Patanjali) gives rules for the accentuation of nouns (ed. Kielhorn, 1866); Hemachandra's *Lingānuçāsana* is a treatise on gender (ed. Franke, Göttingen, 1886). Among European grammars that of Whitney was the first to attempt a historical treatment of the Vedic and Sanskrit language. The first grammar treating Sanskrit from the comparative point of view is the excellent work of Wackernagel, of which, however, only the first part (phonology) has yet appeared. The present writer's abridgment (London, 1886) of Max Müller's Sanskrit Grammar is a practical work for the use of beginners of Classical Sanskrit.

Lexicography.

Zachariæ in *Die indischen Wörterbücher* (in Bühler's *Encyclopædia*, 1897) deals with the subject as a whole (complete bibliography). The Sanskrit dictionaries or *koças* are collections of rare words or significations for the use of poets. They are all versified; alphabetical order is entirely absent in the synonymous and only incipient in the homonymous class. The *Amarakoça* (ed. with Maheçvara's comm., Bombay), occupies the same dominant position in lexicography as Pāṇini in grammar, not improbably composed about 500 A.D. A supplement to it is the *Trikāṇḍa-çesha* by Purushottamadeva (perhaps as late as 1300 A.D.). Çāçvata's *Anekārtha-samuchchaya* (ed. Zachariæ, 1882) is possibly older than *Amara*. Halāyudha's *Abhidhānaratnamālā* dates from about 950 A.D. (ed. Aufrecht, London, 1861). About a century later is Yādavaprakāça's *Vaijayantī* (ed. Oppert, Madras, 1893). The *Viçvaprakāça* of Maheçvara Kavi dates from 1111 A.D. The *Mankha-koça* (ed. Zachariæ, Bombay, 1897) was composed in Kashmir about 1150 A.D. Hemachandra (1088–1172 A.D.) composed four dictionaries: *Abhidhāna-chintāmaṇi*, synonyms (ed. Böhtlingk and Rieu, St. Petersburg, 1847); *Anekārtha-saṃgraha*, homonyms (ed. Zachariæ, Vienna, 1893); *Deçīnāmamālā*, a Prākrit dictionary (ed. Pischel, Bombay, 1880); and *Nighaṇṭu-çesha*, a botanical glossary, which forms a supplement to his synonymous *koça*.

Poetics.

Cf. Sylvain Lévi, *Théâtre Indien*, pp. 1–21; Regnaud, *La Rhétorique Sanskrite*, Paris, 1884; Jacob, *Notes on Alaṃkara Literature*, in *Journal of the Roy. As. Soc.*, 1897,

1898. The oldest and most important work on poetics is the *Nāṭya Çāstra* of Bharata, which probably goes back to the sixth century A.D. (ed. in *Kāvyamālā*, No. 42, Bombay, 1894; ed. by Grosset, Lyons, 1897). Daṇḍin's *Kāvyādarça* (end of sixth century) contains about 650 *çlokas* (ed. with trans. by Böhtlingk, Leipsic, 1890). Vāmana's *Kāvyālaṃkāravṛitti*, probably eighth century (ed. Cappeller, Jena, 1875). *Çṛingāra-tilaka*, or "Ornament of Erotics," by Rudrabhaṭa (ninth century), ed. by Pischel, Kiel, 1886 (*cf. Journal of German Or. Soc.*, 1888, p. 296 ff., 425 ff.; *Vienna Or. Journal*, ii. p. 151 ff.). Rudraṭa Çatānanda's *Kāvyālaṃkāra* (ed. in *Kāvyamālā*) belongs to the ninth century. Dhanaṃjaya's *Daçarūpa*, on the ten kinds of drama, belongs to the tenth century (ed. Hall, 1865; with comm. Nirṇaya Sāgara Press, Bombay, 1897). The *Kāvyaprakāça* by Mammaṭa and Alaṭa dates from about 1100 (ed. in the *Pandit*, 1897). The *Sāhityadarpaṇa* was composed in Eastern Bengal about 1450 A.D., by Viçvanātha Kavirāja (ed. J. Vidyāsāgara, Calcutta, 1895; trans. by Ballantyne in *Bibl. Ind.*).

Mathematics and Astronomy.

The only work dealing with this subject as a whole is Thibaut's *Astronomie, Astrologie und Mathematik*, in Bühler-Kielhorn's *Encyclopædia*, 1899 (full bibliography). See also Cantor, *Geschichte der Mathematik*, pp. 505–562, Leipsic, 1880. Mathematics are dealt with in special chapters of the works of the early Indian astronomers. In algebra they attained an eminence far exceeding anything ever achieved by the Greeks. The earliest works of scientific Indian astronomy (after about 300 A.D.) were four treatises called *Siddhāntas;* only one, the *Sūryasiddhānta* (ed. and trans. by Whitney, *Journ. Am. Or. Soc.*, vol. vi.), has survived. The doctrines of such early works were reduced to a more concise and practical form by Ārya-bhaṭa, born, as he tells us himself, at Pāṭaliputra in 476 A.D. He maintained the rotation of the earth round its axis (a doctrine not unknown to the Greeks), and explained the cause of eclipses of the sun and moon. Mathematics are treated in the third section of his work, the *Āryabhaṭiya* (ed. with comm. by Kern, Leyden, 1874; math. section trans. by Rodet, *Journal Asiatique*, 1879). Varāha Mihira, born near Ujjain, began his calculations about 505 A.D., and, according to one of his commentators, died in 587 A.D. He composed four works, written for the most part in the *Aryā* metre; three are astrological: the *Bṛihat-saṃhitā* (ed. Kern, *Bibl. Ind.*, 1864, 1865, trans. in *Journ. As. Soc.*, vol. iv.; new ed. with comm. of Bhaṭṭotpala by S. Dvivedī, Benares, 1895–97), the *Bṛihaj-jātaka* (or *Horā-çāstra*, trans. by C. Jyer, Madras, 1885), and the *Laghu-jātaka* (partly trans. by Weber, *Ind. Stud.*, vol. ii., and by Jacobi, 1872). His *Pancha-siddhāntikā* (ed. and for the most part trans. by Thibaut and S. Dvivedī, Benares, 1889), based on five *siddhāntas*, is a *karaṇa* or practical astronomical treatise. Another distinguished astronomer was Brahmagupta, who, born in 598 A.D., wrote, besides a *karaṇa*, his *Brāhma Sphuṭa-siddhānta* when thirty years old (chaps. xii. and xviii. are mathematical). The last eminent Indian astronomer was Bhāskarāchārya, born in 1114 A.D. His *Siddhānta-çiromaṇi* has enjoyed more authority in India than any other astronomical work except the *Sūrya-siddhānta*.

MEDICINE.

Indian medical science must have begun to develop before the beginning of our era, for one of its chief authorities, Charaka, was, according to the Chinese translation of the Buddhist *Tripiṭaka*, the official physician of King Kanishka in the first century A.D. His work, the *Charaka-saṃhitā*, has been edited several times: by J. Vidyāsāgara, 2nd ed., Calcutta, 1896, by Gupta, Calcutta, 1897, with comm. by C. Dutta, Calcutta, 1892–1893; trans. by A. C. Kaviratna, Calcutta, 1897. Suçruta, the next great authority, seems to have lived not later than the fourth century A.D., as the Bower MS. (probably fifth century A.D.) contains passages not only parallel to, but verbally agreeing with, passages in the works of Charaka and Suçruta. (The *Suçruta-saṃhitā*, ed. by J. Vidyāsāgara, Calcutta, 3rd ed., 1889; A. C. Kaviratna, Calcutta, 1888–95; trans. by Dutta, 1883, Chaṭṭopādhyāya, 1891, Hoernle, 1897, Calcutta.) The next best known medical writer is Vāgbhaṭa, author of the *Ashṭāṅga-hṛidaya* (ed., with comm. of Aruṇadatta, by A. M. Kunte, Bombay, Nir. Sāg. Press, 1891). *Cf.* also articles by Haas in vols. xxx., xxxi., and by A. Müller in xxxiv. of *Jour. of Germ. Or. Soc.*; P. Cordier, *Études sur la Médecine Hindoue*, Paris, 1894; *Vāgbhaṭa et l'Aṣṭāṅgahṛidayasaṃhitā*, Besançon, 1896; Liétard, *Le Médecin Charaka*, &c., in *Bull. de l'Ac. de Médecine*, May 11, 1897.

Arts.

On Indian music see Rāja Sir Sourindro Mohun Tagore, *Hindu Music from various Authors*, Calcutta, 1875; Ambros, *Geschichte der Musik*, vol. i. pp. 41–80; Day, *The Music and Musical Instruments of Southern India and the Deccan*, Edinburgh, 1891; Çārngadeva's *Saṃgītaratnākara*, ed. Telang, Ānand. Sansk. Ser., 1897; Somanātha's *Rāgavibodha*, ed. with comm. by P. G. Ghārpure (parts i.–v.), Poona, 1895.

On painting and sculpture see E. Moor, *The Hindu Pantheon*, London, 1810; Burgess, *Notes on the Bauddha*

Rock Temples of Ajanta, Bombay, 1879; Griffiths *Paintings of the Buddhist Cave Temples of Ajanta*, 2 vols., London, 1896–97; Burgess, *The Gandhāra Sculptures* (with 100 plates), London, 1895; Fergusson, *Tree and Serpent Worship* (illustrations of mythology and art in India in the first and fourth centuries after Christ), London, 1868; Cunningham's *Reports*, i. and iii. (Reliefs from Buddha Gayā); Grünwedel, *Buddhistiche Kunst in Indien*, Berlin, 1893; Kern, *Manual of Buddhism*, in Bühler's *Encyclopædia*, pp. 91–96, Strasburg, 1896; H. H. Wilson, *Ariana Antiqua*, London, 1841.

On Indian architecture see Fergusson, *History of Indian and Eastern Architecture*, London, 1876; *The Rock-Cut Temples of India*, 1864; Cunningham, *The Bhilsa Topes, or Buddhist Monuments of Central India*, London, 1854; Reports of the Archæological Survey of India, Calcutta, since 1871; *Mahābodhi*, or the great Buddhist Temple under the Bodhi tree at Buddha Gayā, London, 1892; Burgess, Archæological Survey of Western India and of Southern India; Daniell, *Antiquities of India*, London, 1800; *Hindu Excavations in the Mountain of Ellora*, London, 1816; R. Mitra, *The Antiquities of Orissa*, Calcutta, 1875.

On Technical Arts see *Journal of Indian Art and Industry* (London, begun in 1884).

BIBLIOGRAPHICAL NOTES

CHAPTER I.

On the history of Sanskrit studies see especially Benfey, *Geschichte der Sprachwissenschaft*, Munich, 1869. A very valuable work for Sanskrit Bibliography is the annual *Orientalische Bibliographie*, Berlin (begun in 1888). Page 1: Some inaccurate information about the religious ideas of the Brahmans may be found in Purchas, *His Pilgrimage, or Relations of the World and the Religions observed in all Ages*, 2nd ed., London, 1614; and Lord, *A Discoverie of the Sect of the Banians* [Hindus], London, 1630. Abraham Roger, *Open Deure*, 1631 (contains trans. of two centuries of Bhartṛihari). Page 2, Dugald Stewart, *Philosophy of the Human Mind*, part 2, chap. i. sect. 6 (conjectures concerning the origin of Sanskrit). C. W. Wall, D.D., *An Essay on the Nature, Age, and Origin of the Sanskrit Writing and Language*, Dublin, 1838. Halhed, *A Code of Gentoo* [Hindu] *Law, or Ordinations of the Pandits, from a Persian translation, made from the original written in the Shanscrit language*, 1776. Page 4: F. Schlegel, *Ueber die Sprache und Weisheit der Inder*, Heidelberg, 1808. Bopp, *Conjugationssystem*, Frankfort, 1816. Colebrooke, *On the Vedas*, in *Asiatic Researches*, Calcutta, 1805. P. 5: Roth, *Zur Literatur und Geschichte des Veda*, Stuttgart, 1846. Böhtlingk and Roth's Sanskrit-German Dictionary, 7 vols., St. Petersburg, 1852–75. Bühler's *Encyclopædia of Indo-Aryan Research*, Strasburg (the parts, some German, some English, began to appear in 1896). Page 6: See especially Aufrecht's *Catalogus Catalogorum* (Leipsic, 1891; Supplement, 1896), which gives a list of Sanskrit MSS. in the alphabetical order of works and authors. Adalbert Kuhn, *Herabkunft des Feuers*, 1849; 2nd ed., Gütersloh, 1886. Page 11: A valuable book on Indian chronology (based on epigraphic and numismatic sources) is Duff's *The Chronology of India*, London, 1899. On the date of Buddha's death, *cf.* Oldenberg, *Buddha*, Berlin, 3rd ed., 1897. Page 13: *Fa Hian*, trans. by Legge, Oxford, 1886; *Hiouen Thsang*, trans. by Beal, *Si-yu-ki*, London, 1884; *I Tsing*, trans. by Takakusu, Oxford, 1896. Führer, *Monograph on Buddha Sakyamuni's Birthplace*, Arch. Surv. of India, vol. xxvi., Allahabad, 1897; Alberūnī's *India*, trans. into English by Sachau, London, 1885. Page 14: *Corpus Inscriptionum Indicarum*, vol. i., 1877, vol. iii., 1888, Calcutta. *Epigraphia Indica*, Calcutta, from 1888.

Important Oriental journals are: *Indian Antiquary*, Bombay; *Zeitschrift der deutschen morgenländischen Gesellschaft*, Leipsic; *Journal of the Royal Asiatic Society*, London (with a Bengal branch at Calcutta and another at Bombay); *Journal Asiatique*, Paris; *Vienna Oriental Journal*, Vienna; *Journal of the American Oriental Society*, New Haven, Conn. On the origin of Indian writing (pp. 14–20), see Bühler, *Indische Palæographie*, Strasburg, 1896, and *On the Origin of the Indian Brāhma Alphabet*, Strasburg, 1898. Page 18: The oldest known Sanskrit MSS., now in the Bodleian Library, has been reproduced in facsimile by Dr. R. Hoernle, *The Bower Manuscript*, Calcutta, 1897. The Pāli *Kharoshṭhī* MS. is a Prākrit recension of the *Dhammapada*, found near Khotan; see Senart, *Journal Asiatique*, 1898, pp. 193–304. Page 27: The account here given of the Prākrit dialects is based mainly on a monograph of Dr. G. A. Grierson (who is now engaged on a linguistic survey of India), *The Geographical Distribution and Mutual Affinities of the Indo-Aryan Vernaculars*. On Pāli literature, see Rhys Davids, *Buddhism, its History and Literature*, London, 1896. On Prākrit literature, see Grierson, *The Mediæval Vernacular Literature of Hindustan*, trans. of 7th Oriental Congress, Vienna, 1888, and *The Modern Vernacular Literature of Hindustan*, Calcutta, 1889.

CHAPTER III.

On the text and metres of the *Rigveda* see especially Oldenberg, *Die Hymnen des Ṛigveda*, vol. i., *Prolegomena*, Berlin,

1888; on the accent, Wackernagel, *Altindische Grammatik*, vol. i. pp. 281–300 (full bibliography), Göttingen, 1896; on the *Rigveda* in general, Kaegi, *The Rigveda*, English translation by Arrowsmith, Boston, 1886. Editions: Saṃhitā text, ed. Max Müller, London, 1873; Pada text, 1877; Saṃhitā text (in Roman characters), ed. Aufrecht, Bonn, 1877 (2nd ed.); Saṃhitā and Pada text with Sāyaṇa's commentary, 2nd ed., 4 vols., by Max Müller, London, 1890–92. Selections in Lanman's *Sanskrit Reader* (full notes and vocabulary); Peterson's *Hymns from the Rigveda* (Bombay Sanskrit Series); A. Bergaigne and V. Henry's *Manuel pour étudier le Sanskrit Védique*, Paris, 1890; Windisch, *Zwölf Hymnen des Rigveda*, Leipzig, 1883; Hillebrandt, *Vedachrestomathie*, Berlin, 1885; Böhtlingk, *Sanskrit-Chrestomathie*, 3rd ed., Leipsic, 1897. Translations: R. H. T. Griffith, *The Rigveda metrically translated into English*, 2 vols., Benares, 1896–97; Max Müller, *Vedic Hymns* (to the Maruts, Rudra, Vāyu, Vāta: prose), in *Sacred Books of the East*, vol. xxxii., Oxford, 1891; Oldenberg, *Vedic Hymns* (to Agni in Books i.–v.: prose), *ibid.*, vol. xlvi., 1897; A. Ludwig (German prose), 6 vols., Prag, 1876–88 (introduction, commentary, index). Lexicography: Grassmann, *Wörterbuch zum Rigveda*, Leipsic, 1873; the Vedic portion of Böhtlingk and Roth's Lexicon and of Böhtlingk's smaller St. Petersburg Dictionary (Leipsic, 1879–89); Monier-Williams, *Sanskrit-English Dictionary*, 2nd ed., Oxford, 1899; Macdonell, *Sanskrit-English Dictionary* (for selected hymns), London, 1893. Grammar: Whitney, *Sanskrit Grammar*, 3rd ed., Leipzig, 1896; Wackernagel, *op. cit.*, vol. i. (phonology); Delbrück, *Altindische Syntax* (vol. v. of *Syntaktische Forschungen*), Halle, 1888; Speijer, *Vedische und Sanskrit Syntax* in Bühler's *Encyclopædia*, Strasburg, 1896.

CHAPTERS IV. AND V.

Consult especially Macdonell, *Vedic Mythology*, in Bühler's *Encyclopædia*, vol. iii. part 1 (complete bibliography), 1897; also Kaegi, *op. cit.*; Muir, *Original Sanskrit Texts*, vol. v., 3rd ed.,

London, 1884; Barth, *The Religions of India*, English trans., London, 1882; Hopkins, *The Religions of India*, Boston, 1895; Oldenberg, *Die Religion des Veda*, Berlin, 1894; Bergaigne, *La Religion Védique*, 3 vols., Paris, 1878–83; Pischel and Geldner, *Vedische Studien*, 2 vols., Stuttgart, 1889–92; Deussen, *Allgemeine Geschichte der Philosophie*, vol. i. part 1: *Philosophie des Veda*, Leipsic, 1894. On method of interpretation (pp. 59–64), *cf.* Muir, *The Interpretation of the Veda*, in the *Journal of the Roy. As. Soc.*, 1866. Page 68: On the modification of the threefold division of the universe among the Greeks, *cf.* Kaegi, *op. cit.*, note 118. P. 128: On dice in India and the Vibhīdaka tree, *cf.* Roth in *Gurupūjākaumudī*, pp. 1–4, Leipsic, 1896.

CHAPTER VI.

Consult especially Zimmer, *Altindisches Leben*, Berlin, 1879. On the home of the Rigvedic Aryans (p. 145) *cf.* Hopkins, *The Panjāb and the Rig-Veda*, *Journal of the Am. Or. Soc.*, 1898, p. 19 ff. On the *Haṃsa* (p. 150) *cf.* Lanman, *The Milk-drinking Haṅsas of Sanskrit Poetry*, *ibid.*, p. 151 ff. On the Vedic tribes (pp. 153–157), *cf.* Excursus I. in Oldenberg's *Buddha*, Berlin, 1897. On the origin of the castes (p. 160) *cf.* Oldenberg, *Journal of the Germ. Or. Soc.*, 1897, pp. 267–290; R. Fick, *Die Sociale Gliederung im nordöstlichen Indien zu Buddha's Zeit*, Kiel, 1897.

CHAPTER VII.

Sāmaveda: text with German trans. and glossary, ed. by Benfey, Leipsic, 1848; by Satyavrata Sāmaçramī, Calcutta, 1873 (*Bibl. Ind.*), trans. by Griffith, Benares, 1893. *Yajurveda:* 1. *Vājasaneyi Saṃhitā*, ed. Weber, with the comm. of Mahīdhara, London, Berlin, 1852; trans. by Griffith, Benares, 1899; 2. *Taittirīya Saṃhitā*, ed. (in Roman characters) Weber, Berlin, 1871–72 (vols. xi.–xii. of *Indische Studien*); also edited with the comm. of Mādhava in the *Bibl. Ind.*; 3. *Maitrāyaṇī Saṃhitā*, ed. (with introduction) by L. v. Schroeder, Leipsic, 1881–86; 4. *Kāṭhaka Saṃhitā*, ed. in preparation by the same scholar. *Atharvaveda:* text ed. Roth and Whitney, Berlin, 1856 (*index verborum* in the *Journal of the Am. Or. Soc.*, vol. xii.); trans. into English verse by Griffith, 2 vols., Benares, 1897, and (with the omission of less important hymns) by Bloomfield into English prose, with copious notes, vol. xlii. of the *Sacred Books of the East.* Subject-matter: Bloomfield, *The Atharvaveda* in Bühler's *Encyclopædia*, Strasburg, 1899.

CHAPTER VIII.

Aitareya Brāhmaṇa, ed. Aufrecht, Bonn, 1879 (best edition); ed. and trans. by Haug, 2 vols., Bombay, 1863; *Kaushītaki* or *Çānkhāyana Brāhmaṇa*, ed. Lindner, Jena, 1887; *Aitareya Āraṇyaka*, ed. R. Mitra, Calcutta, 1876 (*Bibl. Ind.*); *Kaushītaki Āraṇyaka*, unedited; *Tāṇḍya Mahābrāhmaṇa* or *Panchaviṃça Brāhmaṇa*, ed. A. Vedāntavāgīça, Calcutta, 1869–74 (*Bibl. Ind.*); *Shaḍviṃça Brāhmaṇa*, ed. J. Vidyāsāgara, 1881; ed. with trans. by Klemm, Gütersloh, 1894; *Samavidhāna Brāhmaṇa*, ed. Burnell, London, 1873, trans. by Konow, Halle, 1893; *Vaṃça Brāhmaṇa*, ed. Weber, *Indische Studien*, vol. iv. pp. 371 ff., and by Burnell, Mangalore, 1873. Burnell also edited the *Devatādhyāya Br.*, 1873, the *Ārsheya Br.*, 1876, *Saṃhitā Upanishad Br.*, 1877; *Mantra Br.*, ed. S. Sāmaçramī, Calc., 1890; *Jaiminīya* or *Talavakāra Br.*, ed. in part by Burnell, 1878, and by Oertel, with trans. and notes, in the *Journal of the Am. Or. Soc.*, vol. xvi. pp. 79–260; *Taittirīya Br.*, ed. R. Mitra, 1855–70 (*Bibl. Ind.*), N. Godabole, Ānand. Ser., 1898; *Taittirīya Āraṇyaka*, ed. H. N. Apte, Ānand. Ser, Poona, 1898; *Çatapatha Br.*, ed. Weber, Berlin, London, 1859; trans. by Eggeling in *Sacred Books*, 5 vols.; *Gopatha Br.*, ed. R. Mitra and H. Vidyābhūshaṇa, 1872 (*Bibl. Ind.*), fully described in Bloomfield's *Atharvaveda*, pp. 101–124, in Bühler's *Encyclopædia*, 1899. The most important work on the Upanishads in general is Deussen, *Die Philosophie der Upanishads*, Leipsic, 1899; trans. of several Upanishads by Max Müller, *Sacred Books*, vols. i. and xv.; Deussen, *Sechzig Upanishad's* (trans. with valuable introductions),

Leipsic, 1897; a very useful book is Jacob, *A Concordance to the Principal Upanishads and Bhagavadgītā* (Bombay Sanskrit Series), 1891. P. 226: *Thirty-two Upanishads*, ed. with comm. in Ānandāçrama Series, Poona, 1895; *Aitareya Upanishad*, ed. Roer, 1850 (*Bibl. Ind.*), also ed. in Ānandāçrama Series, 1889; *Kaushītaki Brāhmaṇa Upanishad*, ed. Cowell, Calc., 1861 (*Bibl. Ind.*); *Chhāndogya Up.*, ed. with trans. by Böhtlingk, Leipsic, 1889; also in Ānand. Ser., 1890. P. 229: *Kena* or *Talavakāra*, ed. Roer, Calc., 1850; also in Ānand. Ser., 1889; *Maitri Up.*, ed. Cowell, 1870 (*Bibl. Ind.*); *Çvetāçvatara*, ed. Roer, 1850, Ānand. Ser. 1890; *Kāṭhaka Up.*, ed. Roer, 1850, ed. with comm. by Apte, Poona, 1889, by Jacob, 1891; *Taittirīya Up.*, ed. Roer, 1850, Ānand. Ser., 1889; *Bṛihadāraṇyaka Up.*, ed. and trans. by Böhtlingk, Leipzig, 1889, also ed. in Ānand. Ser., 1891; *Īçā Up.*, ed. in Ānand. Ser., 1888; *Muṇḍaka Up.*, ed. Roer, 1850, Apte, Ānand. Ser., 1889, Jacob, 1891; *Praçna Up.*, Ānand. Ser., 1889, Jacob, 1891; *Māṇḍūkya, Up.*, Ānand. Ser., 1890, Jacob, 1891; ed. with Eng. trans. and notes, Bombay, 1895; *Mahānārāyaṇa Up.*, ed. by Jacob, with comm., Bombay Sansk. Ser., 1888; *Nṛisiṃhatāpanīya Up.*, Ānand. Ser., 1895. P. 242: The parallelism of Çankara and Plato is rather overstated; for Plato, on the one hand, did not get rid of Duality, and, on the other, only said that Becoming is not true Being.

CHAPTER IX.

On the sūtras in general consult Hillebrandt, *Ritual-Litteratur*, in Bühler's *Encyclopædia*, 1897; *Āçvalāyana Çrauta Sūtra*, ed. R. Vidyāratna, Calc., 1864–74 (*Bibl. Ind.*); *Çānkhāyana Çrauta*, ed. Hillebrandt, 1885–99 (*Bibl. Ind.*); *Lāṭyāyana Çrauta*, ed. A. Vāgīça, Calc., 1870–72 (*Bibl. Ind.*); *Maçaka* and *Drāhyāyaṇa Çrauta*, unedited; *Kātyāyana Çrauta*, ed. Weber, London, Berlin, 1855; *Āpastamba Çrauta*, in part ed. by Hillebrandt, Calc., 1882–97 (*Bibl. Ind.*); *Vaitāna Sūtra*, ed. Garbe, London, 1878; trans. by Garbe, Strasburg, 1878. *Āçvalāyana Gṛihya Sūtra*, ed. with trans. by Stenzler, Leipsic, 1864–65; ed. with comm. and notes, Bombay, 1895; trans. in *Sacred Books*, vol. xxix.; *Çānkhāyana Gṛihya*, ed. and trans. into German by Oldenberg, *Indische Studien*, vol. xv.; Eng. trans. in *Sacred Books*, vol. xxix.; *Gobhila Gṛihya*, ed. with comm. by Ch. Tarkālaṃkāra, Calc., 1880 (*Bibl. Ind.*); ed. by Knauer, Dorpat, 1884; trans. by Knauer, Dorpat, 1887; trans. in *Sacred Books*, vol. xxx.; *Pāraskara Gṛihya*, ed. and trans. by Stenzler, Leipsic, 1876; trans. in *Sacred Books*, vol. xxix.; *Āpastamba Gṛihya*, ed. Winternitz, Vienna, 1887; trans. in *Sacred Books*, vol. xxx.; *Hiraṇyakeçi Gṛihya*, ed. Kirste, Vienna, 1889; trans. *Sacred Books*, vol. xxx.; *Mantrapāṭha*, ed. Winternitz, Oxford, 1897; *Mānava Gṛihya*, ed. Knauer, Leipsic, 1897; *Kauçika Sūtra*, ed. Bloomfield, New Haven, 1890; *Pitṛimedha Sūtras* of Baudhāyana, Hiraṇyakeçin, Gautama, ed. Caland, Leipsic, 1896. *Āpastamba Dharma Sūtra*, ed. Bühler, Bombay Sansk. Ser., two parts, 1892 and 1894; *Baudhāyana Dh. S.*, ed. Hultzsch, Leipsic, 1884; *Gautama Dharma Çāstra*, ed. Stenzler, London, 1876; *Vāsishṭha Dharma Çāstra*, ed. Führer, Bombay, 1883; *Hiraṇyakeçi Dharma Sūtra*, unedited; *Vaikhānasa Dharma Sūtra*, described by Bloch, Vienna, 1896; Āpastamba, Gautama, Vasishṭha, Baudhāyana, trans. by Bühler, *Sacred Books*, 2nd ed., Oxford, 1897. *Rigveda Prātiçākhya*, ed. with German trans. by Max Müller, Leipsic, 1856–69; ed. with Uvaṭa's comm., Benares, 1894; *Riktantravyākaraṇa* (*Sāma Pr.*), ed., trans. Burnell, Mangalore, 1879; *Taittirīya Prāt.*, ed. Whitney, *Journ. of the Am. Or. Soc.*, vol. ix., 1871; *Vājasaneyi Prāt.*, ed. with comm. of Uvaṭa, Benares Sansk. Series, 1888; *Atharvaveda Prāt.*, ed. Whitney, *Journal Am. Or. Soc.*, vols. vii. and x. The *Çulva Sūtra* of Baudhāyana, ed. and trans. by Thibaut, in the *Pandit*, vol. ix.; *cf.* his article on the *Çulvasūtras* in the *Jour. of As. Soc. Bengal*, vol. xliv., Calc. 1875. Six Vedāngas, Sanskrit text, Bombay, 1892; Yāska's *Nirukta*, ed. R. Roth, Göttingen, 1852; ed. with comm. by S. Sāmaçramī (*Bibl. Ind.*); *Sarvānukramaṇī*, ed. Macdonell, Oxford, 1886 (together with *Anuvākānukramaṇī* and Shaḍguruçishya's comm.); *Ārshānukramaṇī*, *Chhandonukramaṇī*, *Bṛihaddevatā*, ed. R. Mitra, 1892 (*Bibl. Ind.*); Pingala's *Chhandaḥ Sūtra*, ed. in *Bibl. Ind.*, 1874; in Weber's *Indische Studien*, vol. viii. (which is important as treating of Sanskrit metres in general); *Nidāna Sūtra*, partly edited, *ibid.*; *Sarvānukrama Sūtras* of *White Yajurveda*, ed. by Weber in his ed. of that Veda; ed. with comm., Benares Sansk. Ser., 1893–94; *Charaṇavyūha*, ed. Weber, *Ind. Stud.*, vol. iii. On Mādhava see Klemm in *Gurupūjākaumudī*, Leipsic, 1896.

CHAPTER X.

On the Mahābhārata in general, consult especially Holtzmann, *Das Mahābhārata*, 4 vols., Kiel, 1892–95; Bühler, *Indian Studies*, No. II., Trans. of Imp. Vienna Academy, 1892; *cf.* also Jacobi in *Göttinger Gelehrte Anzeigen*, vol. viii. 659 ff.; Winternitz, *Journal of the Roy. As. Soc.*, 1897, p. 713 ff.; *Indian Antiquary*, vol. xxvii. Editions: 5 vols., Bombay, 1888, Calc., 1894; trans. into Eng. prose at the expense of Pratāpa Chandra Rāy, Calc., 1896; literal trans. into Eng. by M. N. Dutt, 5 vols., Calc., 1896. Episode of *Sāvitrī*, ed. Kellner, with introd. and notes, Leipsic, 1888; *Nala*, text in Bühler's *Third Book of Sanskrit*, Bombay, 1877; text, notes, vocabulary, Kellner, 1885; text, trans., vocab., Monier-Williams, Oxford, 1876. On the Purāṇas in general, consult introd. of H. H. Wilson's trans. of the *Vishṇu P.*, 5 vols., ed. Fitzedward Hall, 1864–70; Holtzmann, *op. cit.*, vol. iv. pp. 29–58; *Garuḍa P.*, ed. Bombay, 1888; ed. Vidyāsāgara, Calc., 1891; *Agni*, ed. R. Mitra, *Bibl. Ind.*, 1870–79, J. Vidyāsāgara, Calc., 1882; *Vāyu*, ed. R. Mitra, *Bibl. Ind.*, 1888; Bombay, 1895; *Matsya*, Bombay, 1895; *Kūrma*, *Bibl. Ind.*, 1890; *Mārkaṇḍeya*, ed. *Bibl. Ind.*, 1855–62; trans. by Pargiter, *Bibl. Ind.*, 1888–99, by C. C. Mukharji, Calc., 1894; *Padma*, ed. V. N. Mandlik, 4 vols., Ānand. Ser., 1894; *Vishṇu*, ed. with comm., Bombay, 1887; five parts, Calc., 1888; prose trans. by M. N. Dutt., Calc., 1894; Wilson, *op. cit.*; *Bhāgavata*, ed. with three comm., 3 vols., Bombay, 1887; 2 vols., Nirṇaya Sāgara Press, Bombay, 1894; ed. and trans. by Burnouf, 4 vols., Paris, 1840–47, 1884; *Brahma*, ed. Ānand. Ser., 1895; *Varāha*, *Bibl. Ind.*, 1887–93. On the *Rāmāyaṇa* in general, consult Jacobi, *Das Rāmāyaṇa* Bonn, 1893; also *Journal of the Germ. Or Soc.*, vol. xlviii.

p. 407 ff., vol. li. p. 605 ff.; Ludwig, *Ueber das Rāmāyaṇa*, Prag, 1894; Baumgartner, *Das Rāmāyaṇa*, Freiburg i B., 1894; Bombay recension, ed. Gorresio, Turin, 1843–67; with three comm., 3 vols., Bombay, 1895; Bengal recension, Calc., 1859–60; trans. by Griffith into Eng. verse, Benares, 1895; into Eng. prose, M. N. Dutt, Calc., 1894.

CHAPTER XI.

On the age of Kāvya poetry consult especially Bühler, *Die indischen Inschriften und das Alter der indischen Kunstpoesie*, in Trans. of the Imp. Vienna Academy, Vienna, 1890; Fleet, *Corpus Inscr. Ind.*, vol. iii., Calcutta, 1888. On the Vikrama era see Kielhorn, *Göttinger Nachrichten*, 1891, pp. 179–182, and on the Mālava era, *Ind. Ant.*, xix. p. 316; on the chronology of Kālidāsa, Huth, *Die Zeit des Kālidāsa*, Berlin, 1890. *Buddhacharita*, ed. Cowell, Oxford, 1893; trans. by Cowell, *Sacred Books*, vol. xlix. *Raghuvamça*, ed. Stenzler, with Latin trans., London, 1832; ed. with Mallinātha's comm., by S. P. Pandit, Bombay Sansk. Ser.; text with Eng. trans. by Jvālāprasād, Bombay, 1895; ed. K. P. Parab, with Mallinātha, Nirṇaya Sāgara Pr., Bombay, 1892; i.–vii., with Eng. trans., notes, comm. of Mallinātha, and extracts from comm. of Bhaṭṭa Hemādri, Charitravardhana, Vallabha, by G. R. Nangargika, Poona, 1896. *Kumārasambhava*, ed. with Latin trans. by Stenzler, London, 1838; cantos i.–vi., ed. with Eng. trans. and comm. of Mallinātha, by S. G. Despānde, Poona, 1887; second part, with full comm., ed. by J. Vīdyāsāgara, 4th ed., Calc., 1887; ed. with comm. of Mallinātha (i.–vii.) and of Sītārām (viii.–xvii.), 3rd ed., Nirṇaya Sāgara Press, Bombay, 1893; ed. with three commentaries, Bombay, 1898; trans. by Griffith, London, 1879. *Bhaṭṭikāvya*, ed. Calc., 1628; cantos i.–v., with comm. of Jayamangala, English trans., notes, glossary, by M. R. Kale, Bombay, 1897; with comm. of Mallinātha and notes by K. P. Trivedi, Bombay Sansk. Ser., 2 vols., 1898; German trans. of xviii.–xxii., by Schütz, Bielefeld, 1837. *Kirātārjunīya*, ed. by J. Vidyāsāgara,

Calc., 1875; with Mallinātha's comm., Nirṇaya Sāgara Press, Bombay, 1885; cantos i.–ii., trans. by Schütz, Bielefeld, 1843. *Çiçupālavadha*, ed. with Mallinātha's comm., by Vidyāsāgara, 1884; also at Benares, 1883; German trans. by Schütz, cantos i.–ix., Bielefeld, 1843. *Naishadhīya-charita*, ed. with comm. of Nārāyaṇa, by Pandit Sivadatta, Bombay, 1894. *Nalodaya*, ed. Vidyāsāgara, Calc., 1873; German trans. by Shack, in *Stimmen vom Ganges*, 2nd ed., 1877; *Rāghavapāṇḍavīya*, ed. with comm. in the *Kāvyamālā*, No. 62. Dhanaṃjaya's *Rāghavapāṇḍavīya*, quoted in *Gaṇaratnamahodadhi*, A.D. 1140, is an imitation of Kavirāja's work: *cf.* Zachariæ in Bühler's *Encyclopædia*, pp. 27–28. For a modern Sanskrit drama constructed on a similar principle see Scherman's *Orientalische Bibliographie*, vol. ix., 1896, p. 258, No. 4605. *Haravijaya*, ed. in *Kāvyamālā*, 1890; see Bühler, *Detailed Report*, p. 43, Bombay, 1877. *Navasāhasānkacharita*, ed. Bombay Sansk. Series, 1895; see Bühler and Zachariæ in *Trans. of Vienna Acad.*, 1888. *Setubandha* (in the Mahārāshṭrī dialect), ed. with trans. by S. Goldschmidt, 1884; ed. in *Kāvyamālā*, No. 47, Bombay, 1895. *Vāsavadattā*, ed. with introd. by Fitzedward Hall, *Bibl. Ind.*, 1859; ed. with comm. by J. Vidyāsāgara, Calc., 1874. *Kādambarī*, ed. P. Peterson, Bomb. Sansk. Ser., 1889; ed. with comm. in Nirṇaya Sāgara Press, Bombay, 1896; with comm. and notes by M. R. Kale, Poona, 1896; trans., with occasional omissions, by C. M. Ridding, Royal As. Soc., London, 1896. *Harshacharita*, ed. by J. Vidyāsāgara, Calc., 1883; ed. with comm., Jammu, 1879; Bombay, 1892; trans. by Cowell and Thomas, Roy. As. Soc. London, 1897. *Daçakumāracharita*, Part i., ed. Bühler, Bomb. Sansk. Ser., 2nd ed., 1888; Part ii., P. Peterson, *ibid.*, 1891; ed. P. Banerji, Calc., 1888.

CHAPTER XII.

Meghadūta, ed. with vocab. by Stenzler, Breslau, 1874; with comm. of Mallinātha, Nirṇaya Sāgara Press, Bombay, 1894; ed. by K. B. Pathak, Poona, 1894. Eng. verse trans. by Wilson, 3rd ed., London, 1867; by T. Clark, London, 1882; into German by

Max Müller, Königsberg, 1847, by Schütz, Bielefield, 1859, Fritze, Chemnitz, 1879. *Ritusaṃhāra*, ed. with Latin and German trans. by P. v. Bohlen, Leipsic, 1840; with notes and Eng. trans. by Sitārām Āyyar, Bombay, 1897. *Ghaṭakarpara*, ed. Brockhaus, 1841, trans. into German by Höfer (in *Indische Gedichte*, vol. ii.). *Chaurapanchāçikā*, ed. and trans. into German by Solf, Kiel, 1886; trans. by Edwin Arnold, London, 1896. Bhartṛihari's Centuries, ed. with comm., Bombay, 1884, trans. into Eng. verse by Tawney, Calc., 1877; *Çṛingāra-çataka*, ed. Calc. 1888. *Çṛingāratilaka*, ed. Gildemeister, Bonn, 1841. *Amaruçataka*, ed. R. Simon, Kiel, 1893. *Saptaçataka* of Hāla, ed. with prose German trans. by Weber, Leipsic, 1881 (in *Abhandlungen für die Kunde des Morgenlandes*, vol. viii., No. 4). Mayūra's *Sūrya-çataka*, or Hundred Stanzas in praise of the Sun, ed. in *Kāvyamālā*, 1889. *Gītagovinda*, ed. J. Vidyāsāgara, Calc., 1882; Bombay, Nir. Sāg. Pr., 1899; trans. into German by Rückert, vol. i. of *Abhandlungen für die Kunde des Morgenlandes*, Leipsic.

CHAPTER XIII.

On the Sanskrit drama in general, consult especially H. H. Wilson, *Select Specimens of the Theatre of the Hindus*, 2 vols., 3rd ed., London, 1871; Sylvain Lévi, *Le Théâtre Indien*, Paris, 1890. *Çakuntalā*, Bengal recension, ed. by Pischel, Kiel, 1877; Devanāgarī, recension, Monier-Williams, 2nd ed., Oxford, 1876; M. R. Kale, Bombay, 1898; trans. by Monier-Williams, 6th ed., London, 1894; into German by Rückert, Leipsic, 1876; Fritze, 1876; Lobedanz, 7th ed., Leipsic, 1884; there are also a South Indian and a Kashmir recension (*cf.* Bühler, Report, p. lxxxv). *Vikramorvaçī*, ed. S. P. Pandit, Bombay, 1879; Vaidya, 1895; South Indian recension, ed. Pischel, 1875; trans. Wilson, *op. cit.;* Cowell, Hertford, 1851; Fritze, Leipsic, 1880. *Mālavikāgnimitra*, ed. Bollensen, Leipsic, 1879; S. P. Pandit, Bombay, 1869, S. S. Āyyar, Poona, 1896; trans. by Tawney, 2nd ed., Calc., 1891; into German by Weber, Berlin, 1856; Fritze, Leipsic, 1881. *Mṛicchakaṭikā*, ed. Stenzler, Bonn, 1847; J. Vidyāsāgara, 2nd ed., Calc., 1891;

trans. by Wilson, *op. cit.;* into German by Böhtlingk, St. Petersburg, 1877; by Fritze, Chemnitz, 1879. *Ratnāvalī*, ed. Cappeller, in Böhtlingk's *Sanskrit-Chrestomathie*, 1897; with comm. Nir. Sāg. Pr., Bombay, 1895; trans. by Wilson, *op. cit.;* into German by Fritze, Chemnitz, 1878. *Nāgānanda*, ed. J. Vidyāsāgara, Calc., 1873; ed. Poona, 1893; trans. by Palmer Boyd, with preface by Cowell, London, 1872. Bāṇa's *Pārvatīpariṇaya*, ed. with trans. by T. R. R. Aiyar, Kumbakonam, 1898; Germ. by Glaser, Trieste, 1886. *Mālatīmādhava*, ed. R. G. Bhandarkar, Bombay, 1876; trans. by Wilson, *op. cit.;* by Fritze, Leipsic, 1884. *Mahāvīracharita*, ed. Trithen, London, 1848; K. P. Parab, Bombay, 1892; trans. by J. Pickford, London, 1871. *Uttararāmacharita*, ed. with comm. and trans., Nagpur, 1895; ed. with comm. by Aiyar and Parab, Nirṇaya Sāgara Press, 1899; trans. by Wilson, *op. cit.* *Mudrārākshasa*, ed. Telang, Bombay, 1893; trans. by Wilson, *op. cit.;* into German by Fritze, Leipsic, 1887. *Veṇīsaṃhāra*, ed. K. P. Parab, Nirṇaya Sāgara Press, Bombay, 1898; N. B. Godabale, Poona, 1895; Grill, Leipsic, 1871; trans. into English by S. M. Tagore, Calc., 1880. *Viddhaçālabhanjika*, ed. J. Vidyāsāgara, Calc, 1883. *Karpūramanjarī*, ed. in vol. vii. of *The Pandit*, Benares. *Bālarāmāyaṇa*, ed. Govinda Deva Çastri, Benares, 1869; J. Vidyāsāgara, Calc., 1884. *Prachaṇḍapāṇḍava*, ed. Cappeller, Strasburg, 1885. (On Rājaçekhara, *cf.* Kielhorn, *Epigr. Ind.*, part iv. 1889; Fleet in *Ind. Antiq.*, vol. xvi. pp. 175–178; Jacobi in *Vienna Or. Journal*, vol. ii. pp. 212–216). *Chaṇḍakauçika*, ed. J. Vidyāsāgara, Calcutta, 1884; trans. by Fritze (*Kauçika's Zorn*). *Prabodhachandrodaya*, ed. Nir. Sāg. Pr., Bombay, 1898; trans. into German by Goldstücker, with preface by Rosenkranz, Königsberg, 1842; also trans. by Hirzel, Zürich, 1846; Taylor, Bombay, 1886.

CHAPTER XIV.

Panchatantra, ed. Kosegarten, Bonn, 1848; by Kielhorn and Bühler in Bomb. Sansk. Ser.; these two editions represent two considerably divergent recensions; trans. with very valuable introd. by Benfey, 2 vols., Leipsic, 1859; English trans., Trichinopoli,

1887; German by Fritze, Leipsic, 1884. The abstract of the *Panchatantra* in Kshemendra's *Bṛihatkathāmanjarī*, introd., text, trans., notes, by Mankowski, Leipsic, 1892. *Hitopadeça*, ed. F. Johnson, London, 1884; P. Peterson in Bomb. Sansk. Ser. *Kāmandakīya Nītisāra*, ed. with trans. and notes, Madras, 1895; text ed. by R. Mitra, *Bibl. Ind.* Calc., 1884. Çivadāsa's *Vetālapanchaviṃçatikā*, ed. H. Uhle (in *Abhandlungen der deutschen morgenl. Gesell.* vol. viii., No. 1), Leipsic, 1881. Sir R. F. Burton, *Vikram and the Vampire*, new ed., London, 1893. *Siṃhāsana-dvātriṃçikā*, ed. (*Dwatringshat puttalika*), J. Vidyāsāgara, Calc., 1881. *Çukasaptati*, ed. R. Schmidt, Leipsic, 1893 (*Abh. f. d. Kunde d. Morgenlandes*), Munich, 1898; trans., Kiel, 1894; Stuttgart, 1898. *Kathāsaritsāgara*, ed. trans. by Brockhaus, Leipsic (Books i.–v.) 1839, (vi.–xviii.) 1862–66; ed. Bomb., 1889; trans. by Tawney in *Bibl. Ind.*, 1880–87. *Bṛihatkathāmanjarī*, chaps. i.–viii., ed. and trans. by Sylvain Lévi in *Journal Asiatique*, 1886. *Jātaka-mālā*, ed. Kern, Boston, 1891; trans. by Speijer in *Sacred Books of the Buddhists*, vol. i., London, 1895. *Kathākoça*, trans. by C. H. Tawney from Sanskrit MSS., Royal As. Soc., London, 1895. Pāli *Jātakas*, ed. by Fausböll, London, (completed) 1897; three vols. of trans. under supervision of Cowell have appeared, I. by Chalmers, Cambridge, 1895; II. by Rouse, 1895; III. by Francis and Neil, 1897. Warren, *Buddhism in Translations*, Harvard, 1896. Bhartṛihari's *Nīti* and *Vairāgya Çatakas*, ed. and trans., Bombay, 1898 (on Bhartṛihari and Kumārila see Pathak in *Journ. of Bombay Branch of Roy. As. Soc.*, xviii. pp. 213–238). *Mohamudgara*, trans. by U. K. Banerjī, Bhawānipur, Bengal, 1892. *Chāṇakya Çatakas*, ed. Klatt, 1873. On the *Nītimanjarī cf.* Kielhorn, *Göttinger Nachrichten*, 1891, pp. 182–186; A. B. Keith, *Journ. Roy. As. Soc.* 1900. *Çārngadharapaddhati*, ed. Peterson, Bombay, 1888. *Subhāshitāvalī*, ed. Peterson and Durgaprasāda, Bombay, 1886. Böhtlingk's *Indische Sprüche*, 2nd edition, 2 vols., St. Petersburg, 1870–73; index by Blau, Leipsic, 1893. *Dhammapada*, trans. by Max Müller in *Sacred Books of the East*, vol. x., 2nd revised edition, Oxford, 1898.

CHAPTER XV.

On Indian philosophy in general see Garbe's useful little book, *Philosophy of Ancient India*, Chicago, 1897; F. Max Müller, *Six Systems of Indian Philosophy*, London, 1899. Garbe, *Sānkhya Philosophie*, Leipsic, 1894; *Sānkhya und Yoga* in Bühler's Encyclopædia, Strasburg, 1896 (complete bibliography); *Sānkhya-kārikā*, text with comm. of Gauḍapāda, ed. and trans. by Colebrooke and Wilson, Oxford, 1837, reprinted Bombay, 1887; ed. in Benares Sansk. Ser., 1883; trans. Ballantyne (*Bibl. Ind.*); *Sānkhyapravachana-bhāshya*, ed. by Garbe, Harvard, 1895, trans. into German, Leipsic, 1889; Aniruddha's comm. on *Sānkhya Sūtras*, trans. by Garbe, *Bibl. Ind.*, Calc., 1888–92; *Sānkhya-tattva-kaumudī*, ed. with Eng. trans., Bombay, 1896, trans. by Garbe, Munich, 1892; Çankara's *Rājayogabhāshya*, trans. Madras, 1896; Svātmārāma's *Haṭhayogapradīpa*, trans. by Walther, Munich, 1893; *Haṭhayoga Gheranda Sanhita*, trans. Bombay, 1895. On fragments of Panchaçikha *cf.* Garbe in *Festgruss an Roth*, p. 74 ff., Stuttgart, 1893; Jacobi on *Sānkhya-Yoga* as foundation of Buddhism, *Journ. of Germ. Or. Soc.*, 1898, pp. 1–15; Oldenberg, *Buddha*, 3rd ed. *Mīmāṃsā-darçana*, ed. with comm. of Çabara Svāmin (*Bibl. Ind.*), Calc., 1887; *Tantravārttika*, ed. Benares, 1890; *Çlokavārttika*, fasc. i., ii., ed. with comm., Benares, 1898; *Jaiminīya-nyāya-mālā-vistara*, ed. in Ānand. Ser. 1892. *Arthasaṃgraha*, as introd. to Mīmāṃsā, ed. and trans. by Thibaut, Benares, 1882. Most important book on Vedānta: Deussen, *System des Vedānta*, Leipsic, 1883; Deussen, *Die Sūtra's des Vedānta*, text with trans. of Sūtras and complete comm. of Çankara, Leipsic, 1887. *Brahma Sūtras*, with Çankara's comm., ed. in Ānand. Ser., 1890–91; *Vedānta Sūtras*, trans. by Thibaut in *Sacred Books*, vol. xxxiv., Oxford, 1890, and xxxviii., 1896. *Panchadaçī*, ed. with Eng. trans., Bombay, 1895. On date of Çankara *cf.* Fleet in *Ind. Ant.*, xvi. 41–42. *Vedānta-siddhānta-muktāvalī*, ed. with Eng. trans. by Venis, Benares, 1890. *Vedāntasāra*, ed. Jacob, with comm. and notes, Bombay, 1894, trans. 3rd ed., London, 1892. *Bhagavad-*

gītā with Çankara's comm., Ānand. Ser., 1897, trans. in *Sacred Books*, vol. viii., 2nd ed., Oxford, 1898; by Davies, 3rd ed., 1894. *Nyāya Sūtras* in Vizianagram Sansk. Ser., vol. ix., Benares, 1896. *Nyāyakandalī* of Çrīdhara, *ibid.*, vol. iv., 1895. *Nyāyakusumānjali* (*Bibl. Ind.*), Calc., 1895. *Vaiçeshika-darçana*, ed. with comm., Calc., 1887. *Saptapadārthī*, ed. with comm., Benares, 1893; text with Latin trans. by Winter, Leipsic, 1893. *Tarkasaṃgraha*, ed. J. Vidyāsagara, Calc., 1897; ed. with comm., Bombay Sansk. Ser., 1897; text and trans. by Ballantyne, Allahabad, 1850. *Sarvadarçana-saṃgraha*, ed. by T. Tarkavāchaspati, Calc., 1872; trans. by Cowell and Gough, 2nd ed., London, 1894.

CHAPTER XVI.

M'Crindle, *Ancient India as Described by Classical Authors*, 5 vols., especially vol. v., *Invasion of India by Alexander*, London, 1896. Weber, *Die Griechen in Indien*, in *Transactions* (*Sitzungsberichte*) *of the Roy. Prussian Acad.*, Berlin, 1890. Sylvain Lévi, *Quid de Græcis veterum Indorum monumenta tradiderint*, Paris, 1890; also *La Grèce et l'Inde* (in *Revue des Etudes Grecques*), Paris, 1891. Goblet d'Alviella, *Ce que l'Inde doit à la Grèce*, Paris, 1897; also *Les Grecs dans l'Inde*, and *Des Influences Classiques dans la Culture Scientifique et Littéraire de l'Inde*, in vols. xxxiii., xxxiv. (1897) of *Bulletin de l'Académie Royale de Belgique.* L. de la Vallée Poussin, *La Grèce et l'Inde*, in *Musée Belge*, vol. ii. pp. 126–152. Vincent A. Smith, *Græco-Roman Influence on the Civilisation of Ancient India* in *Journal of As. Soc. of Bengal*, 1889–92. O. Franke, *Beziehungen der Inder zum Westen*, *Journ. of Germ. Or. Soc.*, 1893, pp. 595–609. M. A. Stein in *Indian Antiquary*, vol. xvii. p. 89. On foreign elements in Indian art see Cunningham, *Archæological Survey of India*, vol. v. pp. 185 ff.; Grünwedel, *Buddhistische Kunst*, Berlin, 1893; E. Curtius, *Griechische Kunst in Indien*, pp. 235–243 in vol. ii. of *Gesammelte Abhandlungen*, Berlin, 1894; W. Simpson, *The Classical Influence in the Architecture of the Indus Region and Afghanistan*, in the *Journal of the Royal Institution of British*

Architects, vol. i. (1894), pp. 93–115. P. 413: On the Çakas and Kushanas, see Rapson, *Indian Coins*, pp. 7 and 16, in Bühler's Encyclopædia, Strasburg, 1898. On the relation of Indian to Greek fables, *cf.* Weber in *Indische Studien*, vol. iii. p. 327 ff. Through the medium of Indian fables and fairy tales, which were so popular in the Middle Ages, the magic mirror and ointment, the seven-league boots, the invisible cap, and the purse of Fortunatus (*cf.* Burnell, *Sāmavidhana Brāhmaṇa*, preface, p. xxxv), found their way into Western literature. For possible Greek influence on Indian drama, *cf.* Windisch, in *Trans. of the Fifth Oriental Congress*, part ii., Berlin, 1882. On chess in Sanskrit literature, *cf.* Macdonell, *Origin and Early History of Chess*, in *Journ. Roy. As. Soc.*, 1898. On Indian influence on Greek philosophy, *cf.* Garbe in *Sānkhya und Yoga*, p. 4. L. von Schroeder, *Buddhismus und Christenthum*, Reval, 2nd ed., 1898. P. 422–23: It seems quite possible to account for the ideas of the Neo-Platonists from purely Hellenic sources, without assuming Indian influence. On the relation of *Çakuntalā* to Schiller (*Alpenjäger*) and Goethe (*Faust*), *cf.* Sauer, in *Korrespondenzblatt für die Gelehrten und Realschulen Württembergs*, vol. xl. pp. 297–304; W. von Biedermann, *Goetheforschungen*, Frankfurt a/M., 1879, pp. 54 ff. (*Çakuntalā* and *Faust*). On Sanskrit literature and modern poets (Heine, Matthew Arnold), *cf.* Max Müller, *Coincidences*, in the *Fortnightly Review*, New Series, vol. lxiv. (July 1898), pp. 157–162.

INDEX

THE END

LITERATURES OF THE WORLD.

EDITED BY EDMUND GOSSE,

Hon. M. A. of Trinity College, Cambridge.

ANCIENT GREEK LITERATURE. By GILBERT MURRAY, M. A., Professor of Greek in the University of Glasgow. 12mo. Cloth, $1.50.

"A sketch to which the much-abused word 'brilliant' may be justly applied. Mr. Murray has produced a book which fairly represents the best conclusions of modern scholarship with regard to the Greeks."—*London Times.*

"An illuminating history of Greek literature, in which learning is enlivened and supplemented by literary skill, by a true sense of the 'humanities.' The reader feels that this is no book of perfunctory erudition, but a labor of love, performed by a scholar, to whom ancient Greece and her literature are exceedingly real and vivid. His judgments and suggestions are full of a personal fresh sincerity; he can discern the living men beneath their works, and give us his genuine impression of them."—*London Daily Chronicle.*

"A fresh and stimulating and delightful book, and should be put into the hands of all young scholars. It will make them understand, or help to make them understand, to a degree they have never yet understood, that the Greek writers over whom they have toiled at school are living literature after all."—*Westminster Gazette.*

"Brilliant and stimulating."—*London Athenæum.*

"A powerful and original study."—*The Nation.*

"Mr. Murray's style is lucid and spirited, and, besides the fund of information, he imparts to his subject such fresh and vivid interest that students will find in these pages a new impulse for more profound and exhaustive study of this greatest and most immortal of all the world's literatures."—*Philadelphia Public Ledger.*

"The admirable perspective of the whole work is what one most admires. The reader unlearned in Greek history and literature sees at once the relation which a given author bore to his race and his age, and the current trend of thought, as well as what we value him for to-day. . . . As an introduction to the study of some considerable portion of Greek literature in English translations it will be found of the very highest usefulness."—*Boston Herald.*

"Professor Murray has written an admirable book, clear in its arrangement, compact in its statements, and is one, we think, its least scholarly reader must feel an instructive and thoroughly trustworthy piece of English criticism."—*New York Mail and Express.*

"At once scholarly and interesting. . . . Professor Murray makes the reader acquainted not merely with literary history and criticism, but with individual living, striving Greeks. . . . He has felt the power of the best there was in Greek life and literature, and he rouses the reader's enthusiasm by his own honest admiration."—*Boston Transcript.*

"Professor Murray has contributed a volume which shows profound scholarship, together with a keen literary appreciation. It is a book for scholars as well as for the general reader. The author is saturated with his subject, and has a rare imaginative sympathy with ancient Greece."—*The Interior, Chicago.*

"Written in a style that is sometimes spasmodic, often brilliant, and always fresh and suggestive."—*New York Sun.*

"Professor Murray's careful study will be appreciated as the work of a man of unusual special learning, combined with much delicacy of literary insight."—*New York Christian Advocate.*

D. APPLETON AND COMPANY, NEW YORK.

LITERATURES OF THE WORLD.

MODERN ENGLISH LITERATURE. By EDMUND GOSSE, Hon. M. A. of Trinity College, Cambridge. 12mo. Cloth, $1.50.

"Mr. Gosse has been remarkably successful in bringing into focus and proportion the salient features of this vast and varied theme. We have read the book, not only with pleasure but with a singular emotion. . . . His criticism is generally sympathetic, but at the same time it is always sober."—*London Daily Chronicle.*

"Mr. Gosse's most ambitious book and probably his best. It bears on every page the traces of a genuine love for his subject and of a lively critical intelligence. Moreover, it is extremely readable—more readable, in fact, than any other single volume dealing with this same vast subject that we can call to mind. . . . Really a remarkable performance."—*London Times.*

"A really useful account of the whole process of evolution in English letters—an account based upon a keen sense at once of the unity of his subject and of the rhythm of its ebb and flow, and illumined by an unexampled felicity in hitting off the leading characteristics of individual writers."—*London Athenæum.*

"Probably no living man is more competent than Mr. Gosse to write a popular and yet scholarly history of English literature. . . . The greater part of his life has been given up to the study and criticism of English literature of the past, and he has a learned and balanced enthusiasm for every writer who has written excellently in English."—*London Saturday Review.*

"The bibliographical list is of extreme value, as is the bibliographical work generally. It is just one of these books which every reader will want to place among his working books."—*New York Times.*

"To have given in a moderate volume the main points in a literature almost continuous for five centuries is to have done a marvelous thing. But he might have done it dryly; he has made every sentence crisp and sparkling."—*Chicago Times-Herald.*

"A book which in soundness of learning, sanity of judgment, and attractiveness of manner has not been equaled by the work of any other author who has sought to analyze the elements of English literature in a concise and authoritative way."—*Boston Beacon.*

"Thoroughly enjoyable from first to last. It traces the growth of a literature so clearly and simply, that one is apt to underrate the magnitude of the undertaking. Mr. Gosse's charming personality pervades it all, and his happy manner illuminates matter that has been worked over and over until one might imagine all its freshness gone."—*Chicago Evening Post.*

"This is not a mere collection of brief essays on the merits of authors, but a continuous story of the growth of literature, of which the authors and their works are only incidents. The book is lucid, readable, and interesting, and a marvel of condensed information, without its seeming to be so. It can be read by nine out of ten intelligent people, not only without fatigue, but with pleasure; and when it is finished the reader will have a comprehensive and intelligent view of the subject which will not only enable him to talk with some ease and confidence upon the merits of the principal creators of English literature, but will also point the way to the right sources if he wishes to supplement the knowledge which he has derived from this book."—*Pittsburg Times.*

"That he has been a careful student, however, in many departments, the most unrelated and recondite, is evident on every page, in the orderly arrangement of his multitudinous materials, in the accuracy of his statements, in the acuteness of his critical observations, and in the large originality of most of his verdicts. He says things that many before him may have thought, though they failed to express them, capturing their fugitive expressions in his curt, inevitable phrases."—*N. Y. Mail and Express.*

D. APPLETON AND COMPANY, NEW YORK.

LITERATURES OF THE WORLD.

EDITED BY EDMUND GOSSE,

Hon. M. A. of Trinity College, Cambridge.

FRENCH LITERATURE. By EDWARD DOWDEN, D. Litt., LL. D., D. C. L., Professor of English Literature in the University of Dublin. 12mo. Cloth, $1.50.

"Certainly the best history of French literature in the English language."—*London Athenæum.*

"This is a history of literature as histories of literature should be written. . . . A living voice, speaking to us with gravity and enthusiasm about the writers of many ages, and of being a human voice always. Hence this book can be read with pleasure even by those for whom a history has in itself little attraction."—*London Saturday Review.*

"The book is excellently well done; accurate in facts and dates, just in criticism, well arranged in method. . . . The excellent bibliography with which it concludes will be invaluable to those who wish to pursue the study further on their own lines."—*London Spectator.*

"Remarkable for its fullness of information and frequent brilliancy. . . . A book which both the student of French literature and the stranger to it will, in different ways, find eminently useful, and in many parts of it thoroughly enjoyable as well."—*London Literary World.*

"Professor Dowden is both trustworthy and brilliant; he writes from a full knowledge and a full sympathy. Master of a style rather correct than charming for its adornments, he can still enliven his pages with telling epigram and pretty phrase. Above all things, the book is not eccentric, not unmethodical, not of a wayward brilliance; and this is especially commendable and fortunate in the case of an English critic writing upon French literature."—*London Daily Chronicle.*

"A book readable, graphic, not overloaded with detail, not bristling with dates. . . . It is a book that can be held in the hand and read aloud with pleasure as a literary treat by an expert in style, master of charming words that come and go easily, and of other literatures that serve for illustrations."—*The Critic.*

"His methods afford an admirable example of compressing an immense amount of information and criticism in a sentence or paragraph, and his survey of a vast field is both comprehensive and interesting. As an introduction for the student of literature the work is most excellent, and for the casual reader it will serve as a compendium of one of the richest literatures of the world."—*Philadelphia Public Ledger.*

"Thorough without being diffuse. The author is in love with his subject, has made it a study for years, and therefore produced an entertaining volume. Of the scholarship shown it is needless to speak. . . . It is more than a cyclopædia. It is a brilliant talk by one who is loaded with the lively ammunition of French prose and verse. He talks of the pulpit, the stage, the Senate, and the *salon*, until the preachers, dramatists, orators, and philosophers seem to be speaking for themselves."—*Boston Globe.*

"Professor Dowden's book is more interesting than we ever supposed a brief history of a literature could be His characterizations are most admirable in their conciseness and brilliancy. He has given in one volume a very thorough review of French literature."—*The Interior, Chicago.*

"The book will be especially valuable to the student as a safe and intelligible index to a course of reading."—*The Independent.*

D. APPLETON AND COMPANY, NEW YORK.

"THE TRUTH ABOUT THE BOERS."

Oom Paul's People.

By HOWARD C. HILLEGAS. With Illustrations. 12mo. Cloth, $1.50.

"He [the author] has written a plain, straightforward narrative of what he himself saw and learned during his recent visit to South Africa. . . . The only criticism of it will be that which Sam Weller passed on his own love letter, that the reader 'will wish there was more of it'—which is the great art of letter-writing and of book-writing."—*New York World.*

"The first systematic and categorical exposition of the merits of the whole case and its origins written by a disinterested observer. . . . An informing book, and a well-written one."—*New York Mail and Express.*

"Gives precisely the information necessary to those who desire to follow intelligently the progress of events at the present time."—*New York Commercial Advertiser.*

"A most satisfactory and timely book."—*Chicago Times-Herald.*

"A most interesting and timely book."—*Boston Herald.*

"Has all the timeliness of an up-to-date newspaper article; in fact, some portions of it read almost like a cablegram from the Transvaal."—*New York Sunday World.*

"A book on the Boer troubles that is free from British prejudices and misrepresentations. . . . It is the best book of the hour in its unbiased presentation of the Boer side of the controversy."—*Chicago Tribune.*

D. APPLETON AND COMPANY, NEW YORK.